READINGS IN
Psychological Tests
and
Measurements

READINGS IN
Psychological Tests and Measurements

THIRD EDITION

Edited by
W. Leslie Barnette, Jr., Ph.D.

Professor of Psychology
State University of New York at Buffalo

THE WILLIAMS & WILKINS COMPANY
Baltimore

Copyright ©, 1976
The Williams & Wilkins Company
428 E. Preston Street
Baltimore, Md. 21202, U.S.A.

Made in the United States of America

Library of Congress Cataloging in Publication Data

Barnette, Warren Leslie, Jr. 1910–   ed.
    Readings in psychological tests and measurements.

    Bibliography: p.
    Includes indexes.
    1. Psychometrics—Addresses, essays, lectures. I. Title.
BF39.B37   1975   152.8   75-12683
ISBN 0-683-00363-1

Composed and printed at the
Waverly Press, Inc.
Mt. Royal and Guilford Aves.
Baltimore, Md. 21202, U.S.A.

To the Reader

The present volume is based on the experience of the editor in teaching undergraduate courses in Psychological Tests and Measurements, largely populated by majors in the Department of Psychology at SUNY/Buffalo. Experience has shown that it is desirable to use readings of recent origin to supplement the basic text used in the course. It is usually impractical to ask fairly large groups of students to read articles directly from journals in the Periodical Room of the campus library; it is also costly to have such material reproduced for local use. For these reasons (among others, for which see below), the present compilation of articles has been assembled.

This selection was also governed by another consideration: that the materials so ably presented in the *Test Service Bulletins*, published by the Psychological Corporation in New York City, would not overlap. It is assumed that this collection of bulletins, still most pleasantly free for the asking, will be utilized in conjunction with the present collection of readings.

At the time of the first edition of these readings (1964), this was the sole such collection available. Since that time, several other volumes of readings dealing with tests and measurements have appeared. Apparently our first edition started a trend. Megargee's volume (1966) has essentially an advanced clinical psychology approach. The Chase and Ludlow collection (also 1966) is designed for use with a second-level measurements course, or a course offering placed at the MA level. This Chase-Ludlow volume, while sharing more overlap with our present edition than that of Megargee, will still be seen as very different from this third edition. The year 1967 saw the publication of three additional collections of readings: one by Flynn and Garber, which is composed largely for use by Education students and has valuable sections on tests as used in school systems; a second by Mehrens and Ebel, composed from a principles of measurement stance and thereby, in the opinion of this editor, introducing statistical and theoretical material more appropriate for an advanced measurements course; and a third by Payne and McMorris, again with an Education emphasis, with a focus on teacher understandings, various ap-

proaches to achievement testing, item construction, prediction and decision-making in regard to high school and college academic success plus
discussions of the management of large-scale testing programs. Finally,
a collection edited by Gronlund (1968) has appeared, again with an Education emphasis, where considerable space is given to classroom tests,
how to evaluate reviews of various types of tests and inventories, trends
and recent developments with standardized tests and how, profitably,
to use these. A new feature here is a table which coordinates these readings with the contents of twenty different measurement texts currently
available.

To complement these six collections, there is the excellent compilation
of papers (Anastasi, 1966) originally presented at the Invitational Conferences on Testing Problems, sponsored each year since 1949 by the Educational Testing Service. The reader will find a few of these papers reprinted in this present volume.

Taken as a unit, these seven books, together with this third revision,
will constitute a very complete and concise library of materials dealing
with psychological tests and measurements in their many phases. The
present editor finds it both surprising and pleasing that the content overlap among all of these volumes is so slight.

So, now, why this additional collection of readings? Up-dating was
clearly needed since the previous edition (1968, and also the year of publication of Gronlund's volume). This new edition, in the editor's thinking,
is the sole such volume designed for advanced undergraduate majors in
psychology who have already been exposed to a required course in Elementary Statistics. Hopefully, such students have also enrolled for one or
two research methods courses (as in Social or Cognitive or Clinical). The
emphasis for this revised collection has been clearly on empiricism and a
conscious attempt on the part of the editor has been to include rather
unusual and interest-promoting material (examples: the studies reported
on altruism and the financial honesty of the general public, the improved
selection of teen-age boys as door-to-door salesmen, the "serendipitous"
validation difficulties met in Vietnam, etc.). Regardless, theory has
not been neglected although not given the primary focus. The aim has
been to demonstrate that psychological tests and concomitant measurement can be exciting and productive and not necessarily confined to the
laboratory.

As with the previous editions, the editorial job has been considerable.
Only a few papers are presented here in their original forms; many have
been condensed or abbreviated in one way or another, all with the explicit permission of the authors. We have consistently kept in mind the
undergraduate psychology major whose knowledge of advanced statistics
is modest. Articles presenting extensive tables and elaborate statistical
analyses have been drastically edited from this point of view. (The editor
has frequently been irritated, when using other collections of readings for

undergraduate courses, when such editing has not been done and, as a result, the student meets up abruptly with F ratios, complex Rorschach nomenclature, analyses of covariance and the like.) This third edition has not entirely eschewed such techniques—and here the instructor will have to supplement—but an attempt has been made to keep them at a minimum. The student reader, in the main, is only expected to understand elementary statistical concepts such as correlation, central tendency and dispersion and the simpler ways of expressing confidence levels. However, in the light of the times, this third edition also presents new material dealing with multivariate regression analysis and computerized programs, but not at a complex statistical level. Clinical material utilizing projectives has been omitted by design.

The bibliography at the end of the book lists all publications mentioned in the main body of the readings. Unlike most collections of readings, the volume has been composed to conform with regular textbook format—tables and figures are numbered sequentially rather than in the manner of appearance in the original sources. Similarly, all references to other and related research cited by the authors of articles have been collected in the final bibliography at the end of the volume.

Buffalo, New York   W. L. BARNETTE, JR.
August, 1975

Acknowledgments

The common attribution of credit to other persons for any merit a book may have is especially appropriate for a book of readings such as this. It is to these authors, herein reprinted and edited with their permission, that the editor owes the first debt of gratitude. In the name of these contributors, a portion of the royalties from this volume has been assigned to the American Psychological Foundation.

In addition, the following journals and publishers and professional associations are to be thanked for their permission to use their copyrighted materials: American Institute for Research, *American Journal of Mental Deficiency*, American Psychological Association, College Entrance Examination Board, *Educational and Psychological Measurement*, Educational Testing Service, Elementary School Principals' Association of Connecticut, *Harvard Educational Review*, Houghton Mifflin Company, *Journal of Criminal Law, Criminology and Police Science*, National Elementary Principals' Association, Penguin Books, *Personnel and Guidance Journal*, Science and Behavior Books, *Scientific American*, Social Security Administration of U. S. Department of Health, Education and Welfare, Society for the Psychological Study of Social Issues, U. S. Department of Labor, and the *Vocational Guidance Quarterly*.

W. L. Barnette, Jr.

Contents

PART ONE
General Measurement Problems

PART TWO
Test Administration Problems

PART THREE
Norms

PART FOUR
Validity

PART FIVE
Ability Testing

PART SIX
Personality

PART SEVEN
Situational Testing

PART EIGHT
Interests

PART NINE
Achievement or Proficiency Testing

PART TEN
Automation, Computers, and Multivariate Techniques

PART ELEVEN
Testing of the Disadvantaged: Bias, Discrimination, and Differential Validities

PART TWELVE
Measurement and Policy Issues

BIBLIOGRAPHY

INDEXES

PART ONE

General Measurement Problems

MEASUREMENT that purports to be scientific in any sense of the word has a logic of its own. Because of historical priority, this logic has largely been developed in the area of the physical scientists. The claims of social scientists, and especially workers in the field of psychometrics, must be evaluated against these same standards. It is well that the beginning student of psychological measurement know something of these principles. Writers such as Bridgman, Campbell, and Carnap have published treatises in this area from the vantage point of physics and mathematics. In the following article, Dr. Comrey, Psychologist at the University of California in Los Angeles and well known for his research in psychometrics, spells out some of the fundamental facts of measurement as these relate to the mental testing movement. However, the reader is urged when he reads this article not to confine his thinking merely to "mental" tests but, rather, to generalize these arguments to the wider field of aptitude testing. The article originally appeared in *Educational & Psychological Measurement* in 1951.

Before attempting to understand all of Dr. Comrey's article, it would be wise for the student to be acquainted with the differences between and among nominal, ordinal, interval, and ratio scales.

MENTAL TESTING AND THE LOGIC OF MEASUREMENT

Andrew L. Comrey

By comparison with measurement in the physical sciences, psychological measurement has always enjoyed a somewhat unsavory reputation and has even been called by some the "queen of the inexact sciences." Many writers have pointed out deficiencies in the techniques employed in psychology; some have based their criticisms upon alleged violations of the traditional "laws of measurement". In a previous article (Comrey, 1950) certain implications of the logic behind measurement were given some attention. The traditional requirements were stated, criticisms of psychological measurement were discussed, and an interpretation of the position of psychological measurement with respect to these requirements was offered.

In the present paper, some of the general problems of psychological measurement will be discussed as they apply to the mental-test field. A brief review of the requirements of fundamental measurement will be given, together with a discussion of some difficulties in applying this model to mental testing. Some of the consequences to these difficulties for measurement practice will be mentioned and, finally, some suggestions regarding criteria for evaluating mental-test methods will be made which depart from the customary criteria of conformity to the pattern of fundamental measurement. The point of view will be expressed that the excellence of measurement methods in mental testing may be judged by the practical validity of those methods for the purposes at hand, in addition to comparing them with the model of measurement in the physical sciences. Reasons for giving greater emphasis to the former criterion will be offered.

CRITICISMS OF MENTAL TESTING

Perhaps the most comprehensive treatment of the requirements for fundamental measurement has been given by Campbell. Some of the more important requirements will be summarized with respect to ordinal characteristics, the relation of equality, and the operation of addition. The requirements for order specify that a class of elements must be defined unambiguously so that the elements vary with respect to some particular property. To be measurable with respect to that property, the elements must vary only in degree, not in kind. Furthermore, a relation "greater," which is transitive and asymmetrical, must be physically defined. That is, if Stimulus A is greater than Stimulus B, and B is greater than C, then A should be greater than C; also, if A is greater than B, B cannot be greater than A.

To satisfy the requirements for equality, a physical definition of the relation "equals" is needed. This definition must be such that physical equality is transitive and symmetrical, i.e., if $A = B$, and $B = C$, then $A = C$; also, if $A = B$, then $B = A$. And, finally, the requirements for addition state, among other things, that some experimental operation must be found whereby two elements possessing the measurable property can be added together to get an element containing an amount of this property greater than that of either element added. For properties which satisfy these requirements, a complete, or *fundamental* measurement is possible. Numbers assigned to elements of such classes of measurables can be manipulated in accordance with the rule of arithmetic. Furthermore, such measurements are made on scales with equal-unit and ratio properties. A few properties so measurable are weight, length, period of time, and electrical resistance.

It is fairly well known that certain difficulties are involved in trying to apply the model of fundamental measurement to the mental-test area. One of the first criticisms laid at the doorstep of mental testing is that classes of measurables are not even defined, i.e., the class of degrees of some property supposedly indicated by different scores on some test do not represent merely differences in degree but differences in kind as well. A Gestalt interpretation of mental organization would tend to contradict the notion that merely a quantitative difference is reflected by different test scores. Furthermore, the relation of equality does not meet the necessary conditions. It is stated that equal test scores do not mean identity with respect to some ability. Individuals may get the same test scores by solving correctly different combinations of items. Furthermore, by this line of reasoning, if $A = B$ (i.e., equal test scores), and $B = C$, there is no reason to suppose that the underlying ability organizations of A and C are the same, even though their numerical test scores are identical.

Interesting as these objections may be, the psychologist can minimize their importance on operational grounds. He can state that by the only measuring instrument available to him, i.e., the test, $A = B$ if they have the same test score. Aside from the question of differences in kind represented by different test scores, no contradiction in the actual numbers assigned can occur with respect to the relations "greater" and "equals." The fact that different combinations of items add up to the same score does not bother him too much because he feels that if the items themselves are of the same sort, the total score should be fairly indicative of the person's level of achievement.

That mental testing has no suitable operation of addition is quite apparent, and critics have not failed to mention this point. There seems to be no way to add physically one psychological magnitude to another to get a third even greater in amount. With fundamentally measurable variables, such as weight, length, resistance, and so on, this can be accomplished easily and, from such an operation, numbers can be assigned such that differences and ratios are endowed with the desired experimental meaning. The fact that the operation of addition is not defined in mental testing leads to considerable difficulty, since this operation is employed in fundamental measurement to endow measurement scales with equal-unit and ratio properties. Thus, it would appear that mental-test workers may not be able to develop test scales with equal units and ratio properties.

Let us consider, for a moment, two opposed points of view which might be adopted with respect to the nature of measurement involved in a mental test. First, it might be assumed that the human mind is composed of an undetermined number of abilities. A test may tap, so to speak, a few of these abilities which inhere basically in the physiological structure of the organism, but the test can be only in indirect measurement in terms of certain behavioral manifestations. A direct measurement is out of the question, at the present state of our knowledge of physiology, for there is no way that variations in these abilities can be directly observed. Behavioral products represent the only available indicators of such underlying variables at the present time.

Taking a simple case, suppose there were such an underlying ability and a test which measured this variable alone, plus some error variance. What is the functional relationship between the performance variable and the underlying ability? If a performance variable is to be used to yield a measure of ability in this sense, it is obvious that such functional relationships must either be determined experimentally, or assumed to follow a certain form. This functional relationship must be known before the task of securing equal-unit scales, with respect to the underlying variable, can be accomplished, for the equality of units must be in terms of the underlying ability, not the performance.

Unfortunately, it is not now possible to determine the nature of such functional relationships. An independent measure of the underlying ability would be necessary before the relationship of such measures to scores on the performance test could be found. Since no independent measurements (e.g., physiological determinations) for the underlying variable can be taken, this method of proceeding is impractical. It should be mentioned at this point that an approach to this problem can be made through the use of certain types of judgments. For example, one might employ fractionation and equal-appearing-interval methods for the scaling of the subjective difficulty of digit series and words in a vocabulary test. These methods do not comprise an experimental verification of unit equality on an underlying mental-ability variable, however. They do allow an operational meaning to be attached to unit differences on the subjective scale, but such units do not represent those of a fundamental type for the underlying variable.

From this analysis, it appears evident that one cannot prove that a performance or behavior test yields equal units along the scale of some basic underlying ability which in itself is not directly observable. It should be emphasized that the task of disproving an assumption of equal units in such cases is equally difficult, for this, too, would require experimental checks of the relationship between the performance variable and independent measurements of the underlying ability.

An opposite position which might be assumed by some persons with respect to the nature of measurement involved in a mental test is the point of view that a test measures a variable of some kind, or variables, and these behavioral products themselves are what concern us. It amounts to behavioristic approach, so to speak, which denies the necessity of dealing in terms of concepts which have no basis in observation. The extreme behaviorist might ask, "What is the point of assuming an underlying ability which cannot be measured, observed, or proved to exist?"

If the second approach is taken, what are the consequences? First, the matter of a functional relationship between the behavior variable and a hypothetical underlying variable is no longer of importance. The behavior itself is the variable, as determined by the performance on some test. The emphasis with this approach is switched from a consideration of whether the test measures the underlying variable properly to that of whether the variable measured is a useful one. It is assumed that the measures obtained from a test represent some variable in a one-to-one fashion. Since the variable is defined by the test scores, there can be no question as to whether the units on such a test are equal, because that is implicit in the assumptions. It follows from the general approach involved that the units of such tests are equal by definition. It is not the intention of the writer to advance either of these positions as his own. These points of view are considered as represented opposed positions which may flank most observers rather than represent them. The point of importance in this dicussion is merely that, regardless of what systematic position one adopts, we do not have equal units of the fundamental type with any mental test and we will not have them until means are devised for direct observation of underlying physiological phenomena.

SOME POSSIBLE CONSEQUENCES OF THE DIFFICULTIES

It has already been suggested that the objections raised against mental-test methods with respect to the requirements for order and equality are crucial. The issues raised by the failure to achieve an operational definition of addition in mental testing are more serious, however. Since equal-unit and ratio properties of measurement scales are based upon addition, mental testing faces the task of evaluating the effects of this deficiency.

The most obvious conclusion which might be drawn is that measurement in this area is confined to the ordinal level. That is, numbers assigned by means of mental tests can indicate only the rank-order positions of performances to which those numbers have been given. This is the sort of conclusion which is often made by critics of psychological measurement.

Now, it is quite clear that many of the statistical procedures which are applied to mental-test results demand something in the way of a unit of measurement. Means, standard deviations, product-moment correlations, and all the statistical procedures based upon these must necessarily depend upon interval sizes along the scale of measurement. This is no less true of the rank-difference correlation method, which is derived from the product-moment formula, and hence involves the same concepts. (Ratio characteristics of measurement scales do not constitute as much of a loss to mental testing as the lack of equal units, for most purposes, since the typical statistical treatments need not involve such relations between test scores.)

These considerations suggest that one of two courses of action must be taken by those attempting to use mental tests for measurement purposes. First, they may show that using methods involving unit assumptions does not introduce serious errors or that certain procedures can be employed to minimize such error in spite of the absence of fundamentally equal units. Secondly, they may avoid the use of methods of analysis which depend upon interval interpretations. The multiple cutting-score methods, for example, do not demand such assumptions. Further, non-parametric methods may be used for statistical tests of hypotheses.

It is likely that further development of measurement techniques in mental testing will proceed along both these lines. Certainly, there is a vast unexplored territory in the area of the second procedure suggested above. With respect to the first program, it can be stated that insufficient attention has been given to the problem of determining the degree and kind of error introduced into the results of measurement by virtue of the fact that such measurements lack certain characteristics they are presumed to have. In the next section, criteria for judging the work of measurement methods will be treated in the light of the discussion to this point.

CRITERIA FOR EVALUATING MENTAL TEST METHODS

The fundamental-measurement model has typically been used as a criterion by which measurement procedures should be evaluated. Those procedures which fit this scheme are termed "good" methods, and procedures which fail to do so are held to be primitive and unsatisfactory as scientific instruments. Mental tests fall in this latter category, for they certainly fail to fit the fundamental-measurement model in at least one important respect, namely, in their defection with respect to the operation of addition. Are there other criteria by which mental tests can be evaluated which may be more useful? Under the first criterion mentioned above, all mental tests are unsatisfactory, and no discrimination among them is provided. Certainly, some tests are better and more useful than others.

The obvious answer to this question is that other criteria are available for judging the value of procedures in mental testing. These criteria are to be found in the validity of such instruments for the practical purposes of assessing and predicting status under a variety of conditions. Lest some misunderstanding on this point arise, it should be hastily added that the logic of fundamental measurement should not be forgotten or ignored. It is a good thing to know where one's methods fail to meet this more exacting pattern in order to avoid the errors which are likely to occur in the absence of this knowledge. The fact that mental-test methods do not satisfy such criteria need not blind us to the possibility and usefulness of evaluation in terms of these other more practical criteria.

Whereas many difficulties are involved in the use of mental tests for the purpose of establishing scientific laws, there seems to be little doubt as to their value for certain practical purposes. It seems reasonable to assert that mental testing is and will be for some time essentially an empirical science with certain rather well-defined practical objectives, rather than primarily a theoretical scientific enterprise. At least, in terms of relative proportion of activity in this area, such a position could scarcely be questioned. Some individuals may object to this point of view, since personal preferences in matters of emphasis are involved. Be that as it may, this position will be adopted with respect to the objectives of mental testing.

These considerations lead to certain conclusions regarding the attitude which practical mental-test workers should adopt toward the logic of measurement. In the first place, they should abandon attempts to manipulate their test scores for the purpose of making their measurements approximate fundamental measurement. It is quite clear that such objectives can never be attained in this manner; they can be attained only through experimental operations upon the underlying physiological determiners of behavior. The practical test worker is not in a position to engage in the type of research activity which might conceivably succeed in reaching such ends. This fact would be evident to anyone familiar with the logic of fundamental measurement, so mental-test workers should by all means be acquainted with measurement theory.

It should be pointed out in this connection that scaling procedures which are apparently designed for obtaining measurement properties beyond rank order are not necessarily bad. What is not defensible is to assume that such procedures can stand on their own because they appear to resemble, in the end result, measurement in the physical sciences. Whether such methods are good or bad can be assessed in terms of their capacity to help achieve the practical objectives of mental tests. Ultimately, methods may become available to checking the claims of such procedures with respect to measurement properties beyond rank-order but, for the present, such claims must rest upon assumptions for which there is insufficient experimental evidence.

Attempts to improve quantification techniques in mental testing should not be confined to the pattern of fundamental measurement but should be spread over a much wider area. Any and all techniques should be explored which might conceivably lead to better predictions or assessments of status, even though such techniques do not appear to have any possibility of making mental-test measurement more like fundamental measurement.

As a matter of fact, some such successful techniques may appear to be in contradiction to a goal in terms of the fundamental-measurement pattern. An article by Richardson (1936), for example, emphasizes the importance of considering the effects of test difficulty on validity. Richardson states that the validity of a test depends in large measure upon whether the test is properly tailored to the job with respect to difficulty. He states:

> Suppose, for example, that a test of clerical aptitude is meant to sort out the best 15 per cent of all applicants. This is on the assumption that the labor market is such that one hundred persons will apply for 15 positions. It is then clear that the optimal difficulty of test elements should be in the neighborhood of plus 1 sigma and that easier tasks would give us discriminations between individuals in whom we are not interested. Under any circumstances involving educational or psychological measurement, the distribution of difficulty of the elements to tasks can be arranged to fulfill more accurately the purposes of measurement.

If, by some procedure, it were possible to develop a test of clerical aptitude which would represent truly a fundamental-measurement scale with a given number of items, the scale would be the same whether 15 percent or 85 percent of the applicants were being selected. Under conditions where error variance is not present in the test, success would probably be equal for any cutting score. However, under the conditions of testing existing, this fixed scale would not do the measuring job at a given level as well as a test tailored for that level, although this fixed scale might conceivably be the best general-purpose scale. Thus, the approach to better measurement through meeting the requirements for fundamental measurement, were it possible, would not necessarily give the best practical methods, since it ignores at least one of the important factors affecting test validity.

The methods to be employed in mental testing, then, have a definite purpose and they can be evaluated in terms of that purpose. From the standpoint of the ideas presented here, the primary value of item analysis and factor analysis, for example, lies in the possibility of using such techniques to increase predictive efficiency. Developing batteries of the pure tests to predict some criterion through factor analysis of tests and criteria, constitutes a method of value of which can definitely be assessed in terms of higher validity coefficients. The same criteria can be applied to other methods introduced into the mental-test field. Where such good means are available for evaluating measurement methods it seems inappropriate to rely principally on comparisons with abstract logical criteria that were designed for a different context.

SUMMARY

1. Many difficulties lie in the path of securing for mental-test measurement the type of rigor found in the fundamental type of measurement. Among these, one of the most serious is the impossibility of obtaining equal units without independent physiological assessment of the variables under consideration.

2. This failure brings up many important problems with respect to the treatment of mental-test data by statistical methods, since many of these methods presume that a unit of measurement has been established. Some justification for the use of such methods should be offered.

3. It would be desirable to attain a fundamental type of measurement for mental testing but, at present, such a goal seems out of reach. If fundamental measurement is made the sole yardstick by which the excellence of measurement procedures is to be judged. mental-test methods are automatically classed as primitive and virtually without prospect of substantial improvement.

4. The objectives of mental testing are held to be primarily empirical in nature. Testing techniques are designed mainly for the prediction and assessment of status. These objectives provide additional criteria by which mental-test methods can be judged, namely, the practical validity determinations for the purposes at hand.

5. Mental-test workers should certainly be aware of what is involved in fundamental measurement, but they should devote their major efforts toward developing measurement techniques which give some hope for better satisfying the practical validity criteria rather than the fundamental-measurement criteria. This position is taken because (a) the fundamental-measurement criteria cannot be attained by the methods available to the mental-test worker, if at all, and (b) the practical-validity criteria and the fundamental-measurement criteria may sometimes be contradictory objectives in the practical situation.

▽ ▽ ▽

The comments that follow represent a condensation of a book review by Dr. Dingle, published in the *Scientific American* (June, 1960). The author was writing about a volume that contained the contributions to a symposium on measurement held at the 1956 meetings of the American Association for the Advancement of Science. Dr. Dingle uses this occasion—which is the reason sections of the review are reproduced here—to write about the general operational approach to valid measurement, something that is applicable to physics as well as to psychology. The author takes issue with the first sentence of this book: "Measurement presupposes something to be measured, and, unless we know what that something is, no measurement can have any significance."

Dr. Dingle is an English astronomer and physicist. He is Professor Emeritus of History and Philosophy of Science at University College, London.

BASIC PROBLEMS OF MEASUREMENT

Herbert Dingle

To understand what measurement means we must turn to the physical sciences as the field affording the potentialities of measurement their widest scope; there alone are all the known processes of measurement exemplified. Consequently a true conception of measurement must cover physical measurements in their widest generality. Such a conception shows that measurement is a self-contained process, a process that implies nothing beyond that of which it gives a numerical estimation.

It is perfectly legitimate to ask an astronomer to measure the area in the sky of the constellation Orion as defined by the International Astronomical Union. But what is the "something" that he measures? We no longer think in terms of a "sky," and from another viewpoint the constellation ceases to exist. There is no "something," but beyond question there is a measurement.

Pursuing the matter, we see not only that all physical measurements are of this kind, but also that, far from starting with a something and then measuring it, we start with a measure and then try to find something to which we can attach it. We measure the weight, W, of a body, and its height, h, above the ground, and form the product Wh. This we regard as significant because it is equal to the kinetic energy with which the body, having been released, reaches the ground. We therefore invent something that Wh measures and call it the potential energy of the body. When the body falls, and h becomes zero, it loses its potential energy. We are delighted, and think we have "discovered" potential energy. But we are now forced to say that when a body moves toward or away from the sun, it similarly loses or gains potential energy. Suppose, then, that our body falls to the earth when the sun is directly overhead. Has it gained or lost potential energy? We can take our choice, which means that potential energy is not "something to be measured," but a quantity devised after the measurement has shown its importance. In its devising we are free to exercise our choice among various possibilities; and, if we do not devise it at all, the measurement has exactly the same status it had before.

Take another example. We make a measurement with a diffraction grating and call the result the "wave length" of light. But we do not first perceive the waves and then measure their length; we make a measurement and then invent "wave length" to attach to it. The invention is just as arbitrary as that of potential energy, and at present it is even less satisfactory. Another observer, moving away from us in the direction of the light, gets a different value. It is the same light. Which observer determines the "right" wavelength? Clearly, at least one of our measurements does not imply a "wave length to be measured." But if the something is not wave length, what is it? We do not know, though there can be no doubt that this measurement is important.

So we could continue. For this reason I some years ago proposed the rudiments of a theory in which measurement was defined as "any precisely specified operation that yields a number; that is, measurement is related to the operation performed and not to the hypothetical "something" on which it is supposed to be performed." This theory appeared in *The British Journal for the Philosophy of Science* (Vol. 1, page 5), and as it seems not to have been noticed by any of the contributors to the present volume, I shall take the liberty of outlining its basic idea. But first of all I think it will be useful to take a step still further back and see how measurement came to be practiced at all. This point is not touched upon in the volume, yet it is of some relevance and is indeed essential if we are to understand fully what measurement signifies. The contributors to the volume take measurement for granted and then discuss— often admirably—what it is, but they do not ask why it must be taken for granted. They tacitly assume the strategy of the campaign, and concentrate on the tactics. Let us see why the strategy commits us to measurement.

The fundamental problem of philosophy is that of making sense of our experience. We are originally aware of a haphazard succession of experiences. After a while some regularities force themselves on our attention— night and day alternate, falling is followed by a pain, and so on. The first philosopher is the man who first conceives the possibility that other— perhaps all—experiences are related; that is, experiences form a rational system. Given a knowledge of some experiences, therefore, other experiences that seem quite independent can be predicted.

The earliest philosophers accepted the obvious relations and tried to supplement them—the alternation of night and day was associated with alternations of heat and cold, falling on grass hurt less than falling on stone—until in such a system as that of Aristotle, with its generalizations in terms of matter and form, a considerable area of experience became organized into a rational system. Two things characterized this approach: first, it was concerned entirely with involuntary experience; and second, progress in it was painfully slow.

By the 17th century the patience of philosophers was exhausted (I am of course describing not what consciously went on in their minds, but what we, knowing the outcome of their actions, can see to be the truest rationalization of them), and they said: "Look here; we aren't getting anywhere with ordinary experience; it is too difficult. Let us make some artificial experiences and find relations between them. Then perhaps ordinary experience will fit in later." So instead of studying the natural motions of birds and smoke and rivers, they made artificial motions— balls rolling down carefully prepared grooves. Thus was born scientific experiment: the deliberate production of artificial experiences more simply related to one another than those that come naturally.

The aspect of the artificial experiences that was examined was the metrical aspect. The rolling ball did not pass from potentiality to actuality; it merely gave readings on a measuring scale and a form of clock, readings represented by numbers. What was the advantage of this? Simply that, since rational relations were required, it brought into operation the most highly developed form of reasoning known: pure mathematics. The artificial experiences were reduced to experiences of numbers, and then metrical science was born. Thus the original aim of relating all natural experience was transformed to that of relating the numbers yielded by contrived operations.

But this was not all understood. It was thought that each measurement represented a property of something in the "external world." The object of philosophy was conceived to be the study of this external world. Our experience—which is ultimately all that is of any importance to anybody—was simply a trivial effect of the casual impinging of the "world" on our bodies; the "world" would be exactly the same if this had never occurred. This idea could persist because there happened to be a pretty close correspondence between the other "things" that were thought to be measured and the "things" that we actually experience, but in fact this correspondence is illusory. Take mass, for instance. This is the name given to something conceived to be responsible for the recordings of certain measuring instruments. But mass was imagined to be "the quantity of matter in a body," and this was plausible, because when the instrument recorded a big number, a large body was usually seen. Hence it was believed that Newton's law of gravitation described the path of a planet around the sun. In reality it describes the path of a mass-point in a gravitational field, and both mass-point and gravitational field belong to an invented world that only in part corresponds to the common-sense world of material objects. If the earth should explode to smithereens through internal stresses, the mass-point (the "center of gravity") would continue on its orbit undisturbed, but there would be no matter where it was situated.

Every symbol in every physical equation stands for the result of a measurement or a combination of such results, and fundamentally for nothing else. In a simple case like that of mass, the correspondence between symbol and some element of ordinary experience is fairly close; usually matters are more complex. Take, for example, Avogadro's number, N—the number of molecules in a cubic centimeter of gas in a certain state. N actually stands for a combination of measurements with thermometers, pressure gauges, balances and so on. (There are various combinations that give the same result; that is why the "number" is important.) Be we describe N as "a number of molecules"—the name given to the result of the operation of counting. And we think of it as such. But in fact the operation of counting molecules is impossible. We can delude ourselves into believing that the operation of weighing is a discovery of the mass of a body, but no honest man can claim that when he is finding N he is counting anything. Yet such is our faith that each measurement is a measurement of "something" that we are ready to make such a claim in order to maintain that faith. Nor is that the worst. We even analyze the intricate concept that we call "the momentum of an electron" as though we had a particle of matter before us and were applying the process for measuring momentum to it; and then we imagine that we are learning something about the world of experience. God help us!

The whole world of physics is a set relations between concepts that represent combinations of the results of measurements, i.e., of artificially created experiences. Nothing that this world contains would ever have happened if we had not made it happen. To verify any of the relations you must adjust the conditions with the greatest care; let experience come naturally, and their supposed requirements are always violated. Go on dropping an object to the ground, and it will come to rest at a different place every time. Go out one day, and you feel warm; do the same the next day, and you feel cold. The laws of falling bodies and of heat are obeyed only in laboratories. Physics tells us a tremendous amount about the world, but it is not the natural world; it is a world of our own making.

How is it, then, that we have turned the results of physical research to such significant account in ordinary life? Simply because of a purely empirical relation between the natural and the artificial worlds. Over a large part of experience they maintain a close parallelism. When a balance gives a big number, we usually do see a big object (but we have seen that a large value of M does not always mean that). When the thermometer has a high reading, we usually feel hot (but in outer space we should probably die instantly of cold, although astronomers tell us that the temperature there can be over 1,000 degrees centigrade). Why the sight of a big object is usually attended by a large M, and feeling of heat by a large O, we understand no more than Thales could have if he had known the facts. With all our science we have learned nothing about the relations existing in the world of natural experience. We have discovered how to create a world between the elements of which rational relations do exist, and we exploit the empirical fact of its close parallelism with the natural world.

This is of the greatest importance in regard to the function of measurement in other sciences such as psychology and sociology. Here exactly the same considerations hold good, but whereas in physics the parallelism between the metrical concepts and ordinary experiences is the rule and its breakdown the exception, in the other sciences the reverse is more nearly true; at least any supposed measurement of psychological attribute is much less uniformly related to actual experience than is normally the case in physics. To take but a single example, the primary importance of Intelligence Quotient is not that it measures "intelligence," whatever that may be, but that it stands in simple relations to other measurements (in particular, a relation approaching identity with further determinations of the same quantity with the same person). We may expect that in time a considerable system of relations between psychological measurements will be built up, but woe betide us if we imagine that its relation to the world of experience is other than purely empirical. A large IQ may go with a good performance in other specified operations, but its possessor may well be a gambling addict, and so one of the most "unintelligent" of persons.

It is in view of such facts as these that measurement must be defined in terms of its origin in the operations we perform, without reference to anything external. Having so defined it, we can begin its analysis. Each measurement includes a manual and a mental part; for example, in measuring length we lay an object along a specified scale (the manual part) and subtract the smaller from the larger of the end-readings (the mental part). We deliberately relax the precision of the specification in two respects. In the manual part we allow one element of the operation to be changed ad lib.; in the example of length we can make "the object" anything we like, and we call the result (merely a name) the length of that object. In the mental part we allow ourselves to multiply the result of any fundamental measurement (that is, a measurement that does not include another measurement as part of its prescription) by any number; we call this (again merely as a name) "changing the unit of measurement." The whole process is thus described without wandering outside into a hypothetical "something to be measured."

∇ ∇ ∇

Much of psychological research, especially concerning personality traits, is limited because of the small range in the choice of subjects upon whom research results are based. Too often is the remark jokingly made that the science of psychology is a science based on only two population samples—white rats and college sophomores. Rather than merely settling for subjects that are conveniently available, we need to be more ingenious in our data gathering techniques and to approach measurement via multiple methods. It is to this point that Dr. Eugene Webb's article is addressed. The paper is also of interest because of its numerous examples of situational types of testing in which the researcher goes directly into the field for data, thereby using highly naturalistic situations, and in which the subjects are usually unaware of being tested at all.

Dr. Webb's paper, slightly condensed for this book, was originally presented at the 1966 Invitational Conference on Testing Problems, sponsored by the Educational Testing Service, the proceedings of which are now in print (ETS, 1967). Dr. Webb is now Professor in the Graduate School of Business at Stanford University.

UNCONVENTIONALITY, TRIANGULATION, AND INFERENCE

Eugene J. Webb

All three of the nouns in this paper's title—unconventionality, triangulation, and inference—are imbedded in a more general concept: multiple operationalism as a way of knowing. With educational psychologists making significant contributions, the mistaken belief in the single operational definition of learning, of performance, or of values has been eroded.

Most students today would agree that it is appropriate to draw simultaneously on multiple measures of the same attribute or construct.

In 1953, E. G. Boring wrote:

As long as a new construct has only the single operational definition that it received at birth, it is just a construct. When it gets two alternative operational definitions, it is beginning to be validated. When the defining operations, because of proven correlations, are many, then it becomes reified.

But just as we ask if a correlated *x* and *y* are more highly correlated with *z*, it is also reasonable to ask if the components being converged or triangulated are truly complementary. Are we fully accounting for known sources of error variance? This is a serious question with most of the multimethod studies now available. "Multimethod" has usually been defined as multiple scales or behaviors collected under the condition in which the subject knew he was being tested. The multiple

TABLE 1

Sources of Research Invalidity

I. *Reactive Measurement Effect*
   1. Awareness of being tested
   2. Role playing
   3. Measurement as change
   4. Response sets

II. *Error from Investigator*
   5. Interviewer effects
   6. Change—fatigue/practice

III. *Varieties of Sampling Error*
   7. Population restriction
   8. Population stability over time
   9. Population stability over areas

IV. *Access to Content*
   10. Restrictions on content
   11. Stability of content over time
   12. Stability of content over areas

V. *Operating Ease and Validity Checks*
   13. Dross rate
   14. Access to descriptive cues
   15. Ability to replicate

methods thus have tended to be multiple variants within a *single* measurement class such as the interview.

Every data-gathering class—interview, questionnaires, observation, performance records, physical evidence—is potentially biased and has specific to it certain validity threats. Ideally, we should like to converge data from several data classes, as well as converge with multiple variants from within a single class.

The methodological literature warned us early of certain recurrent validity threats, and the evidence has markedly accelerated in the last few years. It has been 30 years, for example, since Lorge (1937) published his paper on response set, and 20 years since Cronbach (1946) published his influential paper on the same topic in *Educational and Psychological Measurement*. Further, there is the more recent work of Orne (1962) on the demand characteristics of a known research setting and Rosenthal's stimulating work (1964) on the social psychology of the experiment. All these investigations suggest that reliance on data obtained only in "reactive" settings is equivocal.

As a guide to locating the strengths and weaknesses of individual data classes—to better work the convergent multiple-methods approach— my colleagues at Northwestern and I have tried to develop a list of sources of research invalidity to be considered with any data class. An outline of these sources of invalidity is contained in Table 1.

To bring under control some of the reactive measurement effect, we might employ data classes which do not require the cooperation of the student or respondent. By supplementing standard interview or pencil-and-paper measures, more dimensionality is introduced into triangulation.

In a recent paper which described the use of observation methods in the study of racial attitudes, Campbell, Kruskal, and Wallace (1966) studied seating aggregations by race. Two colleges were picked in the Chicago area—one noted for the liberal composition of its student body and the other more associated with a traditional point of view. Going into lecture halls, they observed seating patterns and the clustering of Negro and white students during class. With a new statistical test developed by Kruskal, they were able to demonstrate a greater racial mixture in the more "liberal" college. They also found, however, that the seating mix in the liberal college was significantly less than that expected by chance.

The linkage of secondary records is another way to develop control over reactivity. An example of this approach is DeCharms and Moeller's (1962) study of achievement imagery. They first gathered the number of patents issued by the United States Patent Office from 1800 to 1950. These data (controlled for population) were then matched to achievement imagery found in children's readers for the same period. There was a strong relationship between the level of achievement imagery in their sample of books and the number of patents per million population. Both data series are nonreactive, and although other rival, plausible hypotheses might explain the relationship, it remains as one piece in the inferential puzzle, uncontaminated by awareness of being tested.

For matching of other archival records, we can note Lewis Terman's (1917) study estimating Galton's IQ (not far from 200) and Galton's own early studies of hereditary genius (1870).

Another class of data comes from physical evidence, one example of which is Fredrick Mosteller's creative study (unpublished) of the degree to which different sections of the *International Encyclopedia of the Social Sciences* were read. He estimated usage by noting the wear and tear on separate sections: dirty edges of pages, frequency of dirt smudges, finger markings and underlinings on pages. He samples different libraries and even used the *Encyclopaedia Britannica* as a control.

Thus far, the emphasis has been on data sources and overlapping classes of data. We might also profitably explore the possibility of using multiple samples. Again, this is different from the usual definition of multiple samples. In addition to sampling a number of different classrooms, or groups of students or cities, one may ask if there are different types or categories of samples available for the variable under study. Is there a group of natural outcroppings among occupations, already formed social and interest groups, or people who have common experiences? Can we economically exploit for research purposes the broad spectrum of already formed groups which may be organized along some principle of direct substantive applicability to the investigation?

Professor James Bryan of Northwestern and I have been interested in the use of these "outcropping" groups as a middle-level sampling strategy—one that straddles the elegant but cumbersome national probability sample and the more circumscribed "$N = 80$ volunteer males from the introductory psychology class" populations.

Because one sometimes doesn't know the universe for a study and because of cost restraints, subjects are most often selected because of proximity. Our subjects are typically drawn from the subject pool of the introductory class, from friends, friends of friends, or those unlucky enough to be members of the same institution as the investigator, be it the school, the hospital, or the prison.

Consider some convenience samples which may supplement conventional groups. Becker, Lerner, and Carroll (1964) used caddies loafing about a golf course waiting for jobs as a subject pool. E. E. Smith (1962) suggested firemen in a fire house. They have almost unlimited time available for questioning and offer the very happy situation of a naturally formed, real group, whose members know each other very well. This is a good setting in which to replicate findings derived from experimentally formed groups in laboratories or from natural groups.

Sometimes these convenient aggregates offer a special opportunity to get a high concentration of usable subjects. To study somatotyping among top athletes in different track and field events, Tanner (1964) went to the 1960 Olympic Village at Rome. In a study of proposed brand names for new products, in which one of the criteria was relative invulnerability to regional accents, MacNiven* sent interviewers to a nearby airport where they asked travellers to read off lists of names while the interviewers noted variable pronunciations.

In trait measurement, one may define altruism by one or by a series of self-report scales. But it may also be profitable to examine extant groups with some face-valid loading on altruism—say, volunteer blood donors, contributors to charitable causes, or even such groups as those who aided Jews in Nazi Germany.

Bryan and Test (1966) have recently reported on a provocative study of the influence of modeling behavior on altruism. Their objective in a field experiment was to see whether or not people stopped to help someone who had a flat tire. The experiment involved two women stranded with flat tires one quarter of a mile apart on a highway and a model, a man who had stopped to help one of them. In one part of the experiment, the traffic passed the women and the model and then, farther up the highway, passed the other woman. In the other part of the experiment, the traffic passed only one woman and no model (see pp. 203–10 for a full report of this study).

---

* Personal communication.

Other clusters of groups may help to define or locate a particular ability. Occupational categories may be particularly useful here. For studies of superior depth perception there are natural occupational outcroppings such as magnetic core threaders, jugglers, or grand prix automobile drivers.

Each of these groups possesses other attributes, and one might consider the same group of automobile race drivers as a high risk-taking sample and link them with other high risk-taking groups such as sport and military parachute jumpers.

Or, for studies of deviance, there are the self-help deviant groups of Alcoholics Anonymous, Gamblers Anonymous, and prisoners who volunteer for therapy. All presumable share a common characteristic, but the setting of the phenomenon is varied.

As an expansion of this idea, consider Ernest Haggard's exemplary chapter on isolation and personality (1964). Haggard reviewed studies of isolation: How is personality affected by the restraint of habitual body movement in restricted, monotonous, or otherwise unfamiliar environments? Instead of limiting himself to the laboratory experimentation on sensory deprivation, he went abroad to the large literature of "naturally" occurring isolation. These are research findings on interstate truck drivers, pilots flying missions alone at night or at high altitudes, orthopedic patients in iron lungs, and anecdotal reports of prisoners in solitary confinement, shipwrecked sailors, and explorers. Haggard reports the commonalities among these widely *differing* groups, which overlapped on the isolation dimension, and which shared common sensory and personality phenomena. He compares, for example, the anecdotal reports of Admiral Byrd (1938) and the scientific investigation of Rohrer (1960) on International Geophysical Year personnel, both of whom found the individual cutting back on information input under isolated conditions—even when a mass of material was available to consume.

In another isolation investigation, Sells considered many of the same data in his applied study, "A model for the social system for the multiman extended duration space ship" (*NASA Report*, undated). Thinking of such long journeys as a Mars shot, Sells assembled data from many isolated groups, both natural and artificial. His analysis was careful and based on theory. He related the findings from different studies to a general model of an isolated social system—evaluating the degree to which results from the individual studies were likely to transfer to a space vehicle setting. Thus, data from submarine and exploration parties were most applicable, while the findings from shipwreck and disaster studies were least likely to transfer.

In this paper, I have stressed two main points. One is the utility of different data-gathering techniques applied concurrently to the same problem. The other is the laying of these techniques against multiple samples which are natural outcroppings of a phenomenon.

E. G. Boring, in a personal communication, wrote:

. . . The truth is something you get on toward and never to, and the way is filled with ingenuities and excitements. Don't take the straight and narrow path of the stodgy positivists; be gay and optimistic, like Galton, and you will find yourself more toward than you have ever expected.

▽ ▽ ▽

PART TWO

Test Administration Problems

TEST wise Americans often expect little difficulty with aptitude testing programs in other cultures, despite extensive anthropological and sociological evidence that culture and individual values were intertwined. In our easy adaptation to aptitude and achievement tests of all sorts, particularly in school situations, we are apt to forget that psychological testing is a very different sort of experience to foreigners, especially non-Westerners. Presumably, "culture free" tests (a clear misnomer, since no psychological tests can be constructed outside of any cultural value system) will minimize some of these difficulties; however, evidence that they can is sadly lacking. The following four articles deal with various aspects of test administration, both in "foreign" cultures and in U.S. subcultures.

The first article of this group relates some of the difficulties, as well as some very amusing sidelights that one psychologist met in his attempt to devise a selection battery for police officers in Vietnam. Dr. Wickert is Professor of Psychology at Michigan State University. During 1955–1957, he was in Vietnam on a technical assistance mission to the Vietnamese government. The article is reproduced in its entirety from *American Psychologist*, 1957.

AN ADVENTURE IN PSYCHOLOGICAL TESTING ABROAD

Frederic R. Wickert

In the room at the north end of the first floor of President Diem's Freedom Palace in Saigon, one day in September, 1955, several members of the "police team" and I were in a conference. We all belonged to the Michigan State University group sent to Vietnam to give technical aid to the government of that new country.

The police team members, one of several teams in the MSU group, had the mission of helping the Vietnam government improve the internal security of the country as rapidly as possible. In the States the police team members had all been engaged in professional police work. Normally, I am one of the regular teaching members of the MSU psychology department. Temporarily I had agreed to go to Vietnam as coordinator and deputy adviser for in-service training.

We MSU technical aides were conferring with Mr. Ro, something like a chief of staff to the Minister of the Interior, whose offices were in the palace. Mr. Ro, in addition to his many other duties, had been named to head the new police academy which our police team had been instrumental in establishing.

During the conference the subject of student selection arose. Mr. Ro asked whether we could give a test in order to make sure that only students who could benefit from the instruction would be included in the class. This request had a familiar ring to a psychologist. Further discussion indicated that the students should have completed the equivalent of sixth grade. From this it was concluded that an "intelligence" (educational achievement type) test, pitched at the level of students at the end of sixth grade, would be in order. We told Mr. Ro that we could, with help from him, prepare a suitable test in the short time remaining before the opening of the academy. Mr. Ro then arranged a visit to the Ministry of Education, where discussion with officials indicated that a test consisting partly of Vietnamese language items and partly of arithmetic items would be appropriate. Two "professors" who taught Vietnamese language and two who taught arithmetic, all at the sixth-grade level, were borrowed from the Ministry of Education. I spent some hours trying to explain to them how to construct objective items in language and arithmetic. The Far East edition of *Reader's Digest* fortunately contains a page of multiple-choice vocabulary items. These items provided a pattern for the language professors to follow. The idea of objective-type items came more readily to the arithmetic professors. It was most difficult to get both the language and arithmetic professors to prepare items of a wide enough range of difficulty. Specifically, they wanted to make difficult items only. Finally, some of the interpreter-translators around the office helped to construct items too. It got to be a game.

Vietnamese language is a tricky thing to work with. Basically it is monosyllabic. Complex, abstract concepts are sometimes expressed by combining two or three monosyllables. Since, however, Vietnamese is basically a peasants' language (with, for example, about twelve different ways of expressing the idea "to carry," a different word depending on what part of the body is doing the carrying), it is poor in abstractions, even when one tries putting Vietnamese monosyllables together to express more complex ideas. It borrows heavily from Chinese monosyllables, and combinations of monosyllables, for abstractions. Vietnamese who would do well on Chinese-type language items were said to be overly pedantic and would not necessarily make too good policemen.

In addition, the Tonkinese or North Vietnam dialect is quite different from the South Vietnam dialect. Almost the only persons available to construct vocabulary items were North Vietnamese intellectuals who had fled from the North as the Communists took over following the Geneva conference. But most of the persons who would take the test would know only the South Vietnamese dialect. Eventually these problems were largely overcome. A 60-item Vietnamese language and 60-item arithmetic test, including test booklet and a separate answer sheet, was finally prepared.

The Ministry of Education was asked to provide a large number of average boys, just beginning seventh grade, as a tryout group. After much negotiating, only one class of about 50 boys was made available. Instead of average boys, they turned out to be probably the best seventh-grade class in all Vietnam. The Vietnamese were out to show how well they could do. Naturally the items were too easy for this group. The item difficulty analyses did not show as much as would ordinarily have been expected.

Administering the test was an eye-opener for us Americans. It turned out to be necessary to give much supplemental instruction on the use of the separate answer sheet, on how to mark answers, etc. Boys would turn to each other for help, notwithstanding frequent instructions that they were not to talk to each other. Maintaining order was all the more difficult because of the Vietnamese habit of thinking out loud as they work problems or even study. How much neighbors listened to each other and benefited from this listening could not be determined. The test administrators and proctors could not be sure whether the students were communicating to each other or were merely doing the usual thinking out loud. The boys all seemed to try hard on the tests and remained in good spirits but looked very puzzled when we tried to keep them from talking. How to maintain "standardized" testing conditions under these circumstances?

Results showed that the arithmetic test took unnecessarily long, while the language test was too easy and too short. Odd–even reliabilities of the two-part scores were reasonably satisfactory, judging by the scatter diagrams of odd-versus-even scores.

In view of the above experiences, the test was reconstructed. The language test was expanded from 60 items to 100; the arithmetic was cut from 60 items to 40. The items were arranged in the order of their difficulty, as well as could be done from the data. Types of items thought to be difficult turned out to be relatively easy, and other types, thought to be easy, turned out to be difficult. Instructions were reworked in the light of specific difficulties encountered in the tryout testing.

The big day finally arrived when approximately 130 candidates, all policemen on the active force, appeared for testing. The two classrooms available for testing held but about 70 students each, so the group was split in two. Group 1 was started without much apparent difficulty. Its members were especially cautioned not to talk, and they stayed surprisingly quiet. We then went next door to Group 2. They had scarcely started when the slight rumble from the direction of Group 1 increased to a roar. We rushed back only to find that they had gone back to thinking out loud, each one trying to outshout his neighbor. In two hours practically all had finished and the papers were collected.

Results showed that we had guessed well on many things. Scatter diagrams showed odd–even reliabilities on both parts of the test to be about in the eighties or low nineties. The correlation between the two tests was probably in the low thirties. This time the items were fairly well arranged in the order of their difficulty. The test was rather easy, so that those subjects toward the lower end of the distribution were well spread out and discrimination among these persons was reasonably dependable. Incidentally, I had no time to work out any statistics. It was easy to teach Vietnamese assistants to score the tests, to make frequency distributions and scatter diagrams and to do simple item-difficulty analysis. In the rush of far more pressing matters, there was no time to teach them how to calculate correlation coefficients, and I had no time to do them myself.

Administratively the decision was made to send back to duty the 26 men with the lowest scores. A number of persons, both Vietnamese and Americans, objected to sending these men back on the grounds that they were the ones who most needed training. It was finally worked out that the low men from four or five classes would be accumulated and put through as a class for which the instruction would be especially adapted.

It developed that about three fifths of the group tested was made up of municipal police and the remaining two fifths were from the "Sureté," the plain-clothes, undercover men. Much to the surprise of the Americans, the Sureté men did no better on the test than the ordinary municipal police. To the Vietnamese this was no surprise. They did say that at least the test results would provide them with ammunition to try to convince the higher-ups that the Sureté should be given better men. The idea of using tests in selecting new men for the Sureté they have not yet been able or willing to grasp.

The staff of the Police Academy were most impressed by the speed with which test results were made available. They said that never before had they seriously considered using selection testing in a crash program like the present one. In the past, tests had always taken weeks and even months to score.

The speed-of-scoring feature of the tests had another by-product. The academy staff decided to give their classes weekly objective tests. Their first attempts to make true-false items were very crude, but they did better on multiple-choice items. In view of their obvious interest, I then gave the instructors some help on how to construct objective items. The students were much interested in the weekly achievement tests and demanded to have their scored papers returned to them quickly. Other parts of the government have begun to hear about the testing and have expressed an interest in learning more about how it is done. However, I have had no time to develop this field further.

Upon the graduation of the first class at the academy in late December, 1955, the candidates for the second class took the test. This time there was far less talking. According to some Vietnamese the word had gotten around with respect to how to behave during Western-style testing. This "word" was apparently far more potent than any test instructions. The volume of talking out loud during testing was down markedly.

A strongly worded request had gone out to all administrators sending candidates to the academy to refrain from sending any but good men in the future. A comparison of the first and second testings showed that in the first class 16 percent of 130 men made scores below 67, a kind of minimum passing score. In the second class, however, a little under 10 percent of the 165 candidates scored below 67. Although these results look as though either the statement to the administrators or other factors were operating to make the performance of the second group better, the difference is not significant.

Some other testing had been done in Vietnam. There is still a large sign over a courtyard leading to a government-type building which indicates that a psychotechnical center once existed there under the French occupation. The Vietnamese military have developed two tests which were used in selecting men to technical military specialties. This little bit of testing, done in the past, had apparently made no imprint on the culture, judging from our experiences.

Testing in another culture, then, can have its surprises. It also can be useful in that culture. With more time and effort, testing in Vietnam could play an increasingly important role in an awakening movement to adopt improved personnel practices and to modernize educational procedures.

▽ ▽ ▽

SCHWARZ has worked in an Africa setting, specifically that of Nigeria, where very little information concerning human resources was available. In any developing nation, it is vital that the most productive use of available manpower be made. A developing country cannot afford high failure rater in training which then means that selection processes must be accurate. The monograph by Schwarz (1961) is of interest as a summary of work, designed originally as a one-year program, to ascertain whether suitable screening techniques could be devised. The Nigerian government agreed to serve as a "laboratory" for this initial evaluation. Then, depending upon the success here, this work might subsequently be extended to other locales. Initially the task was to develop a preliminary set of testing instruments that could be feasibly administered to Nigerians without undue cost. Test administration problems in Nigeria were expected to be vastly different from USA. Out of this experience Schwarz arrived at a series of nine testing principles for use in situations such as these. These, together with the author's comments about certain of the outcomes, should be of interest since some unexpected developments did occur and required some ingenious solutions.*

The following material has been abstracted from Dr. Schwarz' full report (pp. 14–22, 72–74) which was published by the American Institute for Research in 1961, when he was Senior Research Scientist (he is currently Executive Vice-President), in the form of a research report submitted to the International Cooperation Administration in Washington, D.C. The test battery was entirely of the paper-and-pencil variety. A grand total of over 2,000 Nigerians were successfully tested.

PRINCIPLES FOR AFRICAN TESTING

Paul A. Schwarz

The modifications that made the American tests suitable for use in Nigeria can be grouped into nine general principles or rules. Most of these are techniques to be followed in administering aptitude tests, irrespective of the specific content of the items included.

Three of the principles derived from the examinees' inexperience in taking aptitude tests. The standard American procedures pre-suppose a certain degree of "test-wiseness" that our children begin to develop in elementary school, and that matures with increased exposure in the later school years. But the Nigerian has had little if any opportunity to become sophisticated in the accepted testing ritual, and will be at a serious disadvantage if the following modifications are not made:

1. *The testing procedure should not pre-suppose any response as being*

---

* For a more general discussion of adapting tests to differing cultural settings, see Schwarz (1963).

automatic on the part of the examinee. It should include explicit provisions for teaching him every response that he will be expected to make.

This includes not only the responses related to the solution of the test problems, but also all the incidental manipulations that are normally required. The handling of pencils, test booklets and answer sheets (if used) must be explained in detail. This explanation should also include complete instructions for "emergency" situations; i.e., what to do if one of the test pages is blank or unintelligible because of a printing error. Time limits are a special problem that requires specific training and practice sessions.

When a battery of several tests is being administered, it is best to use a sequential training procedure that introduces only one or two new elements with each test, and that gradually builds up to the most complex. In the present study, for example, the first test given to a group was always the one paced by the examiner.

Separate instructions are given for each item, so that the examinees all work at a pre-determined and fairly rapid rate. This paves the way for the introduction of the clock in the second test, selected to be the one with the most generous allowance of time. The last test is the most demanding, requiring the examinees to budget their own time within one-minute limits.

2. *The design of the test booklet should minimize the number of constraints imposed on the examinee's performance in working from the first page to the last. Insofar as possible, instructions and cautions irrelevant to the solution of the problems should be eliminated.*

American tests are super-efficient in layout and design. By such procedures as binding different tests into a single booklet, or printing certain portions upside down, they are able to collapse the material into a shorter and therefore cheaper form. This economy is not feasible with less sophisticated examinees. They will generally not be able to "store" the complex program of instructions that includes choice-points and abrupt changes of procedure.

The examinee should not have to decide when to continue to the next page or column, when to stop and check his work, and when to wait for further instructions. Different tasks should not be printed on the same page, and different tests should not be included in the same booklet. And if a set of tests is to be used during a single session, the mechanics for handling and marking them should be the same.

Because of these changes, the tests developed for this study are generally bulkier than they would have been for use in the United States. But, in retrospect, even more might have been done. It would probably be helpful to split apart also the separately timed parts of the same test, and to collect the completed papers for one part before moving on to the next.

3. *The test should not rely on any printed instructions for teaching or*

controlling the responses to be made. The test booklet should include no such instructions.

This applies not only to the explanatory instructions that usually precede the test, but also to such briefer directions (e.g., *STOP*) as might be interspersed among the test items. The use of printed instructions in Nigeria generally resulted in confusion.

The problem seems not to lie in the comprehension of written materials, but rather in their adequacy as a stimulus for physical action. Apparently, these groups are not accustomed to receiving directions in printed form.

This is illustrated in a study of the *Patterns* test, given to two streams of eighth-year elementary school students in the same school. One group took the test with the standard American directions, while the other took a special form with printed Yoruba instructions. In the English group, 50 percent of the students did not know what to do when the starting signal was given. In the Yoruba group, this percentage dropped only to 40 percent, indicating that language comprehension was not the critical factor. And when the test was given to a third stream with the printed directions entirely deleted, the percentage dropped to 8 percent, as reported below.

The preceding three principles dealt mostly with aspects of testing that cannot be used because of the naivete of the test group. The next two describe approaches that are effective substitutes for the standard procedures.

4. *The most effective means of teaching the test is through the use of visual aids, supplemented by active demonstration. These aids should replicate as closely as possible the exact operation to be performed.*

Visual aids serve two functions. One is to help reduce concepts and "mental" processes to the level of physical operations. If the examinee has to visualize the appearance of an object after rotation, a mock-up of this object can be affixed to a pin and actually turned. If it is to be folded, an articulated model can in a similar manner make tangible the exact folding operation.

The second use of such aids is as a vehicle for demonstration. Working with simulated test items, the examiner can himself do all of the operations that he is asking the examinees to do during the test. This makes the test instructions comparable to the teaching methods to which the students are accustomed, since these usually proceed through rote learning of the cookbook style.

It was such a combination of visuals and demonstration that yielded the dramatic improvement on the *Patterns* test reported above, and that was subsequently used for all the other tests with comparable success. The examiner must take care to avoid any slips in his demonstration, as these will surely be duplicated in the performance of the examinees.

5. *Explanations necessary to supplement the demonstrations should*

be given through oral instructions. Such instructions must take account of idiosyncrasies in local patterns of speech and expression.

Supplementary instructions would probably be most effective if given in the native languages by native personnel. In the present study, this was done only for groups that did not speak English as a second language. But it might well have simplified the test administrations to have adopted this procedure for all groups irrespective of education level.

English instructions can be used *only* after extensive pretryout on representative samples of examinees. The objectives are to eliminate phrases that prove to be not immediately understood, to introduce accepted local (in Nigeria this is British) idiom, and to follow the conventions that have somehow developed for this kind of communication.

One example of such a convention in Nigeria is the appropriate "trigger" for initiating action as a result of oral instructions. Instructions like *"Write your name at the top of the paper—right here"* typically get no result at all. But the slight change to *"Everybody, write your name at the top of the paper—right here"* produces immediate action.

Another useful device is to give preference to words that are also used in the local English vernacular (i.e., Pidgin-English) spoken at the lower levels. The principle underlying such languages is that it is possible to communicate with a small vocabulary of basic expressions that do away with the shadings and redundancies in the formal language. Thus, the word *small* is the only expression that is used to convey the idea of diminution; it encompasses all of the meanings of such words as *few, little, slight,* and the rest. Test instructions that use the local words in lieu of more accurate expressions improved comprehension, even with advanced groups.

The following two principles are additional suggestions related to the design of effective instructions. They are based on certain differences in the attitudes of Nigerian examinees that are not usually found with American test groups:

6. *The training session should include supervised practice in doing the test problems, with a specific provision for feedback to the examiner. Such practice and feedback must cover not only the basic task, but also any variation that may be incorporated in certain of the test items.*

The practice period is not itself an innovation, since this is part of the standard procedure. But in designing practice problems for these groups, it is particularly important to insure that such problems sample even minor differences in the test items. Because of the tendency to mimic the teacher (or examiner) precisely, there is little generalization from the specific procedures illustrated in the instruction and practice phases. If a picture of a fish is the correct answer to one of the sample problems, some examinees will perseverate in choosing the fish in subsequent items without looking for a more appropriate answer. The solution is to make the fish the wrong answer in one of the other sample or practice problems.

The need for explicit provisions for feedback derive from the reticence of the examinees to admit their own confusion, or to question anything that the teacher or teacher-surrogate might be doing. They will seldom ask spontaneous questions, and will uniformly indicate complete comprehension if queried on their understanding by the teacher.

If the practice problems are sufficiently comprehensive, they will require the examinee to display his understanding with respect to all of the important operations he should have learned. The examiner and/or proctors can then check each examinee's paper, and supply additional explanations on an individual basis. The more usual *"Are there any questions?"* is generally a waste of time.

7. *To get maximum examinee cooperation, the testing procedure should differ sharply from the routines to which they are normally accustomed in school. Elements of the dramatic or flamboyant inspire the peak effort that is necessary for effective aptitude measures.*

Because of physical limitations, most testing sessions must be held in a classroom or study hall of an available school. This produces a natural identification with accepted school practices that the testing procedures must try to break down. Many tests require patterns of behavior (e.g., striving for speed rather than accuracy) quite incompatible with the examinees' past experiences in a school setting.

To stimulate greater enthusiasm, it is necessary to conduct the tests almost at the level of a serious but nevertheless enjoyable game. As important as the technical soundness of the test procedures is their appeal as a new form of entertainment.

Accordingly, all aspects of the present procedures were pretried also for their entertainment value. It was found that the introduction of such elements as action, suspense, and humor produced the desired responses much more effectively than stern warnings or admonitions.

The enforcement of a one-minute time limit, for example, could not be managed with normal proctoring procedures. But the problem was solved by a simple change in the demonstration phase. For this test, the examiner flubs his usually perfect demonstration (often amid loud cheers and applause). He insists on stopping as soon as the bell rings, even though he has not completed the exercise, and will get a poor score. The examiner's failure leads to complete cooperation on the part of the examinees.

Application of the foregoing principles can be expected to provide workable testing procedures. The technical content of the test problems, however, is a separate problem. The general finding of this study was that most of the non-verbal test materials used in the United States can also be used with Nigerian examinees, providing that the instructions are properly presented. But there are exceptions, leading to additional principles concerned with the content of the items themselves:

8. *It is seldom possible to predict on logical grounds which tasks foreign examinees can and cannot do. Each new test should be subjected to thorough experimental investigation.*

Test items should not be based on intuitive notions or expert opinions of appropriateness, since these generally underestimate the abilities of the examinees. The instructors and administrators who inspected the present tests prior to their application consistently predicted that the items were too difficult for their students or trainees, and were consistently wrong in their predictions.

Nevertheless, there are certain cultural deficits in the examinees' ability to perform essentially Western skills that they have no opportunity to practice in their own culture. One wellknown example is the interpretation of drawings, especially when they are intended to show depth as a third dimension.

Such factors can have subtle implications. In designing one of the present tests, it was found that the examinees could immediately interpret one drawing of a banana but had great difficulty with another that to American students would be equally clear. In the measurement of three-dimensional visualization, these problems proved too difficult to be resolved by minor adaptations, and an entirely different kind of test had to be devised.

On the other hand, there were no such problems in the *Inspection* test, despite the fact that this contained many drawings of technical and mechanical objects that the examinees had never before seen. On this as on all other tests it was necessary to defer the judgment of appropriateness until empirical data had been collected.

9. *Preference should be given to items that are reasonably independent of individual differences in the tactics or strategies of the examinees. It is usually not possible to enforce a uniform strategy that will be followed by the entire group.*

Many tests require a uniform approach by all of the examinees whose scores will be compared. On these tests, the normal instructions include such advice as *"If you find one problem very difficult, go on to an easier one,"* or *"You should try to answer every item,"* or *"Work as fast as you can without making mistakes."* The American student takes this in stride, and further delimits the task by asking point-blank *"Does this test have a correction for guessing?"*

It is not feasible to try to teach the Nigerian examinee the fine points of testmanship in a session already crowded with more basic instruction. One solution is to avoid using tests in which different strategies will produce widely disparate scores.

Early in the study, for example, a set of *Matrices* was used as a power test with a time limit of 15 minutes. The instructions had been refined in accordance with the above principles, and there were no problems of comprehension or cooperation. But the variability in the ways different examinees budgeted their time during this relatively long testing period could not be controlled. The test was eventually shelved in favor of an alternative procedure that permitted external control on an item-by-item basis.

On some tests, it is possible to correct for different strategies by an appropriate scoring formula. With tasks such as arithmetic computation or the comparison of names, the slow and careful approach can be roughly equated to the rapid but careless tactic by an appropriate weighting of errors. The magnitude of such weights must be determined empirically by rather elaborate research. Because the design of this research proved unworkable when attempted in the present study, the American procedure of triple-weighting errors was provisionally adopted. This is almost certainly not the optimal solution, however, and a more appropriate formula should be determined in future research.

The formulation of these nine principles was the turning point in the project. They made possible the adaptation of a wide variety of test instruments that could then be applied to the main study objectives. It is likely that they can be used in subsequent studies to provide equally effective measure of additional aptitudes and skills important to a comprehensive screening program.

SPECIFIC TESTING PROCEDURES

One of the immediate consequences of the experimental phase was that the testing materials imported from the United States could not be used. New forms had to be developed in Lagos, using available equipment, and abiding by tropical work schedules. The petty routines of preparing, printing, and assembling test materials became major logistic problems.

The upshot was that many compromises had to be made. In some cases, it was necessary to use pictures that could be cut and pasted from published sources, even when significantly better items could have been designed on the basis of the experimental findings. The need was for instruments that would serve the purposes of the preliminary survey, and generate the data needed to prepare improved operational forms after the initial study was completed.

A battery of twelve tests was developed and tried out to sample such basic aptitudes as learning ability, three-dimensional visualization (crucial for most mechanical and technical occupations), various perceptual skills (involving detection of differences and "hidden figures"), coordination, clerical aptitude, arithmetical computation and the like. These test results then provided a comprehensive pool of data from which a battery specially relevant to a particular job could be assembled. But the basic problem was the feasibility of even administering aptitude tests to African examinees. On the basis of prevalent opinion about the rate of learning of the African student, Schwarz comments that, many would have predicted that even this could not have been achieved. Yet the findings show that, in the end, this and more was done and with excellent results. Some 500 students at various education levels and at widely separated geographical locations easily learned the entire set of operations required. The reliability of their performance was comparable to results that are typically secured from American testees in similar amounts of testing time. (Editor's note.)

This suggests that the basic *capacity* of the Nigerian is far greater than has been supposed. The composition of the tests as a set of specific job elements further suggests that this capacity includes the ability for learning Western job skills.

The actual process of producing these skills, however, includes many factors quite different from the African's basic ability to learn. His capacity or maximum performance capabilities refer to the kinds of things that he *can* or *could* do. This is not at all the same as what he *will* do in a practical training situation.

More specifically, the findings of the present study suggest that the African's performance in a typical training program will be considerably below the potential indicated by the above conclusion. He will, as many observers have reported, learn more slowly than the European; and he will attain a generally lower level of skill. Not because of deficient capacities, but because of a number of other external limitations.

One of these limitations was illustrated by the sharp contrast between the experimental and tryout phases. During the initial testing, the examinees were not at all the rapid learners they later proved to be. They were confused, apathetic, and sluggish, and did poorly on all of the test problems. It was not until the American training procedures were discarded that this illusion of incompetence disappeared.

Apparently, the *technique of training* determines the performance of African examinees to a much greater extent than is true in the Western cultures. And, at least in the teaching of test problems, the training methods imported from a foreign country could not be instituted without major adaptations.

The implication is that the improvements in selection afforded by this study must be accompanied by corresponding improvements in training if Nigeria's potential is to be translated into tangible manpower resources. Many of the institutions visited during the project were actively seeking more suitable methods, and on their success may depend the final answer to the trainability of the Nigerian trainee.

A second limitation is suggested by the nature of the adaptations that made the American tests suitable for Nigerian use. Re-examining the nine principles that motivated these changes shows that they were largely directed at one specific area of need. The Nigerian examinee was not prepared for these materials to the same extent as the American student because he had less opportunity for the *incidental learning* that in our culture occurs mainly outside of school. He is prepared for activities traditional to his own culture, and learns many things through experience that the American boy will never know. But when he is placed into a training situation that requires essentially Western skills, he is not adequately prepared.

The class of skills involving eye-hand coordination is a case in point. In America, such skills are developed through many casual activities such as sketching or the manipulation of mechanical objects and toys. But in Nigeria, this kind of activity is relatively rare. And the test intended to measure this skill had to be dropped because it was too difficult for the typical Nigerian examinee.

Nor is the phenomenon found only in the testing situation. One of Nigeria's graduate engineers reported that he sped through all science and math courses in one of the better English institutions, but had to stay in England an extra year to pass the mechanical drawing examinations.

If such countries as Nigeria decide to use Western technology as one tool of development, this lack of incidental learning about things technological will continue to hamper the performance of their trainees. It would be unrealistic to try to introduce the necessary opportunities into the culture as a whole, but the schools could readily take on this responsibility as an adjunct to the classic curricula they now teach. Especially at the primary levels much incidental training could profitably be done.

There are no doubt many other factors, such as attitudes and motivations, that affect the performance of the Nigerian trainee. But for the present it is tentatively concluded that

1. The performance of the groups tested in this study showed higher levels of ability than are traditionally estimated for the African population.

2. These abilities include the capacity for learning needed manpower skills.

3. This high potential may not be realized under existing methods of education and training.

▽ ▽ ▽

ESPECIALLY with psychological tests that require individual administration, such as the Stanford-Binet or the Wechsler scales, to say
nothing of projective tests, all test manuals exhort the test administrator to be neutral and objective, and to establish good rapport with the
testee. Beyond general statements, such as the admonition to the
examiner to remain interested and attentive, and in the instance of
incomplete answers to ask for further information, little more is done
with this general topic of rapport. A little reflection on the business of
interaction between tester and testee, especially in an individual test
situation when some area critical to the testee such as intelligence is
being rated, would lead one to pay close attention to this aspect of
test administration. Partly because the entire situation is supposed to
be objective and because scoring instructions are so detailed, it is
often assumed that this personal interaction phase of test administration can be minimized. The following report, one of the few in the
research literature, shows that significant differences in test scores
can result among testees (accomplices) who put on a warm or cold
facade to the examiner, and that even in an objective situation of this
type relatively experienced examiners can be adversely influenced.

Dr. Masling is Professor of Psychology at the State University of
New York at Buffalo. A previous report by him, employing a projective
test situation (1957), showed significant effects of such warm and
cold facades. In the present report, condensed from the *Journal of
Consulting Psychology*, 1959, the same effects are to be seen in a
more objective and standardized test situation.

THE EFFECTS OF WARM AND COLD INTERACTION ON THE ADMINISTRATION AND SCORING OF AN INTELLIGENCE TEST

Joseph Masling

Several studies have examined the psychologist–subject relationship
in projective test situations. The ambiguity which faces both examiner
and subject here makes it probable that each will be influenced by the
other in attempting to complete their respective tasks. In intelligence
testing, however, the instructions are specific, the stimuli are clearly
defined, and there are right and wrong answers. Here the examiner is
required to read the questions as stated in the test and to evaluate the
answers with the aid of a scoring manual.

The examiner–subject relationship in intelligence testing has not
received a great deal of attention. During the course of their training
most examiners are exhorted to establish "rapport" and admonished to
be "objective." The "objective" examiner is charged with the responsibility of deriving as valid an estimate of the intelligence of the subject as
can be obtained, without regard for his personal attitudes about the
subject. He is thus expected to be standardized and depersonalized. The

purpose of the present study was to investigate the extent to which an examiner could divest himself of personal bias in administering and scoring an intelligence test—in this case, three verbal subtests of the Wechsler-Bellevue I* (hereafter called the "W-B I")—when the subject acted in either a highly approving, interested (warm) manner or in a persistently rejecting, disinterested (cold) manner. The specific hypotheses which were tested were as follows:

1. When an examiner tests two subjects, one of whom acts warm to him and the other cold, he will be more generous in scoring the responses of the warm subject.

2. During the course of administration of an intelligence test to two subjects, one of whom is warm and the other cold, an examiner will: (a) make more reinforcing statements to the warm subject than the cold; (b) ask more questions of the warm subject, giving him the opportunity of clarifying or reformulating an answer.

METHOD

The Interaction

Manipulation of the interaction was effected through the use of attractive female accomplices, posing as test subjects (S's), who acted either warm or cold to the examiner. In the warm condition, the accomplice acted interested in the examiner and in the test; she responded freely to his questions and tried to communicate respect and liking for him. In the cold condition, the accomplice acted disinterested and bored with the test and the examiner; her attitude was that of fulfilling an unpleasant class assignment which she wanted to complete as soon as possible. She tended to answer pre-test interview questions in monosyllables and throughout avoided eye contact with the examiner. In the middle of each cold session the accomplice in a deliberate, calculated fashion put on sunglasses, thereby increasing the psychological distance between herself and the examiner.

Examiners and Procedure

These were 11 graduate students at Syracuse University, all of whom had completed at least one course in the administration of individual tests of intelligence. Six of these also had had further work with individual tests. The most experienced of the examiners had previously given over 200 W-B's. The median W-B adminstrations for the entire group was 21.

Each examiner was told that the author was interested in the comparability of various short forms of the W-B and that he would be asked to administer two or three subtests to subjects chosen at random. The subjects would be two undergraduates participating in the experiment

---

* Listed incorrectly in the original report as "W-B II."

as part of their Introductory Psychology course requirement.

Each examiner administered three subtests (Information, Comprehension, Similarities) to both subjects, one of whom acted warm to him and the other cold. Each accomplice had five cold and five warm roles. To insure uniformity in score, each examiner was directed to use the instructions in Wechsler's manual (third edition). The experimenter prepared a script for each accomplice to memorize and to repeat to each examiner, regardless of whether this was a warm or cold interaction. Fourteen of these responses were written to maximize difficulty in scoring. All test situations were tape-recorded.

RESULTS

There was no mistaking the impact of the warm and cold conditions on the examiners. All reported that one S seemed particularly disinterested in the test, with some emphasizing the notion that this represented "sick" behavior. One examiner correctly guessed that the S's were really accomplices, and he was therefore replaced and his data were not used.

Hypothesis I was tested by comparing the way in which each examiner scored the responses given him under the two conditions. Since the experimenter had intentionally written responses that gave a higher "true" IQ for one of the accomplices than for the other, the bias of the examiner scoring was determined from the mean of the 10 scores given each accomplice, rather than from the raw scores. Once a mean score for each accomplice had been obtained, the extent and direction of differences from each mean were derived for each examiner. A statistical test showed that the probability of obtaining such a distribution of differences by chance was remote ($p = .056$).

Hypothesis I can also be evaluated by looking at scores assigned above and below the subject's mean. Of the five examiners who tested Accomplice A under the warm condition, four gave her scores greater than the mean, while of the five examiners who tested her in the cold condition, four gave her scores smaller than the mean. The identical results were obtained for Accomplice B: four of the five examiners who interacted with her in a warm manner gave her scores greater than the mean, while four of the five examiners who interacted with her in the cold condition gave her scores smaller than the mean.

Hypothesis II was tested by having independent judges go through the tape recordings (all identifying data being removed) and rating examiner statements as reinforcing ("OK," "swell," etc.) or questioning ("Can you be more specific?"). There were 285 examiner remarks culled from the testing sections of the interviews. The judges independently agreed on the ratings of 89 percent of the remarks; the remainder were eventually agreed upon in conference. Once the number of reinforcing and questioning statements had been obtained, a comparison was made of each examiner's verbal behavior during the warm interaction and with his verbal behavior during the cold interaction. All examiners made more reinforcing statements to the warm subjects and they asked more questions of them. The sum of reinforcing and questioning statements was also greater for the warm condition than for the cold.

While the experimental hypotheses were substantiated, the differences between conditions seemed much smaller than the differences among examiners. For example, Examiner 1 made a total of only 14 remarks to his S's, while Examiner 7 made 64. Examiner 8's scoring favored the warm condition by 4.8 points, while Examiner 5's scoring was biased in favor of the cold condition by 1.8 points. Since it was possible that the more experienced examiners were least biased by the interaction, rank order correlations were computed between the number of W-B's previously given and the dependent variables. None of the *rho's* was significantly greater than zero.

DISCUSSION

The results of this study indicate that the examiner–subject interaction influenced the psychologist's behavior in the administration and scoring of the three subtests of the W-B I. When the instructions to the cold accomplice are considered, i.e., to answer in monosyllables, to appear disinterested, and the typescripts of the sessions studied, it becomes clear that the examiners tried to make contact with the Cold S and, in failing to do this, became silent. While the examiners were undoubtedly trained to encourage the S, this was difficult to do when friendly overtures elicited disinterest and rejection. The feelings which the interaction aroused in these examiners obviously influenced the manner in which they administered the tests. With warm, responsive S's they tended to encourage and question; with cold S's they tended to remain silent.

It is difficult to predict the extent to which this particular finding can be generalized to nonlaboratory situations. Probably few individuals taking intelligence tests act as hostile and nonparticipating as the cold accomplice. However, some S's, notably children, may become threatened by the testing situation, responding with belligerence or silence or other variations of avoidance.

The interaction also affected the examiners' "objective" judgment of the scoring of relatively "objective" material. Even though they had the Wechsler manual available, a response given in the warm condition tended to be given greater credit than the identical response given in the cold condition. This bias is even more striking when it is considered that the scoring occurred some time after the testing, allowing the examiners some perspective regarding the events of the session. Again, this study exaggerated the situation found in most clinic settings, since the examiners were given responses that were selected because they were difficult to evaluate. However, an examination of the scoring records indicated that there were systematic differences even for those responses which were cited as examples in the scoring manual.

The artificial nature of this study—the use of accomplices and relatively unsophisticated examiners, the exaggerated nature of the interjection, the use of ambiguous responses—together with the inadequate sampling of both the examiner and accomplice populations limits severely the generalization of these findings to nonlaboratory settings of psychologists and S's. What has been demonstrated is that in giving an intelligence test under these conditions, an advanced graduate student examiner will respond to the way S's interact with him and will act out his feelings about the interpersonal situation in administration and scoring.

SUMMARY

1. Eleven graduate students, each of whom had completed at least one course in the adminstration of individual intelligence tests, administered the Information, Comprehension, and Similarities subtests of the Wechsler-Bellevue I to two subjects. The test subjects were accomplices who acted in either a warm or cold role to the examiners, giving as their responses memorized answers, 14 of which were specifically devised to be difficult to score. One examiner became aware of the purposes of the experiment, and his data were not used. Each accomplice had five cold and five warm roles, and each examiner saw one subject who acted warm and one who acted cold.

2. From the typescripts prepared from these tapes, every examiner remark during the course of the testing part of the interview was rated. Of the 285 examiner statements, two judges independently agreed on the rating of 254 of them, for an agreement of 89 percent.

3. The results indicated that in scoring the responses, the examiners tended to be more lenient to the warm subject than the cold. The examiners also tended to use more reinforcing comments and to give more opportunity to clarify or correct responses to the warm subject. The magnitude of the differences in behavior to the two subjects was generally small, with individual differences more marked than differences due to the effect of the interaction.

Not only may client behavior influence test results and the interpretative comments derived from test protocols, but also client "stimulus input" may clearly influence an interviewer's or therapist's behavior. The behavior of the therapist, for example, may be very specifically determined by the stimulus characteristics of his client. Heller et al. (1963) decided to study these effects by using trained student actors who acted out hostile–friendly and dominant–dependent roles during a half-hour intake interview conducted by 34 graduate student trainees in clinical and counseling psychology. Clear results were obtained (with the exception of the client who portrayed the dependent–hostile role but was, in actuality, not very hostile) to show that clients could evoke reciprocal behaviors from therapist, even though these influences were not perceived. Experience of the inter-viewers or therapists used in this study, incidentally, varied from one semester's clinical practicum to several years of field experience.

In view of the widespread belief that testing conditions have signifi-cant effects on scores, Pierce (1963) was surprised to find little effect on scores for four WAIS subtests administered as part of a psychiatric screening process to several hundred patients over 60 years old. The test administrators rated the test conditions as good, fair, or poor (poor meant one or more disruptive events such as kibitzing of fellow patients). The mean WAIS summed scores did drop as one pro-gressed from good to poor test conditions, but not significantly. Pierce admits that the rating of test conditions was crude, and that one could only conclude here that poor test conditions do not have the gross effects usually thought. He feels that perhaps a more homogeneous group, such as college sophomores, might be better suited to test these effects of noise and distraction. "But at least we have evidence that intelligence tests are more robust than test au-thors have thought"(p. 537).

The Masling report is one of a long series of studies in which experimenter and subject variables, rapport variations, and situa-tional variables (such as discouragement) have been utilized in both intelligence and personality testing. Sattler and Theye (1967) have recently reviewed some 65 studies concerned with departures for what are usually seen as standardized procedures, all involving indi-vidual intelligence testing situations. They conclude that minor changes in test procedures are more likely to affect specialized groups (such as elderly, disturbed, or retarded individuals) than normals. Children, not surprisingly, are more susceptible to situa-tional factors (as discouragement) than are older testees. Effects are greatest with test items or test responses that are ambiguous and less highly structured. Skin color of either the experimenter or the subject has rather unclear effects. Little is known, for example, about the effects of a Negro examiner with a white testee. Sattler and Theye report inadequate research designs in many of the studies they summarize. They conclude that a combination of man and machine test administration may solve some of the problems encountered but that, still, many questions will remain unanswered.

▽ ▽ ▽

EXPERIMENTER–subject differences, especially when visible and obvious, may make for measurement distortions and invalid scores. Such experimenter–subject differences would be particularly significant in regard to intelligence testing, where so much of one's ego may be invested and where, say, the examiner is white and the subject is a southern black youngster. Masling's previous paper, describing warm and cold manipulations, can serve as a fitting introduction to the far more serious business of black-white interrelationships, especially when these concern test situations with ego-involving aspects.

So significant was this issue—especially since experience has shown that conventional intruments of mental testing were too often fashioned to fit the cultural ways of middle-class children, so that minority group children were being excluded from special training opportunities because of "cultural deprivation"—that the Society for the Psychological Study of Social Issues published a report (SPSSI, 1964) on how this unfortunate situation might be remedied.

Related to this broader issue is the following article by Dr. Irwin Katz and his collaborators, all of whom were associated at New York University at the time of this research, which was jointly supported by the university and the Office of Naval Research. The original report first appeared in the *Journal of Social Issues*, 1964, and is presented here in a slightly condensed form. Dr. Katz is now at the Graduate Center of the City College of New York.

THE INFLUENCE OF RACE OF THE EXPERIMENTER AND INSTRUCTIONS UPON THE EXPRESSION OF HOSTILITY BY NEGRO BOYS

Irwin Katz, James M. Robinson,
Edgar G. Epps, and Patricia Waly

It was recently demonstrated that the efficiency of Southern Negro college students on a verbal task can be influenced by both the race of the experimenter and the evaluate significance of the task. Katz, Roberts and Robinson (1963) found that when digit-symbol substitution was presented as a test of eye-hand coordination, Negro subjects scored higher with a white administrator than they did with a Negro administrator. But when the same task was described as an intelligence test, there was marked impairment of performance with the white tester, while subjects who were tested by the Negro experimenter showed a slight improvement. The present study deals with the effect of these experimental conditions upon the arousal and expression of hostility.

There is reason to believe that emotional conflict involving the need to control hostility may have a disruptive influence on the performance of Negro students when their intelligence is evaluated by a white person. Sarason *et al.* (1960) have described the test-anxious child, whether Negro or white, as one who typically reacts with strong unconscious hostility to the adult tester, whom he believes will in some way pass judgment on his adequacy. The hostility is not openly expressed, but instead is turned inward against the self in the form of self-derogatory attitudes, which strengthen the child's expectation of failure and desire to escape from the situation. Thus, he is distracted from the task before him by fear of failure and impulse to escape.

A number of studies support the view of blocking of aggressive impulses as detrimental to intellectual efficiency. Scholastic underachievement has been found to be associated with difficulty in expressing aggression openly. Rosenwald (1961) reported that students who give relatively few aggressive responses on a projective test suffered greater impairment in solving anagrams after a hostility induction than did students who had shown less inhibition on the projective test. Goldman, Horwitz and Lee (1954) demonstrated experimentally that the degree to which hostility against an instigator was blocked from expression determined the amount of disruption on three cognitive tasks.

With respect to Negroes, it is known that segregation engenders a feeling of intellectual inadequacy (for a review of empirical evidence, see Dreger & Miller, 1960), hence they should be prone to experience test situations as threatening. Hostility would tend to arise against the adult authority figure from whom an unfavorable evaluation was expected. The Negro student's hostility might perhaps be stronger against a white tester than against a Negro tester, since the former might be expected to compare him invidiously with members of the advantaged white group. However, previous research suggests that aggressive impulses against a white person will usually be strongly inhibited. There is also evidence (Berkowitz, 1962) that when there are strong restraints operating against openly aggressive behavior, even its expression on projective tests will be blocked to some extent.

In the present experiment, hostile expression was measured by means of a questionnaire that was disguised as a concept formation test. Negro students at a segregated high school in the South were given the questionnaire by either a Negro or a white experimenter, with instructions that described it either neutrally or as an intelligence test. Then scores were compared with those obtained previously by the same subjects in an informal, all-Negro setting. It was predicted that when neutral instructions were used, levels of hostile expression in the Negro-tester and white-tester groups would remain the same, but when intelligence test instructions were used, hostility scores would *increase* under a Negro experimenter and *decrease* when the experimenter was white.

METHOD

Subjects and Procedures

The subjects were 72 male students at a Negro high school and junior high school in Nashville. They ranged in age from 13 to 18 years. Volunteers for the experiment were recruited in classrooms with an offer of one dollar for participating for an hour in a research project. The study was done on two successive days. The first day all subjects met after school in a large room and were administered the hostility scale by the assistant principal of the school. They were told that the purpose of the questionnaire was to aid in evaluation of a proposed new method for teaching vocabulary. Afterwards, they were given their assignments for the following day. For the second session the entire sample was divided into four groups of equal size. Each group was tested by either a white or a Negro adult stranger, with instructions that described the task as either an intelligence test or a research instrument. The two testers worked simultaneously in different rooms, and ran the two instructional conditions in quick succession, to prevent subject contamination. Both experimenters introduced themselves as psychologists from local universities (Fisk and Vanderbilt) and gave oral instructions.

The neutral instructions stated in part:

Yesterday you did some vocabulary items. Today you will do a slightly different version of this task for me. It is *not* a test. I am doing research on the meaning of certain words in American speech. To a psychologist, the meaning of a word refers to how it is used by people who speak the language. So I want you to show me how you use these words. Your answers will not be shown to your teachers. Yesterday you had a practice warm-up. It will not be scored. Today's answers are the ones that count. So answer what you think is correct today.

The intelligence test instructions were in part:

Yesterday you were given a vocabulary test. Today you will do a slightly different version of this test for me. I am interested in this vocabulary test because it will show me how intelligent you are. I am doing research of mental ability, and I want to see how bright you boys are at ——— School. This test will show your knowledge of words, your ability to recognize abstract concepts, and your general intelligence. It will show whether you could succeed in college, or in your chosen field of work. But your individual scores will *not* be shown to your teachers. They will be used only for research on intelligence. Yesterday you had a practice warm-up (rest of instructions same as neutral conditions).

After the instuctions were given, a hostility questionnaire was administered which was the same as the one used the previous day, except that the items were arranged differently.

The Hostility Scale

The instrument used to measure hostile expression was based on a test that had been developed by Ehrlich (1961) to study the influence of aggressive dispositions on concept formation in Northern white adolescent boys. Our test had 58 items, each consisting of four words, with instructions to "circle the word that does not belong with the others." Twenty-nine items contained only nonaggressive concepts; elimination of a particular word resulted in a better concept than did elimination of any other word, e.g.: TUNNEL, BRIDGE, FERRY, TOLL. In the remaining 29 items, one word had an aggressive meaning, one was nonaggressive, and two were ambiguous, e.g.: HOMERUN, HIT, BASH, STRIKE. Here the subject could select an aggressive concept by eliminating HOMERUN, or a nonaggressive concept by dropping BASH. Out of a total of 58 items in our test, 47 were taken from Ehrlich's 84-item test. He found scores on his test to be related to ratings of overt aggression, as well as to hostility scores on a TAT-like projective test. The present version evolved from a preliminary tryout of the original instrument of a sample of Southern Negro college students, under neutral instructions. Items which did not appear to be suitable were dropped, and some new ones were added.

A subject's hostility score consisted of the total number of critical items in which he had included the aggression word, regardless of whether he had used the correct concept. In addition, a score indicative of the level of intellectual functioning was obtained by totalling the number of correct concepts attained on neutral items, and on aggression items. To study the effect of the experimental conditions, change scores were obtained by subtracting each subject's scores on the pretest from his scores on the post test.

RESULTS AND DISCUSSION

The main findings of the experiment by analysis of variance, indicate that there was a significant interaction effect of the two variables, Race of Tester and Test vs. Neutral Instructions, on changes in hostility scores from the previous day ($p < .025$). The group means reveal that in the Neutral condition the change scores of subjects who had a white administrator were only slightly different from those of subjects who had a Negro administrator. But when test instructions were used, the White Tester group expressed *less* hostility than previously, while the Negro Tester group showed an *increase* in hostile expression. This difference between groups was significant ($p < .01$). Thus the experimental prediction was supported.

There were no significant effects of the experimental conditions on changes in the number of correct concepts attained on neutral items, on aggression items, or on all items combined. Within each of the four experimental groups, there were no correlations between the various measures of conceptual accuracy and hostility change scores. Finally, several items in a post-experimental questionnaire, which were intended to elicit information about the subject's emotional state and perception of the situation, failed to reveal any group differences.

Our interpretation of the results is that both task administrators instigated hostility in subjects when they announced that they were testing intelligence; when the experimenter was Negro, students revealed their annoyance by forming aggressive concepts, but when he was white the need to control hostile feelings resulted in avoidance of aggressive words. This view of the data is of course inferential, since all that is actually known about the White Tester–Test Instructions group is that their hostility scores *declined* from pretest levels. There is no direct evidence of increased emotional conflict in this condition. Assuming that our interpretation is correct, the results suggest that inhibited hostility may have contributed to the behavioral impairment that Katz, Roberts and Robinson observed in Negros who were tested intellectually by a white experimenter. Why then were there no effects in the present experiment on conceptual accuracy? Our belief is that the task was not an appropriate one for revealing the disruptive effects of emotional conflict. It has none of the usual features of tasks on which impairment has been found to occur under stress. For example, it was not speeded, and it did not involve complex learning, coordination of responses, or problem solving.

Finally, the results provide a methodological critique of previous research on Negro personality which did not take into account possible effects of the race of the investigator on subjects' responses. For example, the bulk of studies on Negro aggression that were reviewed by Dreger and Miller (1960) apparently were done entirely by whites.

▽ ▽ ▽

PART THREE

Norms

WITH the troublesome concept of test norms, it cannot be stressed sufficiently that norm represents normal: if the average eight-year-old child correctly completes 15 arithmetic problems on Test X, then 15 is the norm. In fact, norms not only give the average; they also provide the relative frequency of the varying degrees of deviation from this norm—i.e., norm tables. There are, furthermore, many kinds of norms—local, class, grade, geographic area, and national norms, to mention only a few. Adequate normative data do not have to be based on millions of cases to insure accuracy and stability. The crux of this problem lies in the standardization procedures that were employed and, most important, the sampling procedures themselves.

In the history of psychological testing, the best sampling procedures have typically been with standardized mental ability scales for which national norm data are to be computed. In the United States, the prime example of this was the work of Terman and Merrill (1937), when they standardized Forms L and M of the Stanford-Binet and where they used a stratified sampling technique.

Random sampling, let alone 100 percent sampling, is rarely employed, but when it is carefully done very accurate results occur. Probably the best example of this sampling technique is the famous Scottish survey in 1939 (Macmeeken, 1940), very likely the most nearly complete testing on an entire population yet managed. All children born in Scotland on four days (February 1, May 1, August 1, November 1) were to be tested. As one might imagine, this meant a diligent, painstaking search to the remotest corners of Scotland in order to secure a final and complete sample. (There was a loss of only one case!) This search resulted in a total of 443 boys and 430 girls between the ages of 8 years, 11 months and 11 years, 9 months. All testees were administered the 1916 Stanford-Binet and eight of the performance measures devised by Pintner and Paterson. To illustrate one of the norm results: for the Stanford-Binet, the researchers secured a generally normal, but not perfect, curve. Here it should be remembered that all these tests were standardized on U.S. children.

With achievement tests, the sampling problems in regard to school and grade populations are no less difficult. Normative data from these types of tests are typically expressed in terms of grade placement indexes. Among the most widely used of such tests are the California Achievement Tests. Robert Dion, Area Director for the California Test Bureau, has written about the sampling procedures employed in standardizing the 1957 edition of these tests. His article, reproduced from the October, 1958, *Newsletter of the Elementary School Principals Association of Connecticut,* is here presented because he spells out so clearly what is involved in a stratified sampling technique.

NORMS ARE NOT GOALS

Robert Dion

After users have compared obtained results with the norms supplied with a test, the following reactions are not too uncommon: "The norms are too high."—"The norms are too low."—"The test must be off because our group is below the norm."—"The test is too easy because our group is above the norm."—"Our group is below the norm, but we'll work to bring it up to the norm."—"More cases should have been used in establishing norms." Searching for reasons for such reactions and other comparable reactions reveals that there is confusion and misunderstanding about norms; misuse of norms; and invariably no consideration is being given to a variety of factors that may account for deviations from test norms. Replies to the foregoing reactions embrace several concepts and procedures.

A test is merely a sampling from a broad area of knowledge, information and skill, and the preparation of a test involves two major aspects— (1) content (items, reliability, validity), and (2) assigning norms which will serve as reference points indicating the typical performance for described groups. This discussion concerns the latter aspect.

Although there are many ways of describing or recording performance on a test, numbers are the least cumbersome and complicated for practical use because they simplify communication, comparison and manipulation. Thus the raw score is an essential or fundamental piece of information. However, the raw score by itself is meaningless. Determining the total number of items in the test and expressing the score in terms of the percent of the total number of items in the test may have more meaning; however, the percent score may indicate a good or a poor score depending upon the difficulty of the items. To interpret raw scores it is necessary to know how others perform on the test. Raw scores have to be related to other types of information that may affect performance, so raw scores are converted into derived scores.

Derived scores can be expressed as grades, ages, percentiles, standard scores, etc., and the use of one type does not exclude the use of others. One of the most commonly used derived scores is the grade placement or grade equivalent, so let us examine what it means. If a pupil makes a raw score of 55 and 55 is the median score made by pupils tested at the sixth month of the fifth grade, he is said to have a grade placement of 5.6. This 5.6 grade placement is the norm and merely reflects or describes the typical performance of all tested in a described group who are at the sixth month of the fifth grade. Consequently, all examinees shouldn't be expected to reach or exceed a norm which has been established by a score achieved or exceeded by only 50 percent of the examinees in a group. Norms should not be considered standards of work, because standards are levels of performance or attainment fixed for an individual school or a pupil and expressed in terms of outcomes of instruction. It cannot be presumed that a given group is doing satisfactory work if the group is up to the norm without considering the objectives of the school and the background and ability of the pupils. For example, the standard of accuracy in arithmetic is 100 percent; however, the norms of sixth graders may indicate that only 85 percent of the computation has been done correctly.

The user of a test must understand the nature of the group upon which the test has been standardized, and he must determine that the norms yield meaning in terms of the particular purpose for which the testing is done. Large numbers of cases are no guarantee of an adequate sampling, and naming the localities (without additional information) where norms were obtained does not indicate the nature of the population. These two elements were established quite forcefully following the huge mail canvasses of ten million or more post-card ballots sent out by the *Literary Digest* back in 1936. Actually the number of cases required for an adequate sampling is a statistical problem, and in view of a number of criteria the amount required is relatively small. If the standardization group is not comparable to the group upon which the test is to be used then comparable results cannot be expected. If the norms are not based on groups with whom it is sensible to compare individuals we are testing, they are meaningless and misleading. Therefore, the main consideration is a definition of the standardization or normative group and the relevancy of the norms. Find the evidence in the manual.

Although standardization is complex and very often one procedure is preferred to some other procedure because of the philosophy of the test maker and the objectives underlying the test, it may be helpful to give an example of the procedures followed in the standardization of a series of achievement tests (Clark and Tiegs, 1958).

SAMPLING

1. Nation-wide Representation. Students from 48 states and the District of Columbia were included in the overall standardization popula-

tion. For selection and statistical purposes, eighteen geographical homogeneous areas were established. Data used in assigning states to an area were from the Biennial Survey of Education in the United States, 1952–54, published by the United States Office of Education and from other sources. Primary consideration was given to the following factors: average expenditures per student for instructional purposes; comparability of average scores on draft deferment examinations; length of school term; urban-rural characteristics; and type of school organization, attitudes and cultural characteristics. The areas were as follows:

Area 1.   Maine, New Hampshire, Vermont, Massachusetts, Connecticut and Rhode Island (5.04% of school population)
Area 2.   New York (7.40%)
Area 3.   New Jersey (2.53%)
Area 4.   Pennsylvania, Delaware and Maryland (7.63%)
Area 5.   West Virginia, Virginia and District of Columbia (4.61%)
Area 6.   Ohio (4.87%)
Area 7.   South Carolina, Alabama, Georgia and Mississippi (9.78%)
Area 8.   North Carolina and Florida (5.73%)
Area 9.   Tennessee, Arkansas and Kentucky (6.55%)
Area 10.   Illinois and Indiana (7.38%)
Area 11.   Michigan (4.00%)
Area 12.   Minnesota and Wisconsin (3.77%)
Area 13.   Iowa, North Dakota, South Dakota, Kansas, Nebraska and Colorado (5.92%)
Area 14.   Missouri, Oklahoma and Louisiana (6.53%)
Area 15.   Texas (5.75%)
Area 16.   New Mexico, Idaho, Montana, Utah, Wyoming, Arizona and Nevada (3.20%)
Area 17.   Oregon and Washington (2.78%)
Area 18.   California (6.53%)

2. Population Density Categories. Within each area the schools were divided into the four population density categories from which the schools draw their pupils.

a) More than 100,000.
b) 10,000 to 99,999.
c) 2,500 to 9,999.
d) Less than 2,500.

3. Basic Sampling Pattern. For each grade level (Grades 1 through 12), representative classes were selected for each of the four population density categories in each of the eighteen geographical areas. Thus, the sampling procedure of the nationwide sample at each grade from 1 through 12 was identical. In computing the norms for the W-X-Y-Z series, the test statistics for each population density category and each geographical area were weighted in direct proportion to the percent the school children in these specific categories are to the school children in the United States as a whole.

4. Data from about 65,000 selected cases were utilized in the dual, two-stage standardization program. The first stage of sampling provided a large pool of subjects from which the second stage sampling drew stratified groups having statistically and educationally controlled characteristics. In addition to the sampling design, a number of other quality restrictions and controls are imposed on the standardization testing. Some of these were:

a) Only one grade per level was utilized in any one participating school. The rationale for this requirement was to avoid undue influence by any school system.

b) Special efforts were made to have the participating schools include only the designated normal or typical classes for the community. Neither accelerated nor retarded classes were included. Even mixed classes, i.e., those consisting of more than one grade level, were avoided. The purpose of this restriction was to maintain the normal homogeneity of classroom units in the standardization program.

c) No classes were included if they had recently been administered either a California Achievement Test Battery or the California Test of Mental Maturity. This restriction was imposed to avoid the possibility of spurious practice effects.

d) Most testing was done on Tuesdays, Wednesdays and Thursdays which did not immediately follow or precede holidays or athletic events. Any detrimental influences of fatigue after a holiday or the disturbance of anticipation of a special event or holiday were thus minimized.

e) Because the total testing required for both batteries was over two hours, testing was distributed over two or three days. The purpose of this was to avoid having examinees become test-weary and fatigued.

In their final form the norms for the California Achievement Tests have been based on a controlled (stratified), two-stage sampling which constituted a normal distribution of mental ability, typical age-grade relationships and other characteristics as follows: the median IQ for pupils in Grades 1 through 8 was 100 with a standard deviation of 16 points; for grades above the eighth, the median IQ for each grade was as follows: ninth—101.5, tenth—103, eleventh—104, twelfth—105; 70 percent were making normal progress through the grades; about 20 percent were retarded one-half year or more; 10 percent were accelerated one-half year or more; the norming sample contained various ethnic and cultural groups and pupils with bilingual problems. The two-stage national sampling design assumes a random sampling of examinees within the required cell design rather than the cluster sampling of total classes traditionally used which can give undue weight to some communities or regions. Weights were applied to obtain the number of sample cases proportional to the total of pupils enrolled in schools over the nation when classified with respect to population, geographic area and school grade.

Note that the above example defines the population, reflects a well-planned sample rather than data collected on the basis of availability, and reports the number of cases and details methods.

Differences in courses of study, materials of instruction, time allotments, emphasis on certain skill areas, differences in the quality of teaching, and age and intelligence of pupils are factors which may account for deviations from test norms. Among the foregoing let us consider three principal factors that influence test scores of pupils from a particular elementary school.

a) Curriculum. If, in a particular school, instructional materials tend to be taught earlier in the school program, then the test performance of that school at this grade will tend to be higher with respect to norms. Conversely, if materials are not taught until later than usual, the test performance of that school at this grade will tend to be lower with respect to norms. However, when all materials have been taught, it is expected (other things being equal) that the performance of the two groups will be about equal. Variations in curriculum primarily influence rate of growth and are detected by analyzing the test results in a longitudinal manner from Grades 1 to 8. The school introducing materials earlier and stressing the basic skills will have results that start out high at Grades 1, 2, and 3, but tend to drop somewhat at Grades 7 and 8. Those schools using a delayed approach start out lower, show more rapid growth, but end up at about the same level at Grades 7 and 8.

b) Age-grade relationship. Acceleration–retardation policies of a school influence test results. Consider a school system with a "no failure" policy. This policy will tend to lower the test results for a school in relation to the norms which are based upon 70 percent of the pupils making normal progress through the grades with 20 percent being retarded and 10 percent being accelerated by one-half year or more. Take a pupil in Grade 5 whose test score is 4.0 grade placement units. Here his performance is 1.0 grade placement units below norms and he tends to pull the class average down. Now assume that this same pupil has been in a school system that followed the policy of retarding pupils low in achievement. In this school the pupil would have been retarded and so would be in Grade 4 rather than Grade 5. At a Grade 4 classification his performance would be the norm and he would not tend to pull the class average down. Thus the more pupils are retarded in a school system the higher will be the average performances of the various grades. An analysis of the age-grade relationships is important in interpreting test results.

c) Mental ability. It is estimated that curriculum and age-grade factors account on the average for about 30 percent of the variations from the norms in test results of a particular school, and about 70 percent of the variations may be attributed to variations in mental ability. Schools whose pupils have an average IQ above 100 (median mental ability of the norm group for Grades 1–8) would be expected to have achievement results above the norm. There are several ways that the median IQ of a school may be raised. In some schools all pupils with IQs below 80 or 70 are withdrawn from regular classes and classified in opportunity rooms. This procedure will raise the median IQ of the general classes. In independent schools entrance requirements establish certain selective criteria. As a result it is found that pupils in these schools usually have median IQs in excess of 100. Consequently, we would expect the median performance for such schools to exceed the norms. Conversely, schools whose pupils have an average IQ below 100 would be expected to have achievement results below the norm.

Test norms should serve as the point of departure both in investigating the reasons for obtained results and in determining the desirability of possible modifications of the factors which account for the obtained results. The elements which constitute a norm provide somewhat of an average of all the combined successes and failures of teachers and pupils ranging from the poorest to the best. To use norms as goals, objectives or standards is to encourage mediocrity.

▽ ▽ ▽

REGARDING 100 percent sampling, reference has been made to the Scottish survey involving the 1916 Stanford-Binet test and certain of the Pintner-Paterson performance indexes. Perhaps at the other extreme would be when researchers are limited to only one subject and where measurements typically are obtained over extended periods of time. It is important to recognize that much valuable data may be obtained in this fashion. Studies of single persons or single events may also be very fruitful sources for hypotheses for further experimental testing. Too often in the field of measurement we insist on large numbers of cases, too easily taking comfort in that a large *N* ensures better sampling (which may be anything but the case). It is for this reason that Dr. Dukes's paper, summarizing researches involving only one subject, has been included here. An *N* of 1 is seen as also appropriate when, for the function considered, intersubject variability is low, when opportunities for observing a given class of events are limited, and when a supposed universal relationship is questioned and the obtained evidence is negative.

Dr. Dukes is Professor of Psychology at the Davis campus of the University of California. His paper originally appeared in a 1965 issue of the *Psychological Bulletin*.

N = 1

William F. Dukes

In the search for principles which govern behavior, psychologists generally confine their empirical observations to a relatively small sample of a defined population, using probability theory to help assess the generality of the findings obtained. Because this inductive process commonly entails some knowledge of individual differences in the behavior involved, studies employing only one subject ($N = 1$) seem somewhat anomalous. With no information about intersubject variability in performance, the general applicability of findings is indeterminate.

Although generalizations about behavior rest equally upon adequate sampling of both subjects and situations, questions about sampling most often refer to subjects. Accordingly, the term "$N = 1$" is used throughout the present discussion to designate the *reductio ad absurdum* in the sampling of subjects. It might, however, equally well (perhaps better, in terms of frequency of occurrence) refer to the limiting case in the sampling of situations—for example, the use of one maze in an investigation of learning, or a simple tapping task in a study of motivation.

As a corollary, the term $N = 1$ might also be appropriately applied to the sampling of experimenters. Long recognized as a potential source of variance in interview data, the investigator has recently been viewed as a variable which may also influence laboratory results (Rosenthal, 1963 and 1964).

Except to note these other possible usages of the term $N = 1$, the present paper is not concerned with one-experimenter or one-situation treatments, but is devoted, as indicated previously, to single-subject studies.

Despite the limitation stated in the first paragraph, $N = 1$ studies cannot be dismissed as inconsequential. A brief scanning of general and historical accounts of psychology will dispel any doubts about their importance, revealing, as it does, many instances of pivotal research in which the observations were confined to the behavior of only one person or animal.

SELECTIVE HISTORICAL REVIEW

Foremost among $N = 1$ studies is Ebbinghaus' investigation of memory published in 1885. Ebbinghaus' work established the pattern for much of the research on verbal learning during the past 80 years. His principal findings, gleaned from many self-administered learning situations consisting of some 2,000 lists of nonsense syllables and 42 stanzas of poetry, are still valid source material for the student of memory. In another well-known pioneering study of learning, Bryan and Harter's (1899) report on plateaus, certain crucial data were obtained from only one subject. Their letter-word-phrase analysis of learning to receive code was based on the record of only one student. Their notion of habit hierarchies derived in part from this analysis is, nevertheless, still useful in explaining why plateaus may occur.

Familiar even to beginning students of perception is Stratton's (1897) account of the confusion from and the adjustment to wearing inverting lenses. In this experiment according to Boring (1942), Stratton, with only himself as subject,

settled both Kepler's problem of erect vision with an inverted image, and Lotze's problem of the role of experience in space perception, by showing that the "absolute" localization of retinal positions—up-down and right-left—are learned and consist of bodily orientation as context to the place of visual excitation [p. 237].

The role of experience was also under scrutiny in the Kelloggs' (1933) project of raising one young chimpanzee, Gua, in their home. (Although observations of their son's behavior were also included in their report, the study is essentially of the $N = 1$ type, since the "experimental group" consisted of one.) This attempt to determine whether early experience may modify behavior traditionally regarded as instinctive was for years a standard reference in discussions of the learning-maturation question.

Focal in the area of motivation is the balloon-swallowing experiment of physiologists Cannon and Washburn (1912) in which kymographic recordings of Washburn's stomach contradictions were shown to coincide with his introspective reports of hunger pangs. Their findings were widely incorporated into psychology textbooks as providing an explanation of hunger. Even though in recent years greater importance has been attached to central factors in hunger, Cannon and Washburn's work continues to occupy a prominent place in textbook accounts of food-seeking behavior.

In the literature on emotion, Watson and Rayner's study (1920) of Albert's being conditioned to fear a white rat has been hailed as one of the most influential papers in the history of American psychology. Their experiment, Murphy (1949) observes,

immediately had a profound effect on American psychology; for it appeared to support the whole conception that not only simple motor habits, but important, enduring traits of personality, such as emotional tendencies, may in fact be "built into" the child by conditioning [p. 261].

Actually the Albert experiment was unfinished because he moved away from the laboratory area before the question of fear removal could be explored. But Jones (1924) provided the natural sequel in Peter, a child who, through a process of active reconditioning, overcame a nonlaboratory-produced fear of white furry objects.

In abnormal psychology few cases have attracted as much attention as Prince's (1905) Miss Beauchamp, for years the model case in accounts of multiple personality. Perhaps less familiar to the general student but more significant in the history of psychology is Breuer's case (Breuer & Freud, 1895) of Anna O., the analysis of which is credited with containing "the kernel of a new system of treatment, and indeed a new system of psychology (Murphy, 1949, p. 307). In the process of examining Anna's hysterical symptoms, the occasions for their appearance, and their origin, Breuer claimed that with the aid of hypnosis these symptoms were "talked away." Breuer's young colleague was Sigmund Freud, who later publicly declared the importance of this case in the genesis of psychoanalysis.

There are other instances, maybe not so spectacular as the preceding, of influential *N* = 1 studies—for example, Yerkes' (1927) exploration of the gorilla Congo's mental activities; Jacobson's (1931) study of neuromuscular activity and thinking in an amputee; Culler and Mettler's (1934) demonstration of simple conditioning in a decorticate dog; and Burtt's (1932) striking illustration of his son's residual memory of early childhood.

Further documentation of the significant role of *N* = 1 research in psychological history seems unnecessary. A few studies, each in impact like the single pebble which starts an avalanche, have been the impetus for major developments in research and theory. Others, more like missing pieces from nearly finished jigsaw puzzles, have provided timely data on various controversies.

This historical recounting of "successful" cases is, of course, not an exhortation for restricted subject samplings, nor does it imply that their greatness is independent of subsequent related work.

FREQUENCY AND RANGE OF TOPICS

During the past 25 years (1939–1963) a total of 246 $N = 1$ studies, 35 of them in the last 5-year period, have appeared in the leading psychological periodicals. Although these 246 studies constitute only a small percent of the 1939–1963 journal articles, the absolute number is noteworthy and is sizable enough to discount any notion that $N = 1$ studies are a phenomenon of the past.

When, furthermore, these are distributed according to subject matter, they are seen to conextend fairly well with the range of topics in general psychology.

The breakdown is as follows:

	f
Maturation and development	29
Motivation	7
Emotion	12
Perception, sensory processes	25
Learning	27
Thinking and language	15
Intelligence	14
Personality	51
Mental health and psychotherapy	66
Total	246

As might be expected, a large proportion of them fall into the clinical and personality areas. One cannot, however, explain away $N = 1$ studies as case histories contributed by clinicians and personologists occupied less with establishing generalizations than with exploring the uniqueness of an individual and understanding his total personality. Only about 30% (74) are primarily oriented toward the individual, a figure which includes not only works in the "understanding" tradition, but also those treating the individual as a universe of responses and applying traditionally nomothetic techniques to describe and predict individual behavior (e.g., Yates, 1958).

In actual practice, of course, the two orientations–toward uniqueness or generality–are more a matter of degree than of mutual exclusion, with the result that in the literature surveyed purely idiographic research is extremely rare. Representative of that approach are Evans' (1950) novel-like account of Miller who "spontaneously" recovered his sight after more than 2 years of blindness, Rosen's (1949) "George X: A self-analysis by an avowed fascist," and McCurdy's (1944) profile of Keats.

RATIONALE FOR *N* = 1

The appropriateness of restricting an idiographic study to one individual is obvious from the meaning of the term. If uniqueness is involved, a sample of one exhausts the population. At the other extreme, and *N* of 1 is also appropriate if complete population generality exists (or can reasonably be assumed to exist). That is, when between-individual variability for the function under scrutiny is known to be negligible or the data from the single subject have a point-for-point congruence with those obtained from dependable collateral sources, results from a second subject may be considered redundant. Some *N* = 1 studies may be regarded as approximations of this ideal case, as for example, Henemann's (1961) photographic measurement of retinal images.

A variant on this typicality theme occurs when the researcher, in order to preserve some kind of functional unity and perhaps to dramatize a point, reports in depth one case which exemplifies many. Thus Eisen's (1962) description of the effects of early sensory deprivation is an account of one quondam hard-of-hearing child, and Bettelheim's (1949) paper on rehabilitation a chronicle of one seriously delinquent child.

In other studies an *N* of 1 is adequate because of the dissonant character of the findings. In contrast to its limited usefulness in *establishing* generalizations from "positive" evidence, an *N* of 1 when the evidence is "negative," is as useful as an *N* of 1,000 in *rejecting* an asserted or assumed universal relationship. Thus Lenneberg's (1962) case of an 8-year-old boy who lacked the motor skills necessary for speaking but who could understand language makes it "clear that hearing oneself babble is not a necessary factor in the acquisition of understanding . . .," (p. 422). Similarly Teska's (1947) case of a congenital hydrocephalic, $6\frac{1}{2}$ years old, with an IQ of 113, is sufficient evidence to discount the notion that prolonged congenital hydrocephaly results in some degree of feeblemindedness.

While scientists are in the long run more likely to be interested in knowing *what is* than *what is not* and more concerned with how many exist or in what proportion they exist than with the fact that at least one exists, one negative case can make it necessary to revise a traditionally accepted hypothesis.

Still other *N* = 1 investigations simply reflect a limited opportunity to observe. When the search for lawfulness is extended to infrequent "nonlaboratory" behavior, individuals in the population under study may be so sparsely distributed spatially or temporally that the psychologist can observe only one case, a report of which may be useful as a part of a cumulative record. Examples of this include cases of multiple personality (Thigpen & Cleckly, 1954), congenital insensitivity to pain (Cohen *et al.*, 1955), and mental deterioration following carbon monoxide poisoning (Jensen, 1950). Situational complexity as well as subject sparsity may limit the opportunity to observe. When the situation is greatly extended in time, requires expensive or specialized training for the subject, or entails intricate and difficult-to-administer controls, the investigator may, aware of their exploratory character, restrict his observations to one subject. Projects involving home-raising a chimpanzee (Hayes & Hayes, 1952) or testing after 16 years for retention of material presented during infancy (Burtt, 1941) would seem to illustrate this use of an N of 1.

Not all $N = 1$ studies can be conveniently fitted into this rubric; nor is this necessary. Instead of being oriented either toward the person (uniqueness) or toward a global theory (universality), researchers may sometimes simply focus on a problem. Problem-centered research on only one subject may, by clarifying questions, defining variables, and indicating approaches, make substantial contributions to the study of behavior. Besides answering a specific question, it may (Ebbinghaus' work, 1885, being a classic example) provide important groundwork for the theorists.

Regardless of rationale and despite obvious limitations, the usefulness of $N = 1$ studies in psychological research seems, from the preceding historical and methodological considerations, to be fairly well established. Finally, their status in research is further secured by the statistician's assertion (McNemar, 1940) that:

The statistician who fails to see that important generalizations from research on a single case can ever be acceptable is on a par with the experimentalist who fails to appreciate the fact that some problems can never be solved without resort to numbers [p. 361].

PART FOUR

Validity

OF all the topics concerning any kind of psychological measurement, but especially techniques that are applied to human beings and focus on subsequent decisions or plans—for example, aptitude or ability testing—that concerning overall validity of the measurements is paramount. (This point of view is reflected in this collection of readings in that the largest section is given over to validity.) As a general succinct introduction to this topic, for the student there probably is no source better than the presentation contained in the revised edition of *Standards for Educational and Psychological Tests and Manuals,* prepared by a joint committee of the American Psychological Association, the American Educational Research Association, and the National Council on Measurement in Education. This is a technical manual concerned with general principles of test construction, together with specific recommendations about how these principles should be implemented. Every student of the field should be acquainted with it.

Introductory comments in this manual indicate that psychological and educational tests are frequently employed in arriving at decisions that may considerably affect the welfare of the individuals tested, decisions on educational points of view and practices, and even decisions on the development and utilization of human resources. Test users therefore need to apply high standards of professional judgment when selecting and interpreting tests; test producers, likewise, are obligated to produce tests that can then be of greatest possible service. Such a test author or publisher has the task of providing sufficient information concerning each test so that the test user can ascertain just how much reliance he can correctly place on it. The manual, therefore, is an important sourcebook or guide for both test authors and test publishers.

The following statements concerning general features of validity are taken verbatim from this manual (APA, 1966, pp. 12–14),* wherein are outlined the three major types of validity—content, criterion-related, and construct. Of particular importance is the notion of construct validity, a concept that has recently come to assume a large place in the area of educational and psychological measurement. Following these remarks, specific recommendations, together with

---

* Revised again recently (1974) by the APA.

committee comments, are provided for both the test author and the test publisher.

VALIDITY

A.P.A. Standards for Educational
and Psychological Tests and Manuals

Validity information indicates the degree to which the test is capable of achieving certain aims. Tests are used for several types of judgment, and for each type of judgment, a different type of investigation is required to establish validity. For purposes of describing the uses for three kinds of validity coefficients, we may distinguish three of the rather numerous aims of testing:

1. *The test user wishes to determine how an individual performs at present in a universe of situations that the test situation is claimed to represent.* For example, most achievement tests used in schools measure the student's performance on a sample of questions intended to represent a certain phase of educational achievement or certain educational objectives.

2. *The test user wishes to forecast an individual's future standing or to estimate an individual's present standing on some variable of particular significance that is different from the test.* For example, an academic aptitude test may forecast grades, or a brief adjustment inventory may estimate what the outcome would be of a careful psychological examination.

3. *The test user wishes to infer the degree to which the individual possesses some hypothetical trait or quality (construct) presumed to be reflected in the test performance.* For example, he wants to know whether the individual stands high on some proposed abstract trait such as "intelligence" or "creativity" that cannot be observed directly. This may be done to learn something about the individual, or it may be done to study the test itself, to study its relationship to other tests, or to develop psychological theory.

Different types of tests are often used for each of the different aims, but this is not always the case. There is much overlap in types of tests and in the purposes for which they are used. Thus a vocabulary test might be used (a) simply as a measure of present vocabulary, the universe being all words in the language, (b) as a screening device to discriminate present or potential schizophrenics from organics, or (c) as a means of making inferences about "intellectual capacity."

To determine how suitable a test is for each of these uses, it is necessary to gather the appropriate sort of validity information. The kind of information to be gathered depends on the aim or aims of testing rather than on the type of test. The three aspects of validity corresponding to the three aims of testing may be named content validity, criterion-related validity, and construct validity.

Content validity is demonstrated by showing how well the content of the test samples the class situations or subject matter about which conclusions are to be drawn. Content validity is especially important for achievement and proficiency measures and for measures of adjustment or social behavior based on observation in selected situations. The manual should justify the claim that the test content represents the assumed universe of tasks, conditions, or processes. A useful way of looking at this universe of tasks, or items is to consider it to comprise a *definition* of the achievement to be measured by the test. In the case of an educational achievement test, the content of the test may be regarded as a definition of (or a sampling from a population of) one or more educational objectives. The aptitudes, skills, and knowledges required of the student for successful test performance must be precisely the types of aptitudes, skills, and knowledges that the school wishes to develop in the students and to evaluate in terms of test scores. Thus evaluating the content validity of a test for a particular purpose is the same as subjectively recognizing the adequacy of a definition. This process is actually quite similar to the subjective evaluation of the criterion itself. Unless, however, the aim of an achievement test is specifically to forecast or substitute for some criterion, its correlation with a criterion is *not* a useful evaluation of the test.

Criterion-related validity is demonstrated by comparing the test scores with one or more external variables considered to provide a direct measure of the characteristic or behavior in question. This comparison may take the form of an expectancy table or, most commonly, a correlation relating to the test score to a criterion measure. Predictive uses of tests include long-range forecasts of one or more measures of academic achievement, prediction of vocational success, and prediction of reaction to therapy. For such predictive uses the criterion data are collected concurrently with the test; for example, when one wishes to know whether a testing procedure can take the place of more elaborate procedures for diagnosing personality disorders. A test that is related to one or more concurrent criteria will not necessarily predict status on the same criterion at some later date. Whether the criterion data should be collected concurrently with the testing or at a later time depends on whether the test is recommended for prediction or for assessment of present status.

Construct validity is evaluated by investigating what qualities a test measures, that is, by determining the degree to which certain explanatory concepts or constructs account for performance on the test. To examine construct validity requires a combination of logical and empirical attack. Essentially, studies of construct validity check on the theory underlying the test. The procedure involves three steps. First, the investigator inquires: From this theory, what hypotheses may we make regarding the behavior of persons with high and low scores? Second, he gathers data to test these hypotheses. Third, in light of the evidence, he makes an inference as to whether the theory is adequate to explain the data collected. If the theory fails to account for the data, he should revise the test interpretation, reformulate the theory, or reject the theory altogether. Fresh evidence would be required to demonstrate construct validity for the revised interpretation.

A simple procedure for investigating what a test measures is to correlate it with other tests. We would expect a valid test of numerical reasoning, for example, to correlate more highly with other numerical tests than with clerical perception tests. Another procedure is experimental. If it is hypothesized, for example, that form perception on a certain projective test indicates probable ability to function well under emotional stress, this inference may be checked by placing individuals in an experimental situation producing emotional stress and observing whether their behavior corresponds to the hypothesis.

Construct validity is ordinarily studied when the tester wishes to increase his understanding of the psychological qualities being measured by the test. A validity coefficient relating test to criterion, unless it is established in the context of some theory, yields no information about *why* the correlation is high or low, or about how one might improve the measurement. Construct validity is relevant when the tester accepts no existing measure as a definitive criterion of the quality with which he is concerned (e.g., in measuring a postulated drive such as need for achievement), or when a test will be used in so many diverse decisions that no single criterion applies (e.g., in identifying the ability of Peace Corps trainees to adapt to new cultures). Here the traits or qualities underlying test performance are of central importance. It must be remembered, however, that, without a study of criterion-related validity, a test developed for diagnosis or prediction can be regarded only as experimental.

These three aspects of validity are only conceptually independent, and only rarely is just one of them important in a particular situation. A complete study of a test would normally involve information about all types of validity. A first step in the preparation of a predictive (*criterion-related*) instrument may be to consider what *constructs* are likely to provide a basis for selecting or devising an effective test. Sampling from a *content* universe may also be an early step in producing a test whose use for *prediction* is the ultimate concern. Even after satisfactory *prediction* has been established, information regarding *construct* validity may make the test more useful; it may, for example, provide a basis for identifying situations other than the validating situation where the test is appropriate as a predictor. To analyze *construct* validity, all the knowledge regarding validity would be brought to bear.

The three concepts of validity are pertinent to all kinds of tests. It is the intended use of the test rather than its nature that determines what kind of evidence is required.

Intelligence or scholastic aptitude tests most often use criterion-related validity to show how well they are able to predict academic success in school or college, but the nature of the aptitudes measured is often judged from the content of the items, and the place of the aptitude within the array of human abilities is deduced from correlations with other tests.

For achievement tests, content validity is usually of first importance. For example, a testing agency has a group of subject-matter specialist devise and select test items that they judge to cover the topics and mental processes relevant to the field represented by the test. Similarly, a teacher judges whether the final test in his course covers the kinds of situations about which he has been trying to teach his students certain principles or understandings. The teacher also judges content when he uses a published test, but he can appropriately investigate criterion-related validity by correlating this test with tests he has prepared or with other direct measures of his chief instructional objectives. When the same published achievement test is used for admissions testing, it may reasonably be checked against a later criterion of performance. In any theoretical discussion of what is being measured by the achievement test, a consideration of construct validity is required. Whether the score on a science achievement test, for example, reflects reading ability to a significant degree, and whether it measures understanding of scientific method rather than mere recall of facts are both questions about construct validity.

Development of a personality inventory will usually start with the assembly of items covering content the developer considers meaningful. Such inventories are then likely to be interpreted with the aid of theory; any such interpretation calls for evidence of construct validity. In addition, a personality inventory must have criterion-related validity, if, for example, it is to be used in screening military recruits who may be maladjusted.

Interest measures are usually intended to predict vocational or educational criteria, but many of them are also characterized by logical content and constructs. This makes it more likely that they can provide at least a rough prediction for the very many occupations and activities that exist and for which specific evidence of criterion-related validity has not been obtained.

For projective techniques, construct validity is the most important, although criterion-related validity using criteria collected either concurrently with the testing or afterward may be pertinent if the instuments are to be used in making diagnostic classifications.

▽ ▽ ▽

THE 1954 treatment of the notion of constuct validity (A.P.A., 1954) generated a great deal of discussion. The revised edition of the A.P.A. publication (1966) expanded the treatment of construct validity and tightened the entire concept with specific illustrations. Prior to this revised edition of testing standards, Bechtoldt published an extended and negative critique of the entire concept in 1959, arguing from a position of the philosophy of science. Bechtoldt felt that the introduction of this concept into psychological theorizing created, at best, real confusion and, at worst, "a nonempirical, nonscientific approach to the study of behavior" (p. 628). Instead, he felt that the techniques of operational methodology were to be preferred.

This provided the springboard for a paper by Campbell (1960) who distinguished the philosophical problems posed by Bechtoldt from the more empirical business of test validation. This led him to suggest additional instances where the concept of construct validity needed to be considered. Campbell was, however, writing prior to the publication of the revised edition of the earlier *Technical Recommendations*. This revision (A.P.A., 1966) did much to clarify the notion of construct validity further and it specifically mentions some of the examples or "additions" that Campbell wrote about.

Still another validity construct, as a sequel to Campbell's discussion, has been suggested by Sechrest (1963) for tests which are intended for applied predictive use. This he has termed incremental validity. Validity claimed for any particular test must be in terms of some increment in its predictive efficiency over and above information that is easily and inexpensively available. There are indications in the research literature where, in spite of better than chance validity, tests may not contribute to, or may even detract from, predictions made from easily obtainable interview or application blank information. Evidence produced for incremental validity would quickly spot this.

A fairly recent, promising development related to validity concerns what is termed "moderator or suppressor variables."

The English & English *Dictionary* (1958) defines a suppressor variable as a variable in a prediction battery that correlates zero with the criterion but high with another predictor in the battery. It has the effect of subtracting from the predictor variable that part of its variance that does not correlate with the criterion, and hence increases the predictive value of the battery (p. 537).

The validity of a certain psychological test or inventory of personality or interests is likely to vary among different population samples. We then must be able to predict these differences. In any distribution of scores that involve two variables, there are always some individuals who earn scores that place them close to the regression line (or the line of "best fit"). Other individuals fall quite wide of this mark, missing the regression line sometimes by large amounts. It might then be asked whether or not there is some special characteristic that might be pinpointed to differentiate between those persons far from or near the regression line. For example, it might be ascertained that a test worked better with middle-class boys or better with neurotics

than with psychotics. Here, then, social class and degree of maladjustment are the moderator variables, since they function in ways to
alter the predictive validity of the measures.

The following report, dealing with a much discussed student issue
of academic motivation, is an illustration of both a study of construct
validity and the workings of a suppressor variable. Dr. Drake, the
senior author, now retired, was Professor of Psychology and Director
of the Student Counseling and Guidance Center at the University of
Wisconsin; Dr. Oetting is now at Colorado State University, where he
is Professor of Psychology. The study originally appeared in the
Journal of Counseling Psychology in 1957.

AN MMPI PATTERN AND A
SUPPRESSOR VARIABLE PREDICTIVE
OF ACADEMIC ACHIEVEMENT

L. E. Drake and Eugene R. Oetting

In a previous study of MMPI profile patterns (Drake, 1956) it had been
found that a group of profiles of male counselees characterized by their
counselors as "lacking academic motivation" could be distinguished
from profiles of other counselees by certain profile codings. Scales 8(Sc)
and 9(Ma) paired among the three highest coded scales with Scale 0(Si)
coded among the two lowest scales constituted a pattern. This pattern 89–
0 was found significantly more frequently in the profiles of the "lacking
academic motivation group" than would be expected from its frequency
of occurrence in the total group of 2,634 profiles. Also, Scale 5(Mf) coded
among the highest three was found to occur significantly *less* frequently
in the profiles of the "lacking academic motivation" group than would be
expected from its frequency of occurrence in the total group.

It was concluded that a profile containing the pattern 89–0(Ma-Sc
paired high with Si low) could therefore lead to a hypothesis of "lacking
academic motivation," to be checked further in the counseling interviews. Also, since Scale 5(Mf) occurred less frequently in profiles for the
above group, the above hypothesis might be modified when Scale 5
occurred coded high in profiles with the 89–0 pattern.

Partly on the basis of the above, two hypotheses were formulated
which could be checked against an independent criterion. It was postulated that, if the profile pattern 89–0 was found more frequently in
persons "lacking in academic motivation," then these individuals as a
group would reflect that characteristic in terms of a lower grade point
average in college studies. This, then, was the first hypothesis.

The second hypothesis has a more complex origin. It was noted above
that Scale 5(Mf) occurred significantly *less* frequently coded high in the
profiles for the nonmotivated group. In addition there are other indications that Scale 5(Mf) is in some manner associated with the ability to

adjust socially and personally to situations where other MMPI patterns indicate difficulties. Hathaway and Monachesi (1953, pp. 133–34) point out in their study of delinquency, "Scale 5 also seems to be negatively related to the occurrence of delinquency in the boys. The frequency is low when 5 is the high point and also in most combinations with 5. Only scale 4 is clearly able to combine with 5 to produce a high rate."

It is hypothesized, then, that Scale 5(Mf) may act as a suppressor variable in some profile patterns. In this instance, individuals showing the profile pattern 89–0 should not obtain lower grades if Scale 5 is coded high.

The two hypotheses to be tested in this study, then, are: *Hypothesis 1.* Beginning freshmen whose MMPI profiles were coded 89–0(MaSc paired high with Si coded low) and whose profiles did not have Scale 5(Mf) coded high would obtain lower grades their first semester in college than the total group of freshmen. *Hypothesis 2.* Beginning freshmen whose MMPI profiles were coded 89–0 and whose Scale 5 was also coded high would *not* obtain lower grades than the total freshmen group.

PROCEDURE

The group form of the MMPI was administered to the entering freshmen during New Student Week in 1949, 1950, and 1951. There were 3,480 male students for whom there were profiles. The grade point averages were computed for the first semester's work for each individual. The MMPI profiles were then coded according to the Hathaway system. All those with the 89–0(MaSc paired high with Si low) pattern were separated from the total group. These were then divided into two subgroups: (a) those with the Scale 5 coded high and (b) those without Scale 5 coded high. The grade point average distributions were then tabulated for the two subgroups, and for the total group. These distributions were then tested for significance.

RESULTS

Table 2 shows the distribution of grade averages for each of the subgroups and the total group. As was hypothesized the subgroup with the pattern 89–0, the pattern which differentiated the group characterized as lacking academic motivation obtained a significantly lower grade point average than the total group as well as the group with the 89–0 pattern with 5 coded high. The X^2 was beyond the .001 level for both of these tests.

The second hypothesis, that the group with the same pattern (89–0), but with Mf coded high, would not have grades below average, also was supported. Not only did this group exceed the 89–0 group without 5, but it also exceeds to some extent the total group. The test for the latter was significant beyond the .05 but not beyond the .01 level of confidence.

Since Scale 5 appears to have such a strong influence on the code

TABLE 2

MMPI Patterns and Distribution of First Semester Grades for Male College Freshmen

MMPI Pattern	Percent with First Semester Averages of			N
	Below C	C to B	B or better	
Total freshman group	41	39	20	3480
89–0, without 5 high	67	27	6	69
89–0 with 5 high	18	59	23	39

Between total freshman group and 89–0 without 5 high: $X^2 = 19^*$
Between total freshman group and 89–0 with 5 high: $X^2 = 9\dagger$
Between 89–0 without 5 high and 89–0 with 5 high: $X^2 = 24^*$

* Significant at .001 level.
† Between .01 and .05 levels of confidence.

pattern one might raise the question as to whether or not Scale 5 could have been used alone to predict academic achievement. The scores on Scale 5 were correlated with the first semester grade point averages for the male students who entered the University in 1950. The resulting coefficient was +.17 for the 857 male students. The correlation between grades and the ACE for these same students was +.46. The coefficient of the multiple correlation, ACE, Mf with grades, was +.47. Scale 5 alone does not appear to be very efficient in forecasting scholarship.

DISCUSSION OF RESULTS

This study demonstrates several things that may be important in personality measurement. In the first place a rather complex pattern was necessary to predict the criterion. Analysis of the individual scales revealed no single scale in this pattern which differentiated the subgroup from the total group. Furthermore, although Scale 5 appeared to suppress the effects of this pattern, it, by itself, did not predict academic achievement to any great extent. It appears that, although the scores on a single personality scale may be related to some underlying construct, factorial or otherwise, the determination of behavior is unlikely to depend on a variable simple enough to be measured by a single scale. In order to predict behavior for a group, the group must be relatively homogenous for the behavior. Consequently the group must be selected on the basis of as many underlying traits as possible. In this study three scales were used to select the group and it was still necessary to include a fourth scale as a suppressor in order to predict the criterion. An important consideration in planning research of this type is to obtain a sufficient number of subjects from which to select subgroups sufficiently homogeneous for predictive purposes. Out of 3,480 profiles only 124 had the 89–0 coding for "lacking academic motivation." Of these 16 were for students who did not complete one semester (13 of the 16 did not have Mf coded high). This left 69 profiles for the subgroup without Mf and only 39 profiles with Mf coded high.

A second point is the demonstration of the effect of a suppressor scale. The prediction of lower grade point averages was made on the basis of pattern analysis of the original data. Scale 5 (Mf) was not used to predict the criterion directly, but rather to predict the errors, or false positives. Scale 5 identified those students who, although possessing the "lacking academic motivation" pattern, did not reflect this pattern in their grades. Whether these individuals were not lacking in academic motivation or whether their interests and emotional structure was such that they can perform in college in spite of a basic lack of motivation is not known. In the opinion of authors the latter is more likely. The original hypothesis was based in part on this interpretation of the action of Scale 5.

The third aspect of this study is that it is an example of Cronbach and Meehl's (1955) "construct validation." On the basis of previous studies and knowledge and experience with the test, an extension of the use of the test and the meanings of certain patterns was hypothesized. This extension was then tested and found to be significant. The fact that the extension could be made and validated not only demonstrates that this particular profile pattern on the MMPI may be used with a high degree of confidence in forming hypotheses in counseling about "lack of academic motivation," but also tends to add slightly to the feeling of confidence about all of the steps taken in making the extension. It suggests that the techniques of the original study of patterns on the MMPI were reasonable, that much further attention be paid to the action of suppressor variables in personality testing (particularly the Mf scale on the MMPI), and that the principles involved in extension of a "nomological net" and its construct validation may be highly useful tools in the difficult area of personality assessment.

A later study by Drake (1962) carried this research further, modifying these results somewhat but still testifying to the suppressor effect of scale 5 (Mf). Approximately 1,000 MMPI profiles for the entering male freshman students in the upper half of the distribution of scores obtained from scholastic aptitude tests were studied for peak scores and checked against grade-point averages. Findings from this large group were then cross-validated on about 1,800 similar profiles for the 1958–59 entering male freshmen. Scales 4 (Pd) and 9 (Ma), either alone or in combination, differentiated best in both the original and the cross-validation groups. In every case studied, however, the size of the differentiation increased when such profiles with scale 5 (Mf) coded high were eliminated from the distribution. Pattern 49 high gives the significant differentiation, and 5 acts as the suppressor variable.

In an industrial setting, Sorenson (1966) has reported the discovery of a suppressor variable where both useful levels of prediction and economics of testing were important. The problem investigated was the development and cross-validation of a test battery to be used in the selection of skilled industrial mechanics. An extensive test battery comprised of aptitude, interests, and personality measures (a total of 34 variables) was developed. The multiple R for these 34 variables against the criterion of job performance (supervisory ratings) for the 43 men used in the development sample was an exciting .92. However, when cross-validated, on the sample of 20 additional mechanics reserved for this purpose, this R shrunk to a vanishing .01! Various combinations of four and five different measures were tried, ending with a three-variable predictor that correlated .44 with the criterion for the development sample and .57 for the cross-validation group. It was here that inspection of the intercorrelations among the three predictors and their correlation with the criterion disclosed the presence of a suppressor variable (a near-zero correlation with the criterion and a relatively high correlation with one of the other predictors). This suppressor variable turned out to be scores on the Bennett Test of Mechanical Comprehension. High scores on this type of test, emphasizing knowledge of elementary physics, contributed negatively to the prediction, whereas high scores on a different type of mechanical aptitude measure (a nuts-and-bolts type of test) contributed positively. Thus, in this study, the ability to achieve a high score on the second type of mechanical aptitude test without benefit of a high score on the more academically oriented Bennett was associated with sucess on the job as industrial mechanic. For another study of a suppressor variable in an industrial assessment situation, see pp. 175-78.

In their extensive review of personality research, Klein, Barr, and Wolitsky (1967), succinctly summarize the role of moderator variables when they say that too often relations that "should have been" found are not because small notice has been paid to the possibility that relations between variables might differ in different subgroups of the larger population. The repeatedly reported differences in correlation matrices for the two sexes is one example. They select especially the Kogan-Wallach (1964) study of risk-taking as an excellent illustration. These researchers used defensiveness (measured by social desirability) and anxiety as moderator variables. They found that the most disturbed subjects—those high on both variables—were highly consistent in risk-taking, whether risky, cautious, or in between, which they interpreted as indicating a need to maintain a consistent self-image. The least disturbed subjects were moderately consistent, limiting their consistency to certain kinds of tasks. The least degree of consistency showed up in subjects whose degree of personality disturbance was intermediate.

▽ ▽ ▽

The research literature is replete with careful studies in which item analysis procedures have resulted in excellent measuring devices, but, as it turns out, only for the group on which the particular item analysis was done. Cross-validation here becomes all important. The following paper by Dr. Cureton is reprinted not only because he makes a strong point but also because of the humorous note in it all—something which is rather infrequent in professional psychological journals. Dr. Cureton, who was Professor of Psychology at the University of Tennessee, before his retirement in 1972, has long been known for his work in test construction and test theory. The paper, reproduced in its entirety, originally appeared in *Educational & Psychological Measurement* (1950).

VALIDITY, RELIABILITY, AND BALONEY

Edward E. Cureton

It is a generally accepted principle that if a test has demonstrated validity for some given purpose, considerations of reliability are secondary. The statistical literature also informs us that a validity coefficient cannot exceed the square root of the reliability coefficient of either the predictor or the criterion. This paper describes the construction and validation of a new test which seems to call in question these accepted principles. Since the technique of validation is the crucial point, I shall discuss the validation procedures before describing the test in detail.

Briefly, the test uses a new type of projective technique which appears to reveal controllable variations in psychokinetic force as applied in certain particular situations. In the present study the criterion is college scholarship, as given by the usual grade-point average. The subjects were 29 senior and graduate students in a course in Psychological Measurements. These students took Forms Q and R of the Cooperative Vocabulary Test, Form R being administered about two weeks after Form Q. The correlation between grade-point average and the combined score on both forms of this test was .23. The reliability of the test, estimated by the Spearman-Brown formula from the correlation between the two forms, was .90.

The experimental form of the new test, which I have termed the "B-Projective Psychokinesis Test," or Test B, was also applied to the group. This experimental form contained 85 items, and there was a reaction to every item for every student. The items called for unequivocal "plus" or "minus" reactions, but in advance of data there is no way to tell which reaction to a given item may be valid for any particular purpose. In this respect, Test B is much like many well-known interest and personality inventories. Since there were no intermediate reactions, all scoring was based on the "plus" reactions alone.

I first obtained the mean grade-point average of all the students whose reaction to each item was "plus." Instead of using the usual technique of biserial correlation, however, I used an item-validity index based on the significance of the difference between the mean grade-point average of the whole group, and the mean grade-point average of those who gave the "plus" reaction to any particular item. This is a straightforward case of sampling from a finite universe. The mean and standard deviation of the grade-point averages of the entire group of 29 are the known parameters. The null hypothesis to be tested is the hypothesis that the subgroup giving the "plus" reaction to any item is a random sample from this population. The mean number giving the "plus" reaction to any item was 14.6. I therefore computed the standard error of the mean for independent samples of 14.6 drawn from a universe of 29, with replacement. If the mean grade-point average of those giving the "plus" reaction to any particular item was more than one standard error above the mean of the 69, the item was retained with a scoring weight of plus one. If it was more than one standard error below this general mean, the item was retained with a scoring weight of minus one.

By this procedure, 9 positively weighted items and 15 negatively weighted items were obtained. A scoring key for all 24 selected items was prepared, and the "plus" reactions for the 29 students were scored with this key. The correlations between the 29 scores on the revised Test B and the grade-point averages was found to be .82. In comparison with the Vocabulary Test, which correlated only .23 with the same criterion, Test B appears to possess considerable promise as a predictor of college scholarship. However, the authors of many interest and personality tests, who have used essentially similar validation techniques, have warned us to interpret high validity coefficients with caution when they are derived from the same data used in making the item analysis.

The correlation between Test B and the Vocabulary Test was .31, which is .08 higher than the correlation between the Vocabulary Test and the grade-point averages. On the other hand, the reliability of Test B by the Kuder-Richardson Formula 20, was −.06. hence it would appear that the accepted principles previously mentioned are called in question rather severely by the findings of this study. The difficulty may be explained, however, by a consideration of the structure of the B-Projective Psychokinesis Test.

The items of Test B consisted of 85 metal-rimmed labelling tags. Each tag bore an item number, from 1 to 85, on one side only. To derive a score for any given student, I first put the 85 tags in a cocktail shaker and shook them up thoroughly. Then I looked at the student's grade-point average. If it was B or above, I projected into the cocktail shaker a wish that the student should receive a high "plus" reaction score. If his grade-point average was below B, I projected a wish that he should receive a low score. Then I threw the tags on the table. To obtain the student's score, I counted as "plus" reactions all the tags which lit with the numbered side up. The derivation of the term "B-Projective Psycho-kinesis Test" should not be obvious.

The moral of this story, I think, is clear. When a validity coefficient is computed from the same data used in making an item analysis, this coefficient cannot be interpreted uncritically. And, contrary to many statements in the literature, it cannot be interpreted "with caution" either. There is one clear interpretation for all such validity coefficients. This interpretation is—

"BALONEY!"

▽ ▽ ▽

THE General Aptitude Test Battery (GATB), the product of years of research by the U.S. Employment Service, is possibly the most successful of the various multi-aptitude test batteries currently in use. Its origins go back to the work of the Minnesota Employment Stabilization Research Institute during the depression years (Dvorak, 1935). Extensive validity data, both concurrent and predictive, are available, and this research is a continuing process. For a general description of these tests, consult Dvorak (1956). Research with these tests is especially significant since aptitude patterns have been developed, which has resulted in a psychological classification of occupation groups into "families." Recently, the test norms have been extended downward to ninth-grade groups (U.S. Department of Labor, 1959) so that now this battery covers a very wide range of talent.

Dr. Dvorak is with the Division of Counseling and Testing Service, U. S. Department of Labor, and it is she who has been largely responsible for the general direction of GATB research. The following material has been abstracted and condensed from Section III of the GATB Manual (U.S. Department of Labor, 1958). This manual, together with that of the Differential Aptitude Test Battery, is a model of completeness, especially in regard to the presentation of extensive validity data.

DEVELOPMENT OF OCCUPATIONAL NORMS

Beatrice J. Dvorak

The basic assumption underlying the GATB is that a large variety of tests can be reduced to several factors, and that a large variety of occupations can also be clustered into groups according to similarities in the abilities required. It is assumed that occupations differ from each other in varying degrees and that occupations can be grouped into families on the basis of similarities in the abilities required. One of the major efforts of this research has been to show that these are differential ability patterns among workers in various types of occupations, and that these patterns have validity. The GATB may then be accurately described as a "multipotential"test battery.

Since the GATB has been designed for use primarily in everyday employment situations, the emphasis has been placed on empirical and predictive validity (although other types of validity have not been ignored.). The GATB is the only multi-aptitude test battery currently available which is based on such extensive "working population" norms. For this reason, the GATB treatment of validity is all-important. The discussion of validity has, therefore, a thoroughly realistic base in the world of occupations.

Since a suitable criterion is essential to the successful conduct of a test development study, the determination of the availability of the needed criterion, or measure of job performance, is made early in the process. It is important here that the criterion be a measure of an important phase of the job which involves the essential job performance abilities, rather than a measure of general job success. For example, although factors such as co-operativeness, dependability and diligence are important determinants of general job success, these factors are not measured by aptitude tests and should not be reflected in a criterion to be used for test development purposes. A suitable criterion for aptitude test development purposes should be a reliable and valid measure of each worker's job proficiency with respect to quantity and quality of production; it should be a good measure of the performance that we wish to predict with the aptitude tests.

TYPES OF CRITERIA

In broad terms, criteria can be classified into two main categories: objective and subjective. An objective criterion is a quantitative measure of quantity and/or quality of production. "Production records" is a general term used to denote a variety of objective criteria. The actual records may be expressed as "units produced," "percent of production standard achieved," "piece-rate earnings," or some other comparable measure to reflect quantity of production; or they may be expressed in terms of the number of errors made or the number of items rejected to reflect quality of production. Sometimes the two types of records may be combined statistically to obtain a single measure of both the quality and quantity of production for each worker. In addition to production records, work samples, such as proficiency tests in typing and stenography, may be used as objective criteria. It is possible to obtain separate or combined measures of speed and accuracy with work-sample criteria.

Subjective criteria involve a judgment of performance, usually made by somebody who is in a good position to rate the performance of each individual in the sample, such as a foreman, supervisor, or instructor.

The rating technique might involve one of a variety of procedures, such as broad category or group ratings, rank-order ratings, paired comparison ratings which yield a rank-order distribution, or the use of a descriptive rating scale. Regardless of the type of rating procedure employed, the objective is to place each individual in the experimental sample in the correct relative position with respect to his job performance ability.

School grades are also used as criteria for test development studies. These may be primarily objective, or to a large extent subjective, depending upon the grading system used in the school. For example, school grades would be considered as objective if the final grades for each course were based solely upon examination marks made by the students. However, school grades become relatively subjective when an instructor uses the examination marks as a guide and assigns final grades in accordance with his judgment of each student's total performance.

Even though traditionally it has been customary to classify criteria as either "objective" or "subjective," it should be borne in mind that there seldom is a clear-cut line between these two types of criteria. There often is an element of subjectivity in a criterion that is expressed in units which appear to be completely objective. For example, when records of the number of rejects are employed to evaluate the quality of workers' performance, the criterion appears to be completely objective. However, there must necessarily be subjective factors involved in setting the standards of acceptability for the items being produced, as well as in the evaluation of finished products in terms of the established standards to determine if they should be accepted or rejected. Similarly, there are subjective elements involved in criteria based on quantity of production. Subjective determinations are made of factors, such as the method of measuring quantity of production and the rate of production considered to be satisfactory.

At one time objective criteria were generally regarded as more dependable measures of job performance than subjective criteria. In the early years of the Employment Service test development program, attempts were made to use only objective criteria for test development purposes. However, objective criteria were just not available for many occupations, and for many jobs for which objective criteria were available, it was not possible to obtain comparable measures on samples of sufficient size for test development purposes. It was also found that objective criteria usually covered only one facet of job performance, such as quantity of production. These factors led to the employment of objective criteria in test development studies. Experience has since shown that it is often advisable to obtain both objective and subjective criterion data for the same sample. Each criterion correlated separately with the test scores can contribute data for meaningful interpretation. In a test development study on the occupation of tile paster, a job in the production of ceramic products, both production records and supervisory ratings were obtained as criteria. The production records showed significant correlation with measures of manual dexterity and motor speed, whereas the supervisory ratings showed significant correlation with measures of form perception as well as with measures of manual dexterity and motor speed. Further study showed that the production records were based solely on quantity of production, whereas the supervisory ratings reflected both quantity and quality of production. The job analysis data indicated that although form perception was involved in quality of production it was not a determinant of quantity. In this instance the subject criterion data not only served to substantiate the findings of the objective criterion, but also revealed a significant relationship between job performance and measures of form perception that could not have been made evident through use of the objective criterion alone. On the basis of experiences similar to the one cited immediately above, it is believed that we should not generalize with respect to the superiority of one type of criterion over another. Both objective and subjective criteria have their specific uses. When both types of criterion data are available, the choice to lean more heavily on either one or to make equal use of both for purposes of test validation must necessarily vary in accordance with the pertinent factors to be considered in each specific situation.

QUALITY OF·CRITERION

The success or failure of a test development study can be determined by the quality of the criterion that is obtained. Therefore, it is of extreme importance to evaluate the criterion data in every way possible. As already stated, it is important that the criterion employed for a test development study be primarily a measure of each worker's job proficiency and that other determinants of general job success, such as cooperativeness and dependability, be excluded from this criterion. Data should be collected which enable a statistical evaluation of the reliability and validity of the criterion. The reliability of a criterion can be measured by obtaining two or more sets of criterion data covering different periods of time and correlating them, or by correlating the ratings on the same people made by different supervisors or foremen.

The validity of the criterion is extremely difficult to measure and usually can be measured only indirectly. For example, we can determine the extent to which factors other than job performance might be influencing the criterion. Significant correlation between the criterion and variables such as experience, age, and education are sometimes indicative that the criterion is not a true measure of job performance. In some instances, it might be possible to apply a statistical correction to nullify the effects of these extraneous factors. Or this objective might be achieved by applying some type of experimental control, such as excluding from the sample those individuals at the extremes of the distribution of the variable that is unduly influencing the criterion. For example, if an analysis of the data has revealed that length of experience on the job has biased the job performance ratings assigned to workers, the experience factor can be held relatively constant by excluding from the sample those workers who have either extremely high or low amounts of experience relative to the other workers in the sample. Sometimes, however, no statistical correction or experimental control technique is applicable and we either have to discard the criterion, or use it with caution and interpret our results with reservations.

It should also be pointed out that in some instances, a criterion may be a valid measure of job performance even though it does exhibit significant correlation with variables such as age, experience, and education. It is difficult to determine when these correlations are indicative of spurious relationships which call for some correction to be made or for the data to be discarded, or when job performance really does have a true relationship to these other variables. Every effort should be made to obtain as much information as possible which might enable a meaningful interpretation of the obtained relationships. For example, in a particular experimental sample the workers who have been on the job longer may actually be the best performers or they may have been given the higher ratings only because the supervisor is better acquainted with them. Sometimes a thorough examination of the experience and criterion data may yield some meaningful clues. The observation that none or very few of the less experienced workers have been placed in the high part of the criterion distribution might be indicative that the ratings are unduly biased. If all workers in the sample have completed the training period, and there has been no significant change in the labor market or company hiring procedures between the time that the more and less experienced workers were hired, then it is unlikely that there would really be a marked preponderance of proficiency among the more experienced workers.

It is important to make certain that objective criterion data are comparable for all workers and are not influenced by working conditions rather than by each worker's job performance ability. Production records as a measure of proficiency are considered a good criterion if each worker has an equal opportunity to produce as many units as he can and production is measured uniformly for all workers. If because of the nature of the job, the flow of work is subject to fluctuations, or if a machine controls the speed of production, production records would not make a suitable criterion. Factors such as lighting, age of machines, availability of materials and additional duties performed by workers must be taken into consideration when the use of production records as a criterion is contemplated in order to insure comparability.

TREATMENT OF CRITERION DATA

In order to make use of the criterion for purposes of statistical analysis, it is necessary for the data to be in a form which enables us to determine the relationships between the criterion and test performance. Usually objective criteria are expressed in units already forming continuous distributions which can be readily correlated with the test results. Sometimes, for the sake of convenience of computation, some conversion of the units might be desirable.

Subjective criterion data usually require conversion to form which enables correlation with the test results. For example, rank-order ratings, which place each individual in his correct relative position, space each person an equal distance from the next, which tends to indicate that the job performance of each individual in the sample varies by an equal amount from the next better and poorer workers. This, we know, is not the case, because job performance tends to be normally distributed. Therefore, before using rank-order ratings to compute product-moment corrlelations, we convert the ranks to linear scores, which are a better representation of the true differences in job performance between each worker and the next. Items on a descriptive rating scale are usually weighted and summed to obtain a numerical score for each person in the experimental sample. Broad category or group ratings, which might merely designate each worker in the sample as either above average, average, or below average, are converted to quantitative values on the basis of the normal distribution curve. These data can then be used to compute product-moment correlation coefficients corrected for broad categories. When ratings are expressed in two categories, such as satisfactory or unsatisfactory, biserial correlation coefficients can be computed.

Since norms on Employment Service test batteries are established for use with the multiple cutoff method, and scores are regarded as either "qualifying" or "nonqualifying," a technique which enables the correlation of a dichotomously expressed variable is employed to evaluate the norms. The criterion, regardless of its original units, is also dichotomized and tetrachoric correlation coefficients are computed. The question arises with respect to the point at which the criterion should be dichotomized, or where should the criterion cutting score be set?

When the criterion is to be dichotomized, it is desirable to find the "true" point of demarcation between the high and low criterion groups whenever possible. This point is not constant for all groups but varies from one study to another. Experience in conducting test development studies and consultation with foremen and supervisors have indicated that, in general, a valid division is obtained by placing approximately one-third of the experimental sample in the low criterion group and approximately two-thirds in the high criterion group. However, this does not mean that the criterion should always be dichotomized with approximately one-third of the sample placed in the low criterion group. To make the best determination of the division point, it is necessary to consult with the foremen, supervisors, or instructors who are familiar with the performance of everybody in the sample and who are in the best position to specify where the line of demarcation between satisfactory and marginal performance falls. It is often difficult for this determination to be made even by foremen or supervisors who are thoroughly familiar with the performance of everybody in the experimental sample. Greater difficulty in making this determination is experience when there are no established quantitative standards available. On the other hand, if production records are available and it is known that production below a specified level is regarded as unsatisfactory by the company, then determining the criterion critical score is not a difficult matter; or if school grades are the criterion and it is known that the passing grade is at a certain point, there is not much difficulty.

It should be recognized that in some samples, where there has already been some restriction in the range of ability, there may not be a "true" unsatisfactory or low criterion group. This would be particularly true for groups of college seniors or samples of experienced workers which include only those individuals who have demonstrated satisfactory performance, and from which those people who have not performed satisfactorily have dropped out. For samples of this type, in which everybody exhibits satisfactory performance, even though some people are better than others, it is necessary to establish high and low criterion groups on a relative basis by setting a criterion critical score at some arbitrary point which divides the most proficient from the less proficient people in the sample.

EXPERIMENTAL BATTERY

After a suitable and reliable criterion has been obtained, the next step is to select the experimental battery. When the United States Employment Service (USES) first began its test research program in 1935, about 15 suitable tests were selected for tryout in a particular study by inspecting the job analysis information to see what abilities might be involved, and by considering the results of previous studies of the same or a similar occupation. Over a period of time a large number of tests were constructed, and by a process of factor analysis, it was found that they grouped themselves into ten families or groups of tests. These were measuring ten significant vocational abilities. Fifteen tests were selected which provided a good measure of all ten of these abilities. These constitute the first edition of the USES GATB, B—1001. From 1945 to 1952 this battery has been used as the standard experimental battery in every test development study that has been undertaken to develop occupational norms. However, in the fall of 1952 another edition of the GATB, the "Separate-Answer-Sheet Form," B—1002, was introduced to the State Employment Services for use also in operational activities and in test development studies. The entire General Aptitude Test Battery is usually administered to every experimental sample.

EXPERIMENTAL SAMPLE

In the USES test development studies, the sample may consist of applicants, employees, trainees, apprentices, or students. The objective is to have the sample large enough to be truly representative of the population from which it is drawn, and to be chosen without bias in regard to the proficiency of the good, mediocre, and poor individuals comprising the sample. It is desirable to include in the experimental sample all the people in the occupation being studied who meet the requirements with respect to factors such as job duties performed, age, education, experience, criterion of job performance, and availability for testing. As the size of the sample increases, the dependability of the statistics computed on the basis of the sample increases.

When a sample of employed workers is tested for test development purposes, it is desirable for the final sample to include at least 50 workers, preferably more, who are all performing the same kind of work and who have survived the training period on the job. It is recognized that some plants may not have as many as 50 workers all performing the same job duties, or perhaps, the management cannot see its way clear to make all the workers on a particular job available for experimental testing, because this would interfere too much with the plant's production. In such instances the study is conducted on a sample of fewer than 50 but no less than 30 workers. Experience in conducting experimental studies has shown that after the data are collected, some workers are excluded because of the incompleteness or inadequacy of the data, or because they are not representative of the workers generally found in the occupation being studied. Thus to have at least 50 workers remaining in the final sample, it is sometimes necessary to include 70 or more workers in the sample initially selected for testing.

When a sample of students, trainees, or apprentices is tested for test-development purposes, the size of the experimental sample depends upon the objective of the study and the time when testing occurs. If the objective is to develop norms for a vocational course, such as machine shop or radio, or for a college or university area of specialization, it is desirable for the final sample to include at least 50 students. If the testing is done at the beginning of a course, it is desirable to include a much larger number of students, since some will drop out before the completion of the course.

When a sample of students, trainees, applicants, or apprentices is tested, the "longitudinal" experimental design is often used. A criticism frequently made by people interested in test research is that little, if any, follow-up work is done to evaluate the operational efficiency of test norms resulting from test development studies based on experimental samples of employed workers. It is generally conceded that ideally it would be preferable to establish occupational norms based on samples as similar as possible in respect to age, education, and experience to the group on which it is expected the test norms will be used; that such samples should be tested prior to hiring; and that such hiring should be done without regard to test results. However, in fact, it is not often possible to achieve this ideal in practice. Similarly, it is difficult to obtain follow-up data showing the predictive value of the established norms in terms of data which readily lend themselves to statistical interpretation. Notwithstanding these difficulties, the USES has obtained data from a number of studies using the longitudinal experimental design in the development of occupational norms. In this type of design the tests are administered to all applicants for a job rather than to those who are already employed in the job. This experimental design is particularly apropos when a new plant is being staffed and hence no workers are available for study. In this design the entire GATB is administered to all applicants that are referred to an employer, but the test scores are not used in making selections. Only regular interviewing methods are used. After the workers have been on the job a sufficient length of time to reach normal production, criterion data are obtained. Criterion data are also obtained on those individuals who did not complete the training period because of inability to perform the job duties satisfactorily. Studies of this type have the advantage of sampling a relatively wide range of ability with respect to both test and job performance. The longitudinal design has the advantage also of using test scores that have not been influenced by training.

The Employment Service makes it a point to utilize the longitudinal design for test development purposes whenever possible. However, all too often it is not feasible to use this type of experimental design because a waiting period which may vary from several weeks to several years is required before test norms can become available for operating purposes. In instances where test norms are required as soon as possible for a particular occupation, the concurrent validation experimental design must be used. The correlations obtained between test results and the criterion in studies of this type are regarded as measures of descriptive or concurrent validity. When studies which yield measures of descriptive or concurrent validity have been conducted, an effort is made to conduct check studies by using the longitudinal design in order to obtain correlations between test results and the criterion that can be regarded as measures of predictive validity.

ANALYSIS OF DATA

After the tests have been administered to an experimental sample and the criterion data have been collected, the data are analyzed to determine the group of tests having maximum validity for the occupation. Various methods for analyzing such data have been used. In the early years of the test research program, when the USES was interested merely in developing one specific battery at a time, the Wherry-Doolittle Multiple Correlation Technique was used to arrive at the combination of tests with maximum validity for the occupation. When the use of the General Aptitude Test Battery was inaugurated, however, the methods of analyzing the data were changed somewhat because the objective became somewhat different. The USES is now interested not only in establishing test norms for a single occupation but also in relating a given set of occupational norms to the norm structure for groups of occupations, so that a single battery of tests can be scored for a large variety of occupations. This means an interest in occupational differentiation as well as in differentiating good from poor workers within an occupation. A shift was made to the multiple cutting-score method. All the aptitudes regarded as significant are considered for inclusion in the final test norms. The data are further analyzed to determine which combination of significant aptitudes and cutting scores will yield the best selective efficiency in terms of the criterion of the experimental sample.

ESTABLISHMENT OF TEST NORMS

Norms on Employment Service test batteries are established for use with the multiple cutoff method, and scores are regarded as either "qualifying" or "nonqualifying." A critical or minimum qualifying score is set on each aptitude included in the final battery for subsequent use in the selection of new workers or the counseling of applicants by means of the multiple hurdle method. In other words, an individual is considered qualified only if he meets the minimum score on *each* of the key aptitudes. There is no total weighted score to be obtained.

Since Employment Service test norms indicate whether an individual is "qualified" or "nonqualified," a technique which enables the correlation of a dichotomously expressed variable is employed to evaluate the norms. Therefore, the criterion is dichotomized and tetrachoric correlation coefficients are computed between trial set of norms and the criterion. The trial norms consist of various combinations of significant aptitudes and minimum scores; the combination which yields the best selective efficiency is established as the final norms or test battery for the specific occupation being studied.

Minimum scores on Employment Service test norms are set so that the proportion of the experimental sample in the nonqualifying test score group approximates the proportion in the low or unsatisfactory criterion group. This usually tends to maximize the tetrachoric correlation coefficient and results in the test norms qualifying the maximum number of satisfactory individuals and screening out the maximum number of unsatisfactory individuals. Of course, factors such as the composition of an experimental sample, labor market conditions, production requirements of a particular plant, caliber of supervisory personnel, training techniques and production methods are determinants of the proportion of a sample placed in the low criterion group as well as the proportion that it is expedient to screen out on the basis of test results. Since it has been found that these proportions frequently approximate one-third of the sample, setting the minimum score on each significant aptitude approximately one standard deviation unit below the mean obtained for the experimental sample usually screens out the desired number and results in good selective efficiency. The number of aptitudes included in the final norms also affects the points at which minimum scores are set, because as the number of aptitudes included in the norms is increased, it is usually necessary to lower the points at which minimum scores are set in order to screen out the desired proportion. In general, if the final test norms include only two aptitudes, minimum scores are usually set at 5-point score levels slightly higher than one standard deviation unit below the sample mean on each aptitude; if the norms include three aptitudes, minimum scores are usually set at 5-point score levels close to one sigma below the mean; and if the norms include four aptitudes, minimum scores are usually set at 5-point score levels slightly lower than one sigma below the mean. Minimum scores are set at 5-point score levels in order to avoid taking undue advantage of chance fluctuations, to effect greater comparability of the results of various studies, and to facilitate use of the norms for operating purposes.

We noted that often there seemed to be a relationship between test scores and job proficiency only to an optimum point. Since there was not a straight-line relationship throughout the entire range, the Wherry-Doolittle Multiple Correlation Technique did not yield that ability in the final norms. For example, finger dexterity might be a crucial ability for some jobs; without a minimum amount of it, persons would not be able to perform successfully on the job; but, beyond a certain point, additional increments of finger dexterity would not be associated with additional production on the job.

Even when a crucial ability does show a straight-line relationship between test scores and success, the method of multiple regression weights permits the possession of other abilities to compensate for a low amount of a crucial ability. In our experience, an employer is not satisfied with a worker who is awkward with his fingers in a certain job, even though he may have an unusually high amount of other abilities required by the job. Hence we use the multiple cutoff method which does not permit such compensation of some abilities for others required by the job.

DETERMINATION OF VALIDITY OF BATTERY

The validity of the test battery composed of the key aptitudes and cutting scores is determined by means of a correlation coefficient showing the relationship between the norms and the criterion. Usually the tetrachoric correlation coefficient is used to indicate this relationship. In the USES studies, a tetrachoric correlation coefficient is not regarded as significant unless it is at least twice its standard error.

The following are two examples of test-development studies. That for mounter is an illustration of the concurrent validation experimental design in which the minimum qualifying scores eliminate approximately one-third of the experimental sample. The study for file clerk is an illustration of the longitudinal design in which the minimum qualifying scores eliminate approximately 30 percent of the experimental sample.

Study of Mounter I (DOT code 7–00.016).

Assembles radio tube mounts and stems of cathode grids and plate by positioning and connecting very small and medium sized parts and wires either manually or with tweezers; spot welds parts in place. Experimental sample of 65 workers with criterion of piece-rate earnings. Statistical results: Table 3 shows that the aptitudes with high mean scores relative to the general population and to each other aptitude are spatial, form perception, aiming, and finger dexterity; the aptitudes with low standard deviation relative to the general population and to each other aptitude are numerical and aiming; aptitudes with correlations significant at the .01 level are finger dexterity and manual dexterity.

The job analysis data for this occupation showed that the aptitudes of form perception, aiming, finger dexterity, and manual dexterity appeared to warrant consideration for inclusion in the test norms. Considering this together with the statistical results, the aptitudes of form perception, aiming, finger dexterity, and manual dexterity were selected. The critical scores were set at 85, 85, 90, and 85, respectively.

To check on the effectiveness of these norms, analysis showed that 14 of the 26 poorer workers (54 percent) failed to achieve the minimum scores established as cutting scores for these norms. Of the 42 workers who made qualifying test scores, 30 (71 percent) proved to be good workers. This indicated that if the norms had been used for selection, 54 percent of the poorer workers would not have been hired and 71 percent of those hired would have been good workers. In statistical terms, this represents an r_{tet} of .49 with standard error of .20.

Study of File Clerk (1–17.02).

Experimental sample here involved 50 workers, tested before they were hired, and who were selected without regard to test scores. Crite-

TABLE 3

STATISTICAL DATA FOR 65 MOUNTERS AND GATB SCORES

Aptitude	Mean	σ	r	σ_r
G—Intelligence	106.9	15.3	−.075	.123
V—Verbal Aptitude	102.2	14.7	−.061	.124
N—Numerical Aptitude	105.8	13.3	.064	.124
S—Spatial Aptitude	109.3	16.6	−.009	.124
P—Form Perception	111.8	15.6	.015	.124
Q—Clerical Perception	106.2	15.9	.097	.123
A—Aiming	107.1	13.9	.229	.118
T—Motor Speed	103.6	15.5	.191	.120
F—Finger Dexterity	109.5	18.4	.437	.100
M—Manual Dexterity	98.7	20.7	.353	.109

rion: supervisory ratings (group ratings in fifths). Test results showed aptitudes with high mean scores relative to the general population and to each other aptitude were: G, V, S, Q, A, and F (see Table 3 for identification of these symbols). Aptitudes with low standard deviations relative to the general population and to each other aptitude were G, P, and Q. Aptitudes with r's at the .01 level are G, V, and Q. In the determination of occupational norms, the job analysis showed that G, V, Q, and F warranted consideration for inclusion in the test norms. Taking this into consideration, together with the other statistical results, G and Q were selected, and the critical scores were set at 100 and 95 respectively.

Regarding the effectiveness of these norms, one study showed that 12 of 17 poorer workers (71 percent) failed to achieve these minimum standards. Of the 36 workers who made qualifying test scores, 31 (86 percent) proved to be good workers. This indicated that, if test norms had been used for selection, 71 percent of the poorer workers would not have been hired and 86 percent of those hired would have been good workers. Statistically these data can be summarized by an r_{tet} of .90 with a standard error of .24.

CHECK STUDIES

The USES people are well aware of the necessity of cross-validation studies. It is always unwise to accept the results of any one study as "true" or "final." Whenever possible such studies are conducted, typically with good results. The interested reader may refer to the GATB Manual (U.S. Dept. of Labor, 1958, Sect. III).

It would perhaps be wise to conclude this section on validity with a cautionary note and a specific reference to the indispensable monograph of Ghiselli (1966), which summarizes an enormous literature on personnel testing and the prediction of occupational success. His review was restricted to aptitude tests, and validity is discussed only in connection with prediction of success in training and in level of job proficiency achieved. Only studies involving adults were surveyed, and only investigations in the United States and with American workers were used. The published professional literature from 1919 to the middle of 1964 was canvassed; in addition, Ghiselli reports that numerous unpublished studies, obtained from sources such as industrial and governmental offices, were included. Occupations were grouped, first, in a broad general occupational classification scheme and then, second, according to the codes in the *Dictionary of Occupational Titles* of the U.S. Department of Labor.

Taking individual tests singly, i.e., not reporting results for an entire battery, the conclusions are sobering. For example, Ghiselli states (pp. 120–21) that the grand average of validity coefficients for training criteria is of the order of .30, and for the proficiency criteria around .20. At their worst, these grand average validity coefficients are quite low (at least they are *not* zero), and at their highest they are at least moderate. "It is apparent that even the most optimistic supporter of tests cannot claim that they predict occupational success with what might be termed a high degree of accuracy. Nevertheless, in most situations tests can have a sufficiently high degree of predictive power to be of considerable practical value in the selection of personnel" (p. 127).

DESPITE the fact that the GATB now has a wide range of occupational aptitude patterns and covers a wide spread of abilities, one still meets clients who are "GATB failures"—individuals who are so handicapped in one way or another that they are not able to score at or above the critical score levels of even the simplest or least complex OAP. For such clients that score so that they fail to qualify for any OAP, the Philadelphia Jewish Employment and Vocational Service has worked out a series of situational evaluation measures, clearly very job-related and which completely avoid the paper-and-pencil test situation. Such situational testing, usually known as work sample testing, is of great value in dealing with clients coming from various disadvantaged groups. Aside from producing clear information as to work skills, attitudinal and personality variables may also be studied.

Dr. Leshner, the author of the following report, prepared this when he was Chief Psychologist at the Jewish Employment and Vocational Service in Philadelphia. The report was prepared for the Bureau of Hearings and Appeals of the Social Security Administration of the U.S. Department of Health, Education and Welfare and was made available to all vocational consultants for this agency in November 1965. Since that time, Dr. Leshner has moved to Temple University where he is Professor of Psychology.

SITUATIONAL EVALUATION OF SUBMARGINAL CLAIMANTS

Saul S. Leshner

The Philadelphia Jewish Employment and Vocational Service has been conducting an experiment on nonverbal, alienated young people who cannot be measured by standardized paper and pencil tests like the General Aptitude Test Battery (GATB) and who therefore have been considered for placement in the most unskilled menial jobs.

The agency has been retesting these so-called "untestables" who failed the General Aptitude Test Battery by means of a carefully graded system of real work tasks. These tasks are given at a workbench in what appears to be a real factory. Substituted for symbols of school failure are job-related materials like wires, screws, pipes, and industrial fabrics.

It appears that the majority of these "GATB failures" have average or low average intelligence. However, they were referred to the agency by the state public employment service for one of 3 reasons: (a) their scores on the GATB were too low to reveal any occupational aptitude patterns, (b) they appeared to be retarded, or (c) they appeared to be too emotionally disturbed to take the 2½ hour test battery.

To reach this special young "untestable" group and other similar physically handicapped individuals with a marginal educational and occupational background, the Philadelphia agency has used work samples since 1957. While a standardized, replicable instrument has not yet been developed, particular principles and a promising format have emerged. Still a clinical tool, the work sample technique has demonstrated its value in yielding reliable and predictive information on more than 2,500 clients who either could not be adequately appraised, or could not be appraised at all, on standard psychological tests.

The total evaluation process covers a period of up to four weeks. This prolonged experience enables the individual to achieve a sense of comfort, to test out and modify his feelings, and achieve successes in progressively difficult work and social activities. Through engagement with a permissive and productive situation he may overcome his emotional resistance and incorporate appropriate work attitudes, motives, and habits. For the Social Security claimant who fears jeopardizing his elegibility for benefits, the setting and its purposive, ego-nurturing activity provide a promising medium through which a positive work identity may be formed. Aspirations for self-determination are heightened and coping behaviors for competitive work are acquired. In the four-week evaluation, the first two weeks use work samples and the second two-week period uses productive, paid work as the medium. The latter phase extends the assessment to include the effects of wages as an incentive and of work performance on production standards.

The setting of the evaluation process is the Work Adjustment Center, a true work environment located in a factory building and equipped with work tables, hand-operated jigs, and fixtures commonly used in sorting, packaging, sealing, assembly, and similar semiskilled and unskilled operations. The work sample tasks were selected from among actual work tasks performed in competitive industry and are distributed within broad occupational categories such as small parts assembly, packaging, sewing, clerical work, building maintenance, etc.

WORK SAMPLE GRADING

The work samples are graded in five levels, each of which represents a different degree of intellectual and motor performance. Each of the gradations are presumed to evoke behaviors which demand higher and more pervasive psychological organization and a greater utilization of the psychological self. They may also be viewed as involving differing degrees of stress for the individual.

The increased complexity of work tasks ranges from those which require simple specific directions to tasks which involve complex directions, abstract reasoning, and problem solving. Likewise, tasks progress from those which can be performed almost reflexively to those which require multi-coordinated sensori-motor activities. The lowest level, Grade 1, reflects behavior of a simple, routine nature. Intellectually, it instigates a repetitive response to a single instruction and requires no comprehension beyond the literal application of elementary knowledge. The motor equivalent is behavior at the reflexive level where spatial and visual arrangement aspects are at a minimum. Grade 2 is slightly more complex, requiring simple choice or the application of two specific alternatives; the performance equivalent is a gross but more controlled motor activity. Grade 3 involves multiple choices requiring moderate discrimination or gross eye-hand coordination and manual dexterity. Grade 4 incorporates judgmental activity and more refined discriminations, interpretation, and functional application of less concrete instructions. Motor activity is at a manipulative level with finger dexterity, spatial perception, and the relationships of multiple components also being present. Grade 5 incorporates symbolic and problem solving activity in which reasoning and judgment of a more abstract character prevails: intricate visual-motor arrangements, sequential processes, delicate tactual, and dexterity factors are involved.

Each level in a category may consist of several tasks which are equated in difficulty. Although these occupational categories can be graded in five levels, some cannot be so classified. Further, the grades assigned to one of the industrial categories are not necessarily equivalent to the same grades in other categories. This is because the character of occupations vary, and a total job sequence, from lowest to the maximum complexity, may not be equivalent to another job series. For example, Grade 5 in the building maintenance group does not correspond to Grade 5 in the small parts assembly group in terms of either aptitudes, interests, or psychological components. But generally, as the client progresses from the lowest to the highest grade in a particular category, he is required to have and to use different and more aptitudes; he experiences increasing levels of internal psychological stresses; and he must reach a higher level of personal achievement.

For illustration, the levels in the electrical work sample series are as follows: Level 1—clipping fuses on to a simple clip board; 2—plug and cord assembly, stripping and placing wires properly on plug terminals; 3—soldering wires into prescribed positions on a plate, using simple tools and equipment; 4—fluorescent light assembly to form a fixture of complex components; 5—small radio assembly from a plan of diagrammatic instructions.

MEASUREMENT VARIABLES AND EVALUATION

The factors selected for measurement were those deemed to be most related to realistic work adjustment. The combined measures present a profile comprising task performance, work behaviors, and personality. Task performance consists of the knowledges and skills the client has for particular kinds and levels of work. Work behaviors include conformance to rules and regulations and relations with supervisors and co-workers. Personality factors involve the learning orientation, adaptability, persistence, competitiveness with self and others, and emotional control or stability.

The task performance aspect of work samples reveals mainly abilities and aptitudes. Each sample has been related, in efforts to standardize the procedure, on all the aptitude factors measured by the General Aptitude Test Battery to establish the extent to which each factor is present in the sample task. A five-point scale has enabled correlational studies of 122 work sample tasks with Occupational Aptitude Patterns of the GATB; tentative results indicate a definite trend in the direction of predicting aptitude from work samples.

Work behavior and personality factors are observed during task performance and general deportment and are rated on a scale from submarginal to competitive industrial standards of performance. These measures assess attitudes toward co-workers, the sense of ease and comfort in applying one's self to the task, how well the client communicates with others, and with other factors that reflect the client's anxiety level and social adequacy. Such observations offer information on the extent to which the client can concentrate, shift his mental set, mobilize his energy and overcome blocking or resistance to the varied forces which are involved in work.

The rate of adjustment or adaptability is the time involved and the extent to which the individual can modify his behavior and functioning. It defines how easily and readily he can accommodate to the changing forces in the environmental situation; it is the variable which may develop and grow with improved psychological integration.

On all factors, the individual is appraised on how he compares with his fellow workers and, as he progresses, how he is similar to or different from others in the group. In addition, how and where his performance reaches or fails to reach normal competitive levels is noted. He is given a standard number of task units and his total time is recorded. The quality of the work is assessed from the accuracy and neatness of the completed units. The evaluator also focuses on psychological processes and observes and records in both narrative form and rating scales such items as learning ability, alertness to detail, concept formation and level of insight or understanding, retention of ideas, goal direction and work planning, steadiness of work tempo, orderliness, neatness, motor coordination, gross and fine dexterity, and general physical adequacy. Similarly, the manner in which the client applies himself, his concentration and distractibility, the immediacy or deferment of reactions, all contribute to the global evaluation of work behavior. The client may, for example, show dependency by requesting repeated instructions or checking of his work by his supervisor; he may aggressively reject supervision or withdraw from engagement with the situation. He may be slow in setting himself and in picking up speed in his work, or the reverse may obtain.

In a final evaluation, judgments about the individual are interpreted in terms of the particular job specifications of his vocational objectives. The ultimate evaluation covers a composite of time and achievement scores obtained in the performance of particular work samples and production tasks together with the rated observations and anecdotes of the dynamic variables which provide a global estimate of the client's adequacy. It sets forth assessments of the individual's development in the building of tolerance for the stresses of work and in the competency for the various activities which constitute work.

EVALUATION RESULTS

A series of studies was made to determine the value of the work sample evaluation technique on various impaired groups. In one study 521 clients with emotional problems were evaluated. The population was classified by primary psychological impairment in the following categories: Psychosis, Psychoneurosis, Character Disorder, Mental Retardation, Organicity, and Psychological Reaction to Physical Disability. Two thirds of the original population were male and one third female. The median age was less than 35 years, a large proportion had less than an eighth grade education, and less than 20 percent had held a job for a year or longer. Evaluation indicated that 399 (65%) clients could profitably enter the agency's personal and work adjustment program. Of the 182 not accepted for this service, 146 (80%) were considered unsuitable for vocational services. Some could not complete the initial evaluation program; 24 were able immediately to enter competitive or sheltered employment or went into vocational training. There were no appreciable differences in outcome with respect to sex, age, education or work history.

Upon completion of an eight-week work adjustment program, 187 of the 339 clients were placed in full-time jobs in competitive industry, 24 entered vocational training, 26 were placed in sheltered employment, 11 were in psychiatric treatment, and 91 continued to be unemployable. This study indicates that the work sample evaluation process was able to (a) differentiate potentially employable from unemployable persons and (b) to predict rehabilitability in 70 percent of the cases.

In another study, a population of 331 hard core school dropouts between the ages of 17 and 19 was referred by the Pennsylvania State Employment Service (PSES) to the JEVS Work Adjustment Center for evaluation. These youth could not be evaluated on the General Aptitude Test Battery for a variety of reasons: some lacked educational or cultural background for coping with the test material and some had personality and physical problems and could not respond to the formal test situation. About evenly divided between male and female, 69 percent left school in the tenth or eleventh grade, 26 percent in grades six to nine, and 5 percent were in special classes; a check of school records indicated a high rate of school truancy; 49 percent had reading levels below the fifth grade and 80 percent were below fifth grade in arithmetic; 48 percent had never worked, and 78 percent had held jobs for less than five months. Initial JEVS evaluation indicated that 69 percent had "inadequate personality," 4 percent were mentally retarded, 5 percent had significant physical handicaps, and 10 percent had multiple handicaps.

Of the total group of 331 evaluated, 69 (21%) were deemed not feasible either for training or employment; 66 (19%) dropped out of the program. A total of 196 were appraised as feasible for Work Adjustment Training and completed the process. All of the 165 who reported to PSES were placed in competitive employment; 12 entered MDTA training courses; 5 entered on-job-training; 14 failed to report to PSES and could not be recalled. It was apparent that the situational evaluation provided an assessment that (*a*) was not available through routine testing and (*b*) resulted in actions that accorded with expectations.

A number of other populations were evaluated through work sample performance, including older impaired workers, long-term unemployed men, and in-school marginal youth. With some variation in administrative approach to meet problems related to the primary impairment and idiosyncratic issues, the procedure demonstrated its value in producing aptitudinal and personality data that either strongly supplemented test information, or was not accessible from tests and case histories.

The range of work samples currently used at the Philadelphia JEVS consists of some 125 tasks, selected from an initial group of more than 500, on the basis of their discriminatory value and their typicality of work performed in competitive industry.

CONDITIONS OF SITUATIONAL EVALUATION

More study and follow-up are needed to develop the procedures described. Tentative conclusions suggest that the range of occupational categories should be extended and more tool and machine tasks added to highlight preferential functional areas. Industrial norms, virtually nonexistent in competitive employment, must be developed and refined so that a more accurate standard of employability is available.

It may be apparent that the process is essentially client-centered and, as noted, involves an interaction of vocational diagnosis and treatment. The treatment aspect inherent in the manipulation and control of situational variables is oriented to the idiosyncratic needs and responses of the client. Since it is an activity, or learn-by-doing procedure, it seems of major importance to insure that the individual has an opportunity to crystallize his feelings and develop insights, to reinforce new behavior patterns through a verbalization of his experience. The combined experience and verbalized insights provide a coherent framework, expressed in concrete terms, and oriented to a reality-based employment objective. The client has clear, specific guideposts around which he can integrate and strengthen his ego functions. Periodic counseling interviews accompany the evaluation as an aid to bringing the meaning of work performance and realistic achievement to the level of awareness, and thereby facilitate the formation of a worker identity.

It is apparent that the factors measured offer a useful definition of employability. As most placement workers are aware, employer job specifications may be phrased in terms of skills and knowledge, but actual hiring practice gives at least equal weight to attitudinal and personality factors. Employee satisfactoriness, and therefore employability, is comprised of good work role behaviors of the kind evaluated situationally. The work experience of the individual while being evaluated represents demonstrated vocational strengths and weaknesses which serve the purposes of the client, the employer, and the rehabilitation worker. The fearful claimant who is caught between fixed Social Security benefits and a socially esteemed self-determination may gain self confidence and move toward a vocational goal. A situational process properly structured permits a more reliable extrapolation of the adjustment curve and is therefore more predictive than a test profile.

A final condition of effective evaluation is the evaluator. Evaluation obviously is only as good, in certain respects, as the evaluator. The control and interpretation of work sample performance should be maintained by a psychologist or counselor who understands the psychodynamics of vocational behavior and the requirements of competitive employment. The actual administrators of the work sample procedure may be subprofessionals under direction of the professional. The latter should be capable of and responsible for organizing evaluation data from work sample and other sources. He should provide assessment material from which vocationally meaningful opinions can be provided for the Social Security Hearing Examiner, and as the situation warrants, for other professional workers, for employers, and for the client himself.

In summary, it is considered that the situational evaluation technique, particularly as it involves the systematic use of work samples, may appear to offer evidence for a reasonable determination of ability to engage in substantial gainful activity.

▽ ▽ ▽

PART FIVE

Ability Testing

THE IQ has come in for a great deal of criticism. An anonymous but facetious critic labeled it "that new tool of infant damnation." This literally becomes very serious business when the IQ score is rigidly used to classify individuals for placement in slow-learner groups in school or, more significantly, when it is used as a basis for commitment to institutions. It is comforting to think that today test users are more sophisticated in IQ interpretation and, in the main, they are. Some school systems, however, still insist that a child's IQ be 74 (and not 75) in order to gain admission to a retarded group. Even more serious are errors that result in commitment to state institutions.

The following report, based on data obtained from the State Home in Beatrice, Nebraska, is by no means a survey of the whole problem. It is to the credit of the professional staff at Beatrice that this study was completed and also that these reexaminations meant the subsequent discharge of the cases reported here. This report is a condensation of the original, which appeared in the *American Journal of Mental Deficiency* in 1960. Dr. Garfield is currently Professor and Director of the Clinical Psychology Training Program at Washington University, St. Louis; Dr. Affleck was formerly Professor of Psychology at the University of Nebraska Medical Center.

A STUDY OF INDIVIDUALS COMMITTED TO A STATE HOME FOR THE RETARDED WHO WERE LATER RELEASED AS NOT MENTALLY DEFECTIVE

S. L. Garfield and D. C. Affleck

The diagnosis of mental deficiency with its concomitant problems is not always as simple a matter as it sometimes appears to be on the surface. Not only are these difficulties in differentiating a mentally retarded person from persons with other types of conditions, but an erroneous diagnosis is one which has very serious consequences for the individual concerned and in many cases for the family as well.

93

Although problems pertaining to the diagnosis and definition of mental retardation have received some attention, comparatively few research studies have been reported on the occurrence of incorrect diagnosis. The concept of "pseudofeeblemindedness," however, has been one evidence of difficulties in this area. More recently, concern has been expressed over problems in the diagnostic differentiation of mental deficiency from childhood autism and childhood schizophrenia. Obviously, the matter of diagnosis is important for proper treatment and disposition.

We became interested in this problem as a result of coming into contact with some cases diagnosed previously as mentally retarded, but who were found on later examination not to be retarded. On a superficial inspection these cases presented a pattern of factors which had led to institutionalization for mental deficiency or to consideration of such action. Usually the individual displayed some behavioral or social difficulty, there was an inadequate home situation, and an intellectual examination had reported an IQ below 75. In several instances, because of behavioral or personality disturbance, such individuals were studied more intensively in our setting and gave indications that they were intellectually above the retarded level. Sometimes the total score on intellectual tests was not too high, but the variability of intellectual performance suggested a state of emotional disturbance which precluded optimal functioning. We were impressed also with the tendency of some psychological examiners to report psychometric data and IQ scores with little sensitivity to other non-cognitive factors which may affect intellectual performance.

THE PRESENT STUDY

As a consequence we were interested in the problem of individuals incorrectly diagnosed as mentally retarded and in the factors that contribute to such problems in diagnosis. In contacts and visits with the staff of the Beatrice State Home, we were informed of 24 individuals who had been reexamined and found not to be mentally retarded. We decided, therefore, to make a study of these 24 cases. We were interested primarily in seeing what types of cases these were, the factors leading to their institutionalization, and the events responsible for their being judged not mentally retarded with subsequent discharge from the institution.

Fourteen of the group were males and ten were females. The group was predominantly white, with only one Negro. The age of institutionalization varied markedly for the subjects in the present investigation. The youngest was four months of age and oldest was 64 years of age at the time of admission. The period of institutionalization ranged widely—from 1 year 8 months to almost 58 years. Seventeen of the patients had some sort of psychological examination prior to admission and, as might be expected, it was the older cases which had no such examination. While the psychological examinations played a role in the initial admission of most cases, psychological reexaminations at a later time also were instrumental in contributing to the revised judgment concerning the lack of mental retardation.

FACTORS ASSOCIATED WITH COMMITMENT

Although some similarity in patterns was noted among the cases relative to the apparent reasons for admission, there were also unique features which are not too easily categorized. One of the more frequent reasons for being institutionalized appeared to be a combination of social difficulty and lack of an adequate home situation. While this was not always the case, it seemed to be reflected in the comparatively large number who were committed to the State Home from other types of institutions—training schools, orphanages, state hospitals. The largest single group of individuals in this study were those who came to the State Home from another type of institution—11 of the current group of 24 were in this category. Various factors appeared to play a role in the eventual transfer or commitment of these patients to the State Home. These included behavioral difficulties, poor educational progress, and patterns of behavior judged to be unusual or indicative of mental disability. Generally, the individual was seen as having some type of personality or behavioral disturbance, and in most instances a psychological or psychiatric examination was then requested. If the latter indicated a low IQ or clinical judgment of mental deficiency, plans for a transfer to the State Home were instituted. This appeared to be the pattern for this group of individuals, but, of course, one cannot state on the basis of our data how frequently such a pattern occurs.

In the other cases listed, a variety of factors seemed to be responsible, including physical disability, a disturbed home situation, death of parents, and behavior judged unsatisfactory by others in the community. In several of these cases definite pressures were exerted to have the individual removed from the home or community. In one case, for example, the individual and his brother were abandoned by their mother while the father was in the service. After the father remarried there was continued bickering in the home. The boy began to act out his difficulties by stealing, setting fires, and fighting. During this period he received psychiatric treatment with somewhat variable results. The stepmother insisted on his removal from the home and he was eventually institutionalized in the State Home. In another case, that of a 15-year-old illegitimate girl, institutionalization was requested by a relative with whom she was living and who was unable to control her. In another instance, a 27-year-old woman living with a man in a common law relationship was committed because of complaints of abuse filed by a domestic relations worker.

Thus, while the specific situations varied somewhat, in most instances there were serious difficulties or problems in the current life situation of the individual. External stresses were particularly notable in the case histories of the 14 individuals who were committed prior to their 18th birthday. Very atypical environmental situations are seen in the fact that eight of these persons were transferred from state or private institutions and three others came directly from a disrupted or inadequate home situation.

PSYCHOLOGICAL TEST RESULTS

Because the results of the psychological examination played a significant role in the commitment or eventual discharge of a number of these persons, it is of some importance to make a separate analysis of these figures.* Seven of the subjects had no psychological examination prior to commitment, and these tended to be those institutionalized some years ago. In some instances the name of the test was not indicated in the reports in the case records. In a few cases also, the individual received an extensive battery of tests including special and less-known instruments, and these results are not included.

The range of scores and the variation in findings are of considerable interest, even though a competent clinical psychologist today would not base his diagnostic impression on the IQ alone. Without question, however, the IQ played an important role in the commitment of the majority of these cases. Where a low IQ was obtained prior to commitment it was apparently seized upon or utilized as a means of committing the individual to the State Home. At least from the material available for some cases, one received a feeling that the individual was viewed as a problem and the opportunity to dispose of the problem was not to be slighted. For example, in one case when the re-examination of the State School revealed the individual was not retarded and this was communicated to the original institution, the latter stated the IQ didn't matter, since the person was a difficult problem. In this instance and in a few others there was decided reluctance to take the individual back.

A few comments can be offered with regard to psychological examinations performed prior to commitment. While most of the IQs obtained were low, little allowance was made in the psychological reports for possible emotional factors which conceivably might have contributed to the lowered level of performance. If a number of these individuals were experiencing difficulties, were away from their home and family, or conceivably were anxious about the test situation, little was said about this and apparently it was not deemed to be of much significance. This

---

* Table 3 in the original report should be consulted for details.

was so, even though other data available on the cases, including psychiatric appraisals, made mention of personality difficulties, frequently of severe degree. It is of interest that seven of the 17 cases examined psychologically prior to commitment had been examined psychiatrically or received psychiatric treatment. Nevertheless, little mention was made in the psychological report of the possible influence of such disturbance on test performance. In some instances mention was made of the negativeness or inadequate cooperation of the subject, but this did not seem to influence the interpretation of the test scores. In general, the emphasis was placed on the IQ score and the interpretation of mental deficiency was followed by a prognostic statement to the effect that the individual would never progress beyond a limited level of mental development. Commitment was also recommended in most instances. By and large, these reports were quite positive in terms of the definiteness and conclusiveness of findings. In most instances, they were performed by psychologists who had not received any extensive training in clinical psychology.

In two cases, IQs in the 80's were reported, but the individual still was committed or retained in the institution. In one of these cases an IQ of 88 by a qualified psychologist was followed by three lower IQs reported by psychologists with limited clinical training. Even though the report containing the 88 IQ mentioned the possibility of significant emotional disturbance in the child, the later IQs carried the day and the child was institutionalized by order of the court. In the other such case, institutionalization occurred prior to the psychological examination. This took place 40 years ago and the data are meager. However, the individual remained in the institution approximately 35 years after an IQ of 87 was obtained.

The IQs secured at a later date in the State Home average considerably higher than those secured earlier. Unfortunately, in not all cases was a psychological examination performed prior to institutionalization, nor was the same test always used in the later examination. This makes the matter of evaluation and interpretation of the data somewhat more complicated. Obviously, different factors might be involved in the various cases, and perhaps no definitive conclusions can be drawn. After reviewing all the available data, however, the present authors believe that the most apparent explanation, at least in a large percentage of those cases tested prior to commitment, concerns the inadequacy of the original examination and the failure to evaluate the importance of emotional factors on intelligence test scores. In over half of these cases, there were data already available pointing to the existence of personality and behavioral disturbance at the time of testing. Secondly, even the brief reports by the examiners made mention of some resistiveness, peculiarity, or other unusual behavior on the part of the subject which was not considered in the evaluation of the test data. To the experienced clinician, this appeared to be definite disregard of personality variables as they affect test scores. Thirdly, in four cases which were examined at our institute, the pattern of test scores and the behavior evident during the testing situation led the clinical psychologist to consider personality disturbance as a significant variable affecting test scores. In these instances, the psychologists felt the patients' intellectual potentials were above that of the mental defective level. Other factors which seemed to play a role in the original test scores were that the individuals were examined at a time when they were experiencing some type of adjustment difficulty, were separated from home and family, were anxious or lacked motivation. It is a time honored colloquialism in mental testing that the examiner must secure rapport and cooperation with the subject in order to secure optimum results. If there seem to be factors interfering with this, the results probably cannot be viewed as valid. This view seemed to be disregarded completely in some of the cases.

While the authors were most impressed with the lack of concern on the part of previous examiners for variables which affect test scores, other explanations are also possible for some of the cases. In two cases (5 and 9), an additional explanation seems obvious. In these two instances, examinations were performed at or before age two, with IQs in the neighborhood of 50. The IQs at later ages on the 1937 Stanford-Binet and WISC were in the 80's. This is in line with other studies indicating the relatively poor predictive ability of infant testing. In the third case tested originally at age two, the differences between the early scores and the later ones were not as marked.

Obviously, the findings discussed do not lead automatically to definite interpretations or conclusions. The writers, in going through the case material, were struck with the very inadequate job of psychological examination in a majority of cases, the lack of sensitivity to the importance of personality factors on test scores, and the almost exclusive reliance on the IQ. To us, this was a disturbing finding with very important social consequences. However, other problems also appear to be raised by our data, even though the latter are limited. One concerns the dangers of relying on the results of tests at or before age two. The other, concerning lack of comparability between tests, also has significant practical implications, since most individuals outside of professional psychology tend to react to all IQs as equivalent, regardless of the test used. When differences occur, which IQs shall be considered as a basis for practical decisions? While it is certainly true that important decisions should be based on more than the IQ, our data strongly suggest that the IQ carries tremendous weight in such decisions.

FACTORS LEADING TO DISCHARGE

The majority of individuals discharged were identified primarily by two means. One of these was a retesting program instituted relatively recently. The other was the result of someone on the staff noting that an individual functioned better than expected. In these instances the individual was given a psychological examination, and if it appeared to indicate that the individual was not mentally retarded, attempts were made to have the individual discharged. Although various staff members were involved with some of these individuals, it appeared that the staff social workers were those most frequently requesting a re-evaluation because certain individuals impressed them as not being retarded. In one instance, a re-evaluation was requested by an outside agency. The psychologist's findings indicated the individual was not mentally deficient, and a recommendation for discharge was made. In three instances, various patterns of acting out or related problems led to evaluation at our own institution. It can be noted also that generally it was more difficult to get an individual out of the institution than it was to get him in. Not only are there numerous problems to consider in getting a person back into the community at large, but in some instances there was definite opposition from the community organizations which played a role in the original institutionalization. This is another reason why errors in diagnosis leading to unnecessary or inappropriate institutionalization have unhappy consequences.

DISCUSSION

Our data appear to lend support for the need to evaluate the influence of emotional and environmental factors on tests of intelligence. Such considerations were rarely suggested in pre-commitment reports in this sample. Apparently in the desire to appear "objective," great reliance was placed on test scores alone. This reliance was not only evident in the reports, but in the reaction of social agencies and the courts to the evaluation. Credence is readily granted a reported test score because of its ease of statement and seeming objectivity. When argument did occur initially in some precommitment cases, it was largely over discrepant IQ scores. The misuse of IQ scores is very evident in subsequent correspondence about the cases. In some instances, the scores are cited as authoritative estimates of intellectual potential or as positive indications of how much ability the person has, e.g., "This boy has 50 percent intelligence." "This girl has an IQ of 66 percent; and since feeblemindedness may be quantitatively defined as any score below 70 percent, she may be considered definitely feebleminded and classified as a moron."

In the light of these misuses, one may question the advisability of reporting IQs. Very few persons who use psychological reports appear to understand that any IQ is only a means of ranking a person relative to a standardization group, and that when emotional disturbance is present, such ranking may not be reliable. For such reasons, it seems preferable to have a qualitative evaluation of intellectual functioning where the clinical psychologist translates his test findings into language which is meaningful to laymen and not as subject to misinterpretation.

Somewhat related to these considerations are the problems concerning the limitations of test results secured at very early ages and the matter of comparability of scores on different tests. Undoubtedly more careful research on these problems is needed, particularly in terms of which tests appear to correlate most with other criteria of social adjustment.

The high percentage (46 percent) of cases in this sample of patients who came from other institutions is also a finding of considerable interest. It would appear that in these cases also, too great attention was given to intellectual factors and test scores when these were in great part symptoms of broader emotional disturbance. The basis for this may rest on the historical availability of institutional care for the mentally retarded and a failure to be adequately sensitive to the total functioning of the person. Where below average (or dull normal) intelligence is combined with anti-social behavior, inadequate home situation or emotional disturbance, institutionalization in a home for the retarded may be viewed as a solution to the problem, particularly if under stress the IQ falls close to the mentally retarded range. It is also possible that unless a child shows grossly psychotic behavior, emotional factors do not receive primary consideration. Related to this may be the fact that institutional facilities for emotionally-disturbed children are relatively scarce and perhaps reserved for those of higher intelligence and grosser disturbance. Outpatient treatment probably is not considered when the home situation is unstable. The net result is that the individual is incorrectly diagnosed and inappropriately institutionalized.

Finally, it should be stated that we have no precise estimate of the extent of the problem reported on here. The current sample is not the result of a statistical survey, and there are undoubtedly variations from setting to setting. Nevertheless, it does emphasize a problem which, though small in number, is important in terms of the welfare of the individual. Periodic reappraisals of the institutionalized individuals in the higher ranges of the mentally retarded would appear justified.

▽ ▽ ▽

In any cross-cultural setting, one of the real difficulties is to find adequate or fair mental ability measures. Usually, nonverbal materials have been applied, but these also can be easily loaded with specific cultural referents. The problem has usually been "solved" by employing matrices of varying degrees of complexity. Cattell and Raven are two British researchers who have prepared such tests. Cattell has produced evidence that these types of tests are loaded with "g," and that this "g" may be separated into "fluid" and "crystallized" intelligence. It is his belief that a culture-fair test should be loaded with the "fluid" kind of "g."

Culture-fair tests would appear to have great utility in testing the various underprivileged groups that elicit so much interest now. It would be helpful here to be able to compare such individuals with this kind of test score as against the more conventional measures of mental ability known to have a built-in cultural bias.

Not all test specialists are so enthusiastic about this possibility. Critics point out the problem has two aspects—measurement of general intelligence and elimination of cultural influences. Simultaneously accomplishing both of these objectives may be impossible. Probably nobody has as yet produced a really satisfactory culture-fair test. Cattell's success in this area is, however, at least partial, and the topic is introduced here as an interesting variant in the area of intelligence testing.

Professor Cattell is Research Professor of Psychology at the University of Illinois, and is widely known for his ingenious and diverse tests of aptitudes and abilities and the like. The following remarks about the culture-fair test (labeled "culture-free" when first published) are taken, with some deletions, from his 1965 book (pp. 301–9).

SOME PRACTICAL IMPLICATIONS OF THE THEORY OF FLUID AND CRYSTALLIZED GENERAL ABILITY

Raymond B. Cattell

The new theory claims that there are actually *two* general ability factors which, from their properties, have been called *fluid* and *crystallized* general ability. In intelligence test practice the quickest way of designating these two is by pointing to the culture-fair and the traditional (verbal and numerical) tests, respectively. Culture-fair tests were implicit in the work of Spearman's students, Fortes, Line, and Cattell, in the late twenties, demonstrating his argument that it does not matter what subject matter is used among the elements between which one asks the subject to perceive relations. Provided the relations are complex enough one can, for instance, generate an analogies test among shades of colour. The systematical application of this to producing tests which would be comparatively free of cultural influences did not begin, however, for nearly another decade, when the present writer, with his students Sarason and Feingold, and Raven in Britain, developed tests which have since been called the I.P.A.T. Culture-Fair Intelligence Scales and the Progressive Matrices. (The Culture-Fair tests include Matrices as one of four subtests.)

The present writer first sought to generate sufficiently complex relations among "fundaments" which are common to people all over the earth and which would not, of course, be presented in verbal symbols, but as pictures. (Intelligence tests given pictorially are, of course, far from culture-free.) It seemed that parts of the human body, sun, moon, and stars were about the only things common to cultures. But, additionally, any shapes on paper, or in plastic, that do not represent objects peculiar to a culture, or have names, proved effective. Figure 1 shows two examples of such material. Such "perceptual" tests were shown by Feingold, Sarason, and other researchers with the present writer, as well as by Raven, (*a*) to correlate very well with general intelligence estimates and the general factor—much better than "performance tests" with form boards, etc., and (*b*) to show no cultural effects. For example, Feingold compared immigrants to the U.S.on these and traditional tests (1) on entering, and (2) a year or more after acclimatizing. The traditional tests were woefully misleading but the culture-fair stood firm. The C. F. tests have since been shown to be effective in China, Africa, India, and across most culture varieties.

What is called the *fluid* general ability factor (because it is free of particular investments) shows itself particularly in the culture-fair tests but also by other characteristics. First, it separates as a distinct but correlated factor from crystallized ability. Secondly, as an ability to perceive relationships in any material, new or old, it reaches its maximum level at about fourteen or fifteen years, as the brain finishes its

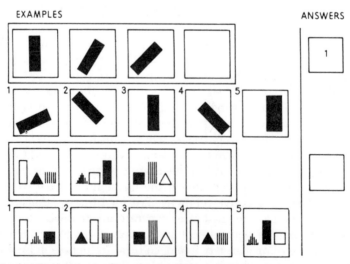

FIG. 1. A series test in a culture-fair intelligence test.

growth. But crystallized ability may go on being deposited with further investments in training, education, and experience beyond this age and in college populations the test performance curve does not "flatten out" till twenty-one or so. Age or brain injury may bring a general reduction of the fluid ability level, but the crystallized ability retains the "shape" which fluid ability and experience have given to it—just as the coral rock formation retains the form reached by the once living coral organism, so that only quite special areas, such as verbal facility, may be damaged.

This metaphor of a coral growth brings us to the crux of the meaning of "two general abilities" and requires that we take stock of our understanding of the statistical pattern which we have all along been calling a "factor." Fluid ability appears as a general factor because it is some sort of active mental capacity or energy, which is thrown now into this problem and now into that. The different performances correlate, i.e., a person high in one tends to be high in all, because people differ in their endowment in it, and it is the same force now exerted here and now there. But the correlation found among the parts of the crystallized general ability, e.g., between judgment in English, in mathematics, in history, etc., is of a different origin. It springs largely from the uniformity of our school curriculum, whereby a person who has been twice as long at school as another will simultaneously know *more* of all these things. If this is the case, one may ask: "What then is the difference between crystallized intelligence and what we simply call general school achievement?" General school achievement includes much that is known merely by rote, i.e. by good memory and school interest, and which required no great fluid intelligence for its acquisition. What we call crystallized intelligence is the collection of *skilled judgments* a person has acquired by applying his fluid intelligence to his school opportunities. It is a sort of "holding company" for what fluid intelligence and school experience have jointly produced, and as such it has a life of its own in that its skills tend to generate more skills like them.

The difference of fluid and crystallized ability is brought out most clearly if we consider persons raised in two different cultures, say in Britain and France. It would be unfair to make any precise inference about an English seventeen-year-old's intelligence from his decisions on the correctness of synonyms in French or the shrewdness of his comment on the domestic policies of Louis Quinze. Within any culture the differences are not so great, but social status, locality, and opportunity differences still make the correlation between fluid and crystallized ability only about +0.6, not the +1.0 which would justify deriving an estimate of a child's natural, fluid intelligence by the traditional intelligence test (crystallized ability) rather than by the fluid intelligence factor (as in a culture-fair intelligence test). Again, this can be sharply brought home by the fact that one simply cannot compare, say, American and Chinese children on an intelligence test by an American or

Chinese intelligence test. Yet, when the I.P.A.T. Culture-Fair test is used, the Chinese in Taiwan and the Americans in Illinois have been demonstrated to possess almost exactly the same average score and scatter. Naturally, the mere fact that the identical test gives the same score in these two circumstances does not alone prove that the test is getting at native ability. A good culture-fair test should *sometimes* decline to show differences between people in different cultures because the cultures may alone distinguish them, but at other times it should even show differences when both groups are within one culture. Such tests, in fact, show lower scores from the north island of Japan than from the south (a fact which Japanese understand), and lower scores in southern Italy than the north (a fact which Italians understand). The finding that Chinese in China score the same as Americans fits other indications of Chinese intelligence, such as the equal performance of their descendants in America in traditional intelligence tests in English. (The prize for Gaelic poetry has recently been given to a Chinese girl brought up in Ireland.) Whether the lower scores found on these tests by anthropologists working in the Congo is to be explained by temporary conditions is something for science to investigate.

Within one country the discrepancy between individual intelligence levels as measured respectively by traditional "crystallized" intelligence factor measures and culture-fair measures of the fluid ability factor is not great *during the growth period*. But after school there is increasing divergence. One person may begin investing his fluid ability in entirely new fields—say mining engineering—while another becomes a school-teacher and another concentrates on the verbal skills of a journalist. Because skilled habits in any field get dusty with disuse, the traditional intelligence test, like the Terman-Binet, the Wechsler, W.A.I.S., etc., will deal rather unfairly with the cowboy, the farmer, or mining engineer, compared with the teacher or journalist, if they are retested at, say, forty years of age. This has been noted in the selection problems of Mensa, a society in England and America, entry to which depends democratically upon the individual, no matter what his background, scoring above a stipulated high IQ level on an adult intelligence test. The selections made by traditional tests (the Cattell Scale III, for superior adults) and culture-fair tests have only a moderate degree of consensus. In Figure 2 the two coordinates represent scores on the two types of test, the angle between them being adjusted to give the correlation of about 0.7, which is approximately correct for such tests among *general adults*. (Among students, having the same educational background, the agreement would be much higher than 0.7.) It will be seen that the same cut-off points—the top 5 percent and the top 10 percent on the two tests—garners a different crop, and that the number in common to the two crops gets lower as the selection point is made higher. In one survey made by the writer the highest score on the I.P.A.T. Culture-Fair was made by a young sailor—a very intelligent man who, through

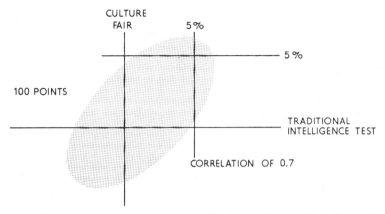

1 percent is in common to the groups formed by the top 5 percent by culture-fair and traditional intelligence tests.

FIG. 2. Differences expected in selection of bright people on culture-fair and traditional intelligence tests.

an adventurous and easy-going temperament, had become a deck-hand—and the highest score in the Cattell Scale III traditional test by a classics student at Oxford. Each was pretty high on the other test too, but if we accept fluid ability as "native intelligence" the sailor was the brighter man. The difference in membership of such a society, according to whether it adopted the fluid or a crystallized intelligence factor as its definition of intelligence, illustrates the general importance of the choice of test in the social application of intelligence tests.

However, the greater discrepancy between fluid and crystallized scores among adults arises not only from the fact that crystallized ability is no longer being "pushed along," just ahead of, and by the growing fluid ability in the common learning environment of the school. For a gap between them develops also from the fact that fluid ability can *sink down* below its late adolescent level. To take an extreme case, a brain injury to the parietal area of Broca may cause some *general* loss of fluid, adaptive ability, but in the crystallized ability measurements it will affect only one of the circle of skills commonly measured in such an intelligence test, in that it will cause specifically some verbal aphasia, i.e. a loss of skilled use of words. Thus if the traditional test used happens to measure the individual on crystallized abilities *not* affected by the locality of injury a wrong impression of his general mental capacity is obtained.

In adult life particularly, when a prediction is required of how intelligently a person will operate in some entirely new field, e.g. in wartime induction testing, assigning new job areas, a fluid ability measure by a culture-fair test is the wiser measure to use. But even at the school age where the two measures are usually in closer agreement, injustices can be done by a test which looks backward to past opportunities rather than forward to potential performance in a new type of school. The work of

Dr. Douglas and his colleagues at the London School of Economics brings this out clearly by showing that on traditional intelligence tests the average IQ of children from lower social status homes drops relative to that of more environmentally favoured children when retested over the age range from eight to eleven plus. For if the alleged intelligence test is actually contaminated with school achievement and home cultural background, the obtained apparent IQ will deviate from its proper constancy in the one case in an upward and in the other in a downward direction.

In the coming decade, with increasing interest of the general public in effective and fair application of mental tests, we are likely to see considerable debate on the proper roles respectively of traditional and culture-fair tests. Against the advantages of the latter, two arguments are likely to appear. First, they do not have "face validity." That is to say it is hard to see from looking at them why they test intelligence. For example, a frequent comment is "This test involves no word skills whatever. How can it possibly predict capacity to succeed in English?" The professional psychologist, but not the general public, has long given up face validity (or "faith validity" as the specialist calls it), recognizing that the first reaction of the general public to the automobile was "How can it possibly go without a horse?" In one group in which varied students were subsequently subjected to intensive English training the culture-fair actually predicted English achievement better than an ordinary verbal intelligence test.

A second criticism is that *within the same year* and among students *all in the same kind of school*, the culture-fair does not correlate with ("predict") achievement quite so highly as the traditional test. This is not only admitted, but treasured by the exponent of the newer tests. The reason that the traditional test gives a better immediate "prediction" is that it already contains an appreciable admixture of the school achievement it is supposed to predict. If all we want to do is predict, in March, children's school achievement in, say, July, we can do better than any intelligence test by predicting from their school achievement scores in March. The very object of an intelligence test, however, is to be *analytical*. As we study any individual child we are interested in the *discrepancy* between his native intelligence and his school achievement, and the more clearly and reliably this is brought out the better the test. The claim of the culture-fair tests is that it will make a more fair selection for future performance when the passage of some years has given a chance for the present accidental inequalities of achievement opportunity to be ironed out.

Beyond two such apparently real criticisms it has been said by shrewd observers that since the professional interest of educators and sociologists is specifically in culture they are not likely to be enthusiastic about a measurement which aims to ignore it. Indeed, it is less than a generation since the majority of sociologists taught their students that there are no innate differences in intelligence, and that "native intelligence" must be a figment of the imagination. The researcher's position is that it is possible to infer the relative contribution of genetic and environment variation to the observed population variance in any trait. What fresh light does this newer analysis of intelligence into two general factors throw on the old and vexed question of how far intelligence is inborn? With tests in use before the advent of culture-fair scales an 80/20 percent ratio in favour of heredity has commonly been found, but recent results suggest that the hereditary determination is higher than this for fluid ability and possibly lower for crystallized ability. However, one must insist that the constitutional determination is still well short of 100 percent for fluid ability, i.e., it is not properly labelled the individual's innate ability level. For its level is affected by accidents of gestation and birth, and thereafter by physiological environment, head injuries, etc., if not by the school environment of the individual. Thus this issue, like many others, is likely to become more understandable as research clarifies the new theory of two general ability factors, fluid and crystallized.

▽ ▽ ▽

A warning is sounded in the following article by Wesman concerning our excessive reliance on verbal criteria in aptitude measurement. Associated with this are Wesman's pertinent and encouraging comments about the depressing downward slide of mean scores from adult measures of intelligence as CA increases. Intelligence is here seen as the summation of learning experiences, a very different concept from Guilford's elaborate factor—analytic structure of intellect model to which Wesman briefly refers to as "mathematicoseductive."

Dr. Wesman, now deceased, was Director of the Test Division of the Psychological Corporation in New York City as well as a Corporation officer. The paper, reproduced in its entirety, was his Presidential Address to Division 5 (Evaluation and Measurement) at the Washington, D. C. meetings of the American Psychological Association, September 1967. The address was later published in a 1968 issue of the *American Psychologist*.

INTELLIGENCE TESTING

Alexander G. Wesman

The nature of intelligence has been a favorite subject for contemplation and disputation for centuries—perhaps from the dawn of man as Homo sapiens. The topic is being studied and debated today by educators sociologists, geneticists, neurophysiologists, and biochemists, and by psychologists specializing in various branches of the discipline. Despite this attention and effort, however—or perhaps *because* of it—there appears to be no more general agreement as to the nature of intelligence or the most valid means of measuring intelligence than was the case 50 years ago. Concepts of intelligence and the definitions constructed to enunciate these concepts abound by the dozens, if not indeed by the hundreds.

With so many diverse definitions of intelligence, it is perhaps not surprising that we cannot agree on how to measure intelligence. It is my conviction that much of the confusion which plagued us in the past, and continues to plague us today, is attributable to our ignoring two propositions which should be obvious:

1. Intelligence is an attribute, not an entity.

2. Intelligence is the summation of the learning experiences of the individual.

We have all too often behaved as though intelligence is a physical substance, like a house or an egg crate composed of rooms or cells; we might better remember that it is no more to be reified than attributes like beauty, or speed, or honesty. There are objects which are classifiable as beautiful; there are performances which may be characterized as speedy; there are behaviors which display honesty. Each of these is measurable, with greater or lesser objectivity. Because they can be measured, however, does not mean they are substances. We may agree with E. L. Thorndike that if something exists it can be measured; we need not accept the converse notion that if we can measure something it has existence as a substance. Intelligence as here defined is a summation of learning experiences. The instances in which intelligent behavior is observed may be classified in various ways that appear to be logical or homogeneous, but they are individual instances all the same. Each instance represents a response the organism has learned; each learned response in turn predisposes the organism for learning additional responses which permit the organism to display new acts of intelligent behavior.

For our present purposes, it matters little whether we are more comfortable with stimulus-response bonds, with experience-producing drives, with imprinting, or with neuropsychological explanations of *how* or *why* learning occurs; whatever the learning theory, the fundamental principle is universal. We start with an organism which is subject to modification by interaction with the environment; as a product of that interaction, the organism has been modified. Further interaction involves a changed organism—one which is ready to interact with its environment in a new way.

Organisms may differ from one another in their susceptibility to modification. One organism may need a more potent stimulus to trigger reaction to the environment than does another. A particular organism may respond to a given class of stimuli more readily than it does to other kinds of stimuli. Organisms may differ from one another in their readiness to respond to different classes of stimuli. There may be important differences in the ability of organisms to modify their behavior in effective ways as a result of experience.

We may develop and investigate hypotheses as to whether such differences in response as are displayed arise from variations in neurological endowment or in conducive environment. All that we can be sure of, at least as of now, is that what we are dealing with is a response-capable organism which has been exposed to environmental stimuli, has interacted in some way with those stimuli, and has been modified thereby.

The bits or modules which constitute intelligence may be information or may be skill; i.e., they may be content or process. Furthermore, they are multidimensional, and some modules may have more dimensions than do others. Each module is subject to essential change as the individual is exposed to further learning experiences. Each act of learning serves to create new modules, change the existing ones, or both. Modules are not independent; rather, they may overlap with several or many other modules; thus, they are complex both in their number of dimensions and in their interrelationships. Even early percepts are rarely if ever simple. A toy ball when first seen has at least size, shape, and color; if it is touched, it has texture and hardness as well. Accordingly, few if any modules of learning are truly simple.

The whole of a person's intelligence at any given moment may well be thought of as an amorphous mass—not a regular geometric figure. Within this mass, modules may cluster with greater or lesser permanence, and may be organized along principles of relatedness. Thus, word knowledge may form a cluster—but the words of which one has knowledge will be components of other clusters as well. A pencil is an object one writes with; it has shape in common with other objects, it has function in common with pens and crayons, it produces color of varying intensity, it has a number property, it is usually associated with paper. The learned module "pencil" may thus be part of many clusters.

One need not posit that a learning module is permanent. It could, presumably, disappear entirely, although far more often we would expect it to undergo essential change by taking on a more complex character. This model does assume that higher learning depends so intimately and essentially on certain previous learnings that the more complex modules cannot exist without the antecedent modules from which they grew. For example, if the ability to subtract numbers should disappear, the ability to do long division could not remain unaffected. Thus, retention of learning is integral to the concept here proposed.

The simple-minded conceptualization outlined above may have horrified those of my colleagues who are even moderately sophisticated with respect to modern learning theories. To those colleagues I apologize, but I also beg their indulgence. Over-simplified as the conceptualization undoubtedly is, I believe it does no *essential* violence to any current theory; it has, I hope, the virtue of permitting a view of the organization of intelligence, and of the nature of the testing of intelligence, which may prove illuminating for several issues which confront us.

ISSUE I: THE CLASSIFICATION OF ABILITY TESTS INTO APTITUDE, ACHIEVEMENT, AND INTELLIGENCE MEASURES

As soon as we have agreed that what we know and what we can do intellectually is learned, the artificiality of the above classification becomes self-evident. Historically, we have recognized that what achievement tests measure is what the examinee has learned. We have been less ready to accord similar recognition to intelligence tests. In their case, we have too often behaved as though what these tests measure is somehow independent of the learning phenomenon. We have played the role of Aladdin seeking a magical lamp, complete with a genie ready to spring forth with full power to accomplish all sorts of wondrous things. We have pondered wistfully on the number of critical issues that would be resolved if we could only somehow measure "intelligence" separately from "achievement."

We have been similarly unrealistic in treating the concept of "aptitude." Our textbooks enunciate the distinction that aptitude tests measure what the individual *can* learn, while achievement tests measure what he *has* learned. Some of our leading theorists aggravate the confusion by ignoring the implications of their special use of the term. "Aptitude" is typically used in laboratory learning experiments as a matching or otherwise controlling variable; it is employed to assure that groups to be compared start the experiment as equal in initial ability. One gets a strong impression that the aptitude instrument is perceived as measuring the innate potential of the individual as distinguished from what is to be achieved (i.e., learned) in the experimental process. If learning theorists recognize that what they are calling "aptitude" (or, for that matter, "intelligence") is "previously learned" (as, clearly, at least some of them do), the artificiality of the distinction between "aptitude" or "intelligence" and "achievement" should be eminently apparent.

I wish that at least a few of my psychometric colleagues would leave off searching for *the* structure of intelligence, and devote their wisdom and energy to learning more about the learning process, and to teaching learning theorists about testing. I am convinced that both specialties would profit immeasurably from the cooperative enterprise. It is my strong impression that the inattention of the psychometrician to the facts of learning is matched fully by the unsophisticated treatment accorded to testing by many learning theorists.

All ability tests—intelligence, aptitude, and achievement—measure what the individual *has* learned—and they often measure with similar content and similar process. Let us take, for example, an item such as this: A square and a rectangle have the same perimeter. The square has an area of 10,000 square feet. The rectangle has an area of 9,324 square feet. What are the dimensions of the rectangle?

This item would clearly be deemed appropriate whether it appeared in an achievement test in high school mathematics, a test of aptitude for mathematics, or the numerical portion of an "intelligence" test. I submit that a great many items can equally readily fit any of the three categories.

Such justification as we have for our labeling system resides entirely in the *purpose* for which the test is used, not in the test document itself. If our intent is to discover how much the examinee has learned in a particular area, such as a school course, we may select items which probe for the distinctive learnings the schooling was intended to stimulate. We label the test an "achievement" test. If our intent is to predict what success an individual is likely to attain in learning a new language, or a new job, we seek those specific previous learnings the possession of which bodes favorably for that future learning, and we label the test an "aptitude" test or a "special aptitude test." If our intent is to predict future acquisition of learning over broad areas of environmental exposure, we seek those previous learnings the possession of which will be relevant to as many, and as important, future learning situations as we can anticipate. This test we label an "intelligence" test. The selection of test items or sample tasks for the three purposes may or may not differ; but in each instance what is measured is what was previously learned. We are not measuring different abilities; we are merely attending to different criteria. It is the *relevance* of the learnings we select for investigation that largely determines how we name our test, and whether we will succeed in our purpose.

ISSUE II: THE UTILITY OF CULTURE-FREE AND CULTURE-FAIR TESTS

The notion of relevance of previous learnings leads naturally to a consideration of some follies we have committed in the search for culture-free or culture-fair instruments. I do not wish to impugn the high social motives which stimulate the search for such devices; I do wish to question that such a search, in its usual setting, is sensible. A culture-free test would presumably probe learnings which had not been affected by environment; this is sheer nonsense. A culture-fair test attempts to select those learnings which are common to many cultures. In the search for experiences which are common to several different cultures or subcultures, the vital matter of relevance of the learning for our purpose is subordinated or ignored.

The implicit intent in the attempt to create culture-free or culture-fair tests is somehow to measure intelligence without permitting the effects of differential exposure to learning to influence scores. This contains the tacit assumption that "native intelligence" lies buried in pure form deep in the individual, and needs only to be uncovered by ingenious mining methods. If we recognize that intelligence comprises learning experiences, it becomes clear that our attempts are not ingenious, but ingenuous.

It is true that we can probe learnings that have occurred in nonverbal, nonnumerical domains. This means only that we can test selected aspects of intelligence. The question immediately arises of the relevance of these special domains to the kinds of learning we will want to predict. The measurement purpose for which culture-fair tests are ordinarily developed is that of predicting academic or industrial performance. Most academic courses and most industrial jobs involve some use of verbal abilities. Since further learning is conditioned by relevant past learning, the individual who has developed more of the prerequisite ability inevitably has an advantage over the individual with less of the prerequisite ability. If we wish to predict whether an individual will profit appreciably from additional exposure to learning, our best predictor must be a measure which appraises what prerequisite learning he has acquired heretofore. Appropriate verbal abilities are more relevant to the largely verbal learning we usually wish to predict than other abilities are.

It has on occasion been suggested that tests be developed which sample the verbal skills or factual information which are peculiar to a given subculture. Such tests are proposed as a "fairer" measure of the "intelligence," or readiness to learn, of the members of that subculture. The response to this proposal is "readiness to learn *what?*" If our purpose is to distinguish members of that subculture from their peers with respect to how much of that special culture they have assimilated, such a test might well be useful. If, as is more likely the case, we wish to predict future learnings of the content of the more general culture (e.g., the so-called white, middle-class culture such as typifies what the majority of our schools are organized to transmit), tests designed for the subculture will be less relevant than those which sample from the general culture. This is not intended to imply that the members of the subculture *could* not learn what the schools as constituted are offering. It does emphasize that, at the moment at which we make our appraisal, what the individual has already learned from the general culture domain is the most significant information as to what he is then ready to learn. The less relevant the previous learnings we appraise, the more hazardous must be our predictions of future learnings.

As long as our educational system and our general culture are dependent on conventional verbal abilities, those who aspire to progress in that system and that culture will need to command those abilities. In a verbal society, verbal competence cannot sensibly be ignored.

ISSUE III: IS "VERBAL ABILITY" SYNONYMOUS WITH "INTELLIGENCE"?

To say that we cannot afford to ignore learnings in relevant verbal areas when we are appraising "intelligence" does not imply that *only* the verbal domain is important. The development of tests of "general mental ability" which sample only the verbal domain implies that since verbal tests predict school criteria best, it is unnecessary to attend to other cognitive abilities the student has developed; in other words, that, in effect, "verbal ability" is synonymous with "intelligence." It would be most unfortunate if, consciously or unconsciusly, we adopted this too narrow perspective.

That verbal tests are typically good predictors of grades in many academic courses is undeniable. *Why* this is the case warrants some thought. Is it because all, or even most, of what constitutes "intelligence" is represented by verbal ability? Certainly the chief symbol system of our society is verbal. Even when we deal with numerical, spatial, or figural problems we often transform them to verbal expressions. It is one thing, however, to recognize the involvement of verbal abilities in all kinds of learning experiences and quite another to grant them exclusive sovereignty over learning domains. Many domains require the possession of other abilities as well, but our appraisal methods are often inadequate to reveal that need. Because it is easier to employ verbal criteria, or more convenient—or because we have given insufficient thought to criterion validity—we predetermine the finding that verbal abilities dominate the scene.

A particularly revealing demonstration of this phenomenon came to the attention of the authors of the Differential Aptitude Tests some years ago. Grades in an auto mechanics course were found to be better predicted by the Verbal Reasoning test of the DAT than by the Mechanical Reasoning test. We had the unusual good fortune of having access to further information about the course. We discovered that early in the course the teacher had been called from the room for almost a half-hour. In his absence, the students had disobeyed his instructions not to fool around with the automobile motors. To let the punishment fit the crime, he conducted the rest of the course almost entirely by lecturing, giving the students minimum opportunity for actually working with the engines. That grades in a course taught by lecture and evaluated by a written test should be best predicted by a verbal test is not too surprising!

An illustration such as the above should force us to stop and think. As we study tables replete with validity coefficients, how many of those coefficients represent similar instances? As we develop hypotheses as to the importance of particular aspects of intelligence, how well do we understand the *criteria* which gave rise to the coefficients on which our hypotheses are based? Would the use of more valid criteria in courses for which curricular goals transcend verbal skills, have produced similar data, or different? Would the admittedly broad pervasiveness of verbal skills seem quite so broad if more appropriate measures of learning were employed? If we remain complacent about criteria composed largely of behaviors from the verbal domain, we are unlikely to see the relevance of other abilities.

In his APA presidential address in 1964, McNemar paid flattering attention to the Differential Aptitude Tests; he quite accurately reported that the verbal tests were most frequently the best predictors of course grades. The data he cited certainly supported the point he was making: Verbal tests predict grades in many academic courses. What might well have been added was recognition that the nature of our educational criteria exaggerates the real importance of verbal skills. If (and it is hoped *when*) grades or other criterion statements become more content valid, the relevance of a number of other skills will be more demonstrable.

Industry has perforce learned this lesson. Few mechanical apprentices are selected solely, or even primarily, because they can describe a process, rather than perform it. The military has learned that the ability to diagnose a malfunctioning torpedo is poorly demonstrated by verbal exposition, but well demonstrated by a work sample requiring actual mechanical repairs. It is to be hoped that education will increasingly become more realistic with respect to what *its* criteria *should* be.

ISSUE IV: THE GROWTH AND DECLINE OF "INTELLIGENCE"

So preoccupied have we been with reifying intelligence as some mystical substance that we have too often neglected to take a common-sense look at what intelligence tests measure. We find ourselves distressed at our failure to predict with satisfactory accuracy the intelligence test scores of a teen-ager from his intelligence test scores as an infant. Why should this occasion surprise, let alone distress? If we look inside the tests, it should be obvious that the kinds of learnings we typically appraise at the earlier ages bear little resemblance, and may have little relevance, to the kinds of learnings we appraise later.

At the earlier age levels, we have typically tested for such characteristics as motor dexterity, perception, and similar features of physical development. When intellectual concepts become available for testing as baby grows to infant, to child, to teen-ager, we change the focus of our testing from the physical domains to the cognitive—we appraise knowledge, concept formation, and reasoning.

It is possible that future research will disclose that possession of certain physical abilities or tendencies is prerequisite to the development of concept formation, and that earlier possession of these characteristics will foretell the future intellectual development of the individual. Interesting and promising research now being conducted is directed toward this goal. It is my opinion that, because learning experiences vary so from one child to another, there is some practical limit beyond which we will be unable to predict, however penetrating our research. In any event, we would do well at this moment to recognize that since we are measuring in different ability domains at infant and school-age levels, we should not expect good prediction from one level to the other— and we should certainly not behave as though the data permitted confident prediction.

At the other end of the age spectrum we have, with similar lack of insight, proceeded to corollary errors. We have accepted the gloomy dictum that once we have passed the age of 18, or 25, or 35 we have passed our peak; from that age, our ability to learn declines. Our texts are peppered with charts showing that depressing downhill slide. What is the basis for this widely accepted conclusion? The principal basis is that when we apply our conventional measures of intelligence to older people, we find that average scores decrease. We have implicitly accepted the idea that intelligence is defined by what is measured by these particular intelligence tests. If, however, we return to our previous information of intelligence as what we know in a wide variety of domains, and hence as a base for what we can learn at a given moment, our perspective changes. We then proceed to compare what the intelligence tests measure with the kinds of learning individuals have engaged in from age 30 or 40 on. The relevance of the tests, except perhaps as measures of retention, is seen as increasingly remote with each passing year. Most individuals have not failed to learn more with added years of life. Their learnings have occurred in areas (science, business, politics, psychology, psychometrics), often relatively specialized, which are not measured by conventional intelligence tests.

It is true that new learnings of adults occur in such a variety of endeavors that it would be virtually impossible to find a common core on which all could be examined. We should not, however, pretend we do not suffer this psychometric disability; we should not continue to use less relevant measures to support deceptive graphs and curves of the decline of "intelligence." We might better recognize the limitations of our measure, until such time as we can devise relevant measures of the significant learnings which do occur. For the present, we can conclude only that with each passing decade older people do less well on tests designed for younger adults.

ISSUE V: THE SEARCH FOR PURITY

A discussion of the nature of intelligence, and of intelligent testing, should not ignore the topic of factor analysis. It is a method which has influenced test construction and test selection. It is a technique which has stimulated the promulgation of theories of the structure of intellect.

The history of psychometrics gives evidence that each new major technique has attained a heyday of popularity, during which unrealistic hopes led to unbridled use. In the 1920s and 1930s, Pearson product-moment coefficients held the stage; everybody seemed to be correlating everything with everything else with wild abandon. We appear, in more recent times, to have been engaging in factor analyses with almost equal frenzy. With so much activity going on, it is perhaps to be expected that some studies, and some conclusions, would be characterized more by enthusiasm than by wisdom.

To criticize factor analysis as a procedure because individuals have misled themselves through its use would be very silly indeed. Among the benefits it has provided are the ability to summarize vast masses of data, and to facilitate the organization of information in a way that inspires, and then leads to investigation of interesting and often fruitful research hypotheses. At the same time, we need not believe that the power of the tool assures the validity of the product. Some of the conclusions which have been drawn, some attitudes which have been adopted, and some theories which have occasionally been treated as though they were established fact might well be exposed to scrutiny.

There have been instances in which a test battery was chosen for practical use *because* it had its origins in a program of factorial research. Presumably, the rationale was that such a battery consists of relatively "pure" tests, and would show near-zero intercorrelation among the tests; it would therefore be more efficient than a battery of similar measures not derived from factorial studies. If this rationale survived empirical study, it would still not of itself be adequate justification for selecting one set of tests rather than another. Efficiency is certainly desirable—but *validity* is *crucial*. How tests were constructed is interesting and even germane; how they *work* is the critical issue.

Let us return, however, to the rationale. Is the leap from "factorial origin" to "purify" defensible? The "pure" tests developed in psychometric laboratories often do correlate very little with one another. To some degree, at least, this low correlation is frequently ascribable to the restriction in range of the various abilities of the subject, or both. For unreliability of short, experimental tests, or to the exploratory and research purposes, these conditions represent a reasonable situation. Practical test use situations are something else again.

When batteries of reliable tests with factorial ancestry, and batteries testing in similar domains but not factor oriented, are given to the same students, the within-battery intercorrelation of scores is ordinarily of about the same order. For example, with one ninth-grade group of boys, the average inter-r among the Differential Aptitude Tests was .37; for the same group, the average inter-r of the Primary Mental Abilities

Tests was .36. Similar results were obtained in a comparison of the DAT and the General Aptitude Test Battery scores for a twelfth-grade group. Thus, there was little evidence of greater "purity" in the factorially derived batteries than in the DAT, which were not so derived. (In the everyday world, it appears, "purity" is all too likely to be an illusion.) Accordingly, we would be well advised when choosing tests for practical use to concentrate on how they work, not on how they were built.

Let us now turn briefly to the role of factor analysis as a stimulator of hypotheses concerning the structure of intellect. Its influence has often seemed to be not so much mathematicodeductive as mathematicoseductive! The power of the method as a way of manipulating great masses of data appears all too often to have led us astray. Even our more eminent protagonists of the technique have not always appeared immune. When expounding on the theory of factor analysis, experts almost invariably agree that factors are merely descriptive categories; they are not functional entities. But when engaged in interpreting the factors which have emerged from their studies, some analysts apparently succumb to the mystic charm of rotating axes and perceive entities which, they have told us, do not exist. The lure of the temptation to discover a psychological structure analogous to the periodic table of the elements is too powerful to resist. We then hear of "primary mental abilities" or are shown "the three faces of intellect." Though the authors of such creations have sometimes demonstrated in other writings that they well understand the difference between the reality of descriptive categories and the illusion of underlying entities, some of their disciples and many of their readers seem less clear in their perception.

If we accept the thesis that the modules or bits which constitute intelligence are themselves complex, a combination of such modules can hardly be expected to be simple or "pure." A 6-year-old who assembles three alphabet blocks to spell out "cat" has employed, at a minimum, verbal and spatial skills; if he is aware that there are three blocks or letters, he has engaged in numerical perception as well. The ability to perform the task has required cognition, memory, convergent thinking, and evaluation. The product is figural, symbolic, and semantic. All this, and we have not yet taken into account such considerations as the motor-manipulative activity, the perception of color, the earlier learning experiences which enabled him to perform the task successfully, or the imagery which the concept "cat" induces in him. We, as analysts, may choose to attend to only a single aspect of the behavior—but the behavior itself remains multifaceted and complex. To assume that we can abstract from a host of such activities a pure and simple entity is to ignore the psychological meaning of intelligent behavior.

Let us continue to explore, by all means available to us (including factor analysis) the nature of man's abilities. Let us *not* assume that the results of research obtained under closely managed conditions in the laboratory will hold true as realities in day-to-day situations. Let us not unwittingly forget that the descriptive categories we adopt for convenience in communication do not have real existence as ultimate psychological entities.

CONCLUSION

To what view of a structure of intellect am I led by the ideas I have enunciated here? Essentially, I believe intelligence is *un*structured. I believe that it is differently comprised in every individual—the sum total of all the learning experiences he has uniquely had up to any moment in time. Such structure as we perceive is structure which we have imposed. We can so select samples of previous learnings to examine as to reveal a general factor, or group factors, or specifics. We can sample from domains that are relatively homogeneous and apply levels such as verbal, numerical, spatial; we can sample from a wider variety of learnings, and apply labels such as "general mental ability" or, simply, "intelligence."

There are many bases on which we may choose which kinds of learnings we will sample. The most reasonable basis, I believe, is that of predictive purpose. Those previous learnings should be probed which are most relevant to the particular future learnings we wish to predict. In addition to criterion—or, more likely, *criteria*—relevance, the principles of band width and fidelity (as enunciated by Cronbach and Gleser) might well serve as guides. If we are interested in forecasting narrow-band criteria, selection of highly homogeneous, directly relevant behaviors is indicated. If we are interested in a wide range of criteria, we have at least two options: we may choose to select small samples from widely scattered domains—as in a Binet, a Wechsler, or a broader gauge instrument still to be devised—or examine more intensively with several narrower gauge tests, as in the Differential Aptitude Tests. The broader gauge instruments will be longer and more time consuming— but the possibility of more direct relevance to one or more particular criteria should permit higher fidelity.

The critical issue, then, is not which approach measures intelligence— each of them does, in its own fashion. No approach except sampling from every domain in which learnings have occurred—an impossible task— fully measures intelligence. The question is rather which approach provides the most useful information for the various purposes we wish the test to serve. Recognition that what we are measuring is what the individual has learned, and composing our tests to appraise *relevant* previous learnings, will yield the most useful information. We, and those who utilize the results of our work—educators, personnel men, social planners—face problems for which intelligence test data are relevant and sometimes crucial. We must remember, and we must teach, what our test scores really reflect. The measurement of intelligence is not, and has not been, a matter of concern only to psychology. It has always been, and continues to be, an influence on educational and social programs. If we are to avert uninformed pressures from government agencies, from school adminstrators, from the courts, and indeed from psychologist colleagues, we must understand and we must broadly communicate what these scores truly represent. Only then can we who build tests and they who use them properly claim that we are indeed engaged in intelligent testing.

ABILITY testing historically began with global measures such as *general* intelligence but with the advent of factor analysis, test batteries sampling not one but several types of aptitudes have been constructed. Such factorially pure test batteries, typically known as "multifactor" batteries, logically would have the advantage since they so economically could measure a wide sampling of different abilities and aptitudes. Research has shown, however, that these multifactor tests tend to be less predictive of school or occupational success than do batteries which have been specifically developed or "tailormade" for that purpose. But for the purposes of guidance and counseling—as against the more specific personnel goal of selection whether for medical school or success on the job—the multifactor test battery has the advantage.

The following article by Dr. Super, reproduced here with only minor editorial changes, served as the introduction to a series of seven specific reviews of multifactor tests which appeared in the *Personnel & Guidance Journal* and beginning in the September, 1956 issue. The batteries later discussed are the Differential Aptitude Tests, the General Aptitude Test Battery,* the Guilford-Zimmerman Aptitude Survey, the Crowder Unifactor Tests, the Primary Mental Ability Tests, the Factored Aptitude Series (by King), the Multiple Aptitude Test (by Segal), and last, the Flanagan Aptitude Classification Test. The idea for this series grew out of the Conference on Using Multifactor Aptitude Tests in Educational and Vocational Counseling and Prediction, held in June, 1953, at the University of California.

Dr. Super is Professor of Psychology and Education at Teachers College, Columbia University, and currently is perhaps best known for his longitudinal Career Pattern Study tracing the vocational development of approximately 275 8th and 9th grade boys from a single New York State community. Data collection for the study was begun in 1951 (Super *et al.*, 1957).

THE USE OF MULTIFACTOR TEST BATTERIES IN GUIDANCE

Donald E. Super

In recent years a number of batteries of tests based on factor analysis have been offered to the public for use in guidance. This represents something new, for in earlier years factor anlysis had served solely as a tool for researchers interested in the structure of mental abilities and human traits. Its practical use has only been recent.

---

* See pp. 72–85 for a discussion of this test battery.

Such being the case, it is desirable to take stock, to see just what is the current state of development of these instruments. It is important to understand the structure of mental abilities, but for the practicing counselor or admissions officer the vital question is the educational and vocational significance of these mental abilities or factors. Counselors need to know what the scientific-appearing batteries of tests indicate as to an individual's prospects of success and satisfaction in various fields of study and of work.

A dim view of multifactor test batteries is taken by Cronbach in the 1956 issue of *Annual Review of Psychology* (pp. 177–178). He writes: "We conclude that while factorial scores may be useful for a theory of abilities, as soon as testors make inferences to behavior in significant situations," *e.g.*, predict success in school subjects, "they encounter the same troubles as personality assessors" who attempt to forecast behavior in known situations on the basis of data on personality structure. "Group factors serve only when regression equations are constructed about the criterion in a single institution." Cronbach goes on to cite the withdrawal of the *American Council on Education Psychological Examination* from the market, and its replacement by a measure of verbal quantitive achievement (the *Cooperative School and College Ability and Test*), as further evidence of the dubious status of differential aptitude testing.

This is in sharp contrast with the more optimistic views taken by both Cronbach (1949, p. 234) and the present author (1949, p. 358) in 1949, when the latter wrote: "The days of the publication of isolated tests of single aptitudes will no doubt soon be past," and Cronbach wrote: 'In due time we may anticipate that pure, psychologically valid tests can be developed which will have empirical validity adequate for vocational and educational guidance."

How justifiable is Cronbach's pessimism concerning multifactor test batteries for guidance? To what extent have they lived, or failed to live, up to the great promise of the 1940's?

THE DESIDERATA OF GUIDANCE TESTS

What are the desirable characteristics of a test or battery of tests to be used in guidance? One could, of course, give an elementary textbookish answer to such a question, but let us take reliability for granted, and talk in terms which are more concrete and operational than the usual language of reliability and validity.

Tests for use in counseling should *describe* a person so that we can see him as he is at the time of testing; they should *predict* what he will be like and what he will do at some future date; they should be relatively *timeless;* and they should, like the people they test, be *multipotential.* Let me elaborate on each of these points.

Tests Should Describe

They should tell something of the make-up of the student or client at the time of testing, how he compares in intelligence, in perceptual speed, in finger dexterity, in computational interest, or in social dominance with other students at the same educational level or of the same age. They should tell what curricular and occupational groups he resembles, and how closely he resembles them. One of the purposes of testing is to get a picture of the person with whom one is dealing, to see to what degree he has a variety of psychological characteristics, where his relative strengths and weaknesses are, and how he compares in each of these characteristics with others who have had comparable experiences and have reached a comparable stage of development, or who are engaged in activities in which he might engage. Having a picture of the stage of development attained by the individual, and of his make-up at that stage, one has a basis for understanding better his recent and present performances, and for setting up reasonable hypotheses concerning the nature of his future development and behavior.

Tests Should Predict

Tests should have some value as indicators of probable status, behavior, achievement, and satisfaction in the future. There are two aspects to this kind of prediction, one being the prediction of what the individual *will be like*, the other prediction of *what he will do* or how he will react, in the future. Both are important, for in guidance one needs to understand what the student or client will be like, and even more to understand what he will be able to do and how he will like doing it. Predictions of achievement need to be educational and occupational: they need to clarify the would-be medical student's prospects of success and satisfaction in the practice of medicine. Too often, in the case of the professions which require long periods of training, only the former type of validity data are available; but it is in these very same occupations that the size of the investment in training makes it especially important that the investment pays dividends in the long run in the vocational success and satisfaction of the person who obtained the training. in these very same occupations that the size of the investment in And as Ghiselli has pointed out (1966, pp. 118–119), the much used training criteria have little relationship to job criteria.

For example, Strong and Tucker's work with physicians (1952) showed that men who completed medical training, but who lacked the interests which are typical of physicians, tended to shift from medical practice to administrative work in which their medical training was not essential. A good instrument such as Strong's could have been used to help these men see that they would in due course find more satisfaction in administrative work than in the practice of medicine. Had this fact been known when they were thinking of entering medicine, and had other opportunities which were equally attractive in income and prestige been made obvious to them, they might have made more economical choices.

Tests Should Be Timeless

Tests can, of course, be timeless only in a relative sense, but differences in the timelessness of aptitude tests are well illustrated by the Meier and McAdory Art Tests, which were first published in 1929. By 1940 the latter test was quite unusable, because many of the items included in the test smacked strongly of the 1920's and looked absurd two decades later, particularly the hats and skirts of the flapper years and the angular automobiles which went with them. The Meier Test, on the other hand, was in this respect as usable in 1940 as in the mid-twenties, for the art forms used in its pictures were good in the Renaissance and are good today, and the forms used in the vases and other items pictured in the test have been good at least since the days of ancient Greece. In such instances, norms collected at some time past, and validities established in longitudinal studies covering a period of years, are not likely to be outdated so soon as to make the test useless. That is, they will not be outdated if the occupation in question has not undergone substantial change, and if the population from which it draws is still substantially the same. Thus Stewart (1947) has shown that, in general, occupational intelligence requirements changed little from 1918 to 1945.

Tests Should Be Multipotential.

People are occupationally speaking, multipotential. They are not square pegs, able to fit only in square holes, nor are they round pegs able to fit only into the round holes. If they were, all one would need would be one test to measure squareness, another to measure roundness, and counseling and selection would be simple. People are polygonal, and so are jobs; in both instances the polygons have so many sides that each person fits more or less easily into a great variety of holes. Test batteries and the tests which make them up, therefore, need to be so constructed that they can be applied to people in a great variety of occupations, and, once normed and validated, used with each person tested for the evaluation of his promise for a number of different fields.

Suppose, for example, that tests useful for predicting sucess in engineering were useful only for that one occupation, and that the same were true also of medicine, dentistry, and chemistry. In counseling a college bound high school senior who is thinking about all four of these possibilities, one would have to find time for four different batteries of tests, of some three to six hours each—an impossible demand both on the time of the student and on that of the counselor. But this is exactly what develops from the construction of one test or battery for the selection or counseling of engineering students, another for use with medical students, and so on. From the point of view of a school or organization selecting students or employees, this may be the most economical procedure, but it does not result in instruments which are economical or useful for counseling individuals concerning educational and vocational choices.

THE PECULIARITIES OF MULTIFACTOR TEST BATTERIES

Factorial Purity

While batteries of tests such as the Differential Aptitude Tests and the General Aptitude Test Battery have not uniformly striven for factorial purity, they have tended to aim at measuring either pure factors or constellations of closely related factors. Thus the GATB is based on one of the most extensive factor analysis studies so far completed, and the test scores are combined to give scores based on the factor loading of tests. While the DAT includes such impure tests as the Mechanical Reasoning Test, with its loadings of heavy spatial, reasoning, and information factors, this was done as an exception to a rule which was observed in the case of less complex tests such as those of spatial reasoning, verbal reasoning, and perceptual speed and accuracy. Other batteries such as Guilford's, Flanagan's, Holzinger's, and King's have striven for factorial purity.

This is, of course, well known. But the fact bears stressing because of what it means in terms of the desiderata of guidance tests. It means that multifactor test batteries *are* likely to be *descriptive, multipotential,* and *timeless*; it also means that they are *likely not to be as predictive* as certain other types of tests. Let me justify each of these brief statements.

The tendency of developers of multifactor test batteries to strive for factorial purity in their tests, resulting as it does in minimal overlapping of the tests, provides scores for traits or aptitudes which, as data accumulate, have a maximum of psychological meaning. While it is true that factor names such as "Factor Q" do not convey much to the user, that even somewhat more descripive labels such as "Memory I" and "Memory II" tell little, and that there is often room for disagreement in naming factors, in due course that study of such factors results in agreement on meaningful names. The terms "spatial visualization," "perceptual speed," "numerical reasoning," all of them derived from or further developed by factorial studies, have come to have considerable psychological meaning, even though at first they were used only as descriptions of what seemed to be the process underlying a particular task with a particular type of test item. These terms have proved to be much more meaningful than terms such as "mechanical aptitude" applied to the scores derived from such diverse tests as the O'Rourke and McQuarrie, useful though these tests have been.

Multipotentiality has, of course, been one of the prime objectives of the developers of multifactor tests, and has been invitable in view of the emphasis on measuring basic psychological characteristics. For if each of the aptitudes measured is important in a variety of occupations and if it is measured in relatively pure form, its true role in each occupation can be ascertained, unobscured by other factors which are specific to one or to a few occupations but are not always associated with the basic factor being measured. For example, a test of spatial visualization will contribute to a prediction of success both in engineering and in art, whereas a test of mechanical aptitude can be used only for the former. This is because the latter is heavily enough weighted with the mechanical information factor that its spatial factor is rendered inoperative in the prediction of artistic success. A battery of tests measuring relatively pure factors can thus be normed and validated for a great variety of occupations and for a great variety of curricula, and a given student's promise for a large number of fields can be appraised in a relatively brief testing session, at least in the institution in which the validity (regression) data are obtained.

The emphasis on factorial purity has meant, also, an emphasis on relatively simple, abstract types of items. Often these are geometric, numerical, or verbal, of a type which lacks easily dated content and which is therefore relatively timeless. The items are, for instance, more likely to resemble those of the undateable Likert-Quasha Revision of the Minnesota Paper Form Board, or the relatively timeless names and numbers of the Minnesota Clerical Test, than the Model-T Ford parts which appear in one form of the O'Rourke Mechanical Aptitude Test.

All of these outcomes of the tendency to aim at factorial purity are good; one other is not so beneficial. This is the unfortunate tendency of factorially pure tests to be less predictive of success in a given subject or occupation than tests which are developed specifically for that purpose. The factorially pure test, we have seen, tends to be abstract and general in its content. It is the direct opposite of the miniature situation test, which attempts to repoduce in a small way the complexity of the subject or job itself. The miniature·situation test, and work sample, copying as it does the tasks of processes of the activity or occupation, taps a great variety of abilities called for in the work. Some of these are measured fairly well by the factor-tests of the battery, but some are specific enough not to be included in the battery. Even the aptitudes common to both tests are, in the miniature situation test, measured in a form more like that in which they are tapped by the job than they are in the more abstract multifactor battery. The specificity of the miniature situation test gives it a validity which is greater than that of the more generally applicable but hence less specific multifactor test. In this way the multifactor test battery is truly a guidance test battery, whereas the miniature situation test is more truly a selection test, and a custombuilt test at that.

This lessened predictive value of the multifactor test is the price of versatility. Apparently one cannot eat one's cake and have it too, at least not in aptitude testing. Custom-built tests for the selection of employees for a given job, in a given organization, are better than standard tests even when the latter are locally standardized for the same purpose. But they are not as good for counseling possible entrants into that occupation in any of a number of companies as are tests which have been standardized on a more varied sample of members of that occupation. Specific factors which make the custom-built test the best for its peculiar situation make it only second best for a variety of situations. Similarly, extraneous factors in the miniature situation test contribute to its validity for some purposes even though they minimize its validity for others. Hence the battery of tests which aim at versatility tends to miss some relatively specific factors and to lose some specific validity. It has been demonstrated that batteries of multifactor tests can have extremely high validities, if those reported in the revised manual for the GATB can be taken at face value. This is, however, made somewhat difficult by the fact that, as Cronbach puts it (1956, p.177): "Striking variation is found in concurrent correlations with different achievement measures in the same field and with different samples. The tests often do not correlate where they are expected to correlate."

THE CHARACTERISTICS OF AVAILABLE MULTIFACTOR BATTERIES

Initial concern with factorial purity in the development of multifactor batteries led to an emphasis on the internal validity of the tests, on questions, that is, of internal consistency and of the independence of the various scores. The work of Thurstone well illustrates this emphasis. The Guilford-Zimmerman Aptitude Survey is another illustration of the primary concern with establishing the factorial purity of the tests, and of the tendency to minimize the importance of external validity.

This emphasis has been rather frustrating to those who use tests in guidance, because factorial purity does not help much unless one knows the practical significance of the factors which are being measured. But it has been an essential first stage in the development of multifactor test batteries; the tool has to be shaped before it can be put to use. The expectation is that the theoretical preoccupations of the test constructors result in better instruments once they are ready for use.

How ready are they for use?

The answer varies, of course, with the battery. One of the functions of test manuals is to give the potential test user the information necessary for judging the readiness of a test or battery for a particular use. The two most widely used multifactor batteries are among the oldest of their types, and are also the two which have been most studied from the point of view of external validity. One of them, the Differential Aptitude Test Battery, has been used primarily in studies of educational success; the other, the General Aptitude Test Battery, has been validated largely for occupational success. In both cases a large number of studies have been completed, and in both cases the results of these studies have been incorporated in revised manuals. Thus users may judge the validity of the tests for their particular purposes and be guided by the known relationships of the tests to success in various types of endeavor whe.ı counseling students and clients. It is no exaggeration to state that no *aptitude* tests have ever been accompanied by such a mass and variety of validity data as are these two batteries; in fact, probably only the Stanford-Binet and Strong's Vocational Interest Blank, both of them considerably older than these batteries, can compete with them in this respect.

It has been shown that even tests which strive for factorial purity generally do not approach it very closely. For example, Thurstone's Primary Mental Ability Tests have moderately high intercorrelations; the median intercorrelations of the test and of the factors in the GATB are, respectively, 0.35 and 0.30; and the Differential Aptitude Tests intercorrelate somewhat more highly than this, as might be anticipated from their lesser emphasis on factorial purity. The intercorrelations of the tests in the batteries result, as the Differential Aptitude Tests manual shows, in a somewhat distressing uniformity of validity, i.e., in a somewhat discouraging lack of differential validity, in the tests and aptitudes measured. By this it is meant that one finds that some tests are *generally* rather good predictors, verbal reasoning for example. Similarly, others are generally rather poor predictors, for instance perceptual speed and finger dexterity. This is true no matter what the type of achievement being predicted. Perhaps this makes the situation seem worse than it actually is, and certainly this is less true of some batteries than of others, but there is a tendency of this type in the validity data. Cronbach thus points out that, according to the FACTS manual, the only difference between printers and professors of humanities is that the latter have good memories (1956, p.178)!

IMPLICATIONS FOR COUNSELING

If the extensive norms and validity data of multifactor test batteries such as the DAT and the GATB prove them to be adequate, the use of singly developed and validated aptitude tests in counseling will in due course be virtually a thing of the past: the multipotentiality of the multifactor test battery gives it too many advantages. The large-scale validation programs which must inevitably be undertaken by the authors and publishers of such batteries, if they are to live up to their ambitious plans, and meet professional standards, give these batteries another great advantage over the singly developed tests.

It would be easy, however, to have too much faith in the general usefulness and comprehensiveness of the batteries which are available, to be over-impressed by large numbers, well-written arguments, or large validity coefficients, and to rely too heavily on these batteries. As technical standards improve, writers of test manuals increase their skill in giving tests the appearance of validity. Sometimes the counselor will deal with special problems or with special occupations on which more light could be thrown by other tests or batteries; he will therefore need to continue to be alert for the development of new tests of special aptitudes not covered by the standard batteries, and for normative data on occupations not adequately included in those sampled by them.

In particular, he should be aware of the fact that the grouping of occupations into broad families, as has been done in the occupational norming of the GATB, obscures differences in occupations which may be of vital significance for some students or clients, even though unimportant for most. Engineers and physicians have much in common, and hence have the same GATB occupational ability pattern, but also differentiating characteristics not brought out by the GATB data; the same if true of tobacco-wrappers and turret-lathe operators.

The test batteries which are considered here still impress me as the most significant developments in the field of aptitude testing since the work of the Minnesota Employment Stabilization Research Institute. The tools which they make available are potentially the most useful, but also the most complex, which we have had. They deserve careful study, before using them, as they are used, and after they have been used. Their special advantages, and their present defects, need to be known if they are to be made maximally useful in guidance.

Dr. Super's previous article on multifactor tests had a generally encouraging and hopeful tone despite the reservations indicated. The article was written some twenty years ago when there was some occasion for optimism for factor analytically derived test batteries. For a negative view of these matters, the student should consult a 1964 article by McNemar who is anything but optimistic. Taking the one multifactor test battery for which there is a very large array of validity data (the DAT of the Psychological Corporation), McNemar comes to the conclusion that such tests are not good differential predictors of school achievement. "The concept of general intelligence," he writes, "despite being maligned by a few, regarded as a second-order function by some, and discarded or ignored by others, still has a rightful place in the science of psychology and in the practical affairs of man" (McNemar, 1964, p.880).

$$\triangledown \ \triangledown \ \triangledown$$

PART SIX

Personality

PSYCHOLOGICAL testing as a diagnostic tool was formerly one of the main professional functions of the clinical psychologist. Especially following World War II, clinical psychologists on hospital staffs spent much of their time in essentially diagnostic work. Extensive test batteries to measure cognitive and emotional functioning were employed (projectives, especially Rorschach and Sentence Completion, the MMPI, WAIS, perhaps Bender-Gestalt for the assessment of brain damage). This would result in a diagnostic workup or psychological report which might run to two single-spaced typed pages. Many man hours were spent in this enterprise. All this is now quite out of fashion. In the early days of Rogerian client-centered therapy, there was a dramatic swing away from any and all testing; diagnosis as such was abandoned. In the article which follows, Breger feels that this artificial separation of diagnosis from treatment may be harmful rather than helpful because such early diagnostic emphasis often will lead to expectations on the part of the patient which will not be fulfilled. The emphasis, rather, should be on research and test validity.

Dr. Breger is a psychiatrist who was formerly on the staff of the Langley Porter Neuropsychiatric Institute in San Francisco and is also a member of the Department of Psychiatry at the University of California School of Medicine. The article which follows appeared in a 1968 issue of the *Journal of Consulting and Clinical Psychology*.

PSYCHOLOGICAL TESTING: TREATMENT AND RESEARCH IMPLICATIONS

Louis Breger

Psychological testing has long been the unique speciality of the clinical psychologist, a fact that stems from the particular history of the field. Recent developments bring out a number of conflicts between the assumptions of this traditional emphasis and clinical practice. For example, Meehl (1960) has reported that only 17 percent of psychotherapists ($N = 168$ drawn from a "wide spectrum of orientations") believe that the prior knowledge contributed by testing is of much value to them. While this change in emphasis has come about first at the level of practice, the recent conference on training in clinical psychology (Hoch, Ross & Winder, 1966) indicated that a reappraisal of the role of psychological testing in teaching and clinical training programs is also in progress. In these and other ways, it seems apparent that conflict exists between the traditional emphasis on testing and current practices. An examination of the history of this conflict and of the issues involved may allow us to break free of certain outmoded assumptions and practices.

Testing should be oriented in two broad directions: first, toward the practical question of what to do about persons and their problems—what might be called treatment in the most general sense—second, toward the comprehension of the nature of problems and effects of treatment—a function which might be labeled research or theoretical understanding. Traditional models of testing have been tied to the concepts of diagnosis and selection, both of which may prove largely inappropriate to much of the data that the clinical psychologist is now faced with and, more particularly, will be faced with in the future. Similarly, a good deal of the traditional research in the testing area (e.g., the innumerable Rorschach studies or the vast literature with intelligence tests directed at controversies over IQ constancy and the like) has not led to significant advances in theoretical understanding. To anticipate, it will be argued that assessment, built around the clinical-therapeutic interview, provides a more appropriate model for practice with that large group of persons referred for personality "diagnosis." First, let us consider a common justification for testing, that it constitutes an essential part of the clinical psychologist's "role."

TESTING AS PART OF THE PSYCHOLOGIST'S PROFESSIONAL ROLE

Deciding how best to help persons can be a very stress-producing affair, particularly when the state of understanding about persons, problems, and treatments is so far from complete. Clinical psychologists, along with their psychiatric and social-work colleagues, are, nevertheless, expected to function as experts in dealing with the persons and problems that face them in mental hospitals, outpatient clinics, counseling centers, and the like. Since it is almost impossible for anyone to continually question everything in his day-to-day functioning, psychologists and others react to this stressful state of affairs by falling back on some generally defined professional role which dictates in what areas they are experts, what kind of activities they will perform, what kind of language they will speak, how their relationships with other professionals will be structured, and other similar considerations. This is inevitable, though the pressure for it is probably greater in situations where there is much uncertainty about how to function ("treat" patients) and about who can function best. In this respect, we find psychiatrists falling back on certain historically established aspects of the physician role. (Physicians treat the sick—hence, they are the ones who must treat the "mentally ill"; physicians have the final responsibility—hence, they must be in charge of the ward or the "psychiatric team.") Similarly, we find clinical psychologists relying on certain historically established role characteristics in defining their functions and their areas of expertness vis-à-vis other professionals.

Psychological testing becomes especially valued in this regard because it is an area in which the psychologist is the unquestioned expert, as contrasted with an activity such as interviewing, where he must compete with psychiatrists, social workers, and others. Thus, testing becomes a key activity in defining the clinical psychologist's role in a way that gives him a sense of expertise in a distinctly outlined area with its own jargon, research literature, and special perogatives.

Certainly not all, or even most, clinical psychologists use psychological testing solely as a rationalization for their lesser status or to gain security by reliance on a clearly defined set of routines, but these factors do enter to some degree in the functioning of many. More to the point is the inappropriateness of professional role considerations as a justification for psychological testing. To say that psychologists should test because this is their professional role makes little sense; it is like saying that barbers should bleed people because this is their professional role or that psychiatrists should give lobotomies because this is their role. Obviously this is a line of reasoning that can be used to perpetuate any existing form of practice, no matter how inappropriate or harmful. Psychological testing, like any other technique, must be evaluated in terms of the adequacy of its basic assumptions, its helpfulness to persons seeking treatment, and its contributions to actual decision making about patients, problems, and treatments. It makes little sense for the psychologist to perpetuate his role as tester in a state hospital where all patients receive the same treatment (or lack of treatment), regardless of what the psychological tests reveal, or in a situation where the individuals making decisions about treatment do not read the psychological report until after they have made their decisions. Testing may also be inappropriate when sources of information that may be more directly related to the decisions to be made can be quickly obtained (e.g., age, job history, length, and number of previous hospitalizations).

HISTORICAL ANTECEDENTS

Beginning with Freud and continuing through the variety of psychotherapies that have branched out from psychoanalysis, there has been a merger of diagnosis with treatment. The psychoanalytic method of therapy is the method of personality "diagnosis." Sullivan's psychiatric interview is both "diagnosis" and "treatment." (Roger's client-centered approach, arising outside the medical framework, has never stressed the need for "diagnosis" before treatment.) The notion of separating treatment and diagnosis derives from different historical sources and cannot be justified within the frameworks of the major therapies themselves. Two such historical influences may be discerned: (a) a belief in the necessity of diagnosing patients before treating them, essentially a reassertion, following the psychodynamic trend begun by Freud, of the medical identification of psychiatry;[1] and (b) a belief in the value of accurate "selection," derived from the mental testing movement within psychology.

The medical diagnostic position is identified with workers such as Schafer (1948) and Rapaport (1946), who used tests to generate descriptions of personality or psychological functioning. Their identification with medical psychoanalysis has led many in this tradition to advocate complete psychological assessment as a part of the comprehensive diagnostic work-up. But, as Szasz (1965) points out, such a commitment to "diagnosis" is logically inconsistent with the basic premises of psychoanalytic therapy.

The belief in the value of selection springs from the mental testing movement, so prominent in clinical psychology's past, as typified by work with the MMPI and the value placed on accurate prediction (whether clinical or actuarial). The confluence of these traditions has reinforced a belief in the value of testing prior to treatment, a belief which begs the central questions concerning test usefulness and validity.

Testing, whether personality descriptive or selection oriented, is wasteful and may even be harmful insofar as it is separated from, and makes no practical contribution to, treatment. Many persons are most in need of, as well as most receptive to, treatment when they make their initial contact with a treating agency. A diagnostic enterprise that is separated from treatment may function as a roadblock at this stage. Commitments to "diagnosis" before treatment or to "selection" both reinforce the fixed position or status of existing treatments. This is inappropriate in a field where little solid knowledge about the relationship between patient-treatment interactions exists. These commitments further the illusion that once a patient is diagnosed or selected, differential treatment will be forthcoming. An honest look at clinical practice reveals that in most instances differential treatment does not follow from differential categorization based on psychological tests. The main reason that testing is not integrally related to treatment is that the

---

[1] A parallel reassertion is represented by the insistance of the orthodox psychoanalytic institutes that their candidates have medical training despite the almost wholly nonmedical nature of both psychoanalytic training and therapy.

central implicit assumption underlying testing—is not true. The basic question of what sort of treatments (insight psychotherapy, group psychotherapy, family therapy, help in getting a divorce, help in changing jobs, etc.) work with what sort of people and with what effects or outcomes remains the central unanswered research question in the clinical assessment area. These points may be illuminated by a consideration of their implications for treatment and research.

TREATMENT

The following discussion is directed at those persons who voluntarily seek psychological help. Their disturbances may range from mild adjustment problems to severe psychosis, and their attitudes towards treatment may be resolute or conflicted; yet in a basic sense these voluntary patients differ from persons who are referred because someone other than themselves—whether parent, friend, or social agency—has decided that they have "psychological problems." Voluntary patients compose the bulk of the population which applies to outpatient clinics, counseling centers, private practitioners, and community mental health programs. What is done with such persons at the time of their initial contact is frequently of great importance. Erikson (1964) directs his attention to what he terms "the problem of the lost momentum of initial commitment." He states:

Hospitalized patients, having been committed, are often ready to commit themselves. They expect "to go to work," both on themselves and on whatever task they may be asked to do. But too often they are met by a laborious process of diagnosis and initiation which emphasizes the absolute distance of patienthood from active life. Thus literally, "insult is added to injury" in that the uprooted one, already considered expendable or abnormal by his previous group of affiliations, finds himself categorized and judged by those who were expected to show him the way through a meaningful moratorium. Many a man acquires the irreversible identity of being a lifelong patient and client not on the basis of what he "is," but on the basis of what is first done about him [p. 97].

The importance of not obstructing the individual's initial attempts to seek help holds equally with the less disturbed nonhospitalized person. Since psychological testing, like history taking and other diagnostic procedures, may obstruct the individual's initial help-seeking attempts, if and when one does test one should have very good reasons for doing so. Most clinician-testers would probably agree that the taking of tests themselves is of no great help to the patient; in fact the process may be harmful insofar as it reinforces his expectations of expert or magical cure and structures the future patient-therapist relationship in an inappropriate way. And as was pointed out above, when one tests during the initial contact, the opportunity to initiate treatment, whether psychotherapy or whatever, at the precise time when the patient is most receptive may be lost.

What reasons can be advanced in favor of testing? Essentially, the reasons are: first, testing can provide valuable information which aids in the decision about what kind of treatment is most appropriate; second, the information from testing is useful to the therapist if and when treatment is begun. Consider the following examples: (a) A patient may be tested to determine if he has sufficient resources (ego-strength) and assets to warrant psychoanalytic treatment, as opposed to brief less intensive psychotherapy;[2] (b) a patient may be tested to determine if he could be more suitably treated as an in- or outpatient.

Examples of how testing could provide useful information to the therapist are: (a) Tests can detect psychotic or suicidal potential that might not become apparent to the therapist for some time and, hence, alert him; (b) it might be argued that the therapist is generally aided by prior knowledge of personality dynamics.

Each of these reasons raises its own important questions. First, can the testing procedures actually indicate which sorts of personalities are suitable for which sorts of treatment? Second, is the personality data supplied by testing useful in treatment? Clear-cut answers do not exist for either of these important questions at this time. In fact, the question of patient-treatment interaction, what sorts of treatments have effects with what sorts of patients, should be the central research concern of anyone working with this material. Unfortunately, a commitment to diagnosis before treatment leads many to bypass this crucial issue.

Assuming that the patient somehow gets placed in treatment, whether group psychotherapy, or whatever, one may again ask whether a knowledge of history and diagnosis is helpful in treatment. Again, there is no clear-cut answer; there are advantages and disadvantages. First, a foreknowledge of personality dynamics may alert the therapist to key conflict areas, key defensive operations, and the like and, hence, increase his sensitivity in responding to these areas. On the other hand, the same foreknowledge may give the therapist a set for certain areas or topics which leads him to overlook or miss the importance of other things the patient is saying. Another consideration regards the effect of foreknowledge on the therapist's conception of himself—does it make him feel like an expert with secret wisdom to impart? If so, how does this affect his relationship with the patient? Many of the difficulties that stem from the untenable assumptions underlying diagnosis and assessment as prerequisites for treatment disappear when treatment is seen primarily as something which the patient himself must seek out and become involved in. Intake or first contact with voluntary patients may be viewed as the initial phase of treatment in which therapist and

---

[2] Such considerations are very likely to be irrelevant in most clinics where staff availability is the overriding concern.

patient together explore the patient's difficulties and desires. The therapist acts as a therapist, giving the patient an opportunity to sample, first-hand, therapy as a way of coping with his problems. On the basis of this sample, the patient and therapist can work toward a decision about further treatment. Approaching the initial contact in this way is consistent with the assumptions of a variety of therapies—psychoanalytic, Sullivanian, Rogerian, etc. Furthermore, it makes good sense in terms of the assessment literature on predicting performance in complex situations. Experience here has shown that the best predictions stem from situations that most closely approximate the criterion situation itself. The best way for both therapist and patient to reach a decision on how the latter will perform in psychotherapy (or whether he wants to try it further) is to sample this criterion situation.

It should be stressed that the question of whether knowledge about personality dynamics is useful for treatment is a very open one that may ultimately depend on the kind of treatment, the kind of personality, and future improvements in both treatment techniques and testing instruments. For the present, it would seem that there are many ways in which testing is unrelated to treatment and may hinder it as well as help. One wonders whether many psychologists resort to tests rather than a direct engagement of the patient in an intake interview, which may be both diagnosis and treatment, for irrelevant professional role considerations. Hopefully, psychologists are beyond the point where they need feel they are infringing on the perogatives of psychiatry when they interview rather than test. After all, what is medical about an interview?

An altogether different set of problems is presented by the chronic institutionalized populations found in many large state and veterans hospitals. Here, the basic treatment goal is to get the patient to the point where he can maintain a minimal level of functioning outside the hospital. In most cases, little in the way of internal psychological change can be accomplished, and treatment becomes oriented primarily to changing the syndrome of institutionalization. Programs in which the patients are formed into semiautonomous groups where they are forced to take charge of their own fates seem much more effective than many traditional forms of treatment. More recent modifications in this social-psychological approach to treatment include the establishment of patient-managed work centers in the community to facilitate the patient's reintegration in society. Traditional assessment and psychological testing activities have little use in these programs; rather, the psychologist turns his attention to the creation of experimental social groups and the evaluation of their effects.

RESEARCH

From the preceding discussion it should be clear that it is the use of tests in the clinical setting that is being considered and not their use for a variety of other research purposes (e.g., work in personality, child development, studies of stress, and the like). Still, within the clinical framework a number of research questions remain. The previous discussion indicated that psychological testing, like other diagnostic procedures, may obstruct the persons' initial effort to do something about his difficulties. In fact, the actual effects of psychological tests on the person's subsequent response to treatment may be directly investigated. In a related form of research Frank (1965) and his co-workers (Frank *et al.*, 1959) have been studying the interaction of patient expectations and response to treatment. They find that patients with the most accurate expectations (i.e., those who were told what to expect in terms of their own and the therapist's behavior, including typical therapy phenomena such as resistance) exhibited the most favorable responses to the therapy. Insofar as testing and other diagnostic activities foster erroneous expectations (which they may do when no differential treatment follows diagnosis or when the therapist never "tells" the person what deep knowledge he has gleaned from the tests), they may be antitherapeutic.

While many persons voluntarily seek what amounts to therapy, there are others who voluntarily seek diagnosis or assessment. Along with these is a sizable group who are referred by others, including young children referred by parents or schools, cases of possible organic involvement, and similar problems. In all these cases, clinical assessment using psychological tests may be quite appropriate. In fact, because they lend themselves to standardized administration and scoring and, hence, may be more readily objectified, tests are superior to the interview for these purposes. Continuing research into the validity of tests for such specific assessment work is, of course, a necessity. There has been a tendency within the field towards identification with single instruments such as the Rorschach or with single approaches such as projective techniques, which really makes little sense when the goal should be the development of valid assessment procedures with respect to some specific goal such as identifying types of organic pathology. One would expect a process of on-going validation to result in the continual modification of the specific tests used in such a procedure. The fact that this has rarely taken place is probably the result of the confounding of two contradictory purposes—the "diagnosis of personality" and the assessment of specific problems such as organic brain damage. While the latter represents a legitimate use of tests in the clinical setting—it may be justified on both clinical and scientific grounds—the former is an unjustified carryover of certain historical assumptions.

Perhaps, by recognizing these different purposes, clinical psychologists may give up, with a clear conscience, the testing of persons who voluntarily seek psychological help and, instead, use tests in those cases where they may make a valid contribution to specific decisions. Such a shift in emphasis has already occurred at the level of practice, but without a clear rationale the clinical psychologist is likely to feel guilty about not fulfilling his professional role. This guilt then tends to perpetuate the traditional emphasis on testing training programs, an emphasis that may take training time away from more important skills. It is skills such as the sensitive use of the initial contact as both treatment and assessment and the continuing research refinement of assessment procedures with respect to specific and answerable diagnostic questions that seem more suited to the future roles of the clinical psychologist.

Breger's plea for a revival of interest in diagnostic work, especially by clinical psychologists, may fall on deaf ears in certain centers. Indeed, the entire future of graduate training in clinical psychology is undergoing change and redirection. Albee, a recent President of the American Psychological Association, has declared traditional clinical psychology as dead (Albee, 1970). But what seems to be happening, as Goodstein (1971) points out is that "Clinical psychology is alive and well, living under an assumed name in the community." There is now a "new breed" of community psychologists and a recent volume (Iscoe & Spielberger, 1970) devotes more than half its space to a description of specific programs of training in this new area. This is a very broad field: at one end of the dimension are psychologists working in schools and out-reach clinics in more or less traditional clinical roles while, at the other end, are psychologists concerned with very broad programs to foster social change (taking on such issues as war, urban sprawl, pollution, and the like). Such re-tooled and re-programmed clinical psychologists thus go directly into the community emphasizing preventative measures rather than confining themselves to the clinic in traditional one-to-one interactions. But others still tread the more familiar channels and steadfastly maintain the role of the clinical psychologist as diagnostician and psychotherapist, as Rotter makes eminently clear in his revision of his text on clinical psychology (Rotter, 1971). "Save the baby...and some of the bathwater" says Goodstein (1970) who believes psychology should continue to maintain its traditional involvement in mental hospitals and, simultaneously, provide for various community intervention approaches.

IT started with Meehl's little volume, *Clinical versus Statistical Prediction* (1954). Meehl reluctantly came to the conclusion that clinical judgment, frequently involved with his favorite test (the MMPI). showed up poorly. He reviewed 20 studies which he thought were relevant to this issue and in which clinical and actuarial methods could be contrasted. In all but one of these, the predictions made actuarially were either approximately equal or superior to those made by a clinician. Meehl did admit, however, that none of these studies had been planned to "test" this issue specifically. This sad report started a host of other studies by hopeful clinicians. Meehl himself returned to the issue in a 1957 report, "When Shall We Use Our Heads Instead of the Formula?" Here he reported on 27 empirical studies: 17 showed the superiority of the actuarial approach, and the remaining 10 showed no difference. None showed a clinical superiority. The cookbook approach again won out.

An example of this type of study is the following report (a 1964 M.A. thesis at the University of Minnesota) by Burton Danet, utilizing the MMPI scaled scores and the prediction of future mental illness in a college sample. Clinicians with varying amounts of experience (up to 21 years) were employed, and their ratings or judgments compared against seven inexperienced graduate students. Correct number of hits were then checked for the two groups against the more straightforward and simple actuarial prediction. The report originally appeared in the *Journal of Consulting Psychology* in 1965.

Dr. Danet is presently engaged in private practice in Riverdale. New York, where he is also a member of the staff of the Riverdale Mental Hygiene Clinic.

PREDICTION OF MENTAL ILLNESS IN COLLEGE STUDENTS ON THE BASIS OF "NONPSYCHIATRIC" MMPI PROFILES

Burton N. Danet

The literature on the Minnesota Multiphasic Personality Inventory (MMPI) contains numerous studies in which more or less successful discrimination between groups of individuals having different characteristics is made on the basis of their inventory profiles. Many fewer reports have been published describing an attempt to predict characteristics of individuals which develop over a span of time. In the present study, the following question was raised. Could clinical judgments be made on the basis of MMPI profiles obtained during college enrollment as to whether college students would be treated for a mental illness within approximately two years following their matriculation? Recent evidence has suggested that in similar prediction problems, statistical methods may ultimately replace much of the clinician's art (Meehl, 1954, 1957). It was, therefore, of interest to devise a simple statistical method of prediction. A comparison could then be made between actuarial prediction and the performance of clinicians.

The contribution of clinicians' or students' experience to the accuracy of the clinical predictions was also studied. Here the question was: Are clinicians with more experience or education more accurate in their predictions than others of relatively less experience and education? Similarly, are clinicians more accurate than a group of inexperienced graduate students who have just completed their first 30-hour course on the MMPI?

METHOD

Samples

Each year prior to entering the University of Minnesota, freshmen take the MMPI as part of their orientation program. From this population of tests obtained during enrollment, 70 were selected from the files of the Student Counseling Bureau. These were all of freshmen and sophomores whose mean age at the time of orientation was 18 years, 2 months. Included were 36 male subjects and 34 female subjects. Among these were three preselected subsamples. One, the *clinic sample*, consisted of 10 male subjects and 14 female subjects who had received 10 or more psychotherapeutic hours at the Mental Hygiene Clinic, University of Minnesota Health Services. The mean number of months between the enrollment MMPI and the time subjects were evaluated at the clinic was 6.4, with a range from 0 to 31 months (SD = 7.8). The second, the *hospital sample*, included 10 male subjects and 6 female subjects who had been admitted to the psychopathic unit of the University of Minnesota Hospitals. The mean time lapse between orientation profile and hospital admission was 18.2 months, with a range from 3 to 54 months (SD = 12.8). The third, the *normal sample*, consisted of 30 college students who had indicated some interest in participating in psychological experiments and had become part of the Psychology Subject Pool at the University. All in the latter sample denied having ever received psychiatric care. They did so within a mean of 18.8 months from the date of the orientation MMPIs, the range being from 7 to 31 months (SD = 11.5). None had been admitted to the psychiatric service of University Hospitals nor were their names on record at the Mental Hygiene Clinic. There were 16 male subjects and 14 female subjects, 26 sophomores and 4 juniors. They listed 18 different majors, suggesting they represented a wide sampling of students at the University.

Procedure

The profiles of students who had been treated for an emotional disturbance (hospital and clinic samples: N = 40) were randomly intermixed with those of students who showed no official record of having received psychiatric treatment (normal sample: N = 30). These 70

MMPI profiles were presented to 41 judges, 34 clinicians, and 7 students just completing a course on the MMPI, who were all asked to make the predictions. The judges were told that the profiles were orientation results for students at the University of Minnesota. The mean age and age range of the sample were given. In addition, the judges were told that some of the subjects, independently of their MMPI testing, had sought out or been referred for psychiatric treatment. The number of subjects in the sample who had received such care was *not* disclosed. The clinicians were also told that other subjects in the sample showed no official record of having received help for emotional problems. On the profile sheet for each subject, the only identifying information presented was age, sex, and marital status at the time of orientation, and the raw scores (*K* corrected) and standard scores for the 3 validity and 10 clinical scales. The profiles were all coded according to the Hathaway (1947) system.

Judges were asked to sort the profiles into 12 categories. Categories 0 through 5 represented a decision that the subject probably *will* develop a mental disorder later on in his college career. Categories 6 through 11 represented the judgment that the subject probably will *not* develop a mental disorder. Within these subgroups, the category of choice depended upon the extent the judge felt it was likely that the subject would develop a mental illness *and* seek out or be referred for psychiatric treatment. No stipulation was made regarding the number of subjects to be placed in each category.

Judges

Among the 34 "experienced" judges, the area of specialization most heavily represented was adult clinical psychology ($N = 21$). There were also seven child clinical psychologists, five counseling psychologists, and one school psychologist. Of these clinicians, 16 held the Ph.D.; 7 others had the equivalent of the doctorate. There were also 11 graduate students in the clinical and counseling psychology training programs at the University of Minnesota. All of these students were at least at the M.A. level and had 1 or 2 years' clinical experience behind them. The numbers of years' experience for the 34 ranged from 1 to 21, with a mean of 7.6 years. Three levels of experience (1–2 years, 3–10 years, 11–21 years) were eventually divided among the judges, with about one-third of the group in each category.

The seven "inexperienced" judges were students without clinical training who had just completed a 30-hour course on the MMPI. Of these, four were in the adult clinical psychology program, two were in sociology, while one was in social psychology.

TABLE 4

NUMBER OF HITS AND MISSES BY SIMPLE ACTUARIAL PREDICTION

Hits		Misses	
Valid positives	29	False positives	10
Valid negatives	20	False negatives	11
Total	49	Total	21

TABLE 5

MEAN PERCENTAGE OF HITS FOR INEXPERIENCED STUDENTS AND CLINICIANS OF VARIOUS LEVELS OF EXPERIENCE AND EDUCATION

Years of Experience	N	Percentage of Hits	Educational Level	N	Percentage of Hits
0	7	65.1	Student	7	65.1
1–2	11	62.3	M.A. equivalent	7	62.8
3–9	11	62.4	M.A.	4	60.7
10–21	12	65.3	Ph.D. equivalent	7	62.2
			Ph.D.	16	64.1

RESULTS

Simple Actuarial Prediction

Table 4 presents the results of predictions made on the basis of the following simple statistical procedure. Profiles were called "likely to develop a mental illness" if at least *one* clinical scale was at or above a T score of 70. In this table, the number of "hits" (valid positives and valid negatives) and "misses" (false positives and false negatives) are presented. A contingency analysis showed that these actuarial predictions were more accurate than chance expectation ($p < .005$).[*] The hit rate was 70 percent which also reliably exceeded chance expectation of 50 percent ($p \leq .008$).[†]

Performance of the Judges

When the number of hits and misses of the 34 experienced clinicians were submitted to contingency analyses, for all but 4, the judges were

---

[*] For the contingency analyses, "chance expectation" was defined as the frequency of "mentally ill" cases in the sample of students whose profiles were given to the clinicians. Since actual base rates in the college population were estimated to be extremely low, between 5 and 10 percent, it was feasible to include only a small group of students in this study with the sample base rate for mental illness considerably higher than in the student population. Thus, it was of interest to determine how well judges could predict the base rate in this sample, when not considering population base rates as level of expectation.

[†] For the analysis of percentage of "hits," a chance level of 50 percent was assumed. The reason for this procedure stemmed from the fact that judges were *not* informed of the frequency of "mentally ill" cases in the sample of subjects and were asked to make their predictions based on MMPI profile data alone. Thus, for each subject for whom the judgment was made there was a 50 percent chance the judge would be correct.

significant at or beyond the .05 level of significance (chi-square). The four clinicians whose predictions were not significantly different from the expected chance values stated they had had 1, 2, 12, and 21 years' experience.

The mean percentage of hits for the 34 experienced clinicians was 63 percent, reliably different from chance or 50 percent ($p < .06$). The hit rate was significantly in excess of chance ($p \leq .06$) for 20 of the 34 judges.

Experience and Accuracy of Prediction

Table 5 presents the mean percentage of hits for inexperienced students and for clinicians having different amounts of experience, as well as for judges of various educational levels. Apparently accuracy of prediction is not different at the various levels of experience and education.

Despite the small size of the sample of inexperienced student judges who had completed the MMPI course, their results were strikingly similar to those of the 34 experienced clinicians. As shown in Table 5 the mean percentage of hits of the seven students was 65.1 percent, reliably different from chance (50%) at the .04 level of significance. This figure is remarkably comparable to the mean percentage of hits for all other judges (63%). The contingency analysis for each of these individuals showed that all but one of the chi-square values were significant ($p \leq$ .05). Similarly, all but two of the students achieved percentages of hits which were significant ($p \leq .05$).

DISCUSSION

The results of this study support the proposition that individual clinicians are able to predict which college students will be treated for a mental illness on the basis of "nonpsychiatric" MMPI profiles better than the chance level of expectation. However, statistical confirmation of this fact does not necessarily demonstrate the applicability of the procedure to any clinical decision-making process. The significance of the clinical predictions is further reduced when it is noted that the method of simple actuarial prediction, that is, calling mentally ill those students with profiles having at least one clinical scale at or above $T = 70$, yielded a hit rate of 70 percent, which was reliably better ($p < .02$) than the mean percentage of hits of the clinicians (63%). It may be concluded that this study once more lends support to the actuarial mode of prediction. Of 34 experienced clinicians, only 4 achieved a hit rate the same as or better than that of the simple statistical procedure (the best clinician's hit rate was 74.38%). Since this conclusion is in agreement with evidence accumulating in recent years, it seems that a natural step would be to turn from the clinical to the actuarial mode of prediction in the use of MMPI data. Kleinmuntz's (1963) study is an excellent example, as he used a digital computer to aid in "shuttling back and forth" to arrive at the most successful set of decision rules.

No evidence was found in this study that experience aids the clinician in making the predictions. It cannot be said that those who performed least well were also least experienced. Further, amount of experience and level of education had no relationship to the ability of expert judges to make the judgments. Students who had no clinical experience were able, *as well as* clinicians with experience, to predict mental illness from MMPI profiles beyond chance expectation. Of these seven inexperienced students, five performed at a level equal or superior to 74 percent of the 34 experienced clinicians.

It should be noted that the failure of experience to aid the clinician in making the predictions may be an artifact of the procedure employed in this study. Since the frequency of treated versus not-treated subjects in the sample was not disclosed, some sophisticated judges may have made the false assumption that subjects were drawn at random from the college population. They may then have concluded that only approximately 1 in 20 would be likely to receive treatment. Their performance, therefore, would be hindered to the extent that consideration of the population base rates influenced their judgments. A tentative conclusion that may be drawn is that a certain fundamental knowledge of the MMPI in and of itself seems sufficient to make the predictions in question under the present procedure. If provided with the base rate of "mental illness" in the sample of college students in this study, more experienced clinicians may then improve their predictions relative to less experienced individuals.

Cooke and Kiesler (1967) have replicated and extended Danet's study by determining whether differences can be seen between the MMPI clinical scales with students who applied for psychological counseling five or more months after entering the University of Iowa. When compared to a randomly selected nonclient group, counseling clients had significantly higher total MMPI mean scores and a significantly higher neurotic triad mean. Danet's specific result that a T-score of 70 or more for an individual on one or more of the clinical scales would spot those who received therapy in the future (in contrast to those that did not) was not replicated here. However, since his data were based on both a clinic and hospital sample there probably would be more individuals with elevated scores, especially with the hospital sample.

At one of the Invitational Conferences on Testing Problems, Zubin (1955) noted that this whole issue is a pseudo problem. The dilemma is nonexistent. Despite Meehl's book, he feels the distinction between clinical and actuarial prediction is heuristic rather than basic. The business of predicting for a group is quite different from predicting from the individual case. And it is the group prediction that can be entirely statistical. Here the prediction might be that there is a .70 probability of "success," but then a decision must be made on this. The two types of prediction supplement each other, and the discrepancies between the two ought to be studied reciprocally to improve each other.

Sawyer (1966) has pointed out that the issue of clinical versus statistical prediction is only half the problem. The prior problem— clinical versus statistical measurement—has been largely neglected. He reviewed a total of 45 studies involving 75 comparisons of the two methods, and concluded that the problem remains unresolved. Improvement along methodological lines is what is badly needed.

In his review of research in personnel selection for the *Annual Review of Psychology* (1967), Guion comments that the clinical versus statistical prediction issue seems to have quieted down, and that no special skill, brilliance, or even prejudice is required to admit that some efforts at so-called clinical prediction are in reality "nothing more than arrogance put up as the facade of ignorance." He states that it is obvious that "careful, competent clinical prediction works, and the fact is particularly valuable where statistical methods cannot even be tried as in executive selection and the Peace Corps" (Guion, 1967, p. 206). It may be remarked, however, that the Peace Corps makes use of the MMPI plus extensive field observation of trainees by clinical psychologists over a period of many weeks.

A perennial problem with all self-report devices is faking—conscious or unconscious. Not only is there the unexpected situation of a testee's desire to "fake good," but also there is the distinct problem of detection of the "fake bad." The second is, for obvious reasons, not encountered so frequently as the first, but it does exist—for example, draftees "faking bad" in order to avoid military service. Earlier psychometricians paid little attention to this problem, other than resorting to exhortations for honesty, not requiring testees to sign names, and the like. In recent years, more sophisticated attempts have been made to cope with faking. These generally are based on giving the testee a real chance to distort answers and then deriving an empirical "fake key" from this. Ruch (1942) was probably the originator of this technique when he first had college students fill out the Bernreuter Personality Inventory under normal conditions and, for a second time, as if they were applying for the job of salesman, which they sincerely wanted and for which they knew the test scores would be used.

With the appearance of the Minnesota Multiphasic Personality Inventory (MMPI), much attention was given to the problem of conscious and unconscious faking. Of all the paper-and-pencil personality inventories, the MMPI has been the subject of the largest amount of research on this issue. Four validity scales were developed by the test authors; other psychologists have continued work toward further refinement. By necessity, most such work has involved college students who are asked to take the MMPI on repeated occasions but under different psychological sets.

In the following report, Drs. Drasgow and Barnette were able to secure a non-student group—candidates in industrial assessments by means of psychological tests for upgrading—for which the application of the $F − K$ index (Gough, 1950) brought promising results. The study was done while both authors were serving as counseling psychologists at the University of Buffalo's Vocational Counseling Center (now State University of New York at Buffalo). The report is a condensation of the original article, which appeared in the *Journal of Consulting Psychology*, 1957.

The *F* scale of the MMPI is composed of items answered true or false by very few normals; any testee that had several of these was probably careless or inattentive in taking the test. The *K* scale is the "suppressor scale" of the MMPI. High scores are secured when the testee wants to place himself in a good light; low scores are earned when the testee is either unusually frank or is adopting a highly defensive attitude. Since *K* is the longer of the two scales, the arithmetical result of $F − K$ is typically a negative number.

F – K IN A MOTIVATED GROUP

James Drasgow and W. Leslie Barnette, Jr.

A recurring problem in the use of any personality test is the question of dissembling. The Minnesota Multiphasic Personality Inventory (MMPI) contains at least four separate scales (?, L, K, F) which directly contribute to evaluating the validity of the scores in the profile. Each one of these four scales assesses validity from a somewhat different approach, but apparently the only promising combination of scales to date is Gough's F minus K.

Several empirical studies have reported on the meaningfulness of the values obtained by subtracting the K raw score from the F raw score. These studies have been especially concerned with establishing optimum cutoff points in the F – K distributions. The distributions that have been studied and reported were obtained from subjects under different conditions, e.g., (a) "normal" subjects who were given no particular instructions designed to affect F – K, (b) normal subjects who were instructed to feign abnormality, (c) normals who were instructed to act more normal, and (d) patients who were given instructions designed to be analogous to those given to the first three "normal" groups. The most rewarding results have been obtained with condition (b). These studies have been well replicated and cutoff scores corroborated. The present study focuses on the unsolved reverse problem of detecting profiles which have been faked to make a "good impression."

In an attempt to discover what precise range of F – K values might be used to discriminate the subjects who were instructed to fake a "good" normal profile, earlier studies have merely concluded that more research was needed.

Why is it that the faked-good profiles have been so difficult to detect? In previous studies with subjects working under fake-good instructions, their motivation is open to question. The choice of motivated subjects by previous researchers appears to have been unfortunate since the probability of finding real differences has been minimized by supplying only instructions to stimulate motivation. The present brief report has therefore focused on this aspect and supplies a group with higher motivation.

SUBJECTS

The University's Vocational Counseling Center provides a job applicant screening service to business and industry. The job applicants from this service formed the group with which we worked. Some of the applicants were applying for jobs with companies without having been previously associated with the company, while others were old-line company employees competing for promotion to a choice spot. All Ss were employed males on their "old" jobs at the time of testing. The jobs for which they were being tested included such titles as foreman, salesman, supervisor, superintendent, and vice-president. The jobs can be seen in a framework of advancement and betterment, so that in this society we can reasonably infer an appreciable degree of motivation to get the better job. Many of the men said that they had been working years for the job in question, and that it was not merely a matter of money.

The total number of "industrial cases" with MMPIs available for use in the present study was 92. Within this total pool, 66 profiles had scores within the normal range (T = 30 to 70), and 26 profiles had one or more scores outside. The normal sample of 66 cases is utilized here.

The modal person in the sample was a 34-year-old white married male with two children and two years of college. He was currently employed, but trying to get a "better" job.

RESULTS AND DISCUSSION

All scores on all MMPI scales on the profile were within the accepted normal range as stated earlier. The mean raw F was 1.6 and the SD was 1.5; the mean raw K was 17.6 with an SD of 3.2. The difference of -16 for $F - K$ is well beyond the .01 level.

Hunt (1948) reported a mean $F - K$ of -11 for the group of Navy prisoners who were asked to make a good impression, but he was dissatisfied with this statistic because too many normals also gave this value. One might then expect an $F - K$ of this size as an indication of a "normal" amount of hypocrisy which may be associated with making a good impression in this society. Gough (1950) gives -7 to -10 as a modal range within which the majority of normals would fall.

A corroborating factor and potential source of explanation for the obtained results appeared in the relationship between a job applicant's $F - K$ and his number of dependents. Because of the restriction in the range of the number of dependents and the non-normal nature of the distribution, a non-parametric correlation technique was used to estimate the association. The correlation was .61 and significant beyond the .01 level. Concomitantly, it is of interest to report that the correlation between $F - K$ and age was zero, while that between $F - K$ and education was $-.18$ (Pearsonian r's in both instances).

The relatively high relationship indicated by the .61 could probably be interpreted in a variety of ways. The writers would relate it to the American middle class value of upward social mobility. We postulate that the more dependents the client has, the greater will be his felt personal responsibility and that, as a partial consequence, the more motivated he will be to make a good impression so as to secure the proposed upgrading on the job.

SUMMARY

Other MMPI studies involving $F - K$ samples where testees have been requested to fake good are criticized on the ground of inadequate motivation or felt responsibility. Results are presented, utilizing 66 normal MMPI profiles obtained from clients tested for upgrading where evidence was available for high motivation. The mean $F - K$ index for this group was -16. Age and years of education had little or no effect; number of dependents, however, was significantly related to this index. It is proposed that the felt responsibility and upward motivation of these clients are the important factors in producing such elevated $F - K$ indices.

Ruch and Ruch (1967) have reported a study in which MMPI scales without K corrections were used with success. Involved were 182 sales representatives from about 9 companies, ranging from beverage sales to business forms. With each sample, the salesmen were divided into upper- and lower-criterion groups. The classifications were based on sales managers' ratings. The five uncorrected MMPI scales, which are normally subjected to K correction, differentiated significantly between the criterion groups in the expected directions. The K suppressor variable, when applied according to the manual's directions, surprisingly decreased validity to almost zero. The uncorrected scales were then better correlated with selling effectiveness.

BOTH to introduce the reader to the California Psychological Inventory, as well as to indicate the extensive cross-cultural validation research study centering on the construct of socialization, the following selection has been included. The CPI was developed in the hope of attaining two main goals: First, theoretical in nature, to employ diagnostic concepts drawn from the ongoing processes of interpersonal life, and which therefore should be relevant for conceptualizing and forecasting behavior in any society or culture; and second, the more practical aim of assessing these "folk concepts" by means of brief and valid subscales which would lend themselves to profile recording and configural interpretation. There are 18 scales in the inventory, including measures of dominance, social presence, responsibility, self-control, achievement motivation, psychological mindedness, and femininity.

The inventory is intended principally for use with "normal" subjects and the subscales are addressed to aspects of personality that are involved in social adaptation and constructive achievement. This does not prevent its application to certain "problem" groups, such as prison inmates (Gough & Sandler, 1964), but the main intent of the author was to make available an inventory for general use in schools and colleges, in business and industry, in clinics and counseling centers whose clientele, as Gough puts it, consists mainly of socially-functioning individuals. Recent reviews of the inventory include those by Goldberg (1972) and Kelly (1965). Much of the published validity data for the CPI are based on USA samples, but there is, in addition, a great deal of evidence from other countries, as would be expected in view of the inventory's emphasis on transcultural diagnostic concepts. It is infrequent that psychological measurements developed within one culture are directly transferable to another culture. This is another feature which makes the CPI unusual.

Indeed, for the CPI as a whole, there is a wealth of cross-cultural evidence and more continued to become available yearly. The Italian literature at present now runs to some 50 titles and touches on such topics as scholastic achievement, optimism versus pessimism, and vocational counseling. There is a published Japanese version of the CPI; a Ceylonese and three Chinese translations are in use. Researches in Switzerland have reported findings on watchmakers and skilled tradesmen. The list continues with Australian and French editions of the CPI and a Polish edition has recently been standardized. Portuguese, Spanish, and Dutch editions are currently (1971) in the process of being standardized. A Hebrew edition is in use and two papers on Israeli samples have been published. "Man is worldwide and behavior is worldwide, and we require at least some tools of assessment that are capable of being used on a worldwide basis" (Gough, 1965, p. 386).

Dr. Gough is a Professor in the Department of Psychology at the University of California, Berkeley, where he is also affiliated with the University's Institute of Personality Assessment and Research to which have come many invited groups of people (such as architects and poets) for psychological study and assessment.

The following material is presented at the suggestion of Dr. Gough. This constitutes a four-page overview of the theoretical basis of the CPI, its aims and goals and its psychometric claims which is the introduction to Gough's chapter on the CPI in Volume I of *Advances in Psychological Assessment* (McReynolds, 1968, pp. 55–58).

THE CALIFORNIA PSYCHOLOGICAL INVENTORY

Harrison G. Gough

The California Psychological Inventory (CPI) is intended for diagnosis and evaluation of individuals, with emphasis upon interpersonal behavior and dispositions relevant to social interaction. Although great care was taken in the development of the test and preparation of the manual (Gough, 1957, 1964), so that interpretation of scale scores and profile patterns would not be unduly difficult, the diagnostic implications of the profile are not always self-evident; for this reason it is important that scores on the test be interpreted by a competent psychologist who has become familiar with this particular device. Validity-in-use is not something that resides purely in the inventory itself; it is an outcome that derives from the interpreter's skill and insight in making manifest what is inherent in the instrument.

The CPI contains 480 true-false items, which can be administered either individually or in group testing. The items are printed in an eleven-page booklet, and a special answer sheet is used. The subject reads each item, decides whether he agrees or disagrees with what is said, and then marks *true* or *false* on the answer sheet. If a subject prefers not to answer certain items, he may leave them blank. Testing time, including the reading of instuctions, is ordinarily about a class hour in schools and colleges, or about forty-five minutes in individual testing.

No special controls or restrictions are necessary for valid administration of the test. Subjects may begin at one session and finish at another. Items may be read aloud, or explained if questions are asked. Completion of the test may occur under supervision, or a subject may be allowed to work on his own. The inventory has even been used on a mail-out/mail-in basis (MacKinnon, 1962b) with successful results.

Reading ability at the fourth grade level or higher is required if the questionnaire is to be administered silently. However, with poor readers or in situations where greater control is needed, the items may be read aloud with listeners recording their responses after each item has been heard. Age of the respondent is a factor which should also be mentioned. Although parts of the inventory have been used with grade school children, testing with the complete instrument may not be fully valid prior to the seventh grade. From the junior high school level through high school and college and on into adult life and even old age (Schaie, 1959), the inventory yields valid findings.

At present, the inventory is scaled and profiled for 18 variables. Items in each scale are assigned unit weights (0–1), and raw scores are converted to standard scores (separate norms for males and females) with means of 50 and standard deviations of 10. The purpose of each scale is *to predict what an individual will do in a specified context, and/or to identify individuals who will be described in a certain way.* These aims are important both theoretically and practically and should be distinguished from the more common goal in inventory measurement of trait specification. If a scale is intended to define a unidimensional trait of personality, then it must meet minimal statistical requirements of internal homogeneity, domain reliability, and factorial independence. However, if the purpose of a scale is to forecast what a person will say or do, and/or how he will be described by those who know him well, then these statistical considerations become relevant if, and only if, it can be shown that the predictive utility of the measure is improved by their fulfillment.

Reference to another well known test, the Strong Vocational Interest Blank, may help to make clear what is being said. An occupational scale on the Strong, such as minister, is not intended to define a personality trait of ministerialism, but rather to identify individuals whose outlook resembles those in the profession and who might (therefore) feel at home in the indicated environment. Similarly with the CPI, a high score on a scale for social status does not mean that the individual tested has a "trait" of high status, but rather that in viewpoint and outlook he tends to resemble people of high status; presumably, therefore, he may be already of high status, or possessed of those talents and dispositions that will lead him toward such attainment.

The significance of the point that is being emphasized lies principally in the kind of evidence to which one should turn for an evaluation of the worth of the measure. For the scales of the CPI this evidence should come from the context of application: do the scales for achievement motivation forecast scholastic attainment, does the scale for dominance predict ascendant behavior, does the scale for socialization forecast behavior on parole or in other settings where observance of rules and prohibitions is essential, and does the scale for social presence identify people who are at ease, self-assured, and natural in their dealings with other?

CHOICE OF CONCEPTS

A key decision in the development of any measuring instrument is the choice of concepts. Frequently, the appeal of the test developer is to a theory or partial theory of personality, and scales are constructed that relate to traits or dispositions assigned central significance in the theory. For example, an Adlerian might seek to develop a scale for "inferiority," as this constellation of feelings would for him be basic in any diagnosis; or, a student of Durkheim might wish to work with a measure of "anomie," and all that it would imply about alienation and disaffection in the life setting.

Another way to proceed in choosing concepts is, more or less, to let the evidence speak for itself. A factor analysis of a broad range of self-descriptive statements could be conducted, and any internal clusters or themes that emerged could be studied and named so as to illuminate their inferred content. Or, clear and obvious features of the test stimuli could be classified and a score defined as the number of times an individual based his answer on them.

Both of the approaches briefly sketched above are frequently encountered in testing, and the reader should have little difficulty in thinking of many standard tests of each type. As examples, we could cite the Allport-Vernon-Lindzey Study of Values, based on the theoretical position of Spranger, to illustrate the first approach, and the Cattell Sixteen Personality Factor Questionnaire to illustrate the second. Another example of the second approach is the score on preference for asymmetrical designs in the Welsh Figure Preference Test (Welsh, 1959).

A third approach to the choice of concepts is that which draws directly on the context of usage. If an instrument is to be applied in vocational guidance and occupational choice, then a plausible basis for scaling would be found in the jobs that clients would tend to seek. The Strong Vocational Interest Blank illustrates this approach, as it is scaled for the kinds of lifework that college students tend to anticipate—e.g., physician, lawyer, engineer, banker, personnel manager, etc.

Another illustration may be taken from the domain of psychiatric practice. If a test is intended for use in the hospital and psychiatric clinic, then a justifiable rationale would be to develop scales for the diagnostic concepts that are in functional usage in these settings. The Minnesota Multiphasic Personality Inventory (Hathaway & McKinley, 1943), scaled for such syndromes as hysteria, paranoia, and schizophrenia, is based on this principle.

The theoretical basis for the choice of concepts in the CPI is of this third type. Because the instrument is intended for the diagnosis and comprehension of interpersonal behavior, the concepts selected are those that occur in everyday social living and, in fact, arise from social interaction. Most simply, such variables may be described as "folk concepts"—aspects and attributes of interpersonal behavior that are to be found in all cultures and societies, and that possess a direct and integral relationship to all forms of social interaction.

Assuming that valid measures of such folk concepts can be developed, important theoretical and practical advantages of an inventory incorporating them would then follow. One of these advantages is an immediate relevance for cross-cultural measurement. If, for example, self-control is a universal variable in interpersonal living, and if in fact all societies and all cultures recognize this variable as well as individual differences in its expression, then a scale developed in any one culture has at least presumptive relevance for the diagnosis of behavior in any other culture.

Many technical problems of measurement immediately come to mind, and of course such relevance must be empirically confirmed and not just assumed. Nonetheless, the wisdom of beginning with folk concepts is that from the very inception of measurement one seeks cross-cultural relevance and validity. A clear and unequivocal goal of the CPI, it may be stated, is to provide measures that retain their validity in cross-cultural application; and the intensive efforts that have been expended in cross-cultural testing follow directly from this theoretical emphasis. Two examples among many are Gough (1966) and Gough & Sandhu (1964)

A second advantage in working with folk concepts as a basis for scaling is that the variables are meaningful and readily comprehended by the user. Any scale will carry latent and potential implications, which the skilled interpreter must learn to appreciate, but at the same time no special instruction or insight is required to recognize the main thrust of scales seeking to appraise such interpersonal qualities as dominance, sociability, responsibility, tolerance, social presence, and flexibility.

A third advantage lies in what might be called the power of these folk variables. Deriving from interpersonal living and tied to consistent and characteristic modes of reaction, they can in turn validly forecast future behavior in the same context. Put as a research hypothesis, the assertion is that scales and combinations of scales on the CPI will be of value in forecasting longitudinal and/or remote criteria as well as immediate and current behavior. These theoretical considerations underlie the great emphasis given to longitudinal study of the inventory, as, for example, in the prediction of graduation from high school (Gough, 1966c), success versus failure on parole over a three-year period (Gough, Wenk, & Rozynko, 1965), choice of major field in college (Goldschmid, 1965), choice of medical specialty (Domino, 1967), and adult social adjustment on the basis of personality testing in adolescence (Stewart, 1962).

To summarize the above, we may say that the theoretical basis for scaling in the CPI is found in the ongoing processes of everyday social life, more specifically in what may be called folk concepts. This emphasis insures the relevance of the inventory to problems and issues in interpersonal behavior, and for validation points unmistakably to cross-cultural, longitudinal, and life-centered inquiry. The purpose of each scale is to reflect to a maximum degree some theme or aspect of interpersonal behavior—one that has clear visibility and is conceptually recognized by all people, everywhere. The desideratum for the set of scales is that any social behavior, of whatever variety, can be forecast and comprehended by either a single scale of the inventory or by some simple and meaningful combination of scales.

▽ ▽ ▽

MORE recent work with the CPI has dealt with the 18 scales in patterns or configurations which measure more complex personality dimensions than any of the 18 scales alone. A recent illustration of this pattern analysis deals with the matter of social maturity. Here (and in the following research report by Gough) one sees that the socialization scale does not work alone but, rather, is more effective (and valid) when moderator variables are brought into the picture. This becomes possible with the CPI because it is a multivariate instrument. Even so, the socialization (So) scale is the largest contributor to this more global measure of social maturity as indicated by the beta weights in the regression equation derived by Gough. Gough (1966) has published both a three- and a six-variable regression equation, the former being recommended when hand calculations are to be made. In the paper which follows, Gough turns his attention to the high score end of the continuum and looks at several persons who are "near paragons of independent probity." * This scale has also been cross-validated on an Italian sample (Gough, 1966).

Dr. Gough's paper appeared in a 1971 issue of the *Journal of Abnormal Psychology* and is here reproduced in its entirety.

And, then, at the other or low-scoring end of this dimension, Lefcourt's brief report on an unpremeditated validity study of this same social maturity index, this time in a college classroom situation where a flagrant instance of antisocial behavior was observed and where this CPI index (again the six-variable one) proved its worth.

Dr. Lefcourt is Professor of Psychology at the University of Waterloo, Ontario, Canada. His paper on "serendipitous validity" appeared in a 1968 issue of the *Journal of Consulting and Clinical Psychology.*

SCORING HIGH ON AN INDEX OF SOCIAL MATURITY

Harrison G. Gough

Nearly all sociological phenomena are dimensional, or latently dimensional, and socialization seems no exception to this dictum. Anyone conversant with the constraints and imperatives of a culture can classify both individuals and behaviors along a continuum of socialization, from

---

* Personal communication from Gough, 1971.

the rule-breaking, wayward, recalcitrant, and impulse-ridden misfit at one end, through individuals of lesser alienation and lesser trespass, through a zone of normality, on to a region of what is probably oversocialization and adherence to rule.

An interesting task for psychological measurement is the development of scale equivalents for these sociological loci. A great deal of the work done in developing and validating the socialization (So) scale (Gough, 1960; 1965; Peterson, Quay, & Anderson, 1959) of the California Psychological Inventory (CPI; Gough, 1957) has been of just this type: to attempt through calibration of self-characterization to estimate a person's proper position along this continuum of asocial to social dispositions. The scale functions reasonably well in this task and has proved able to sustain its validity in exploratory applications in many different cultures and linguistic milieus (cf. Mizushima & DeVos, 1967; Sandhu, 1960; Siegman, 1962).

An obvious philosophical issue arose early in this work with the So scale, having to do with the overconventionality and overconformity already mentioned. The goal of the socialization process is to produce individuals who are in harmony with the mandates of the culture, but at the same time free enough or detached enough to set them aside when they become destructive or illegitimate. We would not want supersocialized paragons walking on all fours or sleeping in trees long after these behaviors had lost any positive value for either the individual or his culture. But a person who is fully socialized—in the way this is connoted by the So scale taken alone—might run the risk of behaving in just this sort of repetitive and fruitless manner.

Another concept or another dimension is therefore needed, a notion with which one can moderate the idea of socialization so as to identify people who can live comfortably with others, who can respond to both ordinary and extraordinary stress, and who can also, when appropriate, rise above or depart from the mores and institutionalized givens of social control. From the standpoint of measurement, the So scale, to serve this broader function, must be supplemented by or even moderated by other scales that can detect the rule-innovating potentialities too little presaged by So alone.

It is obvious, of course, that in using any multivariate instrument one must be alert to patterns and combinations; in fact, the more complex and multifaceted the behavioral syndrome to be forecast, the more likely that a cluster or combination of variables will exceed the best that can be achieved with a single scale.

In any combination of scales on the inventory intended to assess social maturity, one would expect the So scale to appear. However, socialization is not synonymous with social maturity. Socialization involves the internalization of rules, constraints, and values, with an emphasis on their preservation. Social maturity, in oppressive circumstances, will lead to the abandonment of old order and a search for new principles of governance. The highly socialized individual can live by the rules, even when repressive, and may welcome their demands. The socially mature individual, on the contrary, although able to conform, is receptive to change and experiment, and under repressive conditions may set himself against the established order. The implication of this for measurement is that one should expect a combination of scales to be superior to the So scale alone in diagnosing higher levels of maturity.

In a prior study (Gough, 1966), an attempt was made to develop a diagnostic index of social maturity. CPI protocols for 2,146 nondelinquent males, including high school and college students and adults, were contrasted with protocols for a sample of 881 delinquents tested in institutions and juvenile halls. For the purposes of the analysis, the nondelinquents were visualized as more mature and the delinquents as less. Using a stepwise multiple regression routine, the following equation was developed:

$$\text{Social maturity} = 28.062 + .148Do + .334Re + .512So \\ - .317Gi - .274Cm + .227Fx^*$$

This equation was then cross-validated on a new sample of 2,482 nondelinquent males versus 409 delinquents, giving rise to a point-biserial correlation of .63. Weights in the equation are for use with raw scores on the CPI, and the constant of 28.062 is set so that the mean of an unselected sample of males will converge on 50.00. The standard deviation of scores computed on the equation is typically about 3.50.

The differentiation between delinquents and nondelinquents in cross-validating samples may be represented graphically, as shown in Figure 3. The areas under the two smoothed frequency distributions have been adjusted for base rates, so that the ratio of the smaller to the larger is .33. The optimal cutting point for diagnosing immaturity, or more precisely, a disposition toward delinquency, occurs at the intersection of the two curves, at a score of about 45.5.

In addition to this discrimination between delinquents and nondelinquents, the index was able to differentiate between cheaters and non-cheaters in college examinations, delinquents and nondelinquents in cross-cultural testing, and between students nominated as high or low on responsibility by high school principals. Recently, Lefcourt (1968) found the index capable of identifying the single individual in a college class who had committed an antisocial act detrimental to the welfare of all of the students.†

DIFFERENTIATION AT HIGHER LEVELS

Evidence in the initial report dealt principally with distinctions between delinquent and nondelinquent or with diagnostic criteria of under-

---

*The scales in the equation, respectively, are Dominance, Responsibility, Socialization, Good Impression, Communality, and Flexibility.
† See the Lefcourt paper immediately following.

socialized behavior. There is also a need for evidence showing that the index can differentiate within subsamples of adequately or even well socialized males. The ultimate goal of the index, it should be reiterated, is to function at the highest as well as at the lowest regions of the continuum.

One line of inquiry on this topic is found in Table 6. From the author's files, protocols of gainfully employed adult males were selected, wherever an occupational group had been tested that was large enough to provide reliable data.

Fourteen such samples were assembled, representing the occupations listed in the table. Names of the occupations were typed on rating sheets, and samples of 85 male and female University of California

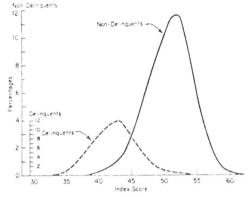

Fig. 3. Graphic representation of differentiation between delinquents and nondelinquents.

TABLE 6

Social Maturity Scores for the Occupational Groups Indicated

Occupational group	N	Ratio scaling		Maturity index	
		Score	Rank*	Score†	Rank*
Industrial research scientists	45	389	1	54.5	4
Dentists	47	369	2	54.6	3
Architects	124	366	3	54.0	6
Bankers	49	319	4	54.9	2
College and high school counselors	66	310	5	57.4	1
City school administrators	200	301	6	54.3	5
Psychiatric aides	180	296	7	52.9	7
Business executives	95	288	8	52.2	8
Correctional officers	192	265	9	45.1	13
Electronic technicians	57	264	10	46.3	12
Shop foremen	45	237	11	47.6	11
Military officers	200	220	12	50.5	9
Regional sales supervisors	85	198	13	49.3	10
Machinists	105	179	14	43.1	14

* Rank-order correlation between the two ranks = .83.

† Scores are in standard form, with a mean of 50 and a standard deviation of 10.

undergraduates were asked to scale them for social maturity, in comparison with "prison inmates," using the constant sum method. In each pairing, using this method, a total of 100 points is divided between the two groups according to the degree of "social maturity" manifested. Thus, if a student were comparing bankers and prison inmates, he might give 62 points to the bankers and 38 to the inmates.

The mean number of points given to each occupational group was then divided by the mean number of points given to the inmates in that same comparison, and this ratio became the scale value for the occupational group. The anchor point, prison inmates, received a scale value of 100. This scaling procedure yields a measure having both additive and multiplicative scale properties. In the judgment of these 170 students, it follows, dentists are 3.7 times as socially mature as prison inmates, and architects are twice as mature as machinists. The internal reliability of scaling was high for each sex, and the male-female corrected reliability was greater than .95. In Table 6, the 14 occupational groups are listed in rank order according to the ratio values assigned.

For each S in the table, a score on the social maturity index was calculated and then the means were computed for the 14 occupational groups. In the previous paper (Gough, 1966), the mean for 2,482 males was 50.76 and the standard deviation, 3.52; these normative statistics were used to convert the 14 occupational means to standard scores with mean of 50 and standard deviation of 10.

The correspondence between occupational rankings by the ratio scaling method and by the social maturity index on the personality inventory is quite remarkable, as indicated by the *rho* of .83. The two largest discrepancies are on the college and high school counselors and correctional officers, the equation ranks the counselors in first place, whereas the students placed them in fifth; the students ranked the correctional officers in ninth place, whereas the equation put them in the thirteenth position.

The sampling of men within each of the occupational groups listed in Table 6 was far too casual and unplanned to permit any firm conclusions to be drawn about true merit, and it is also apparent that there are many important occupations unrepresented. The primary purpose of the analysis was simply to indicate an acceptable correspondence between ratio scale rankings of the occupations and rankings derivable from the social maturity index; this correspondence is indicated by the rank-order correlation of .83. The equation, one may say, does appear to differentiate meaningfully within the more socialized portion of the continuum.

CASE ILLUSTRATIONS

Case history evidence may also be presented to indicate the meaning of high scores on the index. These illustrations are drawn from data on file at the University of California Institute of Personality Assessment and Research in Berkeley. Scores on the social maturity equation were computed for some 400 men who had been assessed in the past 10 years, and from this distribution the two highest-scoring individuals were selected. The raw scores for thse Ss were 59 and 60, which in standard scores would become 73 and 76. It might be mentioned that for approximately 3,000 nondelinquent males on whom the index has been computed, approximately 1 percent have raw scores of 58 and above.

The assessment files for these two individuals were then examined to see how they had been described and evaluated by the psychologists who had observed them. Two kinds of description have been selected for presentation: Q-sort characterizations and a brief personality resumé written by a life history interviewer or assessment director.

The first S had a computed score of 59 on the index, which in standard score form would be 73. He was described by Os on two Q-sort decks, an experimental 50-item set, and Block's 100-item California Q sort (Block, 1961). The six most extremely sorted items from the former deck were as follows:

(a) Most characteristic qualities
1. Independent, intelligent, and self-reliant; values achievement.
2. Honest and direct in behavior; mature and realistic in outlook.
3. Is an effective leader; able to elicit the response and cooperation of others.

(b) Least characteristic qualities
1. Coarse and vulgar; inclined to behave in a crude and impolite fashion.
2. Lazy, indifferent about duties and obligations; generally undependable and immature.
3. Poorly organized; unable to concentrate attention and effort on intelligent problems.

The eight most salient descriptions from Block's deck were:

(a) Most descriptive statements
1. Is a genuinely dependable and responsible person.
2. Is productive; gets things done.
3. Appears straightforward, forthright, candid in dealings with others.
4. Is cheerful.

(b) Least descriptive statements
1. Characteristically pushes and tries to stretch the limits; sees what he can get away with.
2. Is basically distrustful of people in general; questions their motivations.
3. Feels a lack of personal meaning in life.
4. Is guileful and deceitful, manipulative, opportunistic.

The personality resumé for this man comes from the pen of the life history interviewer:

This open-faced, pleasant subject was spontaneous and interested during the interview, requiring a minimum of questioning from the interviewer. At first he appeared to be conventional, somewhat passive, and not too complex a person; but this is deceiving, for he is, indeed, a complex person—and a most effective one.

He has partly internalized a granite-hard New England father of the utmost individuality and a mother with high ambitions for her children. Rather than being at the mercy of these internalized influences, the subject seems to have turned them to his service. He is insightful, sensitive, self-expressive, unconventional in the sense of being free from pressures to conform, and is concerned with social pressures presently in force which demand conformity of the individual. He is self-directed and desires other people to be similarly free.

It should be noted that this resumé stresses the very factor the index seeks to identify: the capacity to be rationally and ethically unconventional.

S 2 had a raw score of 60 on the index, converting to a standard score of 76. From the consensual description provided on Block's Q deck, the 12 most differentiating items have been selected for citation:

(a) Most descriptive statements
   1. Is cheerful.
   2. Is a talkative individual.
   3. Emphasizes being with others; gregarious.
   4. Is a genuinely dependable and responsible person.
   5. Behaves in a sympathetic or considerate manner.
   6. Behaves in an ethically consistent manner; is consistent with own personal standards.

(b) Least descriptive statements
   1. Is guileful and deceitful, manipulative, opportunistic.
   2. Shows condescending behavior in relations with others.
   3. Is self-defeating.
   4. Gives up and withdraws where possible in the face of frustration and adversity.
   5. Is basically distrustful of people in general; questions their motivations.
   6. Reluctant to commit self to any definite course of action; tends to delay or avoid action.

The character resumé for this S was as follows:

Though suffering from a severe physical handicap, this subject radiates a cheerful self-confidence about himself and his career. He expects the world to be good to him, because, as he says, it always has been. His manner in meeting others is cheerful and friendly, indeed warm. He is outward-going and alert, energetic and enthusiastic. Yet there is nothing effusive or pushing about him.

Rather, there is a genuine self-acceptance and warm acceptance of others. He is clearly intelligent and aesthetically sensitive. In his work he rejects a cold analytical analysis of his problems, preferring to give expression to his feelings and intuitions. Though open to and responsive to complexities he seeks simplicity. He is, in summary, a very human being.

In both the Q-sort and narrative descriptions of the S, there is emphasis on his human qualities, acceptance of self and others, and openness to new experience. He appears to be, in short, highly socialized without being over-socialized.

Two brief case examples, it is recognized, do not establish validity, but they do serve to illustrate the kinds of findings one can anticipate in intensive, individual study of Ss scoring high on the social maturity index.

COMMENT

The data presented above are not offered to prove a point, but rather to illuminate a problem. Whenever one deals with dimensional phenomena, he must pay attention to individuals at every interval of severity. Crime and delinquency are pressing social problems, but conceptually and theoretically they represent behavior in only one zone of the socialization continuum. The interest of the psychologist is just as strongly in the deviant at the other pole, and particularly in those deviants who somehow manage to achieve socialization without being subdued by it. Research workers are now paying attention, all over the world, to the intellectually gifted, to the aesthetically talented, and to the creative and innovative. One may hope that equally intensive effort will soon be invested in the study of individuals of exceptional social maturity. The index described in this paper seeks to provide a relatively reliable and convenient method for identifying such individuals.

$\triangledown \ \triangledown \ \triangledown$

SERENDIPITOUS VALIDITY STUDY OF GOUGH'S SOCIAL MATURITY INDEX

Herbert M. Lefcourt

Gough (1966) presented an equation comprised of weighted scale values from the California Psychological Inventory (CPI) which he entitled a measure of social maturity. He reported that the equation differentiated delinquents from nondelinquents in both the United States and Italy and distinguished between cheaters and noncheaters on course examinations and between high school students judged as being more or less responsible.

The following report presents an unpremeditated validity study which suggests that the social maturity index may be a powerful measure for predicting antisocial behavior. Because of the spontaneous, even accidental, way in which the data to be reported in this paper were obtained, a narrative style of relating the findings has been adopted.

METHOD

During this writer's course in personality theory at the University of Waterloo, 66 students were required to complete different personality tests each week, which were subsequently discussed in relation to given personality theories. The first test in this sequence was the CPI. As an exercise for his course in computer programming, the class graduate assistant* developed a program for Gough's six-scale social maturity index. Since the class was large, the writer had little or no opportunity to become familiar enough with the students so that names and faces could be matched.

Toward the middle of the semester, the midterm paper involved the students in a pursuit of all available data regarding one of the mass murderers–Charles Whitman, Perry Smith (from Truman Capote's *In Cold Blood*), or Richard Speck. The students were to gather all relevant behavioral data and attempt to subsume such data within differing theoretical frameworks. Two weeks before the due date, the writer was informed that someone had razored out the newspaper articles from the library newspapers which were most revelatory about the Whitman case. The class members expressed shock, anger, and some embarrassment over such student misbehavior. Rather than being angered, the writer accepted the deed as a challenge and quietly wondered whether he might be able to identify the "criminal" with Gough's social maturity index.

A second criterion for this index was later established in the grading of the midterm paper. The papers were graded from A through D, wherein A represented good use of behavioral data and theoretical constructs, B reflected good use of one but not the other, C reflected mediocre use of both, and D represented not merely a failure but an attempted bluff on the part of the student. If a student received a D grade on the paper, it indicated that he had failed to gather behavioral information about his subject; in addition, it indicated that the student had been unresponsive to the course content, which had stressed the use of theoretical constructs. At best, a paper with this grade would be judged as a bluff. Since this course was largely comprised of third-year

* The author wishes to express thanks to Kirk Blankstein for his help in making the investigation possible.

undergraduates, sheer academic ineptitude would not be the prime cause for such a grade.

RESULTS AND DISCUSSION

Gough (1966) reported that a cutting score of 44 correctly identified 73 percent of his American delinquent sample, while misidentifying only 4 percent of the nondelinquent sample. As indicated in Table 7 the social maturity mean (based on the six-variable index) was 52.4 (SD = 3.2), with only nine students having scores lower than 50 and only one scoring less than the cutoff score of 44 (43.3). At this point, the writer

TABLE 7

DISTRIBUTION OF SCORES ON THE SIX-VARIABLE SOCIAL MATURITY INDEX IN GOUGH'S DELINQUENT AND NONDELINQUENT AND LEFCOURT'S STUDENT SAMPLES

Score	Gough		Lefcourt students‡
	ND*	D†	
62	1		
61	1		1
60	3		0
59	10		0
58	24		2
57	53		3
56	98		2
55	134		4
54	226		13
53	265	2	13
52	289	5	4
51	303	4	6
50	239	4	9
49	210	6	2
48	195	13	3
47	147	18	1
46	101	26	0
45	72	33	2
44	37	45	0
43	31	50	1
42	15	49	
41	12	37	
40	9	34	
39	1	35	
38	6	20	
37		14	
36		9	
35		3	
34		1	
33		1	

* N = 2,482, M = 50.76, SD = 3.52.
† N = 409, M = 42.59, SD = 3.53.
‡ N = 66, M = 52.37, SD = 3.19.

might have been left guessing but for a fortuitous happenstance. In speaking with a student from the class about the offense, he learned that the student knew the identity of the culprit. With assurance that there was no punitive intent, but mere interest in test validity, the student was led to reveal the name of the guilty party. As this writer guessed, the one student below the cutoff point was the offender.

The second validation came in midterm grading, which was done blind, and which produced high interrater agreement (98% between two raters on a subsample of 15). The average grade was 5.6 (B− = 5, B = 6), with SD = 1.7. Of the three lowest persons on the social maturity index (below 45), there were one D and two C− grades. As mentioned above, such low grades were used to indicate bluffing attempts.

One last point of interest involves the students' desire to learn from prior mistakes. When final exams were returned, 64 students came to recover their marked papers. The two students who failed to pick up their finals were the two who had scored at the very bottom of the social maturity distribution.

It may be concluded that Gough's social maturity index provided an amazingly accurate measure for identifying the perpetrator of an antisocial act, singling out a particular individual from 66 possibilities, and for predicting irresponsible behavior in two other instances.

A most comprehensive summary of all details concerning the California Psychological Inventory has recently been published by Megargee (1972), which should be consulted by the interested student concerning the development, validation, and related research dealing with this inventory.

THE usual admonition to the respondent, especially when administering personality and interest inventories, is that he record his first impressions and avoid excessive mulling over of individual test or inventory items. This is one of the means by which the test administrator hopes to minimize social desirability effects or faking good and the like. The result is an expected increase in the validity of the final reporting on the answer sheet. There is also, of course, the matter of avoiding overlong testing sessions that would enormously increase the cost of test administration.

The following report by Oseas, a condensed version of the original which appeared in a 1966 issue of the *Journal of Counseling Psychology*, is of interest because the respondent (who was also the test administrator in this instance) did just the opposite and took, overall, about 9 months to complete a personality inventory that consisted of a mere 187 items. He managed this by attempting to devote exclusive attention to one item per day and by letting his introspections flow as freely as possible. His report is interesting since he then compares this extended administration with the standard administration he began with. Dr. Oseas currently is Professor of Psychology and director of the Psychological Services Center at the University of Cincinnati.

"GIVE THE FIRST NATURAL ANSWER"

Leonard Oseas

In a famous James Thurber cartoon, a colossal, house-engirdling female dominates an entire domestic landscape, including an obviously intimidated little man. The cartoon requires no caption since the look of stern disapproval on the face of the female speaks volumes. It is curious how like Thurber's portrayal of the war between the sexes is the relationship between the principals in the test-taking encounter.

The main actors in both the testing and domestic situations are natural adversaries whose needs for each other somehow manage to overcome apparently instinctive mutual distrust. The dominant partner, especially, attributes to the weaker a certain readiness to equivocate and lie and takes pains to let it be known that this weasel-like penchant does not go unnoticed. Consider, for example, the usual instructions on a personality questionnaire. Almost invariably they include an appeal to the examinee to give honest answers to test questions. At the same time, the ingenuity with which the test-maker provides against lapses from truthfulness, e.g., by presenting the examinee with questions whose intentions are artfully oblique and by building into his instrument subtly contrived (but cynically labeled) "lie" scales, indicates that the test-maker's faith in the efficacy of appeals to reason and fair play is not boundless.

It was in the context of such melancholy reflections that disturbing doubts about the real purpose behind another common innocent-appearing instruction crept into my thoughts. I refer to the caution to "avoid pondering over individual questions." On the surface this appears to be a reasonable condition. But why should the examiner actually prefer ill-considered, superficial answers over those arrived at after careful deliberation? Time considerations excepted, might it not make good sense, and contribute to the development of mutual trust and respect, to permit the examinee to spend as much time as *he* thinks necessary to select an answer *he* could feel confident was truly descriptive of his personality?

Since I was both examiner and examinee in the exercise I am about to describe, time considerations could be managed without prejudice to either party. Moreover, as examiner I would be privy to the innermost thoughts of the examinee, and this arrangement admirably suited the larger purpose of the present undertaking.

THE EXERCISE

The 16 P.F. Test (Cattell, Saunders, & Stic, 1957) was selected for the exercise for practical reasons, the main one being my previous unfamiliarity with it. The test is a product of Cattell and his associates at the Institute for Personality and Ability Testing (IPAT) and is based on his source trait conceptions of personality structure (Cattell, 1957). The instructions to the testee are standard for this type of paper-and-pencil personality inventory. One is urged to give first "natural" answers, to avoid as much as possible resorting to the middle of three possible choices, to answer every question "somehow," and to resist the temptation to impress the examiner by merely marking what seems the "right thing to say."

The first step in the present investigation was to be a good subject: I took the test under standard conditions.

Then, in a second administration, I chose to ignore the admonition against spending too much time on a given item. I pondered each question exhaustively, associating freely to its stimulus, dredging up all pertinent memories, and weighing all the evidence before committing myself to an answer. To do justice to all of the 187 items of Form A at one sitting would be a physical and psychological impossibility, so I decided instead to consider only one item a day. The same time each working day (ten minutes before the morning coffee break) was set aside for undivided attention to the task. One obvious consequence of the one-a-day format was that I exceeded the suggested 30 minutes to complete the entire test. My delinquency extended roughly nine months. During the one-a-day administration, I taped the responses to several widely separated and arbitrarily selected questions.

I repeated the standard administration approximately six weeks after finishing the 187th question. Form A was used for all three administrations, and all were scored after completion of the third test administration.

RESULTS

If the arrangement of being both examiner and examinee nicely circumvents the troublesome matter of confidentiality, there is still the problem of selecting the material to report. In the account which follows, I am not unmindful of the danger of a breach of good taste. Still, the occasion calls for candor if it is to have any relevance at all for a psychology of test-taking.

My suspicions that the task I had set for myself would be a difficult one were quickly and repeatedly confirmed. The expected discomfort of any prolonged introspection was intensified by the effort to stay within the cramped confine of a particular item at a particular time. The flow of associations was anything but smooth. The exhilarating sense of embarking on an adventure (where who knows what undreamed-of treasures might be unearthed) with which each new item was greeted dissipated with disheartening regularity in an arid associational wasteland. Promising trains of thought got derailed or hung-up on maddening broken-record repetitions.

There was a distressingly high proportion of static to substance in the typical response. Distractions came mainly from two sources: from an over-seeing ego which, while observing itself functioning, did not hesitate to make passing comments on these observations; and from the nagging reminders of a hyper-alert superego—I had answered affirmatively question 2, *vis.*, "I am ready to answer each question as truthfully as possible."

No amount of conscious effort succeeded entirely in preventing recollections from prior responses from intruding on ongoing ones. Once admitted to the associational process, these memory traces exerted a definite influence in one of two ways: as an impetus toward response consistency or as a temptation to compensate for response excesses; i.e., to bank deviation credits. ("If I am deliberately deviant now, I will not need to reveal myself in some more damaging way later.") Thus, it proved exceedingly difficult to be indifferent to the personality picture being etched item by item and to resist influencing this process in a favorable way.

Certain answers did indeed seem to be the "natural" ones which the test authors mention in their instructions. These responses seemed so instantaneously right, and they exerted such a strong pull, that it represents no great distortion of the subjective experience of responding to them to note the similarity of this process to tropisms in lower species. The impulse to retreat to these compellingly right answers before the other alternatives were given full consideration had to be opposed with an effort of the will.

The whole range of emotions entered, and in some subtle ways no doubt, influenced the associational process. However, it would be less than candid to fail to note the prevalence of peevish feelings. Most often my annoyance was aimed in a vague and impersonal way at the unknown test-makers who, in my extremity, I was tempted to hold responsible for (*a*) using unclear language, (*b*) my failure to arrive at satisfactory choices and (*c*) subjecting me to an arduous, disagreeable experience! It will come as no surprise that impatience to be done with a question, regardless of the correctness of the answer, was among the more urgent sentiments.

The disagreeable aspects of the exercise were quickly overshadowed by the surge of relief upon completing it and by the quieter satisfaction I found in the conviction that the personality picture that would emerge must be a valid one. How does this "real me" born of nine months labor compare with its 30 minute (or instant) counterpart?

As the profiles in Figure 4 testify, the resemblance is a close one. Comparing the responses on the extended administration with those of

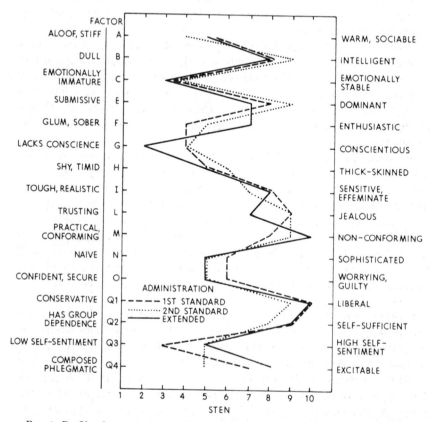

FIG. 4. Profiles from standard and extended administrations of the 16 P.F. test.

the first standard administration, and disregarding the direction of any changes, 138 answers were identical, 38 shifted one position and 11 shifted two positions. The comparable figures for the two standard administrations were 141, 41 and 5. There was somewhat less reliance on noncommittal "b" answers in the extended case: 50, compared with 55 on the first and 61 on the second standard administrations.

On only three factors, F ("Surgency"), G ("Superego strength"), and L ("Pretension," or paranoid orientation) does the difference between the extended and *both* of the standard administration scores equal or exceed two stens. (Stens are ten-step equivalents of the more familiar stanines.) The higher F in the extended case indicates a greater degree of happy-go-lucky optimism, the lower G suggests less perseverence and more indolence, and the lower L depicts a more trusting outlook! Thus, the very qualities demanded by the task were the ones to diminish in the personality portrait that is the end product of that task, as though they were somehow depleted in the process.

That such anguish as characterized the experience apparently could father a picture of light-hearted optimism is one of the darker mysteries and ironies of the undertaking. It is all the more mystifying in view of the fact that I am confident my mood was elevated on the day I took the test the first time. Consider the following verbatim extracts from notes made just prior to the first administration: "Spirits good . . . slight undercurrent of apprehension (anticipation?) . . . F's visit stirring up some excitement . . . Kids doing well . . . Health fine, beat C. at handball . . ." It appears that either (a) I was deluding myself about the true quality of affect I was experiencing on both the standard and extended administrations, or (b) the choice of answers to questions pertaining to feelings is not positively related to the actual emotional state while responding, and may, in fact, be inversely related to it.

The result that most tempts me to self-justification, however, is the reduction in G, the superego factor. The test authors say of G:

This factor . . . is characterized most by energy and persistence. The hypothesis may be set up that (G) corresponds to the super-ego in psychoanalysis. On the whole, it best depicts the regard for moral standards, the tendency to drive the ego and to restrain the id, which are most frequently regarded as marks of the super-ego (Cattell *et al.*, 1957, p. 13).

Since I consider myself to be not less well endowed in these qualities than the next man, I indignantly reviewed my responses to the ten items listed by the test authors as high scoring for G for a clue to where I might have incriminated myself. The three sample items below are quite representative of the ten. In each, the "a" answer is the high contributor; my responses are in italics:

Item 134: I think the police can be trusted not to ill-treat innocent people. (a) yes, (*b*) in between, (c) no.

Item 160: I always make a point, in deciding anything, to refer to basic principles of right conduct. (a) yes, (*b*) in between, (c) no.

Item 184: Everyone could make a success of his life with reasonable effort and perseverance. (a) yes, (b) in between, (*c*) no.

In my judgment, the *G* items are of the kind most likely to elicit socially desirable answers where such a set exists (and I would argue that it exists to some extent in the vast majority of persons). More to the point, however, is the fact that *G* was higher under the rushed conditions of the standard administrations. Thus, the succession of rapid, ill-considered decisions called for by the standard instructions appear to have encouraged the development of a response habit, even in the context of a personality not especially predisposed to it (if I interpret the entire test profile correctly). The "me" of the orthodox administrations is admittedly somewhat "nicer" by conventional standards, but I retain a strong personal preference for the more painfully arrived-at soul-searching *G* answers of the extended administration, incriminating though they may be.

The 16 P.F. Handbook provides 28 occupational and six clinical profiles against which an individual test profile may be compared by a simple goodness-of-fit procedure. The handbook gives no profile for the occupation of clinical psychologist, though the test authors suggest that the high *H* ("parmia") persons among them are likely to be the better group therapists. Similarly, they judge that sensitive clinicians may be distinguishable from ordinary psychometrists, and presumably from the tougher-minded actuarial-learning clinicians, by their greater "premsia" or high *I*. High *I* persons are said to be demanding, impatient and subjective, but these liabilities are apparently offset by the imaginativeness of their inner life and their ability to act on intuition.

CONCLUSIONS

I remember an almost off-hand comment made many years ago by a senior professor to a student who had cavalierly dismissed the meaning of a pure *C* Rorschach response. It was to the effect that the solutions to many of the fundamental riddles of human psychology were imbedded in that response if we had the wisdom and techniques for extricating them. The remark has equal cogency for the process of responding to a personality questionnaire item. Even allowing for the artifacts introduced by amplifying the response process in the manner of the present exercise, the subtlety, richness and complexity of that process was made abundantly evident. Any significant improvement in the efficiency of personality measurement devices might well depend upon our success in unravelling this inherent complexity. Concepts such as response set, focused as they must be on the end products of a process rather than on the process itself, may be inadequate to the task. Perhaps what is needed now is an imaginative assault on the intricacies of the examinee's interactions with the test parameters that stimulate and provoke him.

This experience has had its rewards on a purely personal level. It permitted me to become familiar with a sophisticated instrument and opened new possibilities for empathy with fellow examinees. I believe I know myself better for having gone through the experience; having done so, I would summarize it in the way that 15 million veterans are prone to speak of their army experiences: I would never willingly go through it again, but I would not have missed it for the world.

THE personal interview still remains probably the principal technique of assessing personality despite all that is known concerning its unreliability. The employment interview, in particular, is an example where the interview is used as a basis for decision (for example: to hire or not to hire). In an interesting series of studies in this type of interview situation conducted at McGill University, the focus was entirely on how judgments, both good and bad, were reached (Webster, 1964). Many of these studies reported were Ph.D. theses with, in the main, personnel officers of the Canadian Army cooperating as interviewers who talked with young men who wanted to enlist. (Enlistment in the Canadian Army differs from civilian employment only in that the recruit signs up for three years; the military competes in the open labor market with civilian employers who also see people who want to change jobs.)

The Webster summary of these researches is largely a mournful one. A bias is clearly established early in the interviews, and it tends to be followed either by a favorable or unfavorable decision about the candidate. The stereotype is not unique to the individual interviewer but is common to all such persons who have a modest amount of experience. Unfavorable impressions carry far more weight than do favorable ones. One of the McGill studies reported that even one unfavorable impression is followed by rejection in 90 percent of the cases (Webster, 1964, p. 87). The summary section of this volume begins: "This chapter would have been easier to write had the experiments reported not been undertaken. Furthermore, it would have been written differently and with more assurance. The studies reported have shaken the principal investigator's faith in the interview as an appraisal technique" (p. 101).

An example of these McGill studies, the research report by Dr. Rowe, utilizing the concept of "category width" derived from the cognition studies of Bruner at Harvard, is included. The original research constituted her Ph.D. dissertation at McGill and appeared in the *Journal of Applied Psychology* in 1963.

INDIVIDUAL DIFFERENCES IN SELECTION DECISIONS

Patricia M. Rowe

It is a well documented observation that when several personnel interviewers separately assess the same applicant they arrive at very dissimilar decisions. One conclusion frequently drawn from this finding is that personnel selection decisions based on interviews are extremely unreliable and, consequently, that selection procedures should be drastically modified. However, the observed individual differences among personnel interviewers should be of intrinsic interest to psychologists, and their study might eventually make it possible to control interview unreliability at its source—in the interviewer himself. In the closely related area of categorization of simple, inanimate objects, investigators have taken the approach of regarding unreliability as an individual difference problem. These investigators have been successful in isolating a number of "response styles" underlying individual differences in categorization or judgment.

One of these response styles has been termed "category width" by Bruner and his co-workers. A typical category-width study is that by Bruner and Tajfel (1961). Subjects first viewed a slide containing a cluster of 20 dots. Subsequently, they were presented with slides containing clusters of 20–30 dots and asked to judge for each stimulus whether or not it contained 20 dots. Category width was defined by the number of stimuli judged "20 dots," and subjects were classified as broad or narrow categorizers depending on whether they made many or few such judgments. In another paper Bruner (1957) suggested that the accessibility of a category (and thus category width) is determined by two factors— the learned probabilities of occurrence of events in the individual's world, and the search requirements that are dictated by his need states.

If the principle of category width applies to decisions about persons, it may be that much of the "unreliability" of selection decisions could be accounted for in terms of individual differences in the width of the category "acceptable applicants" among the interviewers. The present investigation was designed to test this notion, and, further, to examine the role of Bruner's two factors of past learning and present motivational state in determining category width.

METHOD

Subjects

Because previous studies (Webster, 1964) indicate that selection standards vary as a function of company employment practices and job requirements, it was necessary to use as subjects interviewers employed by the same company and regularly selecting employees for the same position. The most readily available group meeting these requirements was the Personnel Selection Service of the Canadian Army. Of the 263 Personnel Selection Officers (PSOs) first approached for this study, 146 completed all tests and constituted the sample of subjects.

Two characteristics of the Canadian Army should be mentioned here because of their relevance to the analysis of the data: (*a*) All Canadian servicemen are volunteers; in recent years there have been many more applications than openings. Consequently, the PSO must *select* some applicants and reject many more on other than medical grounds. (*b*) The PSOs in this study are of two types: Regular Force PSOs are those employed in the Army on a full-time basis; Militia PSOs are roughly equivalent to members of the Active Reserve in the United States, and serve in the Army for approximately one-half day per week.

Test Materials

Pilot studies had indicated that applicants themselves change as a function of being interviewed several times; therefore, written descriptions of applicants were chosen as stimuli. One hundred fictitious "applicant" descriptions were constructed from 60 characteristics, 30 favorable and 30 unfavorable. Each applicant description was composed of 6 of the 60 characteristics. Three of the characteristics were favorable, the other three unfavorable, arranged in random order. By using an equal number of favorable and unfavorable characteristics, individual differences were probably exaggerated, but on the other hand, the likelihood of obtaining spurious agreement among the subjects was reduced. The following is a sample item:

This applicant has no commitments: he is completely independent. He seems cocky, a bit of a smart aleck, ready to tell anybody off. He tends to be an active participant in outdoor activities. The applicant makes a good impression; his appearance, language, all round ability and bearing make him stand out in a group. He has often left jobs following disagreements with superiors. The applicant seems to be an argumentative person.

All descriptions were presented to the subjects as applicants for the Regular Force, Canadian Army, who had met minimum Infantry standards on all criteria. The task for the subject was to accept or reject each applicant. In addition to the 100 descriptions, a Characteristic Rating Scale was included in the test material. The subjects rated each of 119 characteristics, which included the 60 used in constructing the applicants, on a 7-point scale from 1 (very unfavorable) to 7 (very favorable). Thus the more favorably a characteristic was rated, the higher was its score.

Procedure

All test materials were mailed to the subjects, who returned the completed forms to the investigator. In order to get a better estimate of the reliability of the decisions, the applicant descriptions were mailed in three groups (consisting of 35, 35, and 30 descriptions, respectively). The Characteristic Rating Scale was mailed separately after the judgments had been received.

RESULTS

The mean number of applicants (descriptions) accepted by the 146 subjects was 34.86 out of 100, with a standard deviation of 20.02, and with a range from 0 to 92 applicants accepted. An analysis of variance, in which the variation between subjects was compared to the variation within subjects from one mailing of the test to another, yielded an F of 17.00 ($p < .01$), and thus demonstrated significant individual differences in the number of applicants accepted. Moreover, the correlations between the numbers of applicants accepted in the three mailings of the descriptions showed a high degree of within-individual consistency. The correlation between Parts 1 and 2 was .849; between Parts 2 and 3, .863; and between Parts 1 and 3, .828. It may be concluded, therefore, that there are both significant between-individual differences and within-individual consistencies in the width of the category acceptable applicants.

Not only do the subjects vary in the number of applicants accepted, but also, the applicants themselves differ in their likelihood of being accepted. The mean number of acceptances received by the 100 applicants was 50.89 out of 146, with a standard deviation of 26.51, and with a range of 8–116 acceptances received. Because of these differences in applicant acceptability we may raise the question of whether the differences in the category widths of the subjects are nonrandom—that is, do the subjects, regardless of the number of applicants they accept, tend to select those applicants most frequently accepted by the group as a whole? Such an analysis is equivalent to determining the scalability of the subjects.

In the present study scalability was determined with Bryden's (1960) rank-biserial correlation. In all, 142 coefficients were calculated (in four cases the statistic was not applicable) of which the mean coefficient was .569, the standard deviation was .141, and the range was from .179 to .873. Of these coefficients, 132 were significant beyond the .01 level, 7 were significant at the .05 level, and 3 were not significant. It is clear that the subjects in this study are scalar—almost all PSOs, regardless of the number of applicants they accepted, tended to select those applicant descriptions most acceptable to the group as a whole.

Is the dimension of acceptability of the applicants related to any other properties of the applicants? The mean rating of each characteristic making up the applicant descriptions was determined from the Characteristic Rating Scale. These scores were then combined appropriately to yield two scores for each applicant description: the mean rating assigned the three favorable characteristics, and the mean rating assigned the three unfavorable characteristics. The correlations of the number of acceptances received with these two scores were .471 and .616, respectively; with the total of the two scores, .713; the multiple correlation was .801. Correlations of such magnitude indicate that the more favorably an applicant's characteristics were rated, the more frequently was he accepted by the subjects.

Now let us turn to a consideration of the sources of individual differences in category width. Table 8 presents the findings of an analysis of number of applicants accepted as a function of kind of service (Regular Force or Militia) and rank (Major, Captain, or Lieutenant). The difference between the Regular Force and Militia PSOs was determined by a *t*

TABLE 8

ANALYSIS OF NUMBER OF APPLICANT DESCRIPTIONS ACCEPTED BY KIND OF SERVICE AND RANK

Group	N	M	SD	t or F
Regular Force				
Majors	8	27.38	4.18	
Captains	28	28.78	20.04	$F = .06$
Lieutenants	5	31.00	10.22	
Militia				
Majors	31	26.29	15.29	
Captains	58	41.83	20.33	$F = 7.09†$
Lieutenants	16	41.81	21.38	
Regular Force	41	28.76	17.95	
Militia	105	37.24	20.28	$t = 2.33*$
Total Group	146	34.86	20.02	

* $p < .05$.
† $p < .01$.

test; differences between ranks were tested by one-way analyses of variance and the means compared two at a time. Regular Force PSOs accepted fewer applicants than did Militia PSOs, thus reflecting the different standards of acceptance in the ordinary duties of the two kinds of officers. Moreover, Militia Majors accepted fewer applicants than did Captains or Lieutenants, which suggests that with increasing experience in personnel selection the interviewer learns that not all men make good soldiers, and consequently reduces his number of acceptances.

The number of applicants accepted was also found to be related to the manner in which the subjects responded on the rating scale. For purposes of the present study the Characteristic Rating Scale consists of four types of characteristics: favorable ($N = 30$) and unfavorable ($N = 30$) characteristics used in constructing the applicants, and favorable ($N = 26$) and unfavorable ($N = 33$) characteristics not used in the descriptions. For each subject the mean rating assigned to each of these four subgroups of characteristics was computed. (The higher the mean, the more favorably were the characteristics of any type rated.) The correlations between the number of applicants accepted and the mean ratings of the characteristics used in the applicant descriptions were .308 (favorable) and .608 (unfavorable); for the characteristics not used in the descriptions they were .348 (favorable) and .495 (unfavorable); all correlations are significant beyond the .01 level. These correlations show that both favorable and unfavorable characteristics are rated more favorably by subjects who accepted many applicants than by those who accepted few.

DISCUSSION

To the extent that between-individual differences and within-individual consistencies in the width of the category acceptable applicants have been demonstrated, the present investigation has shown that the concept of category width is applicable to decisions in personnel selection. Although written descriptions were used as applicants in this study, this conclusion is at least warranted in the area of selection decisions (e.g., those concerning applicants for graduate studies) made on the basis of letters of recommendation to which the present descriptions bear much resemblance. It is not unreasonable to expect that similar, large individual differences may be found in other decision-making areas. For example, we might find that dentists vary in their judgments about "enough decay to necessitate extraction of the tooth," that judges differ regarding "seriousness of a particular crime," and that baseball umpires disagree on decisions of "within the strike zone."

Interviewers differ in the number of applicants they accept, but agree as to the relative acceptability of the various applicant descriptions. That is, regardless of the number of applicants a subject may accept, he tends to select those who are most acceptable to the group as a whole. It follows from this finding that in most cases a fairly accurate prediction of whether or not a particular subject will accept a particular applicant can be made from the knowledge of two variables: the rank order of that applicant in the whole group and the category width of that subject. Moreover, applicant rank order is not necessarily an ad hoc measure, but may be determined from how favorable his characteristics are. The importance of applicant rank order in decision making is not surprising; what the present study contributes is the fact that, because the interviewers are scalar, category width also plays a significant role in accounting for differences associated with selection decisions.

Several characteristics of the subjects were found to be indicative of the sources of individual differences in category width. Kind of service, rank, and ratings assigned to applicant characteristics were all related to the number of applicants accepted. Differences as a function of kind of service and rank are evidence for the importance of Bruner's (1957) two factors of motivational states and past learning in determining category width. The finding that subjects show closely related differences in their standards of acceptance of both applicants and single characteristics is further support for the notion that category width is a general trait displayed in a variety of decision situations.

To summarize, then, this study has emphasized certain characteristics of the interviewer in producing individual differences in selection decisions. Apparently, applicants can be meaningfully ordered along a dimension which is defined by how favorable their characteristics are. Whether a particular applicant will be accepted is a joint function of his position on this dimension and the category width of the interviewer he sees. Future investigations should be directed toward the relation between individual differences in category width and such variables as the accuracy of decisions, prescribed numbers of applicants to be accepted, and personality and motivational characteristics of the interviewer.

Interviews may also be studied for their effectiveness in the selection process, probably the most frequent use to which the interview is put. Mayfield's (1964) published review of all the relevant studies concerning selection interviewing goes back to the early 20th century. He concludes that structured interviews are to be preferred, especially because of their greater reliability; non-structured interviews, where the dialogue is allowed to flow without much direction, simply do not adequately cover the necessary topics. Regardless, the validities are usually of low magnitude. A characteristic prominent in all such studies is the paucity of replication. The McGill studies (Webster, 1964) are cited as an example of productive and promising research on the the interview, which if pursued further will pay off dividends.

ANOTHER useful measure of personality characteristics, frequently in a disguised form, is the application blank. These printed forms have been frequently turned into valid assessment devices after appropriate study and revision. The literature discussing this type of research is very voluminous and has typically concerned itself with the selection of sales personnel, although, clearly, such research could be valuable with many other groups such as college freshmen where such data has been validated and cross-validated to predict college success (Anastasi, Meade, & Schneiders, 1960).

One of the more "lowly" types of sales personnel is the door-to-door sales group recruited from teenage boys. (Offhand, it would be hard to imagine a potentially more difficult group with whom to work and especially when all recruiting and selection is done by mail.) For this reason, we have chosen to include the following study which successfully demonstrated how a research design, clearly at variance with the opinions of the sales departments for the company, produced clean results and which could be cross-validated. The study is a very clear illustration of how the employment of an objectively scored questionnaire, part of the application blank itself, could be economically handled via the mails and how it greatly reduced both sales and marketing costs.

Dr. Appel is Senior Vice President of Appel, Haley, Fouriezos Incorporated (consumer psychology research) in Mohegan Lake, New York; Dr. Feinberg is Professor of Psychology at Baruch College of the City University of New York. The article appeared in a 1969 issue of the *Journal of Applied Psychology.*

RECRUITING DOOR-TO-DOOR SALESMEN BY MAIL

Valentine Appel and M. R. Feinberg

The company which is the subject of the article is a direct seller, that is, a company which distributes its merchandise by means of door-to-door salesmen. The National Association of Direct Selling Companies, the trade association for the industry, reports that there are about 1,200 such companies doing business in the United States; and although the total volume of business done by these companies is not precisely known, the total volume of the 200 members of the association is approximately five billion dollars annually.

Like many direct sellers, this particular company recruits its sales force almost entirely by mail. Every week about 2,000 teenage boys apply for jobs as salesmen in response to direct mail solicitation and to newspaper and magazine advertisements. Applicants are then mailed sales materials following examination of their application blanks and a delinquency check of the company records. For many years, the application blank consisted only of the applicant's name address, age, sex, and a parental endorsement; and virtually all of the applicants who applied were accepted. Although this company has long been established and operates a very profitable business, under this system a large majority of the boys who were started each week failed to perform to the company's minimum standard of sales performance. A sales failure was defined as someone who did not return a sales volume more than sufficient to recover the cost of recruiting and the mailing of materials. Generally this was a person who voluntarily discontinued selling in the first month.

The situation presented an unusual research opportunity for improving the efficiency of the company's selection procedures. To add to the gravity of the problem, there are very few organizations—outside of the armed forces—where such large samples of personnel are continuously recruited to perform exactly the same job. Moreover, data were economically available. Since the company policy is to recruit through the mails, mail questionnaires were mandatory, and there was no question of nonrespondent bias, which is a major problem in most mail surveys.

THE RESEARCH PROGRAM

The research naturally divided itself into four basic parts: (a) a preliminary qualitative investigation (b) the development of questionnaire items, (c) tests using nonreturn of the questionnaire as a screening device, and (d) revision and validation of the questionnaire items. Although each phase of the program has been duplicated one or more times as more data were required, for simplicity of presentation only one study from each of the four phases will be described here.

Qualitative Investigation

The initial step was to conduct a series of informal personal interviews in various parts of the country among boys who had been previously classified as successful or unsuccessful. In addition, prior to interviewing the salesboys, personal interviews were conducted with members of the company's sales department having responsibility for recruitment and selection. As a result of the investigation, it became obvious that most of the company executives believed that the potentially successful salesboy was one who came from a lower income home in which money was not easy to come by, and where it was necessary for the children to earn their own spending money. The following quotations, each from a different interview, will illustrate:

A boy whose family is . . . preferably in the lower income brackets. Generally speaking, boys from higher income families can get money much easier than by selling.

A boy from a home with a number of brothers and sisters . . . from a home where his parents cannot give him too much. If he wants money, he must find a way to get it himself.

A boy from a broken home who needs to find a way of life . . . a boy who wants additional money because of limited parental income.

In contrast to these Horatio Alger expectations, the interviewers who visited the boys in their homes reported that the successful boys appeared to be ordinary middle class teenagers. The unsuccessful boys, however, showed a marked contrast. They were difficult to locate, because they did not appear to live in one place for any length of time; and the homes in which they had previously lived appeared typically to be run down. When the children were located, they were frequently found in households which had been deserted by one parent or the other, and in general their families were depressed economically.

Questionnaire Development

On the basis of the preliminary qualitative investigation, a series of eight multiple-choice questions was prepared for use in a mail questionnaire. These questions were specifically written to resolve the severe contradiction which existed between the prevailing opinion in the sales department and the reports of the interviewers who contacted the salesboys in the field.

Because of the sensitive nature of the data which were required, plus the fact that a mail questionnaire was to be employed, some disguise in questioning appeared to be in order. Accordingly, questions were written which were known or believed to be correlated with family cohesiveness and socioeconomic status, but which on the surface appeared not directly related. Such questions related to bicycle ownership, telephone subscription, participation with parents in recreational activities, use of money earned, and size of family.

The questionnaires were mailed to all the boys (approximately 2,000) who had been started as salesboys in a given week. By the close of tabulation exactly two-thirds of the questionnaires had been returned. The sample was then divided into random halves on an every other questionnaire basis. Using one of the random halves, the questionnaire responses of the successful boys were compared with those who were less successful.

This comparison, which is illustrated in Table 9, essentially confirmed the findings of the original qualitative study in which the boys were visited in their homes. Moreover, the data contradicted the prior opinions of the sales executives who believed that sales success came of economic need. Paradoxically, the reverse appeared to be true. Those who appeared least in need of money also appeared most likely to exert themselves to earn it. The successful boy, when compared with his unsuccessful counterpart, was more likely to own a bicycle (75% vs. 52%), participate in recreational activities with his parents, have a telephone at home, come from a family of less than six children, and so forth.

On the basis of this comparison, a unit-weighted scoring key was developed in which those responses which were characteristic of successful boys were scored +1 and those which were characteristic of unsuccessful boys were scored −1. All other responses were scored zero. This key was then applied to the remaining half-sample which had not been examined to this point. The total scores on the questionnaire were then related to whether or not each boy met the company's minimum standard of sales success.

The results of this analysis are summarized in Table 10 which divides the second half-sample into four groups: those who failed to return the questionnaire, and those who did return and who scored in the top, middle, and bottom thirds using the scoring key which had been independently developed using the first half-sample. By this device the percentage of successful applicants was increased from 8 to 59 percent, depending upon whether or not the questionnaire was returned and how well it scored.

Nonreturn as a Screening Device

Our intention in developing the questionnaire items was to produce material for inclusion in the application forms which were to be part of

TABLE 9

SOME OF THE DISCRIMINATING QUESTIONNAIRE RESPONSES

Questionnaire responses	Successful applicants	Unsuccessful applicants
Has a bicycle	75%	52%
Family receives a newspaper	72%	52%
Attended show or circus with parents	64%	43%
Has a telephone at home	63%	38%
Signed application in pen	59%	46%
Saves money earned	57%	38%
Family less than 6 children	54%	30%
Base: all returns*	195	365

* Actually these data are from a later mailing—a sample independent of the one upon which the original analysis was conducted and which confirmed the original findings.

TABLE 10

RELATIONSHIP BETWEEN QUESTIONNAIRE RESPONSE AND JOB SUCCESS

Applicants	Failed to return	Returned questionnaire and scored in		
		Bottom third	Middle third	Top third
Successful	8%	22%	46%	59%
Unsuccessful	92%	78%	54%	41%
Base: all applicants	309	221	205	198

the recruitment ads. It was never the intention to send a questionnaire to sales applicants as a second and separate mailing. The possibility, therefore, of using a second mailing and of screening out all those who failed to return the questionnaire, as implied by Table 10, was frankly unexpected. Moreover, due to the high cost of recruitment plus the limited availability of applicants, there was resistance by the sales department to the use of a second mailing because of the possibility that a large percentage of successful boys might be lost through their failure to return the questionnaire. In addition, there is a common belief among direct sellers that even a brief delay in placing sales material in the hands of sales applicants reduces the probability of their being successful. Any delay is presumed to reduce the motivation of the applicant.

There was the additional question of whether the failure of the unsuccessful applicants to return the questionnaire would be predictive of their later failure or whether the nonreturn was caused by their prior failure. After all, the questionnaires were received by the applicants following receipt of merchandise to sell, and it was entirely likely that the decision not to return the questionnaire was prompted by their prior sales failure.

In order to resolve these doubts a special test was conducted involving 483 sales applicants who were divided into two matched samples on an every-other-name basis. One sample—the screened sample—was mailed a questionnaire and then merchandise to sell only upon return of the completed questionnaire. The unscreened sample was mailed merchandise immediately as per the usual procedure, and no questionnaire was sent at all. The results of this test are summarized in Table 10 from which two conclusions may be drawn: (a) The screening did not reduce the percentage of successful applicants (10% in the screened sample and 9% in the unscreened sample), and (b) the use of the questionnaire as a screening device had effectively eliminated half the unsuccessful applicants (45 out of 90%).

Armed with this information, the company adopted the technique of using a separate mail questionnaire. The nonreturn of this questionnaire was then employed as a screening device.

Questionnaire Revision

To this point, the scoring of the questionnaire was not included as a step in the selection procedure for the same reason that the company was initially reluctant to use the nonreturn of the questionnaire as a screening device. The limited supply of applicants and the need to maintain sales volume made it necessary to maintain a minimum sales staff, however inefficient that sales staff might be. Moreover, because the scoring key had been developed upon a sample of boys who may have already experienced some measure of success or failure prior to having received the questionnaire, there was a natural reluctance to adopt the scoring key under conditions where the questionnaire had to be returned before the merchandise could be sent.

However, since use of the new questionnaire had now been adopted as standard procedure, it became a simple matter to conduct additional screening studies to add questionnaire items, to delete others, and to improve the scoring key. Finally, as a result of a series of tests involving over 20,000 boys, a 7-item questionnaire, printed on a $4^{1}/_{2} \times 8$ business reply card, was developed to be mailed out on receipt of a sales application. On the basis of these tests the questionnaire was demonstrated to predict with sufficient accuracy as to be made operational which applicants would later be successful and which would not.

The data from the most recent such tests are summarized in Table 11 which divides 560 applicants who returned the questionnaire into two groups: those who were successful and those who were not. For each of these two groups the percentages of applicants scoring in top, middle, and bottom thirds are shown. From this, it can be seen that by rejecting all those who failed to score in at least the middle third, 44 percent of the potentially unsuccessful candidates who returned the questionnaire at the cost of 16 percent of the success could be eliminated.

The estimated utility of the entire program, including the use of nonreturn of the questionnaire as a screening device plus the additional screening following scoring of the questionnaire, can be calculated from the data presented in Tables 11 and 12. Table 11 determined that nonreturn of the questionnaire eliminated 50 percent of the unsuccessful applicants at a cost of virtually none of the successes. Table 12 further determined that if all questionnaire returnees who scored in the bottom third were rejected, 44 percent of the failures who were not screened out on the basis of questionnaire nonreturn would be eliminated. Since we estimate that 50 percent of the potentially unsuccessful applicants were already screened out by their failure to return the questionnaire, it follows that 44 percent of unsuccessful returnees represents an additional 22 percent of all unsuccessful applicants. From this comes the estimate that the program was able effectively to eliminate about three fourths (50 plus 22%) of the sales failures at a cost of about one fifth (16%) of the successes.

TABLE 11

NONRETURN OF THE QUESTIONNAIRE AS A SCREENING DEVICE

Type of applicant	Screened sample	Unscreened sample
Successful	10%	9%
Unsuccessful	45%	91%
Screened out*	45%	—
Base: all applicants	241	242

* Questionnaire not returned.

TABLE 12

PERCENTAGES OF SUCCESSFUL AND UNSUCCESSFUL APPLICANTS REJECTED AT THREE
CUTTING POINTS

Cutting point	Successful applicants	Unsuccessful applicants
Top third	57%	27%
Middle third	27%	29%
Bottom third	16%	44%
Base: all returns*	195	365

* Individual item responses reported in Table 8.

DISCUSSION

Although the use of biographical data in the selection of sales personnel has a history dating back nearly fifty years, the present study provides an unusually clear example of how the use of an objectively scored questionnaire, economically administered through the mail, was able effectively to reduce sales and marketing costs. The study again points up the substantial discrepancy which sometimes exists between management opinion and what the market facts actually are. A similar discrepancy was previously demonstrated in a study by Blum and Appel (1961) relating to package design. That study showed the complete inability of industrial designers and marketing management to predict consumer tastes and perceptions. The present study demonstrates how seriously the discrepancy between what the facts actually were and what they were believed to be had seriously limited the effectiveness of the company's sales and marketing program.

ESPECIALLY in the area of personality measurement, one is often forced to rely on trait ratings for criterion data simply because few, if any, objective standards of performance are available. Ratings by supervisors are certainly the most frequently used device for learning about an individual's merit, temperamental characteristics, research competence, and a host of other traits in which an organization or immediate supervisor is interested. Writers of letters of recommendation frequently are asked to fill out some form of graphic rating scale on a candidate about whom they are writing; this scale may determine, in the last analysis, whether the candidate gets the post or gains admission to a graduate school or passes through the selection screen. It should then be obvious that the reliability and validity of the ratings given should be known, and that the rating scales used should be true psychological scales. However, the usual trend is to employ merely intuitive scales where large halo effects are typically demonstrated.

In the following research paper, Smith and Kendall have described a technique by which rating scales—in this case to be used in the evaluation of nursing performance—are anchored to examples of expected behavior. The scales they finally produce, while obviously fakeable, call for the voluntary cooperation of the rater and ask the rater questions he can honestly answer, rather than attempting to trick him in the manner of a forced-choice situation. And the reliabilities are impressive.

The Smith-Kendall technique has recently been successfully implemented at Cornell with approximately 900 short interviews for various student positions (Maas, 1965). The usual adjective rating scales were originally tried; each candidate was interviewed twice, but only very modest reliabilities resulted. Significant improvement on this score was observed when the scaled expectation technique was introduced.

Dr. Smith, at Cornell University when this research was done, is now Professor of Psychology at Bowling Green University, Ohio. She is also an industrial consultant to Cain-Smith Associates, where her work is largely concerned with management assessment.

Dr. Kendall at the time of this publication (*Journal of Applied Psychology,* 1963) was Chairman of the Department of Psychology at Simon Fraser University in British Columbia.

RETRANSLATION OF EXPECTATIONS: AN APPROACH TO THE CONSTRUCTION   UNAMBIGUOUS AN- CHORS FOR RATING SCALES

Patricia Cain Smith and L. M. Kendall

In many situations, the use of rating as criteria for validation of tests and as indices of effectiveness of educational, motivational, and situational changes involves extreme demands upon the quality of the ratings. Ratings from different raters in different situations should be really equivalent, since they are almost always treated as if they were so. This demand for comparability means that interpretation of the rating must not deviate too widely from rater to rater or occasion to occasion, either in level (evaluation) or in dimension (trait, situational characteristic, job demand, temporal requirement, etc.). The present report covers the development of a rationale for a series of scales with such characteristics, and the testing of a procedure for their construction.

Psychologists seeking to establish reliable and valid rating systems have tended to impose their own values, interpretations, and beliefs about behavior upon the raters. Those who believe in trait theory construct scales based on presumably orthogonal dimensions established by factor analysis or by their own clinical intuitions. Those who believe that evaluation is either one general summary judgment or a composite of a large number of specific observations set up undifferentiated lists of good and bad statements, perhaps item-analyzed against some summary rating. In neither case is the rater consulted about the interpretation he would made of his own report.

This imposition of psychologists' values presupposes both understanding among psychologists concerning the organization of traits, and agreement among raters about the interpretations of various forms of behavior in relation to these traits. Without agreement, at least among a plurality of psychologists, impositions of their interpretations upon others seems presumptuous to say the least. Without consensus among the raters, more importantly, the raters cannot be expected to utilize the scales offered to them with any conviction or agreement.

This kind of consensus can be achieved only if the persons who will be rating indicate, in their own terms, what kind of behavior represents each level of each discriminably different characteristic, and which trait is illustrated by each kind of behavior.

Moreover, the rater must be "sold" upon the desirability of completing the ratings honestly and carefully, which means that the rating scales must have face validity for the purposes of the rater (which include guidance and counseling) as well as those of the researcher. Participation in the rating program must be elicited by virtue of the apparent usefulness of the procedure. These requirements are superimposed upon such essential measurement requirements as interrater reliability and independence of scales.

The present scales were constructed to meet the needs of raters in extremely diverse situations—head nurses rating the performance of staff nurses in a variety of hospitals, under a wide range of working loads, and with a diversity of previous training of both raters and ratees. Despite the differences in raters, they can be reasonably expected to share some common core of experience and of values concerning behavior on the jobs they will rate. The situation is similar to that in most executive, administrative, and technical positions, in which jobs with a single title are seldom comparable in either level of performance required or dimensions of performance considered important. In many of these situations, moreover, participation in the rating program cannot be demanded or even "persuasively encouraged" by higher echelon personnel, but must be voluntary.

The format proposed for the rating scales is a series of continuous graphic rating scales, arranged vertically, in a manner similar to that of the Fels scales. Behavioral descriptions, exemplifying various degrees of each dimension, are printed beside the line at different heights according to their scale positions as determined by judgments of head nurses similar to those who will be expected to use the scales. The examples are intended as anchors to define levels of the characteristic, and as operational definitions of the dimension being rated. Ratings are to be made by checking at any position along the line. Provision is made in the format for support of each check by notes concerning actual observed behavior.

This format was chosen as a means of combining the relevance to direct observation of critical incidents and similar techniques with the acceptability to raters of graphic rating scales. Rating errors associated with lack of definition of either dimensions or levels militated against the use of any of the traditionally used rating scales. Use of critical incidents, although extremely desirable because of reference to observed behavior, was eliminated since pretests had indicated that because of variations in the nursing situation a specific critical behavior often could not occur and hence could not serve as a basis for rating; and since most critical incidents cited tend to be too extreme for good psychometric policy which requires most accurate rating near the mean, rather than at the extremes. Use of forced choice was eliminated because of potential fakeability despite format and lack of validity in some important field tests (Kay, 1959).

The unacceptability to the rater of the forced-choice format was the most crucial deciding factor. The experience of the Army with this system led to its abandonment in 1950. Raters found it so unacceptable to rate without knowledge of the final outcome that they concentrated on finding ways to beat the system. In addition, forced-choice scales and home-office-scored checklists were both rejected because, in our experience, these scales include items almost as vague as those in the traditional rating scales.

The examples we used, therefore, represent not actual observed behaviors but inferences or predictions from observations. Raters are asked to decide whether a given behavior they have observed would lead them to expect behavior like that in the description. Instead of statements such as "shows interest in patients' description of symptoms," the anchors consist of expectations such as "If this nurse were admitting a patient who talks rapidly and continuously of her symptoms and past medical history, could be expected to look interested and listen." Calling for the rater to make such predictions implies that he is willing to infer from observations of behavior, that he has his own—at least implicit—belief about the intercorrelation of behaviors. The present procedure gambles that among a relatively homogeneous group of judges such as head nurses, these beliefs will be reasonably well standardized. It demands that such predictions be organized into areas not by theoretical similarity, but by judged similarity as indicated by the raters, and that the areas represent dimensions meaningful to the raters. It also provides checks in that each rater records briefly the behavior on which his prediction was based.

The use of an open, obviously fakeable format assumes that raters will, under proper circumstances, give conscientious estimates of the level of performance of ratees.

We believe that most rating errors are not due to deliberate faking. Moreover, no rating scale is really proof against distortion by a rater who really wants to do so. Better ratings can be obtained, in our opinion, not by trying to trick the rater (as in forced-choice scales) but by helping him to rate. We should ask him questions which he can honestly answer about behaviors which he can observe. We should reassure him that his answers will not be misinterpreted, and we should provide a basis by which he and others can check his answers.

The use of expected behaviors is intended to encourage such conscientiousness by making the predictions (a) so concrete that, in view of previous agreement by the peer (head nurse) group, central tendency or hedging effects will be minimized; and (b) so verifiable that the insight, judgment, values, etc., of the rater are potentially challenged if later behavior of the ratee should fail to confirm the prediction.

The basic procedure for scale construction resembles that employed to ensure that translations from one language to another adhere to the connotations as well as to the denotations of the original. Material is translated into a foreign language, and then, by an independent translator, retranslated into the original. Where "slippage" occurs, translations are corrected. Similarly, we required that examples, or expectations, be classified as indicative of a given dimension of nursing performance, and that independent judges indicate what dimension is illustrated by each. In addition, we defined the dimensions in the judges' own terminology and scaled the examples along these dimensions.

The submission of examples and subsequent reallocation by the raters' peers seems to ensure a high degree of content validity for the items and the scales.

PROCEDURES

Four groups of head nurses were sent by their hospitals to participate in conferences concerned with the use of evaluation in improving nursing performance. Data were gathered by mail from the remaining head nurses from the same hospitals from which two of the conference groups were drawn. One sample was held out for an independent replication. The samples are diversified and probably representative of head nurses who would be likely to use such a rating instrument.

The procedure used was essentially an iterative one, work performed by one group being checked and revised by others, so that the number of judges differs for different parts of the data. The content area was restricted to that of medical-surgical nursing.

1. First, qualities or characteristics to be evaluated were listed by each group; the most frequent dimensions were selected for further analysis. The nurses' own terminology was retained. Coverage of important aspects was further insured by gathering and classifying critical incidents in the customary way (for one sample only).

2. The groups formulated general statements representing definitions of high, low, and acceptable performance for each quality.

3. The groups submitted examples of behavior in each quality, and these were edited into the form of expectations of specific behavior.

4. Judges indicated, independently, what quality was illustrated by each example. *Examples* were eliminated if there was not clear modal agreement as to the quality to which each belonged. *Qualities* were eliminated if examples were not consistently reassigned to the quality for which they were originally designed.

5. Other judges used the examples to describe a specific nurse with outstandingly good nursing performance and another nurse with unsatisfactory performance. The difference between the outstanding and unsatisfactory nurse was computed for each pair of ratings to determine the discrimination value for each example.

6. Each vertical scale, together with the general definitions, was presented with a list of items previously judged by other raters as belonging to that quality. Judges rated each item from 0 to 2.0 according to the desirability of the behavior illustrated. Items were eliminated if the dispersion of judgments was large, or if the distribution was multimodal. All of the items which met these criteria were assembled for each scale, and the mean scale positions assigned to them for each group of judges were intercorrelated to give estimates of scale reliabilities. It was recognized that mean values were distorted somewhat by skewness in the distributions of judgments at the extremes, but it was felt that since the effect of skewness would be to reduce the stability of the means as estimates of central tendency, correlations using means would give at least a minimal estimate of agreement among groups of judges as to the relative position of items on a scale.

In addition, a comparison among samples of means and variances for all items in each scale indicates the similarity in the absolute location of the items by the various groups of judges.

RESULTS

The qualities which were most frequently considered important are listed in the first column of Table 13. An attempt was made to construct a scale and it proved possible to write general definitions about which there was considerable agreement in each of these areas. Examples of expected behavior were submitted which met the standard of group agreement for each.

The retranslation procedure, however, eliminated many items and several qualities. Table 14 shows the number of items surviving for each. Some of the eliminations are interesting in themselves; items designed to illustrate Reaction under Pressure, for example, were frequently allocated to Organizational Ability or Knowledge and Judgment, on the grounds that a certain degree of crisis is normal in nursing and ability to meet it involves primarily establishing priorities and knowing what to do. Communication Skills terms were allocated to Skill in Human Relationships or Conscientiousness because the items involved, to a large extent, either explaining to patients or keeping records. Both Reaction under Pressure and Communication Skills were eliminated at this step. Flexibility was also considered unpromising,

TABLE 13

AGREEMENT CONCERNING ALLOCATION OF ITEMS TO CHARACTERISTICS

Characteristic	High Agreement (above 59%)	Lower Agreement (49%–59%)
Knowledge and judgment	16	7
Conscientiousness	11	8
Skill in human relationships	21	9
Organizational ability	16	4
Communication skills	1	4
Objectivity	2	8
Flexibility	5	1
Reaction under pressure	1	1
Observational ability	7	4
Total number of items	80	46
Percentage of 141 items presented	57%	33%

TABLE 14

AGREEMENT BETWEEN ONE SAMPLE AND ALL OTHERS ON ASSIGNMENT TO MODAL QUALITY

Quality	Number of Items Assigned by Both Groups	Geisser's Concomitance Measure R
Knowledge and judgment	16	.52*
Conscientiousness	12	.55*
Skill in human relationships	23	.84*
Organizational ability	18	.90*
Objectivity	9	.71*
Observational ability	11	.83*

* $p \leq .01$.

although attempts were made to retrieve it in later institutes not reported here.

The significance of agreement of judges in assigning items to the same modal classification was tested for six scales (see Table 14) by a test of concomitance (Geisser, 1958) for all items which, after editing, had been presented for allocation to areas or qualities. This coefficient showed agreement to be significantly above chance when the judgments of one sample were compared with judgments of previous groups. It should be noted that this agreement was tested for examples presented in a scrambled order and judged one at a time; much better agreement can be expected when several examples of the same quality are grouped together on a single page as in the proposed rating scale format. A separate test of allocation of a few pairs and triads of items showed very high agreement.

Discrimination of items was checked by comparing average rating assigned to outstanding and unsatisfactory nurses. For all items passing the previous criteria the differences were significant by the chi-square test. Also, virtually all differences for individual judges were positive. Therefore all retained items were clearly relevant in discriminating extreme levels of performance.

Scale reliabilities for the first four samples of judges for all retained items were ascertained. The mean evaluation of each of these items for four samples was correlated with that given to it by the holdout sample. The lowest scale reliability is .972. Grand means and variances for all items in each scale were calculated for each sample. Differences among the grand means within each scale were not significant by F tests.

Parenthetically, there are no consistent or significant differences in intercorrelations, means, or variances between Conference and Mail groups.

DISCUSSION

In general, the procedure seems satisfactory, with adequate agreement concerning allocation of examples, excellent discrimination, and high scale reliability. The potential advantages of scales based on such procedures are obvious; they are rooted in, and referable to, actual observed behavior; evaluations of the behavior have been made by judges at least reasonably comparable to those who will eventually use the scales; whatever we think of the terminology, the traits of qualities covered are operationally defined and are distinguishable one from another by the raters. Both dimension and level have been agreed upon, so that there is a fair change of treating ratings by different raters as comparable just so long as they agree with the interpretations of the expectations. Even though different specific behaviors may be observed in different situations, they are referred to the common set of expectations which serves as a mutual frame of reference. Moreover, the chance to supplement predictions with documentation of the actual observed behavior upon which the predictions are based (as is provided by the scale format) permits checking and revision of examples and scales. Also, the use of these supporting anecdotal records, as well as the ease with which predictions can later be checked, favors honest and conscientious rating.

The disadvantages are equally obvious. The decision to use the raters' own theory of traits, and retranslation as a method of checking items, implied that raters would eventually be able to make decisions concerning what characteristics were involved in a given observed behavior. Most behavior is complex, and certainly not attributable to a single cause in the makeup of the individual, without regard to interaction of needs or to the influence of the situation. The use of trait names, and of general statements concerning levels of performance, in addition to the behavioral anchors may make for ambiguity in ratings, especially if one set of raters is less critical than another and displaces the items in relation to the general standards. One set of raters may also be more likely to attribute complex behavior to one cause while another set may prefer another. There are also too many scales for easy handling.

We hope that the number of qualities can be reduced after actual field use permits computation of scale intercorrelations and interrater reliabilities under normal rating conditions. We expect that experience and training with the scales will enable the rater to evaluate complex items of behavior on several relevant scales (and that this evaluation may serve some useful function in improving the rater's ability to interpret, diagnose, and improve the behavior of the person rated). We further hope that the general trait names, with their accompanying general definitions, will "wither away" and be replaced in use by the operational definitions provided by the behavioral expectations. Grouping the expectations on a single page will improve agreement as to qualities also. We expect, moreover, that as higher standards of performance become generally accepted, examples may appear that may be placed even higher in the vertical scales than the present items.

Weights for combining scales in order to give a summary rating, where needed, should be determined empirically by the use of multiple regression against a reliable rating of overall performance obtained in the field and probably separately for each nursing situation.

The consistency of judgments renders tenable the hypothesis that homogeneous groups of judges do share a common belief about the manner in which behaviors are intercorrelated and can extrapolate from observed to predicted behavior.

The procedure seems promising not only for nursing, but also for other complex tasks. Parenthetically, we should point out that reliabilities are so high that procedures similar to this one could certainly be attempted with smaller .numbers of judges, and that sampling differences seem to be a relatively trivial source of error. Wherever behaviors may be expected to be reasonably comparable or interpretable from one situation to another, as in many professional and administrative jobs, and in research settings where observations can be made under fairly uniform conditions, the procedure seems applicable. We hope that it will prove useful in industrial, educational, and social areas of research.

Ratings have been traditionally employed to summarize personality data or interview impressions or actual performance. A new and rather unusual use of ratings is to be found in the work of Carkhuff and Berenson (1967, Ch. 1) and their colleagues. These authors have developed a series of five-point rating scales to measure counselor-therapist effectiveness with clients where a rating of 3 is the minimally facilitative level of interpersonal functioning. One of the scales measures counselor empathic understanding of the client's frame of reference; others measure genuineness and self-disclosure on the part of the counselor (i.e., lack of facade or how fully the counselor is himself to the client); still others deal with the counselor's respect and concern for client feelings and the degree to which the counselor enables the client to deal concretely and specifically with client feelings. Finally, other scales deal with the extent to which the client, in turn, is able to explore himself and experience himself with immediacy. Research has shown these to be reliable scales which can succinctly measure necessary conditions for therapeutic change. This research has shown to a distressing degree that few individuals—professionals included—cast in a helping role attain an average rating of even 2 of these scales; furthermore, graduate students in traditional clinical training programs tend to show declines in overall ratings as their graduate training proceeds!

One further example of a measurement study where *self*-ratings were employed in a most unusual situation and with most interesting results is reported here. This was a study involving experienced and inexperienced parachute jumpers and their felt magnitudes of their approach and avoidance gradients as the actual jump became more imminent (Fenz & Epstein, 1967). Thirty three experienced chutists, all with more than 100 jumps, made up one group; 33 novice chutists, none of whom had made more than five jumps were used as contrast. All subjects were told to place a rating of 1 at the time on the jump sequence series (see Figure 5) when the avoidance feeling was least and to rate 10 when this avoidance feeling was greatest. They were then to rate all intervening points on the jump sequence continuum after establishing these two "anchors" or extremes. Similarly, both groups were asked to supply ratings for feelings of approach. Note here, however, one can say nothing about the magnitude of the fear responses here; all that may be done is to make comparisons of these fear patterns over a period of time. The peak avoidance for novices occurs at the "Ready" signal. Note that the maximum avoidance for

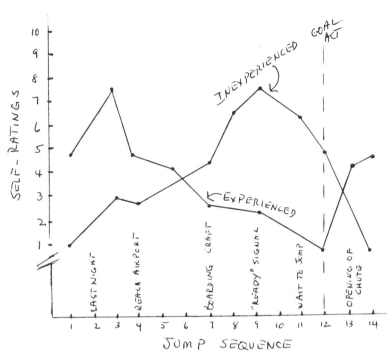

Fig. 5. Self-ratings of thirty-three (33) experienced and inexperienced chutists at points (1–10) where anxiety feelings were least and greatest.

this group does not come at the period just before the chute opens (which would be the maximum point of uncertainty and danger). Anxiety here is adaptive because it reaches its peak when it can influence the outcome. Once the commitment is made, fear declines but it is still high at the moment of the jump. Turning to the self-ratings for the experienced chutists, we see practically a reversed curve: avoidance rises one week before the jump (point 1) to the morning of the jump (point 3) after which it declines over a long period. It reaches its lowest point at the freefall (point 12) and then rises after landing. For this group, the morning of the jump is the decision point; here they decide whether they will jump or not; once they have decided, no further anxieties seem to occur. Fenz and Epstein comment, however, on the after-discharge of anxiety to be noted for this experienced group *after* the jump, suggesting that there has been considerable inhibition of anxiety before all this. An interesting additional question here is, whether with still more jumps, the fear peak and the avoidance reaction would be displaced still further. The authors were able to locate a few chutists with over 1,000 jumps (rather rare persons). They report that most of these men returned the fear-rating forms blank because they said that jumping was now so routine that they experienced no fear. Here all showed approach gradients—a straight line—increasing from one week before to the moment of the jump.

PART SEVEN

Situational Testing

A topic always of great interest to students in courses devoted to psychological testing is performance measures of personality, or situational testing. Typically, in such situations either the subject is quite unaware that he is being observed at all—as illustrated by the first article in this section, dealing with the pecuniary honesty of the public—or else the subject is unclear about the purpose of the test situation in which he has been placed. More often, when situational tests are devised it is the second type that can be laboratory based. With the first, of course, the test administrator must go directly into the field.

The designs for such tests often are very ingenious. Understandably, it is easier to design these performance measures for children than for adults, but good results have been achieved with both such groups. Perhaps the earliest large-scale studies using performance measures with children are the monumental reports of Hartshorne and May (1928–30), whose intensive and detailed studies for the Character Education Inquiry included tests of traits such as honesty, money handling, truthfulness, persistence, cooperativeness, and generosity. A famous and well publicized World War II situational testing program was one for the Office of Strategic Services, the predecessor of today's Central Intelligence Agency. This testing program, of which performance measures of personality were only a part, extended over some three and one-half days, and was conducted on an estate outside Washington, D.C. The psychologists hoped that they could successfully measure, by situational testing, such complex traits as emotional stability, reaction to stress, frustration tolerance, and creative problem-solving ability. For details about this ambitious program consult the volume published by the OSS Assessment staff (1948).

The reader's attention is called to the Webb paper (see pp. 15–20), wherein many examples of ingenious situational testing were presented.

The first article deals with a public, or field, situation where individual testing was not the focus. The study involves imaginative and entertaining observations about the pecuniary honesty of the public.

The study was published in 1948 in the *Journal of Abnormal & Social Psychology,* and is reproduced here in its entirety. At that time, Dr Merritt was Associate Dean of the Graduate College at the University of Arizona; Dr. Fowler was a physicist at the University of Oklahoma.

THE PECUNIARY HONESTY OF THE PUBLIC AT LARGE

Curtis B. Merritt and Richard G. Fowler

INTRODUCTION

Honesty has been described by some investigators as a general characteristic or trait and by others as an aggregation of specific habits. While the question of the existence or nonexistence of some traits cannot be regarded as finally settled, the authors incline to the view that there are fundamental dispositions which influence human behavior. Without attempting to identify honesty itself as a basic human characteristic, the purpose of this study is to sample the trustworthiness of the public in a situation involving financial honesty and to provide some measure of the trait underlying the obliging acts which were manifested during the course of the experiments.

Human honesty is unusually difficult to investigate because of the influence of surveillance on the results. It is believed that the technique to be described largely obviates this criticism. How many human beings will remain honest when there will never be any judge of their dishonesty other than themselves? How many will be sufficiently tempted by the suggestion of a small financial gain to react dishonestly? Within the limits of a particular situation this study proposes to answer these questions as completely as possible. By extension of the experimental method it was found possible to answer other questions as well.

METHOD

The necessary conditions for an objective test of honesty were achieved by use of the United States Postal Service. Nearly everyone has had the experience of recovering lost articles or mail through the grace of the public. If stamped and addressed letters seemingly containing money were judiciously distributed, the number returned should give some indication of the honesty of the finders as a group. The success of the tests depended upon the reliability of the mails. This was found to be perfect in a score of checks made on it, and is known to be excellent in general knowledge.

If the result is to be the completely undisturbed reaction of the individual it must be assured that he is alone when he finds the article. This could not always be guaranteed, and so the experimental data are perturbed by the gregariousness of human beings. It is our impression that a large majority of the letters were found by single pedestrians, but group morality must certainly have influenced a number of the cases. This could have been eliminated by observing the discovery of each lost article but time did not permit this. An estimate of the departure of the result obtained by random tests from individual morality could be made at any time by a study of the frequency of groups of pedestrians as a function of number in a group.

The actual method of procedure in these experiments was generally as follows. Stamped, self-addressed, and sealed letters of two types were "lost" by depositing them prominently but discreetly on the sidewalks of various cities in the East and Midwest. Type A contained only a trivial message, while type B contained, besides a message, a lead slug of the dimensions of a fifty-cent piece. The accompanying message indicated that the lead disc as such was of value to the addressee. Care was taken to drop the letters in locations sufficiently removed from one another to preclude the possibility of any one person finding more than one of the letters. All were put down in clear weather so that the envelopes would not become soiled and hence lose their appearance of value. Tests were made by night and day in both business and residential districts. The technique of dropping the letters was to let them fall to the ground through a hole in the experimenter's trouser pocket. It was possible to drop letters in this manner, even on crowded streets, without establishing ownership by attracting the attention of passers-by.

The envelopes used were standard $3^1/_2$ by $6^1/_2$-inch size. They were addressed in ink and stamped. No return address was given, nor was there any clue as to the owner, other than the potential owner, the addressee. The moneyless (type A) letters contained a simple message on a single sheet of paper to keep their general appearance normal in every respect. The loaded (type B) letters were similar except that they contained a lead disc the exact size and thickness of a fifty-cent piece. The disc was roughened to enhance as much as possible the impression that it was an actual coin. Also the lead disc was enclosed in a smaller envelope to prevent its breaking through and being lost.

The letters were dropped on many different days and in many different cities to insure a representative sampling of the public at large. No attempt was made to watch the pickup of all the letters. However, in order to eliminate the possibility of any selective factor operating to affect the random sampling, the places where the letters had been dropped were checked in about a third of the cases, from fifteen minutes to an hour afterward. This check revealed the pickup to be 100 percent. About twenty specimens were watched until picked up. This brought out that in 90 percent of the cases the first person who noticed the letter picked it up, whether walking alone or in a group. To obtain preliminary information on the reliability of the public at returning lost mail before investing money and effort in the main research problem a test was made by distributing postcards. Here, in spite of the difficulties attending because light cards were blown around by the wind and defaced by rain, three quarters of the one hundred cards were returned. This made it certain that some information would be obtained from the experiment and accordingly it was carried out.

DATA AND DISCUSSION

A summary of the data obtained is given in Table 15. The table is self-explanatory.

Eighty-five percent of the control type letters were returned. This is roughly comparable with the result of the postcard test in which 72 percent were returned. The difference between the two figures probably represents the number of postcards dispersed and lost by natural forces, together with those judged by the finder to be not worth mailing because of the triviality of the message. In the 15 percent of these control letters lost we see very little reason for random losses except in the case of those which may have fallen into the hands of small children. Times of day and locations were in general chosen to minimize the effect of children on the experiments. Of perhaps twenty cases in which the pickup was observed, only one was by children, and they gleefully hurried to the nearest box and posted the letter. The factors which seem most important in the missing 15 percent of controls are dishonesty, curiosity, forgetfulness, and carelessness. Procrastination and forgetfulness probably combined to lose a few letters. This does not seem likely to be very important in view of the experimental fact that, out of the many tests made, no missives were postmarked more than forty-eight hours beyond the time of distribution, and only one showed the folding marks which would be present from being carried in a pocket for any length of time. Curiosity over the nature of the message and the sender probably stimulated several finders to open controls. Subsequent disappointment and chagrin at the triviality of the message then operated to cause the destruction of the letter. No doubt the ancient human principle of salvage rights was next invoked, although illegally, to acquire the stamp. In some cases it is possible that the finders may have applied this principle to the stamp *ab initio*. The factor of curiosity, with or without accompanying dishonesty, seems satisfactory to account for these losses.

The type-A letters cannot be regarded as acting as a perfectly effective

TABLE 15

Article	Number Dropped	Number Returned	Returned Opened	Percentage Returned
Type A (blanks)	33	28	0	85
Type B (test letters) ...	158	86	11	54
Type C (postcards)	100	72	0	72

control on the type-B letters. Their failure to do so derives from two factors, the first of which is curiosity. Fewer type-B letters should be lost from curiosity than those of type-A, since the presence of a specious fifty-cent piece in the letter should act as a deterrent for most of the curious but intrinsically honest, while honest individuals, whose curiosity still carried them away, could be expected to mail the opened letters. Seven percent of such previously opened slug-bearing letters were received. This figure of course must also include people whose dishonesty applies only to money and who, on finding the slug to be worthless to them, but valuable to the addressee, mail it. It can be said of them that their honesty undergoes a transition between the postage stamp fee and fifty cents. The second factor which tends to invalidate the controls as such is the probable lower random loss of the slug-bearing letters. These remained in place more satisfactorily and, once found, it seems unlikely that they would have been neglected as the blank letters may have been. Since the blank letters could not be regarded as a good control, we were compelled to establish the degree of certainty that a given letter is picked up by someone.

To attain this information it was customary to make the distribution in circuits, going over the same course after an interval of time had elapsed. This was done in at least half of the tests made, and in every case it was found that the missive was gone within an hour. It seems likely, therefore, that the honesty coefficient is more nearly related to the actual percentage of slug-bearing letters returned than to the control.

Losses among the slug-bearing letters can be attributed to dishonesty, salvage, and random loss. It is doubtful that the random loss was very large, and on the basis of the sampling previously described it seems unlikely that it extended to more than one or two letters. Even one letter which was found by a paper-picker was not deposited in his waste basket, but in his pocket, and later mailed. Loss occasioned by forgetfulness, carrying the letter home, mislaying it, etc., does not seem to be important, for certainly no one is likely to throw a stamped envelope apparently containing fifty cents into the discard without examination. The chief distribution of losses must therefore be between dishonesty and salvage.

By salvage we mean the ancient law that lost articles are the property of the finder. Legally, this is the case with unidentifiable articles only. The potential owner of the pseudo-fifty-cent piece was clearly indicated. Although it does not seem likely that many of those who actually opened these letters did so as an assertion of right, it must be conceded that cases may have occurred in which the finder erroneously believed the property to be legally his.

The eleven letters which were returned opened were especially interesting. Each contained the imitation fifty-cent piece and three had even been placed in new envelopes with another stamp. The remaining eight had been patched up in various ways before being mailed. Because of the factor of curiosity mentioned before, it cannot be said how many of these cases are human obligingness combined with dishonesty or financial need. These eleven letters seem to support the contention of previous investigations that there are varying types and degrees of honesty. It would be worthwhile to perform a similar experiment with coins of a different denomination in order to throw additional light upon this point. It would be most interesting if actual bills could be included conspicuously in glassine windowed envelopes to determine the irreducible minimum of honest people.

Watching the pickup of the letters proved to be a most entertaining pastime. Some were picked up and immediately posted at the nearest mailbox. Others were examined minutely, evidently precipitating quite a struggle between the finder and his conscience, before being pocketed or mailed. Some were carried a number of blocks before being posted, one person carried a letter openly for nine blocks before mailing it. A lady in Ann Arbor, Michigan, found a letter and carried it six miles in her car to deliver it personally, although she was not acquainted with the addressee. One letter, picked up in Harrisburg, Pennsylvania, was mailed from York, Pennsylvania. Another, picked up in Toledo, Ohio, was mailed in Cleveland. Still another from the Toledo streets was mailed from Monroe, Michigan. Two missives left on the steps of the cradle of liberty in Philadelphia failed to find their way into a mailbox. Two of five letters left on church steps during Sunday services failed to return.

INTERPRETATION

The first human quality which we believe that the tests begin to measure is that trait underlying the obliging acts, consideration, and altruistic responsibility. We believe that this is the case because the letters were placed carefully and conspicuously with their stamp side up so that they were easily recognizable for what they were as they lay. The observations of actual pick-ups clearly demonstrated that, in the majority of cases, the first person to see the missive accepted the responsibility for its care. In only one case observed was a letter passed over by a man who had seen it. This man stopped, bent down and glanced at it, and passed on. He may have concluded that the owner would come back after it. On this basis we feel that a high percentage of the American public at large, between 80 and 90 percent, have this generally altruistic attitude.

The second quality of which some estimate was possible was intrinsic financial honesty. The word intrinsic is used here to differentiate these honest acts from those cases in which the individual may have wrongly believed his act of salvage to be legally defensible. It was found that at least 55 percent, and at most 70 percent, of the individuals tested were intrinsically honest about such a financial matter. It is our belief, from the analysis of the sources of loss in the experiments, that the lower figure is the more accurate.

It is an old question whether a person can be financially dishonest and still intellectually honest in other respects. The possibility can usually be proven by selected instances. It is possible that the 7 percent of letters returned opened indicates the extent to which this is true, if we exclude the likelihood of extreme curiosity in truly honest people.

SUMMARY

We conclude from the evidence presented that the public at large is very strikingly altruistic, manifesting obligingness, consideration, and responsibility. A sharp decline in the reliability of the public sets in under the effects of suggestion of financial gain. One third of the altruistically minded are converted to selfish behavior. It is probable that an even larger proportion of the public at large is unreliable in such a financial matter.

The success of these experiments indicates the possibility of their extension to more elaborate tests on the response of general and specialized groups. However, general disclosure of the method will in all probability destroy its effectiveness.

$$\nabla \ \nabla \ \nabla$$

Two further examples of situational testing in the field are cited because of their entertaining nature and also because these are attempts to study highly abstract personality traits—altruism, in the first instance, and "social responsibility" in the second. Both situations were designed as highly naturalistic, something few laboratory investigations can manage. One can therefore expect that the behavior elicited is entirely spontaneous and that the situations have few, if any, of the demand characteristics known to operate with volunteers and in laboratories.

Bryan and Test were both at Northwestern University at the time of these studies. The Bryan-Test study is one of four experiments that appeared in the *Journal of Personality and Social Psychology* in 1967 under the general title, "Models and Helping: Naturalistic Studies in Aiding Behavior." The second report, by Bryan alone, is included as a kind of student dividend, especially for the reading pleasure of hitchhiking persons. This study is as yet unpublished; a mimeographed version was distributed a few years back by the Educational Testing Service in Princeton. Dr. Bryan is currently Professor of Psychology at Northwestern University; Dr. Test is presently a clinical psychologist in the Department of Psychology at Nendota State Hospital, Wisconsin.

A LADY IN DISTRESS: THE FLAT TIRE EXPERIMENT

James H. Bryan and Mary A. Test

Attention has been directed recently toward the study of altruistic behaviors, i.e., those acts entailing self-sacrifice for no apparent personal gain. While such actions have generally been ignored by the psychological community, perhaps because of this community's biological orientation, such behaviors have important practical and theoretical implications. At the very least such behaviors are useful to the survival of a variety of social institutions, man's included. Additionally, the study of such actions will further clarify the nature of reinforcement.

Several recent experiments have suggested that one important determinant of helping behaviors is the presence of models. Rosenhan and White (unpublished) have demonstrated that significantly more children will donate gift certificates, a highly valued secondary reinforcer, to a fictitious orphanage after having seen an adult model do so than will Ss who were not exposed to such models. While many of the studies on modeling effects have been based on children, several investigations have suggested that models might be effective in eliciting self-sacrificing behavior in adults. Rosenbaum and Blake (1955) found that college students exposed to a model who volunteered, upon the personal request of the E, to participate in an experiment would be more likely to consent than Ss not exposed to such a model or who observed a model refuse to cooperate. Pressures toward conformity in these experiments were great, however, as the request was made directly by the *E* and in the presence of a large number of other students. The present authors, under conditions designed to maintain *S* anonymity, but within a college laboratory, found that college students who were either helped or observed others being aided were more likely to offer help to a stooge than *S*s who were provided with no model or a model who refused to help.

Investigations of modeling that employ adults as *S*s and that demand self-sacrifice on the part of *S*s are limited in number, exploit strong pressures toward conformity, and rely upon college students as *S*s. The present experiment was designed to assess the impact of models upon subsequent spontaneous offers of help by using adults other than college students in an experimental setting other than a university.

METHOD

The standard condition consisted of an undergraduate female stationed by a 1964 Ford Mustang (control car) with a flat left rear tire. An inflated tire was leaned upon the left side of the auto. The girl and the flat and the inflated tires were conspicuous to the passing traffic.

In the model condition, a 1965 Oldsmobile was located approximately a quarter of a mile from the control car. The car was raised by jack under the left rear bumper, and a girl was watching a male changing the flat tire. Stooges played the same role throughout the experiment.

In the no-model condition, the model was absent; thus, only the control car was visible to the passing traffic.

The cars were located in a predominantly residential section in Los Angeles, California. They were placed in such a manner that no intersection separated the model from the control car. No turnoffs were thus available to the passing traffic. Further, opposite flows of traffic were divided by a separator such that the first U turn available to the traffic going in the opposite direction of the control car would be after exposure to the model condition.

The experiment was conducted on two successive Saturdays between the hours of 1:45 and 5:50 P.M. Each treatment condition lasted for the time required for 1000 vehicles to pass the control car. While private automobiles and trucks, motorscooters and motorcycles were tallied as vehicles, commercial trucks, taxis, and busses were not. Vehicle count was made by a fourth member of the experiment who stood approximately 100 feet from the control car hidden from the passing motorists. On the first Saturday, the model condition was run first and lasted from 1:45 to 3:15. In order to exploit changing traffic patterns and to keep the time intervals equal across treatment conditions, the control car was moved several blocks and placed on the opposite side of the street for the no-model condition. The time of the no-model treatment was 4:00 to 5:00 P.M. On the following Saturday, counterbalancing the order and the location of treatment conditions was accomplished. That is, the no-model condition was run initially and the control car was placed in the same location that it had been placed on the previous Saturday during the model condition. The time of the no-model condition was 2:00 to 3:30 P.M. For the model condition, the control car was placed in that locale where it had been previously during the no-model condition. The time of the model condition was 4:30 to 5:30 P.M.

Individuals who had stopped to offer help were told by the young lady that she had already phoned an auto club and that help was imminent. Those who nonetheless insisted on helping her were told the nature of the experiment.

RESULTS AND DISCUSSION

The dependent variable was the number of cars which stopped and from which at least one individual offered help to the stooge by the control car. Of the 4,000 passing vehicles, 93 stopped. With the model car being absent, 35 vehicles stopped; with the model present, 58 halted. The difference between the conditions was statistically significant.

It should be noted that the time of day had little impact upon the offering of aid. Fifty vehicles stopped during the early part of the afternoon; 43, during the later hours. Likewise, differences in help offers were not great between successive Saturdays as 45 offers of aid were made on the first Saturday, 48 on the second Saturday.

The results of the present study support the hypothesis that helping behaviors can be significantly increased through the observation of others' helpfulness. The data further underscore the importance of modeling for the adult S. It is noteworthy that under conditions where conformity pressures are rather weak, that is, conditions where the direct confrontation with the requester can be easily avoided, where requests are not made directly, where the anonymity of the actor is so easily maintained, and where self-gain is so minimal, that adults are still affected by the presence of models.

While it is clear that the behavior of these motorists was not dictated by a variety of situational or social pressures usually associated with study of modeling in adults (Rosenbaum & Blake, 1955) or experiments in academic settings (Orne, 1962), the mechanisms underlying the model effects are not obvious. Berkowitz and Daniels (1963), for example, have provided evidence that dependency states in others will elicit helping behavior from college students. They have argued for the existence of a "norm of social responsibility," a norm dictating the helping of dependent others. It is perhaps possible that the presence of a helping model served as a reminder of such a norm. If this were indeed the case, the model may not only serve to define normative behavior to adults, but also may serve to activate already internalized norms.

Whatever the mediating events, the present study does support the contention that models are important in eliciting helping behaviors under those conditions where nonconformity would produce no interpersonal consequences and conformity would produce very little personal gain in adults other than college students in situations other than academic settings. The findings thus lend support to the generality of laboratory findings regarding the impact of models upon behavior.

$\triangledown \ \triangledown \ \triangledown$

HELPING AND HITCHHIKING

James H. Bryan

Recently, concern has been directed toward the relationship of dependency and helping behaviors. Berkowitz and his colleagues (Berkowitz, Klanderman, & Harris, 1964) have argued that there exists in our culture a "norm of social responsibility," which dictates the aiding of dependent others, irrespective of potential rewards.

While their findings supporting the relationships between dependency and helping are impressive, the data from various investigations rest upon strikingly similar experimental procedures. The experiments have been conducted within a university laboratory setting. They have typically utilized students as subjects. Finally, the experimental manipulations creating dependency have relied upon a particular type of dependency, that concerned with the experimental task—that is, in their experimenter's ratings of the competence of an anonymous other on an assigned task are contingent upon the S's performance. The degree to which E's ratings of the "supervisor" are dependent upon S's behavior defines the degree of dependency.

Studies conducted by other investigators in other contexts using other procedures have yielded contradictory results. Schopler and Bateson (1965) found a sex-by-subject and dependency interaction in three separate experiments. They found that more males will volunteer to help a low dependent than high dependent partner, while the converse held for females. This interaction was found whether volunteering for an experiment or a decision-making task was employed as the dependent variable. Test and Bryan (unpublished), on the other hand, failed to find either the number of help offers or the amount of aid given on a rating and sorting task affected by the stooge's simulation of a broken writing hand.

Since most of the work in the area of nonrewarded helping and dependency is closely tied to a particular experimental method and subject population, the present study was designed in an effort to extend the generality of the findings of Berkowitz and his colleagues. The present investigation's setting was naturalistic, its subject population, passing motorists, the dependent variables, the rides offered a hitchhiker.

METHOD

A male undergraduate, clean-shaven, with closely cropped blond hair, dressed in walking shorts (Bermudas), a white T shirt, and tennis shoes, served as the stooge. His task was to solicit rides from passing motorists. The dress was not only appropriate for summer wear in Los Angeles but was such that the passing motorist would have opportunity to observe a simulated physical infirmity. The high dependency (HD) condition was created by having him wear, while hitchhiking, an Ace bandage around his left knee and lean upon a cane. The bandage and cane were omitted in the low dependency (LD) condition.

The experiment was conducted during the summer of 1966 (Wednesdays of July 13, August 3 and 10, and Thursday, July 14) at one of two main thoroughfares. On the first test day, the hitchhiker was located by a signal on a four-lane road (Road I) from the hours of three to five in the afternoon. For the first hour, the HD condition was imposed, for the second, the LD condition. Unfortunately, the pattern of the traffic light on Road I was changed on the following day, and traffic speed was seriously disrupted. The experiment was thus moved to Road II, another four-lane thoroughfare. Again, the stooge located himself by a traffic signal. On Thursday, the HD condition was run from three to four in the afternoon, the LD from four to five. Road II was used throughout the remainder of the experiment. On the third day of testing, the LD condition was initially conducted (from three to four in the afternoon), followed by the HD condition (from four to five). On the last day, treatment conditions were run for a two-hour period as before, except that they were imposed twice for a 30-minute duration rather than once for a 60-minute period. This latter procedure was followed in order to allow a comparison of the treatments while approximately counterbalancing the time of day and holding the day of week constant.

While it was impossible to keep the stooge unaware of the experimental conditions, care was taken to insure his constant behavior across experimental conditions. Finally, if the hitchhiker was offered a ride, he accepted and rode a distance of 12 blocks. He then hitchhiked back. The same experimental conditions held for his return trip.

RESULTS AND DISCUSSION

To assess the possibility of changing traffic patterns over time, the number of vehicles on Roads I and II were counted on two successive Wednesdays. Tally was made of the number of autos stopping at a red traffic light in a 10-minute period during the critical afternoon hours. For the east to west traffic, counting was completed during the period of 3:00–3:15, 4:00–4:15, and 5:00–5:15 P.M. For west to east traffic, the tally was made between 3:15–3:30, 4:15–4:30, and 5:10–5:25 P.M. The results suggested that little traffic change would be likely during the course of the experiment. The number of autos going in a particular direction during the time sampled did not fluctuate more than 12 autos per 10-minute period.

Data as to the number of ride offers given the stooge under the two conditions classified by time and day of week are presented in Table 16.

Scores were combined, irrespective of road or day of week, and analyzed by the chi-square method. The difference in ride offers elicited by the HD condition and the LD condition was significant ($\chi^2 = 5.48$, $df = 1$, $p < .05$, two-tailed). It should be noted, however, that in this comparison, experimental conditions were confounded with the time of day in which the conditions were imposed and day of week. Using the data compiled from all four observations confounds the HD condition with early afternoon and LD with late afternoon traffic. It may be argued that early afternoon drivers are less hurried than the end-of-the-day commuter, thus more likely to stop. Eliminating observations made on Thursday, a chi-square analysis was performed using only those results made on the Wednesday run in which treatment conditions were counterbalanced. The resulting chi-square approached significance ($\chi^2 = 3.28$, $df = 1$, $p < .10 > .05$, one-tailed). This analysis, however, confounded location with experimental conditions. As will be recalled, the first day of observations were made on Road I, the remaining on Road II. Furthermore, the traffic patterns on Road I were such as to weigh the results in favor of the HD condition. That is, the HD condition was run between the hours of 4:00–5:00 P.M., at the period of maximum east to

TABLE 16

FREQUENCY OF RIDE OFFERS CODED BY TREATMENT CONDITION, TIME OF DAY, AND OCCASION OF OBSERVATION*

Date of Observations	Treatment	
	HD	LD
7/13	9 (3:00–4:00)	6 (4:00–5:00)
7/14	4 (3:00–4:00)	0 (4:00–5:00)
8/3	7 (4:00–5:00)	4 (3:00–4:00)
8/10	4 (3:30–4:00)	2 (3:00–3:30)
	4 (4:30–5:00)	1 (4:00–4:40)

* Numbers in parentheses indicate time of day of observation.

west traffic, while the LD condition was run during the preceding hour at which time there was less traffic. Even though the effects of this traffic flow difference in the east to west direction would be somewhat attenuated by the reversal in traffic rate going west to east, a third chi-square was computed, eliminating the observations taken on the first day. The resulting chi-square equaled 5.54 ($df = 1$) and was significant beyond the .05 level (two-tailed).

In general, the results of this experiment support the prediction that dependency elicits helping behavior under those circumstances where the likelihood of material reward is rather remote. That significant findings were obtained is perhaps more surprising in light of the experimental procedures. In the dependent condition, more of the total time of the hitchhiker was spent within an automobile, thus the LD hitchhiker had more opportunity (i.e., more traffic) to solicit a ride.

At least one plausible rival hypothesis exists that may account for the data. It might be argued that a crippled hitchhiker elicits less fear in motorists than his healthy counterpart. The offers of rides then do not constitute a reflection of the social responsibility norm but rather the difference in the threat components of the HD and LD conditions. While it is impossible to assess this alternative hypothesis from the present data, it should be remembered that the debilitated hitchhiker did carry a formidable appearing cane. The presence of such a potential weapon may have tended to lessen the difference in the threat value of the HD and LD hitchhiker.

The current findings thus extend the generality of the previous work of Schopler and Bateson (1965) and of Berkowitz, Klanderman, & Harris (1964) on the social responsibility norm.

Two other experiments by these same researchers (Bryan and Test) found shoppers contributed more to a Salvation Army kettle in the twenty seconds or half-minute after a model gave than in the same time interval before he gave. Two explanations were offered. One suggested that the effects were due to the information supplied about the pleasant consequences of helping. The second explanation suggested that these effects were due to the comparison between the observer and the model which resulted in shame. Krebs (1970), who has reviewed the experimental literature on altruism, feels that the first interpretation is really not tenable in the flat tire experiment where the consequence of helping was hard work—unless, as he adds, those who stopped had a pick-up in mind. He also feels that the second interpretation runs into some difficulty in all three experiments due to the fact that most shoppers and motorists did not act altruistically. A more conservative interpretation for these findings would seem to relate to the increased salience of the altruistic behavioral alternative (Krebs, 1970, pp. 268–269).

Another ingenious situational test of altruism was conducted on the New York subway trains—what the authors termed "Good Samaritanism" (Piliavin *et al.*, 1969). An express train of the 8th Avenue Independent line, a train with no stops between West 59th and 125th Streets, was used as a laboratory on wheels. Four teams of students, each one composed of a victim, model, and two observers, staged standard collapses where type of victim (drunk or ill), race of victim (black or white), and presence or absence of a model were varied. Records were made of the number and race of observers, the latency of the helping response, race and number of helpers, the amount of movement out of the "critical area," and any spontaneous comments. Major findings indicated that an apparently ill person is more likely to receive aid than an inebriated one; the race of the victim has little effect on the race of the helper, except when the victim is drunk. What about the total number of people who helped? In 60 percent of 81 trials where the victim received help, he received it not from one good Samaritan but from two or three or even more—and there was no difference here between black or white victims or between drunk or ill in the number of helpers subsequent to the first who came to his aid. It was noted that most of the spontaneous first helpers were male (90%) but it should also be pointed out that all the victims were male. Furthermore, the longer the emergency continues without help being offered, the more likely someone will leave the area of the emergency. The expected decrease in speed of responding as group size increases—the "diffusion of responsibility effect" found by Darley and Latané (1967)—does not occur in this situation.

— — —

SITUATIONAL tests have had much appeal to psychologists involved in the development and validation of selection batteries. Almost all such workers use the World War II work of the OSS Assessment staff as a base, as would be especially apt in selection of policemen when usually one wants to measure effective behavior under stress. Situational tests make possible the observation of personality characteristics that appear only infrequently. Dishonesty would be another example, as the previous report by Merritt and Fowler illustrates. It has also been pointed out that with tests of this type the subject's usually strong desire to do his best does not invalidate the results. The investigator is typically looking for a maximum performance on the part of the testee, and he is also trying to obtain this performance in the most naturalistic setting he can devise. However, the problem of long-range validity will always remain. Situational tests are typically rather short, and they tend to be fairly specific (i.e., measuring stress or frustration tolerance in a single and specific situation). How far one can generalize from such test situations is a critical issue. As the OSS staff found, the long-range validity of their own ingeniously devised situational tests was very modest.

The following report on situational testing for an urban police assessment is a condensed version of a more complete report that appeared in the *Journal of Criminal Law, Criminology and Police Science*, 1966. Dr. Mills, the senior author, is Professor of Psychology at the University of Cincinnati and departmental Chairman of Criminal Justice. At the time of this research, Miss Tonkin was a graduate assistant in the Department of Psychology at the University of Cincinnati and Dr. McDevitt was a practicing psychiatrist in Cincinnati.

SITUATIONAL TESTS IN METROPOLITAN POLICE RECRUIT SELECTION

Robert B. Mills, Robert J. McDevitt
and Sandra Tonkin

The emerging profession of law enforcement, as it is perceived in municipal police departments, has started to place greater emphasis upon careful selection of recruits. Careful screening is required because of the complex demands upon a modern metropolitan officer, and a closer look at psychological selection procedures is in progress.

A recent survey of assessment procedures in 55 U.S. cities revealed that 85 percent use some type of "police aptitude" test, which in most cases was little more than an unstandardized intelligence test (Narrol & Levitt, 1963). While 16 percent utilized some psychiatric interviews, critical motivational-emotional-personality dimensions were largely untapped. Whether these deficiencies can be remedied by addition of standardized personality inventories to police selection test batteries is questionable. While standardized objective personality tests may be suited for preliminary rough screening, the police candidate seems quite guarded, and a questionable extrapolation from nonpolice norm groups must usually be attempted.

Even intelligence as measured in paper-and-pencil tests, may not always be translated into equally intelligent decision making in an emergency field situation. This quality of clearheaded use of intelligence under pressure was termed "effective" intelligence by the OSS staff during WW II (1948). A possible answer to the limitations of current police selection procedures may be use of situational-type tests.

METHOD

Three situational-type tests were designed for inclusion in an overall psychological selection program of Cincinnati police recruits. Situational tests, except for the Bull Session, did not enter into final ratings of candidates. Situational tests were administered in the course of an intensive five to six hour psychological evaluation conducted in small groups of eight to ten candidates. Intent of the situational tests was to create a microcosm of a "natural" field problem an officer might encounter and to observe closely the candidate's reaction and performance under stress.

Design of the testing tasks observed the following criteria:

1. The tasks should have a close relation to an activity in which an officer might commonly be engaged.
2. Tasks should present a standard stimulus situation to each candidate. Conditions should not vary, if possible.
3. Each task should have several alternate solutions.
4. Accomplishment of task should not require very specialized abilities, so no candidate would be handicapped by lack of experience.
5. Task should be complex and difficult enough to engage the candidate fully, and stressful enough to produce a variety of emotional reactions. It should differentiate between candidates' performances. Still, care should be exercised not to harm or alienate candidates, who were voluntarily presenting themselves as job applicants.
6. Some measure of group activity should be included.
7. A "debriefing" session should be provided in order to encourage a climate of high morale, encourage expression of anger or anxiety, and help to restore emotional equilibrium.
8. Staff observers should have ample opportunity to confer after completion of a testing session, in order to synthesize observations, reconcile differences, and arrive at final ratings on each candidate with a maximum of information.

Foot Patrol Observation Test

Candidates were instructed to proceed on foot, unaccompanied, over a prescribed route, having been advised to "observe everything closely" along the way. The route proceeded for six blocks through a busy, downtown, predominantly Negro business section to Police Headquarters. Upon arrival the elapsed time of their "patrol" was noted, and 25 multiple choice questions of facts concerning number of intersections traversed, key stores, type of street paving, etc. were administered. Number of correct answers became their score. An open-end essay questionnaire was also administered in which candidates were asked to describe impressions of persons living in the neighborhood, unusual incidents they observed, and their feelings about "keeping the peace" in this district. Questions were designed to tap latent attitudes about law enforcement, minority groups, poor people, and motivation for a police career, as well as providing a written sample of grammar and self-expression.

Clues Test

This situational test was adapted from the "Belongings" test described in *Assessment of Men* (OSS, 1948). An area was roped off containing a desk, chair, and miscellaneous office equipment. Within this area a selected set of "clues" was planted which suggested hypotheses about the personality, habits, whereabouts, and possible flight of a hypothetical city employee. Racetrack sheets, Scotch bottles, tranquilizers, aspirins, "cold" checks, dunning letters from local department and jewelry stores, perfumed love letters, passport application, and a memo from the City Manager requesting audit of accounts were included.

Candidates were given ten minutes to "investigate" the mysterious disappearance of this hypothetical city employee, while a staff member working quietly in another part of the room observed the approach of the candidate to the task. Candidates then completed blank spaces in a questionnaire form requiring information ranging from simple factual data to hypotheses (more heavily weighted in scoring) regarding whereabouts, motives, probable mental state, and possible basis for prosecution. False leads and alternative hypotheses were possible. A final score from 0–60 points was derived.

Bull Session

The so-called "Bull Session" was a group diagnostic procedure which borrows heavily from the principles of group psychotherapy. Candidates from each testing session, eight to ten in number, were assembled around a large table in a conference room. Two group leaders and two observers, previously briefed on each candidate, formed the evaluation team. During the two-hour session group leaders initiated discussion by asking for introductions, present occupation, and reasons for choosing a police career. While discussion generally proceeded spontaneously, group leaders occasionally framed key issues of police work, called upon silent candidates, and pointed out the necessity for participation by each candidate. A typical session included discussion of use of force, handling of fears, use of alcohol and narcotics, mental illness, prostitution, homosexuality, administration of justice in the courts, minority groups, and use of authority. Questions were posed by group leaders in the form of concrete, practical situations.

No separate ratings were derived from the Bull Session; however, immediately after each diagnostic session the evaluation team met together to decide Overall Performance Predictions (OPP) for each candidate. Group participation was evaluated, together with earlier test results. Differences between team raters were discussed and reconciled, and final OPP ratings assigned as follows: 4, Superior; 3, Above Average; 2, Average; 1, Below Average; 0, High Risk. Only the High Risk category was recommended for rejection by the Civil Service Commission.

RESULTS

The situational tests, as part of a comprehensive selection program, were initially administered to a group of 62 Cincinnati police candidates. Of this group, 42 eventually completed recruit training in the Police Academy and were termed the "success" group; 20 did not accomplish police training and were termed the "failure" group (12 of the "failure" group were recommended for rejection by our evaluation team). Foot Patrol and Clues were not included in OPP ratings in order to test their value as independent predictors. The Army General Classification Test, Civilian Edition, was included as a reference measure, since its relationship to police performance has previously been demonstrated. Comparison of mean scores of the initial "success" and "failure" groups on Foot Patrol, Clues, and AGCT showed that the successful group had achieved higher mean scores than the unsuccessful group, but such differences did not reach statistical significance.

The 42 successful recruits were ranked according to their final standing in the Police Academy, which was a weighted measure based upon weekly examinations and notebooks during the three-month training period. Situational and AGCT test scores were then ranked for the group, and Spearman rank-order correlations computed. It was demonstrated that AGCT scores correlated .595 with final standing, which is significant at the .01 level. The Clues Test correlated .375 with final standing, which is significant at the .05 level. Since Clues and AGCT correlated only .105 with each other, it is possible that Clues represents a nonintellective test measure related to police performance, which tends to enhance the validity of the situational test rationale. No other correlations were significant between any measures.

In order to cross-validate results of the initial trial, an identical procedure was followed with a second group of 25 candidates. Fifteen candidates successfully completed Police Academy training, and ten did not accomplish this goal. Mean differences between the successful and unsuccessful group again failed to be significant. Following graduation from the Police Academy, rank-order correlations between final standing and test measures were again computed. AGCT correlated .708 with final standing, which is significant at the .01 level. Clues correlated .425 with final standing, which is significant at the .10 level (just misses .05 level). AGCT and Clues correlated .340 together, which is nonsignificant, so that findings from the initial group were substantially confirmed.

Bull Session evaluation must be indirect, since no separate measurement resulted; however, team members agreed that these diagnostic sessions were the single most valuable technique used in recruit selection and weighted Bull Session results heavily in their OPP ratings. The correlation between OPP ratings and Police Academy performance might, therefore, be used as an estimate of the efficiency of the Bull Session as a predictor. For this purpose, the Kendall rank-order correlation (tau) was used owing to the restricted ranks on the five-place OPP ratings. Results were converted to z scores and level of significance taken from a normal-probability table.

For the initial recruit group a Kendall rank-order correlation of .359 was obtained, which has a probability beyond the .0005 level. The second group correlated .473 between OPP and final Police Academy standing, which is significant at the .007 level of probability. It was concluded that the evaluation team's overall ratings were highly predictive of later recruit performance. By implication, the Bull Session accounted for a large proportion of this accurate prediction.

Unsuspected character traits and attitudes which had not been noted during previous tests and one-to-one interviewing sometimes emerged during the Bull Session. For example, a group leader proposed a hypothetical situation in which a patrolman, working alone in a "rough" neighborhood, encountered several men fighting in a cafe. The question was asked, "If you were that patrolman, what would you do?" As general discussion developed around this theme, a consensus was quickly reached that the lone officer should summon aid before committing himself to stopping the fight, even though it might mean walking away from the scene to summon assistance.

One candidate vociferously disagreed with this solution, insisting that "You'd never be able to show your face again on that beat if you walked away." When he was challenged by several candidates with previous Military Police experience, he became red in the face and sat glowering with clenched fists. Another group member finally offered the comment, "I'd never want to be on patrol with you, buddy, that would be a good way to get myself killed." At this point, the isolated candidate exploded, "I think all of you guys are a bunch of yellow-backs!" This explosive outburst was a valuable clue in establishing the poor judgment and emotional instability of this candidate under stress; the stubborn pseudomasculinity he displayed within the group was almost a promise of inappropriate behavior in police service.

On another occasion a candidate displayed very rigid and dogmatic attitudes on every issue and as the group began to warm up, he commenced to orate in an almost evangelical manner. This man, quietly referred to as "the preacher" by another group member, began to set everyone's teeth on edge, and they attempted to stop him by sarcasm and talking over him. However, this candidate, apparently insensitive to the reactions of the men around him, continued to rant about his pet religious beliefs, and to moralize about the duty of the policeman to correct moral injustices in the community. This candidate's reaction formation against his own unrecognized hostile impulses toward his fellow citizens would have made him an unreliable and sadistic officer, and the other candidates quickly sensed how difficult it would be to work alongside this fellow.

In some cases a candidate was encountered who appeared to be unable to organize his thoughts in any coherent fashion during the group sessions. Some of these men had previously performed adequately on paper-and-pencil tests, but in the Bull Session became disorganized, rambling, and circumstantial. They were unable to react in a realistic and appropriate fashion to the other group members, and displayed completely inadequate social judgment in their responses to questions about practical matters. The evaluation team suspected that these candidates were making a borderline psychotic social adjustment, and sought a police career to give themselves a firmer self-identity and to move toward a more assertive role in life.

These examples have been given to illustrate the usefulness of the Bull Session in confirming psychological test signs whose meaning may have been somewhat tenuous, and in ferreting out behavior not revealed by conventional methods.

DISCUSSION

It appears promising that a simple situational task (Clues) could be constructed on an a priori basis, and on its initial trials manage to correlate with a performance measure. The failure of the Clues Test to correlate with a standardized intelligence measure (AGCT) makes it reasonable to infer that situational tests may be sampling behavioral dimensions not present in paper-and-pencil intelligence tests but important to police field performance. It is premature to speculate on the behavioral constructs sampled by situational tests, since it is characteristic of these tests to require a broad spectrum of skills for this solution. In fact, their life-like quality comes from this breadth. If situational measures can be devised within a setting of continuous cross checks with eventual police field performance, they can be a promising supplement to more conventional techniques of assessment.

The failure of the Foot Patrol Test to correlate with other measures may represent the narrow range of scores obtained or other inadequacies of test construction, and illustrates the pitfalls of attempting untried tests without reliability or validity checks. The selection process occurred with a highly homogeneous, preselected group from an original pool of more than 600 applicants, which places a severe task upon any unverified test instrument.

The limitations of using final grades in a Police Academy training program must also be recognized. It is not necessary to document here the disappointing patrol performance of some men who showed promise during the training period. And later, even the most painstaking rating system in the field is subject to multiple biases. For example, it is common practice to start "rookie" patrolmen with rather low ratings of efficiency, so that adequate differentiation between field performance of starting patrolmen becomes quite difficult. A weighted measure of activity level based upon systematic reports of arrests, citations, etc., is under study by the authors, and this activity field measure may ultimately vindicate the situational test approach to selection.

It may be important to note that, despite the rigor of the selection process, no candidate has yet withdrawn or failed to complete the psychological evaluation phase of selection. Candidates have reported that they enjoyed the lifelike quality of the situational tests, thought this type of test "made sense" to them, and apparently preferred the action-centered tests to the conventional paper-and-pencil approach. Some candidates have expressed the feeling that the careful evaluation reflected the importance of the position they were seeking, and that finalists must be a hand-picked "elite" group, which is true. The group spirit generated during the Bull Session, with its overtones of competition and camaraderie, tended to counteract any anger or anxiety caused by the protracted testing session. The teasing and joking with examiners was an emotional catharsis which seemed to be helpful in restoring emotional equilibrium.

▽ ▽ ▽

RESEARCH in social psychology in field situations, especially with workers coming from lower socioeconomic classes, would stress the value of worker participation when it comes to a management decision to change pay incentive plans. Many such research reports have demonstrated the value of actual and real personal involvement on the part of workers so that they feel they have had a real stake in the control of conditions which directly concern them. Concomitantly, management plans which are merely imposed from above are frequently sabotaged. In the brief report given here, certain of the results—especially with imposed conditions—are the opposite of what one might expect. There was an effective transfer from the original participative group to other and later noninvolved employees. On the other hand, social psychology research would predict that if management discontinues the pay incentive plan in a participative group, then there would be a large and immediate effect. And this is exactly what occurred. The report is an interesting example of a simple situational test situation utilizing a group of workers rarely studied. At the time of the study, all three authors were members of the Department of Administrative Sciences of Yale University and what follows is their complete follow-up report, one year later, which appeared in the *Journal of Applied Psychology* in 1971.

LONG-TERM IMPACT OF EMPLOYEE PARTICIPATION IN THE DEVELOPMENT OF PAY INCENTIVE PLANS: A FIELD EXPERIMENT REVISITED

Kenneth C. Scheflen, Edward E. Lawler III, and J. Richard Hackman

In a previous study, Lawler and Hackman (1969) examined the effects of employee participation in the development of pay incentive plans. The *S*s were part-time unskilled workers who cleaned buildings in the evening. In the experiment, three autonomous work groups developed their own incentive plans to reward good job attendance (participative condition). These plans were then imposed by the company on two other work groups (imposed condition). There were two control groups: one group talked with the researchers about job attendance problems but received no treatment, and the other received no attention from the researchers. Attendance was monitored for 16 weeks following the introduction of the new pay plans. A significant increase in attendance appeared only in the participative condition. Before the change, the average employee in the participative condition worked 88 percent of his scheduled hours; after the plan went into effect, the average employee worked 94 percent of his scheduled hours. In the imposed condition, the comparable pretreatment figure was 83 percent and the posttreatment figure also was 83 percent. No changes were observed in the control groups.

It is possible that the increase in attendance in the participative condition was due solely to an initial burst of enthusiasm on the part of the workers in the participative groups and that the effects observed during the 16-week postexperimental period were only temporary. Alternatively, it is possible that the imposed plans were, in the long run, equally as effective as the participative plans—but that it simply takes longer for an imposed plan to have effect. To examine these questions, follow-up attendance data were gathered from the original work groups approximately 1 year after the pay plans were initially implemented.

In addition, the study examines the effects of a naturally occurring reversal of the original experimental treatment. After the pay plans had been in effect for 6 months in the case of one group and 11 months in the case of another group, company management unexpectedly discontinued the incentive plans in two of the three participative groups. Workers in both of these groups had shown a significant increase in attendance when the new plans had been instituted. The present data show the effects on the attendance of the employees in these groups when they reverted to the preexperimental pay arrangements.

METHOD

The research site was a small company that provides building maintenance services on a contract basis. The Ss were part-time employees who cleaned buildings during the evening. The Ss worked in groups which ranged in size from 2 to 25 and which were responsible for doing cleaning work in one building. Although the work groups did similar work, they were highly autonomous and there was very little communication among employees in different work groups.

The employees tended to have very low educational levels and most were members of minority groups. They ranged in age from 16 to 70 years. Although the employees from whom data were collected in the present study are very similar to those in the original study, about 60 percent of the original participants had left the company by the time data collection for this study had been completed. This high turnover rate is characteristic of all maintenance employees in the company and was not higher in the experimental and control groups used in this research. The research site and Ss are discussed in greater detail by Lawler and Hackman (1969).

Attendance data were collected for the present study from the five work groups which had participated in the earlier study. Two of the groups had incentive plans imposed on them by management in the earlier study, and the plans were still in effect when the present data were collected. One group had participatively developed an incentive plan in the earlier study, and the plan was still in effect. Two groups had participatively developed incentive plans in the earlier study, but the plans subsequently had been discontinued by company management.

A weekly percentage attendance figure was obtained for each group by dividing the number of hours scheduled to be worked each week into the number of hours actually worked. In addition, employees in three of the groups were given semistructured on-the-job interviews about their reactions to the incentive plans, and company managers were interviewed regarding their views about the way the plans had been introduced and how they were functioning.

RESULTS

Results for the participative groups are presented in Figures 6 and 7. In the single participative group in which the pay plan was still in effect at the time of the present data collection, the average employee worked 93 percent of his scheduled hours (see Figure 6). This compares to 94 percent during the 16-week observation period immediately following the introduction of the plan, and 88 percent prior to the introduction of the plan. Thus, the plan appears still to be effective for this group.

Data for the two participative groups for which the plans had been discontinued by management are shown in Figure 7. (Although the plans were discontinued at different times, the data for the two groups have been combined.) In the weeks immediately prior to discontinuation, average attendance in these two groups was 92 percent; in the weeks after the plans had been discontinued, attendance dropped to an average of 82 percent. The 92 percent attendance is comparable to the 94

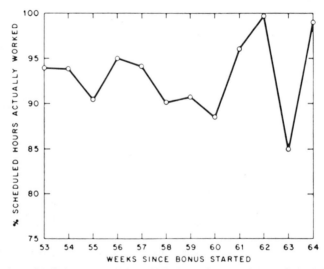

FIG. 6. Attendance in one participatative group for a twelve-week period one year after the plan started.

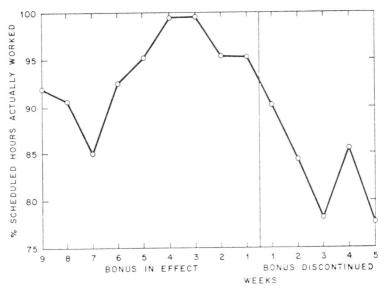

Fɪɢ. 7. Mean attendance of two participatative groups for the nine weeks before the plans were ended and for the first five weeks after they were ended.

percent average obtained for the participative groups in the original study. The drop from 92 to 82 percent is statistically significant (by median test, $\chi^2 = 7.78$, $p < .01$), suggesting that discontinuation of the plan did decrease average employee attendance.

Data from the two imposed groups are presented in Figure 8. During the 12-week observation period, attendance in these groups averaged 87 percent as compared to 83 percent for the 12-week period immediately preceding the installation of the plan (by median test, $\chi^2 = 6.00$, $p < .05$). Thus, attendance in the imposed groups is somewhat higher 1 year after the plans were imposed than it was immediately following their implementation.

DISCUSSION

It is significant that the attendance data were still high in the participative groups 1 year after the plans were installed, despite the fact that a majority of the workers in these groups had not themselves been involved in the development of the plans. It would appear that the norms for good attendance which seemed to have developed in the participative groups when the plans were introduced were effectively passed on to new workers as they joined the work groups. In one group, for example, employees expressed feelings of ownership of the plan despite the fact that most of the group members had not actually participated in the design of the original plan. These data suggest that the initial success of the participative plans was not simply a function of an initial and temporary enthusiasm about the opportunity to partici-

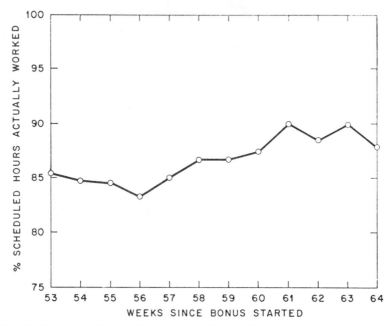

FIG. 8. Mean attendance of the two imposed groups for a twelve-week period one year after the plans were started.

pate in the development of a pay plan, and that groups seem to have norms that do not depend on a stable membership for their maintenance.

The small increase in attendance observed for the groups in which the pay plans were imposed was not entirely unexpected. Although employees did not respond to these plans immediately after they were introduced, the company did administer the plan fairly and consistently throughout the year preceding the present data collection. Experience with the plan over this longer time period may finally have convinced the workers that the plan was "on the level," and that if they came to work more regularly they would receive more money. Further, the workers in the imposed groups simply may have taken longer than their colleagues in the participative groups to learn the mechanics of how the plans worked. The net result, it appears, was that both the workers' trust of management and their understanding of the plan and its implications for the amount of pay they could earn increased slowly over time as did their attendance. It should be noted, however, that even after a year of slow improvement, the imposed groups had not reached the level of attendance attained and maintained by the participative groups.

Probably the most compelling finding of the present study is the large and immediate drop in attendance when the pay plans were discontinued in two of the three participative groups. The decision of company management to drop the two plans created a second manipulation in the study and, in effect, produced a natural field experiment. This second manipulation provides dramatic evidence for the effectiveness of the participative plans: dropping them reduced attendance just as substantially as installing them had increased it.

The decision by company management to discontinue two of the plans came as a complete surprise to the researchers. Financial considerations probably did not play a role in the decision, since hourly rates were raised when the plan was discontinued. Indeed, discontinuance of the plans appeared to cost the company more money in increased hourly wages than it saved in unpaid bonuses.

Further, the decision did not seem to hinge on misperceptions of company managers about the effectiveness of the plans. The researchers had shown the relevant managers the article written about the earlier study and most of these individuals accepted the fact that the participative plans were working as intended. Interviews with several managers responsible for administering the plans did suggest that these managers felt little or no ownership of the plans or commitment to them. They had been told by top management to work with the researchers in instituting the experimental program, but they themselves had little to do with developing it. It is not surprising, therefore, that these managers felt little commitment to the plans and that they were ready to discontinue them when the first opportunity presented itself.

Viewing the long-term impact of the experimental program on organizational effectiveness, it appears that the researchers' failure to gain the commitment of the managers was a very significant one indeed. The two imposed pay plans persisted and even showed a small increase in effectiveness 1 year later. But two of the three plans in which employees participated to a significant degree were dropped. Thus, the net result is that the three participative plans were not as effective over the long term as were the imposed plans. The reason, it should be emphasized, is not that employees respond better to imposed plans. The data suggest just the reverse. In summary, it appears that the present data support the view that long-lasting change can be introduced effectively in organizations only when the changes are accepted and owned by all levels— employees and managers alike—who are or will be involved in the new program.

THE emphasis in most courses and textbooks dealing with the problems involved in psychological measurement focuses on the quantitative aspects—reliability and validity of scores, norms, dispersion, scaling, etc. Any psychological test is also a situation into which the individual is placed. It may be viewed as a standardized situation where the actual test is seen as the independent variable and the individual's responses to the test items become the dependent variable. From this vantage point, much "extra test" data becomes available and the experienced psychometrician pays close attention to these "extras." There are, then, additional nuances to be obtained from any test situation other than mere scores checked against norm tables. The following article by Mrs. Barbara Kirk, who is Director of the Counseling Center at the University of California at Berkeley, spells out some of these extra measurement gains. The paper originally appeared in the *Personnel and Guidance Journal* in 1961.

EXTRA MEASUREMENT USE OF TESTS IN COUNSELING

Barbara A. Kirk

The use of tests for purposes of measurement has been extensively investigated over a number of decades. During and following World War I, tests came into extensive service for population description and comparison, in the assessment of a variety of traits. Then, and most importantly, measurement devices were applied to problems of placement prediction. From their application in mass terms, instruments were developed which had validity and reliability to a degree commensurate with their utilization for selection, placement, and counseling of the *individual*. Testing became a fundamental technique for processes of educational and vocational counseling and constituted a major step forward from vocational guidance based primarily upon occupational information.

In the current status of the field of educational and vocational counseling, testing is an integral and indispensable technique. What part does it play? Are only tests which have acceptably high levels of validity and reliability, and for which probabilities can be adequately calculated, of value to individuals who are faced with educational and vocational choices and decisions? Without, in any sense, gainsaying the value of quantification and the relation of individual scores to normative standards, the contribution of standardized tests to the counseling process must be viewed qualitatively to appreciate their full yield. There are three contributions in particular which may be emphasized, although to the resourceful counseling psychologist, this list should not be considered exhaustive. The three areas under consideration here might be called clinical diagnosis, self-assessment, and interactive facilitation, and represent the values directly to the counselor, to the counselee, and to the interaction between them.

Before describing the three primary extra measurement uses of tests in counseling, it might be well to indicate for whom these uses are appropriate. The interpretation of test results, either quantitative or qualitative findings, is a highly skilled activity of the fully qualified, experienced clinical or counseling psychologist. The counselor, teacher-counselor, or dean is commonly dependent upon a school psychologist or consulting clinical or counseling psychologist for evaluation of test data. An article by the staff of the University of Maryland Counseling Center, "A Check-List for Recording Test-Taking Behavior" (1960), attempts to study the reliability of observations of such behavior. It shows how complicated and difficult making such observations can be. Because of the inherent difficulty in soundly interpreting behavior on tests or in a test-taking situation, such reports must be regarded as tentative within counseling and not fully accepted until proven out in the counseling process. Of the extra measurement use of tests subsequently delineated, *Clinical Diagnosis* is the prerogative of the clinical and/or counseling psychologist whose analysis may be of assistance to the counselor; *Self-Assessment* is an area open to all counselors who are either competent with counseling techniques or who have the good judgment and restraint to permit a counselee to work out his problems himself to the full extent of his capacity! *Interactive Facilitation* again applies to the use of test data by competent counselors.

CLINICAL DIAGNOSIS

This is undoubtedly the best known and the most common extra measurement use of tests in both clinical and counseling practice. We are concerned here with observation of test-taking behavior, of intellectual and emotional functioning, and of demonstrated habits and attitudes. From such observations, conclusions can be obtained by the clinician for habitual and characteristic performance. The presentation of a standard situation gives unique opportunity to observe individual modes of reaction, deviations from usual behavior, and particular trends and quality of intellectual and emotional functioning. Usually tests implicated for this purpose are those which are individually administered, allowing for intensive observation of a sample of some type of performance. On mental ability tests, kind of approach to mental tasks is demonstrated, *i.e.*, trial and error, problem solving, insight gaining. There is also opportunity to learn quality and kind of functioning in relation to such traits as memory, judgment, comprehension, reasoning, and abstraction. Furthermore, malfunctioning may be seen and distinguished from healthy mental functioning. Also observable are personality traits such as confidence, persistence, security, dependence, defensiveness, etc. The observations and clinical determinations of the psychologist are accurate, subtle, deep, and enlightening to the degree of his particular skill, competence, and experience. Here, and only here, can determination be made of true intellectual capacity as distinguished from and discrepant from performing capacity.

Similarly, tests of manual dexterity, manipulation, and so forth, can provide information of great value about attitudes toward work and habits of work. What are the counselee's standards, and what is his approach? Does the counselee improve with practice and continue on to an ever-better performance? On the other hand, does he tire with a prolonged task and tend to reduce his energy output and decrease his motivation? Is he careful, meticulous, accurate, or does he tend to try to rush or be inaccurate and careless? Does he have pride in his performance and to what degree?

Not only is observational material obtainable from individually administered tests, but approach to paper-and-pencil tests, administered in a testing room with other counselees, also is revealing. Consideration for the examiner and other test-takers, dependency on the examiner, fear, demandingness, efficiency, and organization are some of the behaviors which may be most helpful in understanding and counseling the counselee.

Subjective examination and analysis of test content of other than individual ability tests is also a major aid to clinical diagnosis over and beyond and apart from the quantitative test result. We are accustomed to analysis of content of projective test responses for broad and deep understanding of the individual. Other tests also, when their content is analyzed, can make similar contribution. Whether it be an item review and analysis on an inventory-type personality test, or a paper-and-pencil mental ability test, or study habits and attitudes questionnaire, each has something of real significance to offer. Greatly impoverished is the counselor and the counseling when this rich source of knowledge is overlooked.

Analysis of content wherever we implicate it may afford bases for hypotheses and clues for exploration. Even though they do not provide the *"answers,"* they may each and all supply a part of the jigsaw puzzle which when put together gives us the formulation or diagnosis.

SELF-ASSESSMENT

This refers to self-assessment only as part of the process of counseling and not independent of it.

A vitally important contribution of tests is that of gain in self-knowledge for the purpose of self-evaluation and thus development of insights. Even a biographical form, with the opportunity to put together information about oneself, both historically and cross sectionally, can give a counselee sufficient objective self-perception and clarification of problem and goal to facilitate the solution of his problem or determination of a choice or a decision.

To an even greater extent, this function can be served by the range of tests which compel self-inspection and self-inquiry. All of the inventory type personality tests are of this character. Similarly, tests of general college adjustment; tests of attitudes and values; and tests of study habits, attitudes, methods, and techniques serve this purpose. The very "taking" of such tests as these, with the necessity for recording a response, compels thought and self-investigation, which activity in itself is both part of, and accelerative of, the process of counseling. Subsequently bringing to the counseling interview the counselee's conscious reaction to any or many of such items may lead to further insights and to reconstruction of many aspects of the self-concept.

The counselee can benefit from his own content analysis. For example, a counselee, in responding to adjustment or personality inventory tests, begins to recognize that he replies to items in a way which indicates to him that he must be rather passive. His passivity may thenceforth become a concern in his counseling. In self-assessment, the counselee has found clues to explore and pursue in his counseling.

Tests of the sort called special aptitude tests may often be most informative in the area of occupational information. Not only do such tests present situations and problems which occur in the occupation in question, as, for example, law, medicine, teaching, nursing, etc., but also give the counselee an opportunity to relate for himself his own attitudes and inclinations to the occupational demands. An example might be that of a counselee considering the possibility of preparing for teaching who, on responding to a teaching attitudes inventory, learns of the practical disciplinary problems in the classroom and who can thus visualize himself in such situations and try them on for size. Tests which reveal special knowledge in other than professional fields may provide some of the same direct view of occupational characteristics. In this category may be considered such tests as sales aptitude and comprehension, comprehension of mechanical principles, and knowledge of supervisory principles. Even vocational interest tests, such as the Kuder, may be directly helpful to a counselee in this fashion since they describe the function or content of occupations rather than simply list them.

INTERACTIVE FACILITATIONS

Here we are concentrating on the use of tests specifically within the interview framework for assisting in both the counseling relationship and communication and in furthering the counseling itself.

For the inarticulate uncommunicative person, testing may offer the means not only of immediate communication but may also be an impetus factor toward overcoming long-standing habits. For those who find it difficult to communicate orally in an interview, a Sentence Completion Test, for example, where thoughts are communicated in written form, may be most helpful in that they can be talked about directly in the interview. If the counselee has been able to say in writing what he cannot say directly to the counselor, he has at least communicated and has expressed his willingness for the counselor to know what he has said and thus to begin to use it to help him to talk. A Thematic Apperception Test will perhaps draw on a counselee's unconscious attitudes and feelings, forming the basis for his communication on a deeper level than he has formerly been capable of in an interview.

We have indicated that both counselor and counselee can gain from tests very valuable information about the counselee's behavior and traits, again despite the fact that from a quantitative point of view validity and reliability coefficients might be less than desired.

In a sense, the testing situation can be likened to a laboratory in which one learns about oneself in a real life situation and then can gain perspective upon it from counseling discussion. After test taking, both the counselor and counselee have the opportunity in the counseling relationship to share the impressions which come from the testing experience. Any of the information and impressions so derived can be used as an interview aid, as a method of entering into exploration and discussion. For example, with personality inventory type tests, it may be very useful in the counseling process for the counselee in the interview to evaluate with the counselor the presence or absence of a tested trait and the degree to which he feels it pertains. For the counselor, tests provide limitless material for introducing ideas, for exploring hypotheses, for presenting interpretations, for clarifying, for reinforcing insights. In communication regarding the counselee's reactions to the tests, their items, and his performance, the counselee has opportunity for greater self-understanding, leading to resolution of problems. Working in this way utilizes the resources of the counselee in involving him actively in the counseling process.

▽ ▽ ▽

A type of situational test that may strike the reader as ususual is the research using the College and University Environment Scales (CUES), whose antecedent was the College Characteristics Index (CCI). The CCI was developed over a period of years by Dr. C. Robert Pace in collaboration with Dr. George Stern at Syracuse University. The instrument in its present form (CUES) is composed of 150 statements about college life—campus features and facilities, campus rules and regulations, items concerning student life and extracurricular organizations—all of which help to pin down the intellectual—cultural—social climate of the campus. When students take the test, they merely indicate whether they feel the statements on the questionnaire are true or false about their own campuses. CUES is therefore a way of obtaining a description of the college from the students themselves. These are not new or entering students, as are those in the Astin (1965) research; rather, as recommended in the preliminary manual (Pace, 1963), students must fill out CUES from a position of real acquaintance. For this, ideally, the entire junior class might be used. Normative data are currently based on a total of 50 schools. Scores from CUES provide a measure of the college environment, along five dimensions developed by factor analysis. The dimensions are:

1. Practicality—the degree to which personal status and practical benefit are emphasized.
2. Community—the extent to which the campus may be said to be friendly, cohesive, group—oriented.
3. Awareness—how much emphasis is placed on self—understanding and personal identity, wide range of appreciations and a personal involvement with world problems.
4. Propriety—the degree to which politeness and protocol and consideration are stressed.
5. Scholarship—how much in evidence is competitively high academic achievement, shown by such things as concern for scholarship and intellectual discipline, interest in knowledge and ideas.

From these five factor scales, institutional patterns may then be constructed for individual colleges and universities, or even for smaller subdivisions within these organizations. What is done here is to take the early CCI scales (there were 30 of these) and then do a factor analysis based on the 50 colleges and universities. The 50 colleges now become the variables, and the CCI scale scores for each college become the number of observations. A factor analysis of this matrix will thus produce institutional patterns or clusters. This relatively small number of institutions obviously does not constitute a representative sample for all U. S. schools, and so the subtypes of institutional patterns cannot be delineated with much confidence. Pace feels, regardless of the tentative results, that even this small—scale search for pattern may be of some interest and might also stimulate new speculation.

The following report by Dr. Pace is a brief summary of these results, which are given in the CUES Preliminary Technical Manual (Pace, 1963, pp.71–76). Dr. Pace, formerly a collaborator with Dr. Stern at Syracuse University, and for many years the Director of the Psychological Research Center there, is now Professor of Higher Education at the University of California at Los Angeles.

CUES INSTITUTIONAL PATTERNS

C. Robert Pace

From these analyses, one can tentatively group colleges and universities into six patterns. First, there is a group of very selective, private liberal arts colleges—scholarly, aware, somewhat more proper than rebellious, and unconcerned with practicality. Most similar to this group is a group of large academically oriented public universities which are also typically high in scholarship and awareness, generally low in practicality, but which differ from the selective liberal arts colleges in that they have uniformly low scores on the community scale and are generally lower than the liberal arts colleges on the propriety scale. Most dissimilar to the selective liberal arts colleges is a group of large nonselective universities, both public and private. A fourth group consists primarily of small strongly denominational colleges characterized by high scores on the practicality, community, and propriety scales and by low scores on awareness. The fifth pattern consists of universities with a strongly technical emphasis. Most of these schools have an average to strong emphasis on scholarship but very low scores on community and awareness and average to slightly below average scores on practicality. And the sixth pattern consists of moderately denominational colleges and a few teachers colleges. These are characterized by low scores on scholarship and awareness and by high scores on practicality and community.

ILLUSTRATIVE PROFILES

Although there are certain general institutional patterns described in the foregoing section, and although there are certain general correlations between various CUES scores, there are nevertheless some unique qualities in each institution and many significant exceptions to all general tendencies. For this reason, profiles are presented of specific institutions which are alike in certain ways, or which one might think would be alike, but which differ significantly in other ways.

The first set of profiles—for Antioch, Swarthmore and Reed in Figure 9—shows all three schools to be high on scholarship and awareness but very low on practicality. Antioch shows a much higher score on community than Swarthmore or Reed and each college is noticeably unique on the propriety scale.

The second set (Figure 10) describes three public institutions—Purdue, UCLA and San Francisco State College.* Purdue and UCLA scored high on the scholarship scale. UCLA and San Francisco State scored high on the awareness scale, but Purdue had a fairly low score. All three universities are rather low on the community scale, with San Francisco State and UCLA being particularly low. On the propriety scale San Francisco State is much higher than either of the other two. Purdue is uniquely high on the practicality scale. In this second set of profiles, it is evident that high scholarship and awareness are not always correlated and that high scholarship is not necessarily incompatible with high practicality.

Certainly one generalization which clearly emerges from these studies of college environments is that it is risky to generalize. Many institutions of the same presumed type are, in fact, quite different from one another. Indeed, diversity of institutions is a characteristic of American higher education and this will remain true as long as it is a goal of American education to serve a diversity of students. It is partly for this reason that CUES are potentially useful both for the institution and for the prospective student. If colleges and universities are different from one another, with many being unique in significant ways, knowledge of the perceived atmosphere of a campus could lead to planned modification or planned preservation, whichever is wished by the faculty and administration, and to hopefully wiser choices on the part of selective students who are as eager to know more about the college as the college is insistent on knowing a lot about them.

Stern (1970) has published a summary of such data gathered over a 10 year period from some 100 institutions and almost 10,000 students. The book is actually a study of student perceptions about themselves and about their satisfactions (and gripes) with college life. As Kelly (1971) remarks, in his review of this volume, this is not a study of the college environment *per se*; it is, rather, a descriptive account of the range and level of student views about themselves and about their campuses in the 1960s; secondly, it is a rich reference library for hypotheses to identify interrelationships of student and college; it is also a call for the redesigning of much of what now passes as college education

Another and similar approach to arriving at a measure of college environments has been developed by Astin (1965). His method involves a set of 25 student attributes (typically, specific examples of nonacademic student achievement such as placing among the top three in a science contest, having a lead role in a play, being elected

---

* A more detailed report on San Francisco State has been published by Pace (1962).

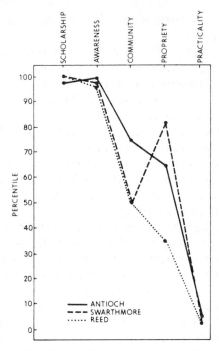

FIG. 9. Three private liberal arts college institutional patterns.

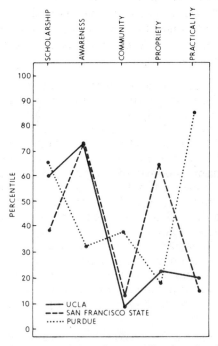

FIG. 10. Institutional patterns of three large public educational enterprises.

to one or more student offices) in the form of a simple questionnaire given to entering freshmen during orientation week at some 250 colleges and universities. In addition, the students were asked about their probable future major field and later occupation, the eventual college degree they planned to obtain, and father's occupation and educational level completed. Finished forms were obtained from over 127,000 students. From the replies to the open-ended questions concerning these last four items, students were classified according to Holland's (1963) occupational classification scheme, which corresponds to six basic personality types: realistic (as mechanic or tool designer); intellectual or scientific (botanist, anthropologist); social (speech therapist, foreign missionary); conventional (bank teller, statistician); enterprising (salesman, diplomat); and artistic (playwright, symphony conductor). These same six groupings may also be used to classify a student's major field. Thus, if a large proportion of entering freshmen reported they planned to become engineers, this student body would then receive a high rating on "realistic." (Astin com-

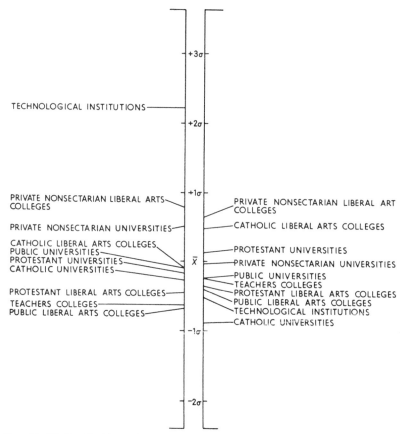

FIG. 11. Median intellectualism scores (*left*) and aestheticism scores (*right*) of student bodies entering ten types of institutions (Astin, 1965, p. 33).

ments on the remarkable variation among entering classes regarding future plans. For example, the percentage of first-year students eventually planning on graduate work varies from 6 to 98.) The questionnaire items answered by the students (52 input items made up the total) were factor analyzed into six factors—intellectualism, aestheticism, status, leadership, pragmatism, and masculinity. The result of all this made possible, then the characterization of individual college environments in cookbook fashion. Figure 11 compares various college and university grouping on two of these factors obtained from the student input data—intellectualism and aestheticism. Astin specifically lists individual colleges by name and locale, followed by scores on all these variables. It is a very entertaining pastime for the reader to check scores of institutions with which he is well acquainted and compare these indexes with his own subjective impressions. Astin's handbook is a very useful compendium for both high school students and guidance counselors when involved with the proper selection of a collegiate institution.

All such information about college environments may be effectively put to use to aid college applicants, a group which has long been at some disadvantage because they typically know much less about the colleges to which they apply than the colleges know about their applicants. Centra (1970), in a study for the College Entrance Examination Board has developed a Questionnaire on Student and College Characteristics (QSCC) which combines both the Pace and Astin approach: upperclass students at college were asked about their perceptions of their college and also were asked to provide self-reports of their activities, interests, and demographic family characteristics. Data were also obtained from the institution itself, such as the average academic aptitude of students who enroll, faculty-student ratio, college income per student, etc. The QSCC was administered at over 200 institutions, all College Board members, in the fall of 1968. This means that *public* universities and colleges are underrepresented and the "independent" colleges are overrepresented. Factor analyses were run on all of these data. Eight perceptual factors, analogous to those described by Pace and Astin were identified (an activism factor, of interest to certain groups of students, points up a fairly recent emphasis on the college campus). Six factors seemed to summarize best the dimensions along which colleges differ and in which applicants would be interested: athletic versus cultural, size with cliquishness, elitism, activism with flexibility, student satisfaction, social life. Centra states "there is no reason to believe that colleges would be objective in selecting items to write their own environmental descriptions" (p. 39) and that, undoubtedly, another outside agency is needed for this purpose. Eventually one might imagine high school students interacting with easily accessible computers to secure such information about colleges they are considering and thereby learn both about the diversity within each institution as well as the differences between college averages. Centra believes the first point about diversity is significant because, in the large university where subenvironments exist, such diversity is an important consideration.

▽ ▽ ▽

MORE recently, and since these previous papers on college environments, there has been a more sweeping proposal to provide this information to prospective college applicants and to make this available to high school students through the auspices of the College Entrance Examination Board (CEEB).

CEEB in 1966 appointed a Commission on Tests whose job was to undertake a thorough and critical review of the College Board's testing functions in USA education and with instructions to consider possibilities for fundamental changes in the present College Board tests and their utilization and also to take charge of making recommendations to the Board on their conclusions. The College Board program originally served only a small number of high prestige eastern USA private colleges; it now serves a very diverse range of institutions and even a more diverse range of students. New programs and new services seemed clearly in the offing. Thus, in 1967, Commission members were appointed for a three-year term and their report to CEEB has now been published in two volumes (CEEB, 1970).

From the second volume, called *Briefs*, comes the following Pace report. *Briefs* are materials composed by various Commission members for the enlightenment and edification of all members and which usually contained specific recommendations for new practices or reforms of current CEEB procedures. The following brief by Pace is one of these. It is a provocative essay on how measurements of college and university environments might be put to better use for potential college applicants.

A PROGRAM FOR PROVIDING INFORMATION ABOUT COLLEGES TO APPLICANTS

C. Robert Pace

Granted the virtue of a greater symmetry of information between applicant and institution in the process of deciding who goes where to college, the College Entrance Examination Board will need to develop a program for doing this that is relevant, feasible, and impartial. Specifically, what information about the institution is relevant? How is relevance determined? How is impartiality assured? How is validity judged?

And what is feasible? These questions cannot be wisely answered overnight. They require systematic, scholarly, and imaginative consideration. The consequences of the inventions and answers that are arrived at may be as significant as the consequences have been of previous inventions of measures of scholastic aptitude and achievement and grade point averages.

The purpose of this brief is threefold: (1) to recommend that the College Board support a research and development program along with the earliest possible introduction of a mutual information exchange system between applicants and Board member colleges; (2) to suggest something of the content and complexity of such a research and development program; and (3) to suggest possible forms that an information system might take.

ESTIMATING THE DIMENSIONS OF THE PROBLEM

Realistically, I assume that the College Board is concerned with providing information about Board member colleges to the applicants to those colleges. Idealistically, I assume that the Board is concerned with a potentially nationwide program without regard to what institutions belong to what organizations—at least that would be true if the Board accepted the student as its potential client just as it now accepts the college as its actual client.

Accepting the student as a client, however, does not necessarily mean that the Board would be dealing with several million high school graduates in relation to more than 2,000 colleges and universities in some mutual information exchange system. The question "Who goes where to college?" can be answered; but the question of how much choice is involved in this distribution of students to colleges cannot be answered with quite the same assurance. For many students no choice (realistically) is open. "The opportunity for students to choose where they will go depends on several conditions: on what is available near at hand, on knowledge of what is available elsewhere, and on the students' talents and financial resources. The combined possession of high academic talents, money, and scholarship will enable some students to make national choices among the best public and private institutions. . . . There are selective students as well as selective institutions. . . . For most students going to college, however, the choices open to them will be more limited, based mainly, as they are now, on the circumstances that the place is near and the price is right. . . . Any national effort toward selective assignment, which told people where to go and what was good for them, would be contrary to our deepest traditions of freedom and morality. Distinctive institutions and distinctive individuals will just have to find one another, as they often do now; and they will be more likely to do so as information about each becomes more available to both, and as the resources which permit mobility are increased. . . ." (Pace, 1966, pp. 160–170).

The point of these comments is simply that how one defines the magnitude of the problem will have a bearing on what kind of information about colleges is really relevant and useful for the applicants. If the clientele is limited to the students who can afford to be nationally selective, then it is important and useful to make subtle distinctions between Harvard, Yale, and Princeton. But if the clientele is larger and more heterogeneous, then such distinctions are of minor utility; whereas differences between those institutions and, for example, the University of Northern Iowa, Ouachita Baptist College, and Eastern Oregon State College are more important. The content of the information system will depend on the kind of discrimination the system is designed to facilitate. One needs to face this policy issue before one can realistically consider the question of what information will be useful to the applicants.

EXAMINING THE INFORMATION THAT IS AVAILABLE FROM OPEN SOURCES AND PUBLISHED INSTRUMENTS

A very substantial literature has accumulated, especially over the past dozen years, that has a bearing on the characteristics of college environments. Basically, researchers have used one or more of five rather different approaches in describing college environments.

1. Colleges have been characterized by the kind of people who go to them. California Institute of Technology can be characterized as a place in which all students have scores of 700 or higher on the mathematical sections of the College Board's Scholastic Aptitude Test (SAT). The *College Handbook*, published by the Board, provides information of this type—SAT scores, high school class rank, and so forth of applicants and enrolled freshmen. Bennington can be characterized as a place where 80 per cent of the entering students have traveled abroad, whereas at the University of South Dakota perhaps no more than 5 percent of the entering students have traveled abroad (this is a guess, not a known fact). Educational Testing Service's College Student Questionnaire (CSQ) is used in several hundred institutions. From the CSQ one can characterize the student body according to educational and vocational plans, family independence, peer independence, liberalism, social conscience, cultural sophistication, and with respect to value orientations described as academic, collegiate, vocational, and nonconformist. Another widely used test is the Omnibus Personality Inventory (OPI). From the OPI one can characterize student bodies along such dimensions as thinking introversion, theoretical orientation, estheticism, complexity, autonomy, religious orientation, social orientation, impulse expression, personal integration, anxiety level, altruism, practical out-

look, and masculinity-femininity. The Stern Activities Index and the Edwards Personal Preference Inventory describe students, and student bodies, with respect to the strength of various personality needs such as needs for understanding, affiliation, dominance, deference, order, and so forth. The Allport-Vernon-Lindzey Study of Values assesses that relative priority of theoretical, esthetic, social, religious, political, and economic values. From Holland's Vocational Preference Inventory, and from other such tests, one can describe student bodies with respect to a variety of occupational orientations and interests. Conservatively, considering only the most widely used measures, I would estimate that they contain about 2,000 more or less different items and produce about 100 more or less different variables or measures along which one could characterize and compare the student bodies of different colleges and universities.

2. Colleges have been characterized by their programs. One does not go to Sweet Briar to study engineering nor to South Dakota School of Mines to study music. The catalog is the basic source for this type of information. But the catalog is not enough. What is also relevant to the atmosphere of the institution is the proportion of students in different fields. A college in which 40 percent of the students are in engineering is quite different from one in which 40 percent of the students are in education.

3. Colleges have been characterized along various census or demographic variables. Again, many of these are common and familiar— such as size, form of control, for men, women or both, highest degree offered, rural or urban, residential or commuter, and so on. Astin (1965) grouped information of this kind into five general dimensions that he calls affluence, size, masculinity, homogeneity of offerings, and technical emphasis. These overlap somewhat with what I have classified as program variables. There are others that may be important, such as class size, ratio of undergraduate to graduate students, ratio of part-time to full-time students, and so on.

4. Colleges have been classified by how students behave in them. Peterson's surveys for the Educational Testing Service giving the incidence of organized student protest are an example of this approach. Astin, in some of his research for the American Council on Education, has been following a similar line, asking, for example, how many students report that they have had a blind date, have drunk beer, slept in class, argued with a professor, and so forth. From factor analysis of information of this kind Astin develops indexes for characterizing the peer environment, the classroom environment, and the administrative environment.

5. Colleges have been characterized by what the students who attend them perceive to be generally true about them. This collective perception or consensus approach is typified by the College Characteristics

Index, the College & University Environment Scales (CUES), by similar scales developed by Thistlethwaite (1965), by some of the semantic differential scales developed by Pervin (1967), and by similar but much less widely used sets of items that other investigators have tried out. The College Characteristics Index, originally developed by Pace and Stern and now used exclusively by Stern, produces measures described as intellectual climate, vocational climate, aspiration level, student dignity, self-expression, group life, and social form. One of these, intellectual climate, is parallel to various intellectual needs measured by Stern's Activities Index. The other environmental press scales are not parallel, or at best are only slightly parallel, to corresponding needs scales in the Activities Index. Pace's CUES, distributed by ETS, produces characterizations of the environment along dimensions labeled scholarship, awareness, community, propriety, and practicality. In the new second edition there are additional scales labeled campus morale and quality of teaching and faculty-student relations. Thistlethwaite's instrument is divided into 12 faculty-press scales and 11 student-press scales, with titles such as faculty press for vocationalism, faculty press for advanced training, faculty press for affiliation, faculty press for independent thinking, student press for academic achievement, student press for estheticism, student press for opposition to faculty influence, student press for reflectiveness, and so on. Astin has also developed some "college image" items, which produce factors labeled academic competitiveness, concern for the individual student, school spirit, permissiveness, snobbishness, emphasis on esthetics, flexibility of the curriculum, and emphasis on social life. Pervin's semantic differential scales include 52 concepts, which can be collapsed into 13 factors having such labels as impulsivity-inhibition, liberal idealism-conservative pragmatism, optimism-alienation, and cosmopolitan-provincial. Altogether, in the most widely used consensus or perceptual measures there are probably about 1,000 more or less different items, which in various combinations produce some 20 to 50 more or less different scales or variables.

In a nationwide study of college students, alumni, and environments that we are currently conducting at the University of California, Los Angeles, we are searching for some reasonably parsimonious set of environmental characteristics that have a bearing on what happens to students. In the process of doing this we are trying out some new measures of such characteristics as learning styles, peer-group patterns, discipline and freedom, and so forth; and we are deriving various indexes for such possibly useful variables as institutional diversity, teaching orientation, involvement in campus life, and cosmopolitanism of student body.

There is a vast amount of published information, and data from test responses, that should be carefully examined. It is quite probable that the essence of this information can be reported in a relatively small number of crucial variables. But no such effort at data reduction has yet been attempted. The reason for some optimism that it can be done comes from the fact that, despite differences in method and content, different methods do not produce conflicting (negatively related) results; and even with some variations in content, certain variables continually emerge. Overall, there is a set of positive intercorrelations among different data sources that "should" be related, which range generally from the .30s to the .60s. Admittedly these are not "high" correlations, but they are about as large as are the typical correlations between SAT scores and college grades.

COLLECTING JUDGMENTS FROM POTENTIAL USERS AND CONTRIBUTORS

It would not be sufficient to base an information exchange system solely on the results of some data-reduction process applied to the thousands of pieces of potentially useful and available information. The ultimate selection of what information is made available, and in what form, should also be guided by the expressed desires and suggestions of the potential consumers (applicants, parents, and counselors) and the judgments of those who would have to provide some of the information (current college students and college officials).

From high school students, parents, and counselors one needs to find out (or be assured that he knows) what they really want to know, what things they consider, or would want to consider in making a choice among colleges. It will probably be discovered that some of their questions cannot be answered—questions like "Will the credits be accepted by another institution?" which can only be answered by the "other" institution. Or "What percentage of the students smoke marijuana?" (Who knows? Is it legitimate public information?) Some questions that can be answered are probably of interest to a great many people; others may be of interest to very few people. A series of interviews and group discussions can help to identify and give some perspective to these consumer concerns. Structured and unstructured questionnaires, both for high school students and for parents, could be distributed at regional test centers. In the structured questionnaires one could present various types of information and ask for some ratings of their relative importance; in the unstructured case, one could simply ask what sort of information they seek or think would be most helpful to them. Some studies of this kind have been made; but new studies are needed because the relevant questions and concerns today may not be the same as those reported by researchers 5 to 10 years ago.

Similarly, from college students and college officials (faculty and administration) one needs to learn what it is about the college that they think prospective students should know—that is, if someone is interested in coming to this place, what are some of the things he ought to know about it. Again, interviews, group discussions, and answers to structured and unstructured questionnaires would be important sources of information.

All this is not to say that consumer surveys should determine what information is put into the system; but it is to say that the questions that researchers ask and that result in assorted scores and indexes are not necessarily the same as the questions of most relevance to consumers. The inquiries and insights of both are important, so that the system produces answers people want, and also answers they need regardless of their awareness of the need.

DEVELOPING GUIDES FOR DECISIONS ABOUT THE SYSTEM

At the beginning of this brief, I used the words "relevant, feasible, impartial . . . and valid." Information about the college should make sense theoretically, educationally, and practically. By theoretical sense I mean that it cannot be a miscellaneous assortment of data that some people think might be useful, nor a presentation of vast amounts of unstructured data. There need to be guiding principles for selecting and grouping information. By educational sense I mean that the information should be relevant to institutional purposes and to the larger purposes of personal development and enrichment. By practical sense I mean that the information must be usable and interpretable by the people for whom it is intended. The result of a research and development program should be a system that makes sense in all these ways.

Moreover, information in the system must be defensible in the sense of fairness and impartiality and reliability. If opinions or collective judgments are part of the system they must be based on honestly selected cross sections of reporters. If characteristics of the student body are part of the system they must be based on reliable and sytematically applied measures. If various pieces of information are combined to produce a score or index, then the psychometric properties of the score must be known. If typologies or broad classifications are part of the system, then there must be statistical support for them.

OPERATING THE SYSTEM IN SUCCESSIVE STAGES

One need not await the results of extensive research before putting parts of a system into operation.

The computer systems that enable applicants to identify colleges having various characteristics (such as their location, size, programs, scholarships, and so on) can be adopted now. An interactive system, such as the one Tiedeman has constructed, might be the recommended model for expanded application. Presumably the content or software that can be put into the system initially would be limited to public information obtained from catalogs, directories, and other documents.

In fact, initially, the software may have to be in printed form until the computer hardware is available. In any case, the public information can be "interpreted" so that applicants will be helped to understand what it means. These interpretations can be based on present research knowledge, including at least some comparative information about the range of differences that exist among institutions of different types.

While this initial information is being prepared for the system, a second stage of research can be started. I conceive this stage as being the consumers' and producers' surveys that have been previously suggested. They would be intended to provide guidance for further amplification of both the student and college input.

A third stage of the research, which can begin whenever the first two stages begin, but which will take somewhat longer to complete, is that of examining the vast range of variables, items, and scores currently in existence, for the purpose of arriving at a more compact and manageable set of variables about student bodies and college environments to use in the final system. This kind of information, psychological and educational, will ultimately give a more meaningful base for mutual choices.

One needs to recognize that it may not be possible, or if possible may not be desirable, to envision a system that says to a student "These six colleges will be best for you" or to a college that "These students will be most compatible with your institutional environment." Whether continuity and homogeneity or whether change and diversity are more productive of personal growth and development and of institutional adaptability is a question to which present research offers no solid answer. The sort of "advice" one puts into a system—whether advice to applicants or to colleges—must be considered with more than a little humility, with a great deal of conservative caution, and with due respect for the possible results of research that has not yet been conducted. This does not mean that there is nothing useful one can say. Rather, it means that a combination of frankness and humility is precisely what ought to distinguish the College Board's program from the programs of commercial or less professional agencies.

The fact that college applicants are required to submit a good deal of information about themselves—answers to questions on an application form, scores on standardized tests of ability and achievement, and a record of high school courses and grades—has had major educational, personal, and societal consequences. It was partly an awareness of these consequences that led to the creation of the Commission on Tests. If, now, the College Board develops a system of information about colleges— parallel in intent and comparable in scope to what colleges require to know about applicants—it is reasonably certain that the results will also have major educational, personal, and societal consequences.

RECOMMENDATIONS

It is recommended that the College Entrance Examination Board:

1. Support a research and development program to assemble, evaluate, and interpret information about colleges, taking into account the kinds of issues, sources, and technical matters described in this brief.

2. Regard this program as contributing, in stages, to the necessary software underlying a computerized information system.

3. Present information developed from the program in some printed form to be determined by the College Board, pending its incorporation into a computerized system, so that as much as possible will be available to applicants at the earliest feasible time.

PART EIGHT

Interests

OF the many kinds of psychological measurements, research has shown that the most valid, long-term results have been achieved with the Strong Vocational Interest Blank for males. Dr. E. K. Strong, Jr. has pioneered in this research for many years and has become famous for persistent follow-up studies. It would be very difficult to find another psychological test or inventory about which so much long-range data are obtainable. This has, of course, made the SVIB one of the most useful counseling tools for college students.

The revised version of the blank for males was finished in 1966 and published by the Stanford University Press. Professor Strong, who had retired from Stanford in 1949, began thinking then about this completed revision, since he wanted to eliminate some of the dated items and to incorporate certain psychometric improvement. At that time, he was totally involved in his large follow-up study of Stanford students of the 1930s (which eventually resulted in his 1955 volume, *Vocational Interests 18 Years After College*).

The job fell, eventually, to people at the University of Minnesota. In 1959, all of Strong's criterion data, consisting of about 40,000 completed interest inventories were transferred to Minnesota and prepared for computer input and analysis. The Center for Interest Measurement Research was established, and Dr. David P. Campbell became the director. The research eventually involved two complete revisions of the inventory, plus the addition of a number of new scales (Campbell, 1966). The women's form has undergone a similar revision and became available in the fall of 1968.

Strong (1951) published data on the permanence of interest scores for men ranging from 17 to 32 years of age, and for intervals of time from 3 weeks to 22 years. The coefficients of correlation were amazingly high for this test-retest data: .84 for 5 years, .83 for 10 years, .75 for 22 years. Campbell has continued this research, and, among the many reports issuing from the Center for Interest Measurement Research, has published data for a 30-year follow-up. This involved the Banker scale, and meant locating and retesting the original group which was tested in 1934. The Campbell study, condensed from its original version in the *Journal of Applied Psychology* in 1966, is also of interest because of the ingenious way of locating and constituting the 1964 group that would be involved in the retesting. This research has now been incoporated in the revised SVIB Manual (Campbell, 1971).

STABILITY OF INTERESTS WITHIN AN OCCUPATION OVER THIRTY YEARS

David P. Campbell

The Strong Vocational Interest Blank (SVIB) is one of the most widely used psychological measuring instruments. Its validity has been established in a variety of settings (see Berdie, 1960, for a review) and data collected over long periods of time have demonstrated the stability of measured interests over intervals as long as 22 years (Strong, 1955). The SVIB accomplishes this by providing an index of the similarity between an individual's likes and dislikes and those of successful men in a wide range of occupations. The results are particularly useful in guidance situations where counselors are trying to help young people plan their future.

The use of the SVIB, or any other empirically developed instrument, requires two assumptions of stability. The first is that the individual remains stable over time; the second is that the characteristics of the criterion groups remain constant. Specifically for the SVIB, the first assumption requires that the individual show some consistency over time in the activities that he finds interesting, thus allowing him to plan his future career on the basis of current likes and dislikes; the second requires that successful men in a specific occupation, say bankers, have the same interest today as did the bankers who were studied in 1934 to establish the SVIB Bankers Scale.

This study tests this second assumption.

The validity of the first assumption, that of consistency within the individual over time, has been well established; data concerning this are extensively reported in the SVIB Manual (Campbell, 1971). The individual is consistent enough in his measured interests over several years, particularly if he is tested during his college days, to make this information useful in laying plans for a career several years in the future.

The second assumption mentioned above, that of constancy within a single occupation over several years, has received less attention. And it perhaps deserves less. Certainly any inventory successfully developed to distinguish between occupations is going to be useful for many years after its development because the membership of most occupations remains stable. Any inventory that distinguishes between a specific occupation and men-in-general in 1934 will certainly separate the two groups in 1935. The question under study here is whether it will do so 30 years later in 1964. This point is becoming more crucial as it has been over 3 decades since the original SVIB standardization data were collected and there is some concern as to whether the scales are still relevant.

What is needed is some method of holding the sampling technique constant over a substantial period of time. One possible procedure would be to study a group of individuals who today hold the identical positions held by the men in an occupational group studied years ago. This procedure has been used in this study with the group of bankers who were used to establish the SVIB Bankers Scale in 1934.

Essentially, this is a study of the interests of bankers who today hold the identical jobs held by the men in the banker criterion group 30 years ago.

METHOD

The group originally used to establish the Bankers Scale, collected in 1934, included 250 individuals. In the SVIB Manual, Strong described the group as follows:

172 were members of the Minneapolis Federal Reserve System; of these 172, 95 were bankers from state banks in Minnesota which opened immediately after the 1933 Bank Holiday and 77 were bankers from national banks and designated as "good bankers" by a qualified expert. The remaining blanks were obtained through The Psychological Corporation, New York, and from miscellaneous sources. Average age 45.5; Education 12.2 grade.

Using a 1935 bank directory, it was possible to identify the position held in 1934 by 189 individuals from the original criterion group. First, an attempt was made to locate and retest these men to determine the amount of change in interests within the individual over 30 years. Second, the individuals who held these 189 jobs in 1964 were approached and asked to fill in the SVIB.

Retesting the Original Group

The first phase of this study involved the follow-up study of the original criterion group. Table 17 reports the results of attempts to locate and retest these individuals.

As Table 17 indicates, most of the group—90 percent—were located or accounted for, but death and illness greatly reduced the potential sample size. The 48 usable respondents represented only about one fourth of the original group, although they constituted approximately two thirds of the current survivors.

Was this group of respondents a representative sample from the earlier group of 189? Certainly they were younger; one would expect a bias in age, simply because the older ones would die sooner. These respondents averaged 38 years old in 1964, their average age was 68, with a range from 54 to 81 and a median of 71.

However, this age difference should not affect the use of this sample to represent the interests of the total group as prior research has shown that interests are stable after about age 25. Further, a comparison of the average 1934 profile of this subgroup with the 1934 profile of the entire original criterion group showed virtually no differences between the measured interests of the two groups.

Testing the Current Bankers

The major part of this study involved the comparison of the SVIB profiles of the original 1934 sample of bankers with the matched profiles of the men who in 1964 held the identical jobs.

This job matching was accomplished by using Commercial West Bank Directories. The 1935 directory provided the job titles of the men in the original sample, and the 1964 directory provided the names of the men holding those positions currently.

This latter group was contacted and asked to fill in the SVIB. For example, if the President of the First State Bank of Duluth, Minnesota, was one of the original sample, the current president of that bank was asked to fill in the SVIB.

There were some problems with this matching. Occasionally the bank had changed names or organizational affiliation, and sometimes the job

TABLE 17
DISPOSITION OF ORIGINAL SAMPLE

	N	Percentage
Couldn't be located	20	10.6
Deceased	91	48.1
Seriously ill	6	3.2
Refused to participate	18	9.5
Filled out inventory incorrectly	6	3.2
Usable respondents	48	25.4
Total	189	100.0

TABLE 18
DISPOSITION OF MATCHED MATES OF BANKERS IN ORIGINAL GROUP

	N	Percentage
Bank had gone out of business	26	14
Woman held job in 1964	9	5
1934 individual still in same job in 1964	13	7
1964 job-holder refused to participate	38	20
Usable respondents	103	54
Total	189	100

had been changed considerably. When in doubt, we erred in the direction of including the current individual in the sample even though it was not certain that he was working in precisely the same job as the earlier individual. But this was true in only a small percentage of the cases.

The results of the attempt to collect matchmates for each of the 1934 participants are summarized in Table 18.

The total possible sample was 189. Disregarding those cases where the bank was no longer in business, where the job was today filled by a woman, and where the 1934 individual was still in the same job, the sample shrank to 141. Of these, 103 (or 72%) completed the Strong Blank.

RESULTS

The results of the retesting of the 48 subjects over an interval of 30 years show the same type of consistency that we have come to expect in interest measurement, though the median test-retest correlation of the occupational scales of .56 is lower than the .75 reported for college seniors over 22 years and the .72 for college freshmen over 19 years reported by Strong in his follow-up study (Strong, 1955). Though the characteristic interests of the group remained very stable, the individuals moved around somewhat in their rank orders. It is likely that these correlations were lowered slightly by the relative homogeneity of this group. Strong's data (1955, p̂. 68) indicate that the average retest standard deviation for 14 scales over 18 years was 11.7. For the retested bankers, the average standard deviation on the same 14 scales was 9.8.

The results of the comparison between the 1934 bankers and their matched mates in 1964 show that while the profiles were essentially similar, there were some differences, some of them as large as one standard deviation. No apparent pattern appeared in these differences; some of them were on scales where the 1964 bankers might be expected to score higher because of the generally increasing level of education— scales such as Psychologist, Physician, and Senior CPA. But other scales usually associated with technical, nonprofessional interests, such as Industrial Arts Teacher and Vocational Agriculture Teacher, also showed differences in favor of the 1964 bankers.*

In general, because the 1964 bankers scored lower on the Banker Scale than did the 1934 bankers (46 to 52, respectively) and slightly higher on most of the other 44 scales (on the average, 27 to 24), it appears that the Banker Scale is slightly less effective in differentiating bankers

---

*The profiles for test-retest results over 30 years and for banker scores compared with their matched mates, contained in the original article, are not reproduced here. The 1971 SVIB Manual reproduces these (p. 318), but for only 93 rather than 103 bankers here. Both sets of profiles are visually very close.

from men in other occupations than it was in 1934. However, some of this regression can be explained by cross-validation shrinkage as this comparison is essentially comparing the validation group with a cross-validation group collected 30 years later.

Although some shrinkage did occur, the most noteworthy result shows the SVIB Banker Scale is still valid 30 years later—current bankers score higher on it than on any other scale.

IMPLICATIONS

The results of this study indicated there was substantial similarity between the likes and dislikes of the bankers in the original SVIB criterion group and a group of bankers in identical jobs 30 years later. This finding clearly upheld the continued use of the SVIB Banker Scale for counseling purposes.

Can these results be generalized to other occupational scales of the SVIB? The answer to that question depends on whether the banking profession is more or less stable over time than other occupational groups, and this can only be conjecture. It would certainly seem that the changes in the banking business over the last 30 years have been as substantial as those in almost any other occupation. The original criterion group was collected in 1934, just after the banks reopened after the national bank holiday; in many ways, a new era began. Accounting procedures have evolved from hand-written records to the most elaborate electronic computer systems. To the naïve observer, it appears that the banking business has attempted to change its public image from that of a somber, staid old patriarch to that of an aggressive, hard-driving public servant. This is particularly reflected in the architecture of bank buildings; frequently the bank is the most modern building in the small midwestern town, the setting that most of these bankers were drawn from.

In spite of these many changes, considerable stability was found in the characteristic interests of bankers over 30 years. If the above speculations have any veracity at all, if the banking profession is changing at least as fast as other occupations, then it seems safe to generalize to the other SVIB scales and assume that they also remain appropriate for use today. It would, of course, be comforting to have comparable follow-up data on other scales to buttress this generalization.

The test-retest results from the 48 individuals over 30 years deserve brief comment. Strong has earlier said that interests remain very stable from age 25 until about age 55, the upper limit of the age of men in his follow-up studies (Strong, 1955). Based on the sample in this study, that is, men tested once at about age 40 and again at age 70, it seems safe to conclude that measured interests remain stable well into old age.

▽ ▽ ▽

AN interesting sidelight on the predictive efficiency of the SVIB has emerged from the follow-up reports of the Study of Adult Development (formerly known as the Grant Study) at Harvard. Here the SVIB has been shown to work more effectively in one subculture than in another, and it is because of this new insight that the article by Dr. McArthur is presented here. What follows is a considerably condensed version of the original report, which appeared in the *Journal of Applied Psychology* in 1954. Dr. McArthur, at the time this article was written, was a psychologist at the Harvard University Health Service.

LONG-TERM VALIDITY OF THE STRONG INTEREST TEST IN TWO SUBCULTURES

Charles McArthur

Surprisingly few long-term follow-ups have been made on the Strong Vocational Interest Blank, when one considers that the test has now been in use two decades.* Strong (1943) adduces support of four rather indirect propositions:

1. Men continuing in Occupation A obtain a higher interest score in A than in any other occupation.
2. Men continuing in Occupation A obtain a higher interest score in A than other men entering other occupations.
3. Men continuing in Occupation A obtain higher scores in A than men who change from A to another occupation.
4. Men changing from Occupation A to Occupation B score higher in B prior to the change than in any other occupation, including A.

A special 20-year follow-up by Strong (1952) dealt with medical interests only but was reported in a more direct manner. Of 108 Stanford alumni who were physicians 20 years after testing, Strong reports that 70 had A ratings on the physician scale in their undergraduate tests and 14 received a rating of B+. In all, then, 78 percent of these men who made careers as doctors had had a "high" physician score when tested in college.

PROCEDURE

The Sample

A series of 61 participants in the Study of Adult Development were given the Strong Vocational Interest Blank in the academic year 1939–1940. These young men were part of a longer series selected for interdisciplinary long-term study on the basis of their apparent "normality." All

---

* But see the previous Campbell article (ED.).

were sophomores at the time in Harvard College. We can now test the predictive power of the Strong over a 14 year interval from 1939 to 1953.

SVIB as a Predictor

How well did the Strong test taken in college predict the occupations of these men 14 years later? In Table 19 an assessment of the correctness of prediction is made in herms of "Good Hits," "Poor Hits," and "Clean Misses." The definitions of these terms are implicit in the claims made by Strong; he feels that a good hit may be counted when a man enters an occupation for which he scored A or which had the 1st, 2nd, or 3rd highest ranking score on his test. Less credence is given to a B+ score when it is outranked by many others, yet such scores are usually regarded as "worth some consideration" in counseling. They are here called "Poor Hits." Anything below these criteria is taken to be a "Clean Miss."

The table also specifies whether or not a scale offered a "Direct" or "Indirect" measure of interest. The indirect measures are often no fair test at all, yet a counselor might in practice be forced to make just this sort of inference (as using the Author-Journalist scale to assess the advisability of teaching drama) for lack of other evidence.

Sixty cases could be used for validation, one man being in an occupation for which no scoring scale seemed even indirectly pertinent. It becomes apparent by inspection of Table 19 that some accuracy is lost through the necessity of using indirect measures. The fairest evaluation of the Strong's predictive power may be had from the 43 men whose occupations can be directly tested. Of these, only one third are Clean Misses. Just half were hit well.

These figures are slightly lower than those given by Strong in his follow-up of medical interests. There, about one out of four tests turned out to be complete misses. Yet one must remain pleased with an instrument that under "blind conditions" (these tests were all unscored until 1952) predicts future behavior even half the time.

STRONG'S FIRST PROPOSITION

Had a counselor used these tests in 1939 to suggest to the boys their likeliest future vocation, he would have been downright misleading only

TABLE 19
FOURTEEN-YEAR VALIDATION: STRONG VOCATIONAL INTEREST BLANK

Validity	Direct	Indirect	Total
Good hit	22	5	27
Poor hit	7	5	12
Clean miss	14	7	21
Total	43	17	60

once in every three attempts. Yet even the "good" tests would have presented him with a grave difficulty: the tests containing accurate predictions also contain too many "extraneous solutions." Like a mathematician solving a cubic equation, the counselor must enter the problem with the expectation that not all the answers offered will be real and pertinent.

Whatever its latter rating, the scale most pertinent to future choice of occupation ranked anywhere from 1st to 33rd highest out of the 44 scales for which each test was scored. The median rank of the most pertinent scale was 5th. That means that the counselor using these tests could have expected, on the average, four "extraneous solutions" with higher-ranking scores than the true solution. It is, of course, true that the "extraneous" quality of certain high scores is obvious: few would counsel a tone-deaf boy to be a musician.

Strong (1934) states that "a college student who continues ten years in the same occupation enters an occupation in which he ranks second or third best." Like our group as a whole, our men who continued in the same occupation (not considering interruption by the war) entered occupations in which, on the median, they had ranked fifth best. Once again, our figures are slightly less impressive than Strong's. It is certainly not true among our cases, men "continuing in Occupation A obtain a higher inherest score in A than in any other occupation."

STRONG'S SECOND PROPOSITION

The proposition that men engaged in an occupation score higher on that occupational scale than all other men is well supported by our data. That is, doctors outscore controls on the physician scale, lawyers outscore controls on the law scale, etc. (Controls are simply all the rest of the 61 cases.) This is true for every directly scaled occupation that occurs more than once.

Strong's second proposition seems to be valid.

STRONG'S LAST TWO PROPOSITIONS

Seventeen of our 60 men have made changes in occupation other than shifts enforced by entering the armed services. Often, these men abandoned two or more vocations before settling on the job they are engaged in today. Strong's follow-up data showed that men who abandoned an occupation were likely to possess lower scores on that occupational scale than the scores made by men who continued on the job. Strong found that rule to hold "except for the records of two individuals," while we, except for one instance of tie, find it to be entirely so.

Another generalization Strong offers about men who change vocational fields is that they will proceed from a field in which they have a low score into a field in which they score high. That was true of nine of our changeable men, seven men going contrary to their tests and entering new jobs for which their test scores were lower. (One man changed between jobs with identical scores.) These figures run faintly in the right direction, probably looking even less convincing than the data from which Strong felt that Proposition 4 was "almost but not quite sustained."

CONTENTMENT IN OCCUPATION

As Strong has pointed out (1952), "the validity of an interest test should be measured in terms of satisfaction" but for this "there is no satisfactory measure." The Study of Adult Development has accumulated much data on expressed satisfaction and dissatisfaction with occupational choice, through the use of annual questionnaires.

The 1953 questionnaires were still coming in when this was written. Of the 60 men in whom we are interested, 37 had returned their questionnaires. There was, as a matter of fact, some tendency for the men engaged in occupations for which they possessed a favorable Strong score to return their questionnaires early! (Three quarters of them had done so, as against half the men with lower scores.) For this, Fisher's p comes out .09. This is not so trivial an indication as it may appear; the study staff has long been aware that among people who are hardest to hear from are those who have a sense of not having succeeded.

Several 1953 questions were pertinent to an inferrable sentiment of job satisfaction. There were 13 men, in all, who showed some evidence of discontent, in answer to one or another of the questions. These 13, who are "less than completely happy about their jobs, only three scored A on the Strong.

OTHER EVIDENCE

These findings, although not so favorable to the test as Strong's results, nonetheless suggest that the test has its usefulness. Furthermore, someone familiar with the study participants cannot help feel that, however inaccurate its predictions of behavior, the test is measuring interests. There is the evidence, for example, of the correlated pair of scores: lawyer and public administrator. Some men enter the law because they have politics in mind. Cases 20, 25, and 27 are examples. In Case 27, the public administrator score matches that for lawyer. In Case 25, the lawyer score is low; the choice of lawyer would seem to have been contraindicated. That would have been correct. Case 25 escapes being one of our dramatically unhappy group only because the practice of law is rationalized as a means to a political end. The Strong has measured the relative interest in law and politics quite accurately. Some indication of the injustice of "occupations entered" as a criterion of interest may be had from Case 20. This man is reported as a lawyer, and his low

score on that scale makes him count in the validation as a "poor hit."
Yet he, too, intends to use law as a steppingstone into politics, a fact
that was not shown in the table, since circumstances have prevented his
carrying out his plans. His score on public administrator is an A. That is
also the scale on which he ranks first.

One is impressed by the logic underlying the relative efficiency of the
test in predicting well or poorly certain occupational choices. Engineers,
ministers, and teachers seem to be highly predictable; all three are
likely to choose their vocation in response to an inner "call." By contrast, men who are in their own business the Strong simply does not
predict. Another way of saying these facts would be to assume that the
Strong tested interest and that the difference in prediction represented
differences in the importance of interest as a factor in various sorts of
career choice. The very patterning of the failures of the test therefore
confirms its validity as a measure of interest.

PRIVATE AND PUBLIC SCHOOL RESULTS

Suppose we explore the consequences of postulating that the Strong
does measure interests. We infer that the test will predict future job
choices only for those men who (consciously or unconsciously) give
weight to their own interests when they choose a career. For men who
do not follow their interest, the test will not predict. We therefore expect
the Strong's "validity" to vary between groups known to take their own
interests more or less seriously. A major instance of such a prediction is
provided by our tests from men who prepared for Harvard at public and
private secondary schools.

The public school boy has usually been raised in the "American
success culture," described by many anthropologists. His parent's efforts
focused on preparing the boy for future vocational achievement. Job
choice has been for him a vital matter; his future self-esteem will hinge
on his job-title and on how well he does within his occupational field. As
one study participant explained it, "I have satisfied myself as to my
ability to compete successfully with most of my contemporaries."

The private school boy will often have been reared in a variant
orientation, ably described by Kluckhohn (1950), where child-rearing
was intended to perpetuate in him a "preferred personality." Occupational role will have been subordinated to family social patterns. In our
1953 questionnaires, eleven private school boys, but only three public
school boys, put family interest or personal breadth ahead of achievement values when discussing their "personal future." As Kluckhohn so
nicely phrased it, the contrast is between two subcultures, one emphasizing a "doing" and the other a "being" orientation.

One consequence of this subcultural contrast is a difference in the
importance assigned to interests when men make their vocational
choice. In the "success culture" a son is expected to surpass (therefore

often bypass) his father's occupation. Choosing a job is for him a vital matter, the more so because the choice is so greatly "up to him." So much hinges on his making a "right" choice, calculated to yield maximal success, that he will often consult his own interest pattern, either introspectively or with formal aid from a vocational counselor. By contrast, the purest case of the upper class variant is a man whose permitted choices are limited to three: trustee, lawyer, or doctor. (The study has witnessed dramatic conflicts within upper-class men when personal "calls" gave way before the pressure of tradition.) While the average private school boy is not subjected to so focal a pressure, he will nevertheless possess values reinforcing the tangible demand that he join his father or uncle in "business," and the intangible expectation that he will first of all be the "right sort." As one participant wrote, "As near as I can tell, I have those (personal) qualities in some small measure, so I think it foolish to spend time thinking about my future."

If all this is true, we arrive at the prediction that interests will matter less, and therefore the Strong will be less valid when applied to the behavior of private school boys. Table 19 shows this to be the case. Chi-square suggests p less than .05; if we combine cells (avoiding the low cell and isolating the relation between public school attendance and "Good Hits"), we can apply Fisher's formula and arrive at p below .01. Our proposition seems well validated.

If we translate Table 20 into percentage, we discover that three quarters of the public school tests gave some sort of "hit" on the occupation engaged in fourteen years after testing. That is exactly the figure reported by Strong (1952) for his 20-year follow-up. If, on the other hand, we try to apply the test to private school boys, our predictions will be useless almost half the time.

Splitting out the public school cases, we can try revalidating Strong's four propositions. Proposition 1 fares better: men engaged in Occupation A still do not have "a higher interest score in A than in any other occupation" but the median rank of the pertinent scale is third, where formerly it was fifth. That is more consistent with Strong's claim, quoted earlier, that the occupation continued in will have ranked first, second, or third. Proposition 2 is no better for the public school group alone; that is because some occupations (engineer, chemist) attract high scores from public school, while others (lawyer, minister) attract higher

TABLE 20

VALIDITY OF STRONG TEST APPLIED TO PUBLIC AND PRIVATE SCHOOL BOYS

Validity	Public	Private	Total
Good hit	19	8	27
Poor hit	4	8	12
Clean miss	8	13	21
Total	31	29	60

scores from private school. At any rate, Proposition 2 was already verified sufficiently. Proposition 3 was already verified in every comparison, and so cannot be improved. There is one scale (public adminstrator) on which Proposition 3 is false for the private school group but true for the public school group. Proposition 4 is about equally valid in both groups.

DISCUSSION

This finding will raise various questions, some of which can be answered from our data. To forestall one, the "private school effect" cannot be explained in terms of income. It is true that the Strong is less accurate when applied to families receiving over $16,000 per year, but this figure marks only the upper quartile of our income statistics, while the "private school effect" is visible at all income levels. For example, in the second income quartile, with income held reasonably constant between four and six thousand dollars, public school tests score good hits 75 percent of the time, private school tests only 40 percent. In all income quartiles that are adequately represented by public school cases, the proportion of misleading tests remains about one in four; in all income quartiles that are adequately represented by private school cases, the proportion of misleading tests remains about one in two.

These figures suggest that it is the fact of having attended private school (or of being reared in a subculture from which one is sent to a private school), rather than income, and somewhat independently of social class that depressed the validity of the test. Several explanations suggest themselves. The most obvious would be that the Strong was validated against public school graduates. Next most obvious might be that attending private school is one of those "experiences affecting interests" that Super warns us have been too little studied.

SUMMARY AND CONCLUSIONS

A 14-year follow-up was made of Strong Vocational Interest Blanks administered in 1949 to participants in the Study of Adult Development. The validity of the test as a predictor of occupational choice at first appeared to be slightly lower than that reported by Strong. Of Strong's four validation propositions, two were confirmed, one (that lawyers outscore non-lawyers on the law scale, etc.) Strikingly, the other (that lawyers obtain one of their best scores on the law scale, etc.) less so. The median test offered four "extraneous" predictions.

It was possible to demonstrate a relation between conformity to choices commended by the test and future vocational happiness. Choosing a job for which one had (some years before) scored "A" also seemed to reduce the likelihood of developing fatigue, irritability or other symptoms of strain.

The proposition was offered that SVIB validly measured interests, but that failure to predict what job a man would choose could be explained in terms of his making the choice on some basis other than interest. Certain case histories supported this idea as did the apparent pattern in occupations which the test predicted accurately and which it did not.

As a corollary of this proposition it was predicted that the Strong test would be applicable to boys who attended a public secondary school but less useful for boys who had prepared in a private preparatory institution. That was the case. The predictive validity of the test among the public school group was almost exactly that originally reported by Strong. Among private school boys, the test was inapplicable half of the time. Further, Strong's first validation proposition was improved in the public school group, the median test record offering only two extraneous predictions.

The import of this finding may be real in one of two ways. If we assume the anthropological theories about the American middle and upper classes to be true, then this is a demonstration that "invalidity" in the Strong test arises because interests do not determine choice rather than from failure of the test to measure interests. On the other hand, the implication that there may be a distinct psychology of the upper class is also pointed out.

From all this may be drawn the following conclusions:

1. The Strong test has at least the validity claimed for it as a measure of interests.

2. Its most rigorous validation criterion will be the prediction of actual behavior, but even that criterion is met at least 1 time in 2.

We may regard as critical for understanding the use of the test Strong's proposed "future calculations as to how much other factors, such as economic conditions, family pressures, etc., affect a man's occupational career." In this respect, attention should be called to upper class variants of the American personality.

Further study of: (a) the effects of environmental pressure in conflict with interests measured by the Strong, and (b) the differences between public and private school personalities will be made from Study of Adult Development data.

And now, thirty years after the publication (1943) of Strong's large work, *Vocational Interests of Men and Women*, a major revision of this interest inventory has been realized (Campbell, 1974). Two major changes here should be noted: one, the introduction of a theoretical framework to guide the profile layout and score interpretations; two, the merging of the men's and women's forms into a single inventory. As Campbell comments, these changes would probably have made Strong uncomfortable. In a similar vein, the old Masculinity-Femininity scale has been dropped because it caused more "trouble" in counseling situations than seemed justified.

These changes, along with the abandonment of the blue form for males and the pink form for females (which Campbell ruefully admits was just about the worst public relations tactic of the year) have resulted in a greatly revised measurement instrument. Items with a sexual bias have been eliminated as have all out-of-date items. New scales have been developed to allow for scoring of both males and females on the same scale (example: advertising man has become advertising executive). New Men-in-General and Women-in-General samples have been constructed which now show 15 percent or greater differences on 163 of the 325 items on the 1964 form. The two sexes do differ in their interests, on the average, the range within each sex being so large that the two samples overlap almost completely. The scoring strategy adopted in this new revision is to score each person on all scales but only scores for appropriate sex scales are plotted graphically. Letter grades, prominent on the earlier profile forms, have been eliminated; more simple clarifying adjectives ("similar," "very similar," etc.) have been substituted. A computer-generated interpretative printout, which might run to eight pages, is also a new feature.

This does not mean, however, that sex differences have been eliminated. The research shows that these male-female differences over time, if anything, have grown larger. Campbell reports that of the 36 comparisons (four items over nine occupations), 25 show larger differences now, 11 show smaller differences. Generally speaking, the gap between men and women on these items is presently as great as, and perhaps greater than, it was in the 1930s. The four items chosen in this regard were selected because they were typical of male-female high contrast items. The research shows, not suprisingly, that the appropriate sex scale is usually superior. Empirical scales developed on male samples still work better for men and those developed on female samples work better for women.

The special scales, of which there were several on earlier forms, have now been reduced to two: Academic Orientation and Introversion-Extroversion.

Mention was made above that about the elimination of dated items. A few, however, have been retained: one example of such an obvious item is "pursuing bandits in a posse." To quote Campbell (1974, p. 6): "No one ever complained about it; the validity statistics are good, with "Like" responses ranging from just five percent among ministers, school superintendents, and physicians to 80 percent among policemen and highway patrolmen; it usually evokes a smile or a chuckle and, falling as it does about midway through the inventory, it offers a welcome departure in tone."

Holland's theoretical structure of occupations has been added to this revised edition and it is included in the profile layout where each occupational score has been coded according to this scheme (Holland, 1973). Holland's hexagonal model is reproduced in the new Campbell manual with intercorrelations for both male and female samples (Campbell, 1974, p. 34).

All in all, this is a major advance in the area of interest measurement and this new Strong-Campbell inventory should be of enormous value to counselors.

These three recent revisions of the Strong test were the work of Dr. David Campbell at the University of Minnesota where he was Professor of Psychology. All of Strong's archives at Stanford University, where he did his original work, were transferred to Minnesota where Campbell went to work on the revisions and up-dating. For this purpose, the University of Minnesota founded the Center for Interest Measurement Research with Campbell as director. It is said that the walls of his office there were literally papered with computer printouts of intercorrelations obtained from the inventory. Campbell has now left Minnesota and he is currently Vice President in charge of research programs at the Center for Creative Leadership at the University of North Carolina.

PART NINE

Achievement or Proficiency Testing

STANDARDIZED achievement or proficiency testing is perhaps the oldest form of psychological examining. Various forms of civil service agencies have long made use of such tests, not only in the West but also in the East. The following historical piece by Dr. DuBois relates some of the procedures adopted by the Chinese as early as 2200 B.C. Later, these testing programs involved millions of men. As the author indicates, since the selection ratio was so small the issue of test validity was not a significant one. But the testing program became a very significant tool of the government. The United States and some European countries made use of this Chinese system when they began to construct their own civil service testing machinery.

Dr. Dubois, at the time this article was composed, was Professor of Psychology at Washington University in St. Louis, Missouri. His original paper appeared in the *Proceedings of the 1964 Invitational Conference on Testing Problems,* a conference sponsored by the Educational Testing Service. The article was reprinted in the Anastasi collection (1966) of representative papers from these conferences.

A TEST-DOMINATED SOCIETY: CHINA, 1115 B.C.– 1905 A.D.

Philip H. DuBois

Our negative enthusiasm for the present government in Peking should not lead us to a lack of appreciation for great Chinese achievements of the past. They have been many.

It is often said that the Chinese invented gunpowder and, quite humanely, used it to frighten, rather than to kill, their enemies.

Certainly they solved the problem of diverse languages with the remarkable invention of a common written language–a code by which peoples who could not communicate with one another orally were able to

communicate freely by means of writing. This invention was so successful that the Chinese came to regard themselves as a single people.

They invented paper, which the West did not know how to make until
some Chinese papermakers were captured by Arabs at Samarkand in
751 A.D. They invented printing. They developed the arts. But, more
importantly for our purposes, they invented the psychological test,
applying it to government, the very framework of their society, in such a
manner that the test makers, in effect, determined over many centuries
much of the format of Chinese society.

The prolonged and intensive Chinese experience with testing seems to
have been completely ignored by contemporary psychometricians. In
none of the writings on psychometrics with which I am familiar is there
any mention of some 3,000 years of examinations in the Chinese empire.
This is rather surprising because in civil service procedures it is easy to
trace the continuity of Eastern and Western methods. Continuity between Western educational and psychological examining methods on
the one hand and Chinese civil service testing on the other is more
difficult to demonstrate, but some influence is probable.

Even if Western psychometrics had been completely independent of
Chinese testing, the Eastern experience would have been of great
interest to us. It affords the one historical example of a society in which
examining methods introduced to attain certain restricted objectives
actually began to determine many characteristics of the society itself.

It should be noted that through the ages the Chinese empire, unlike
the West, did not have a numerous hereditary aristocracy to constitute
its governing class. The chief way to a political career was through
passing a series of examinations in which competition was very severe.
Moreover, China lacked another invention of the West: the university.
The learned Chinese was one who had been successful in passing
competitive examinations, and whose success brought changes in his
attire and in his title as well as public recognition of his abilities, and
employment in government service.

For long periods of time the system worked very well indeed. Only
occasionally were examinations suspended, one notable period being the
time in which the Mongol emperors ruled Peking. (The accounts of
Marco Polo, who spent a number of years in China during their rule,
make no reference to the Chinese civil service examining procedures.)

The Chinese scholar seems to have been a reasonably successful
public administrator. Public office was often distributed by lot among
the mandarins who passed three successive sets of examinations.

Millions of men prepared for the tests, often for decades, and relatively few achieved final success. The selection ratio was so small that
the tests themselves would not have had to be very valid in order to be
useful. That they were useful is perhaps indicated by their long history
and by the fact that for many centuries, with relatively few interrup-

tions, the government of the Chinese empire preserved internal peace, provided security from many would-be invaders, and permitted a flowering of civilization that in many respects was far more advanced than that prevailing contemporaneously in the West.

The earliest development seems to have been a rudimentary form of proficiency testing. About the year 2200 B.C., the emperor of China is said to have examined his officials every third year. After three examinations, he either promoted or dismissed them from the service. There seems to be no record of the exact content nor of the methods of testing, but the precedent of periodic examinations was to continue for many generations.

A thousand years later in 1115 B.C., at the beginning of the Chan dynasty, formal examining procedures of candidates for office were established. Here the record is clear. Job sample tests were used requiring proficiency in the five basic arts: music, archery, horsemanship, writing, and arithmetic. Of the five, at least two, writing and arithmetic, still have validity for public office. Knowledge of a sixth art was also required—skill in the rites and ceremonies of public and social life.

It should be pointed out that this examining system, which was later to be centered upon the Confucian classics, was actually in existence long before the time of Confucius (551–478 B.C.).

While the procedures changed from time to time, and the sources to which I have had access are somewhat contradictory, a few dates seem to be clear. In 165 B.C., by which time Confucian ethics had become current, moral standards were introduced in the selections of competitors. District magistrates were required to send to the capital candidates who had acquired a reputation for filial peity and integrity. Those whose moral character had been sufficiently attested were then examined with respect to their intellectual qualifications. At this time, the test included not only measures of the six arts, but also familiarity with the geography of the empire, civil law, military matters, agriculture, and the administration of revenue.

After 622 A.D., open, competitive examinations took place at more or less regular intervals. By 1370 A.D., three levels of examinations were well established. The candidate who passed the examination in his district became eligible to take a test at the provincial capital, and those successful at the provincial capital were eligible for final examinations in Peking. For about 500 years the system was stable and a description by William A. P. Martin (1870) is pertinent.

. . . The candidates for office—those who are acknowledged as such, in consequences of sustaining the initial trial—are divided into the three grades of *siu-ts'ai, chu-jin,* and *tsin-shi*—"Budding Geniuses," "Promoted Scholars," and those who are "Ready for Office." The trials for the first are held in the chief city of each district. . . . They are conducted by a chancellor, whose jurisdiction extends over an entire province, containing, it may be, sixty or seventy such districts, each of which he is required to visit once a year, and each of which is provided with a resident sub-chancellor, whose duty it is to examine the scholars in the interval and to have them in readiness for the chancellor's arrival.

About two thousand competitors enter the lists, ranging in age from the precocious youth just entering his teens up to the venerable grandsire of seventy winters. Shut up for a night and a day, each in his narrow cell, they produce each a poem and one or two essays on themes assigned by the chancellor, and then return to their homes to await the bulletin announcing their place in the scale of merit. The chancellor, assisted by his clerks, occupies several days in sifting the heap of manuscripts, from which he picks out some twenty or more that are distinguished by beauty of penmanship and grace of diction. The authors of these are honored with the degree of "Budding Genius," and are entitled to wear the decorations in the lowest grade in the corporation of mandarins. The successful student wins no purse of gold and obtains no office, but he has gained a prize, which he deems a sufficient compensation for years of patient toil. He is the best of a hundred scholars, exempted from liability to corporal punishment, and raised above the vulgar herd. . . .

Once in three years these "Budding Geniuses," these picked men of the districts, repair to the provincial capital to engage in competition for the second degree—that of *chu-jin*, or "Promoted Scholar." The number of competitors amounts to ten thousand, more or less, and of these only one in every hundred can be admitted to the coveted degree. The trial is conducted by special examiners sent down from Peking and this examination takes a wider range than the preceding. No fewer than three sessions of nearly three days each are occupied instead of the single day for the first degree. Compositions in prose and verse are required, and themes are assigned with a special view to testing the extent of reading and depth of scholarship of the candidates. Penmanship is left out of the account—each production, marked with a cipher, being copied by an official scribe, that the examiners may have no clew to its author and no temptation to render a biased judgment.

The victor still receives neither office nor emolument; but the honor he achieves is scarcely less than that which was won by the victors in the Olympic games. Again, he is one of a hundred, each of whom was a picked man; and as a result of this second victory he goes forth an acknowledged superior among ten thousand contending scholars. He adorns his cap with the gilded button of a higher grade, erects a pair of lofty flag-staffs before the gate of his family residence, and places a tablet over his door to inform those who pass by that this is the abode of a literary prize-man. But our "Promoted Scholar" is not yet a mandarin, in the proper sense of the term. The distinction already attained only stimulates his desire for higher honors—honors which bring at last the solid recompense of an income.

In the spring of the following year he proceeds to Peking to seek the next higher degree, the attainment of which will prove a passport of office. This contest is still with his peers, that is, with other "Promoted Scholars," who like himself have come up from all the provinces of the empire. But the chances are this time more in his favor, as the number of prizes is now tripled, and if the gods are propitious his fortune is made. . . . If his name appears among the favored few, he not only wins himself a place in front ranks of the lettered, but he plants his foot securely on the rounds of the official ladder by which, without the prestige of birth or the support of friends, it is possible to rise to a seat in the grand council of state or a place in the Imperial Cabinet. All this advancement presents itself in the distant prospect, while the office upon which he immediately enters is one of respectability, and it may be of profit. It is generally that of mayor or sub-mayor of a district city, or sub-chancellor in the district examinations—the vacant posts being distributed by lot, and therefore impartially, among those who have proved themselves to be "ready for office."

Before the drawing of lots, however, for the post of a magistrate among the people, our ambitious student has a chance of winning the more distinguished honor of a place in the Imperial Academy. With this view, the two or three hundred survivors of so many contests apper in the palace, where themes are assigned them by the Emperor himself, and the highest honor is paid to the pursuit of letters by the exercises being presided over by his Majesty in person. Penmanship reappears as an element in determining the result, and a score or more of those whose style is the most finished, whose scholarship the ripest, and whose handwriting the most elegant, are drafted into the college of Hanlin, the "forest of pencils," a kind of Imperial Institute, the members of which are recognized as standing at the head of the literary profession. These are constituted poets and historians to the Celestial Court, or deputed to act as chancellors and examiners in the several provinces.

But the diminishing series in this ascending scale has not yet reached its final term. The long succession of contests culminates in the designation by the Emperor of some individual whom he regards as the Chuang-Yuen or model scholar of the empire. . . . Provinces contend for the shining prize, and the town that gives the victor birth becomes noted forever. Swift heralds bear the tidings of his triumph, and the hearts of the people leap at their approach. We have seen them enter a humble cottage . . . and, amid the flaunting of banners and the blare of trumpets, announce to its startled inmates that one of their relations had been crowned by the Emperor as the laureate of the year. And so high was the estimation in which the people held the success of their fellow-townsman, that his wife was requested to visit the six gates of the city, and to scatter before each a handful of rice, that the whole population might share in good fortune of her household. . . .

It is obvious that which excites so profoundly the interest of a whole nation must be productive of very decided results. That it leads to the selection of the best talents for the service of the public we have already seen; but beyond this— its primary object—it exercises a profound influence upon the education of the people and the stability of the government. It is all, in fact, that China has to show in the way of an education system. She has no colleges or universities—if we except one that is yet in embryo—and no national system of common schools; yet it may be confidently asserted that China gives to learning a more effective patronage than she could have done if each of her emperors were an Augustus and every premier a Maecenas. She says to all her sons, "Prosecute your studies by such means as you may be able to command, whether in public or in private, and when you are prepared, present yourselves in the examination hall. The government will judge of your proficiency and reward your attainments."

Nothing can exceed the ardor which this standing offer infuses into the minds of all who have the remotest prospect of sharing in the prizes. They study not merely while they have teachers to incite them to diligence, but continue their studies with unabated zeal along after they have left the schools; they study in solitude and poverty; they study amidst the cares of a family and the turmoil of business; and the shining goal is kept steadily in view until the eye grows dim. Some of the aspirants impose on themselves the task of writing a fresh essay every day; and they do not hesitate to enter the lists as often as the public examinations recur, resolved, if they fail, to continue trying, believing that perseverance has power to command success and encouraged by the legend of the man who, needing a sewing-needle, made one by grinding a crowbar on a piece of granite.

This quotation from Martin, describing and praising the Chinese testing system, is by no means unique. The use of competitive examinations for the selection of state officials was praised by many Western observers and writers, including Voltaire. In fact, it is clear that initially all civil service examining in Europe and in the United States used the Chinese system, directly or indirectly, as a model. Civil service testing was introduced in France as a 1791 reform, only to be abolished by Napoleon. In England the first competitive examinations in connection with public office were instituted for the selection of trainees for the civil service in India by men familiar with the Chinese system. Later, when the question of civil service examinations for Great Britain as a whole was debated in Parliament, the Chinese model was discussed with both favorable and unfavorable comments. As a part of an extensive study, Congressman Thomas A. Jenckes, one of the fathers of the United States Civil Service, wrote 12 pages on the civil service of China.

Westerners seem to have been particularly impressed with the fact that competition was open, that distinction came from merit, and that a highly literate and urbane group of public officials resulted from the examination system.

The great crisis in Chinese affairs came, of course, when the Chinese realized that they were militarily inferior to the West. They quickly discovered that equality in military power could not be achieved without modern science and technology. Accordingly, technological schools and universities were set up, but as long as the civil service examinations, which were largely literary in character, continued to be the way for an ambitious man to have a career, modern education was not sufficiently attractive. Consequently, in 1905, the Chinese examination system was abolished as a reform measure.

So much for a description and a bit of the history of an ancient Chinese venture in psychological examining as a tool of government. What can be said about their testing techniques from the point of view of the modern psychometrician? In the first place, I find no evidence to indicate that they invented either the multiple-choice format, the test-scoring machine, or item analysis. They did, however, recognize that a relatively short performance under carefully controlled conditions could yield an estimate of the ability to perform under less rigorously controlled conditions and for a longer period of time. I think there is no doubt that the procedure selected capable public servants.

They recognized the problem of objectivity, concealing candidates' names, and sometimes using a bureau of copyists to copy examination material before it was graded. In some cases, tests were read by two independent examiners who handed their sealed evaluations to a third examiner who reconciled any differences. Scores seem to have been in terms of rank order.

The need for uniformity in testing conditions was well recognized. Considerable attention was given to proctoring the examination halls, which were large and permanent installations consisting of hundreds of small cells. Sometimes candidates died during the rigors of the examinations, which went on day and night.

Now, when psychological tests are being used more and more extensively at critical points in the careers of all our citizens, we will do well to consider their effects on individuals, on specific institutions, and on society. The long Chinese experience is a pertinent case history. It is a plausible hypothesis that much of the great strength of the Chinese empire came from the intellectual vigor of men who were bright enough to compete in examinations requiring the writing of poems and "eight-legged essays."

Certainly the opportunities that were opened up by success in the examinations stimulated millions of individuals to long years of scholarship. Perhaps the greatest drawback was that the scholarship was not always pertinent. In the nineteenth century, China suddenly found herself surpassed in technology by the West. While Chinese civilization had been relatively static, Westerners invented the steam engine, the power loom, and the iron-clad. It was then that the Chinese, in order to preserve their country and their institutions, began to desire progress according to the Western model. At that time the age-old examining system was discovered to be a hindrance.

So far, with 60 years of experience, we Westerners have not found our psychological examining a hindrance. But it is becoming increasingly apparent that our test-makers, like those of ancient China, established goals for individuals and influenced the shape of social institutions. Item writers as well as song writers mold the patterns of a culture.

▽ ▽ ▽

SEVERAL objections to school reliance on achievement tests have
been voiced—for example, they eventually will dictate the curriculum. Such objections also relate to teaching objectives. In the article
that follows, Dr. Ebel discusses some of the common objections that
have been raised and interprets the validity of these points.

The article is reproduced, in slightly abbreviated form, from the
National Elementary Principal for 1961. It has also been reprinted in
the collection of readings by Chase and Ludlow (1966). Dr. Ebel is
Professor of Education and Psychology at Michigan State University.

STANDARDIZED ACHIEVEMENT TESTS:
USES AND LIMITATIONS

Robert L. Ebel

Standardized tests of educational achievement are essential educational tools, especially in the elementary school. They can be used to
improve the effectiveness of the competent teacher or school admistra-
tor. They can help motivate and reward the child. They can provide a
basis for constructive cooperation between parents and teachers in
guiding the child's educational development. They can help the school
staff and the community it serves assess the effectiveness of the school
program.

A demonstration of how standardized tests can focus public attention
on an educational need occurred recently in New York City. Results of a
city-wide standardized reading test showed that the average reading
ability of school children in New York was below the national average.
A few years before, it had been above the national norm. While these
findings were doubted, discounted, and rationalized by experts and
spokesmen inside the schools and out, there was almost universal
support for the vigorous action taken by the Board of Education to
strengthen the program of reading instruction. Among other things, the
number of specialists in remedial reading on the school staff was sharply
increased.

This use of standardized tests as a basis for judging and effectiveness
of a school program has been criticized by some educators. They point
out that half the pupils or schools *have* to be below the norm and that
remedial programs can never alter this situation. Further, they say, it
is unreasonable and unfair to expect the same levels of achievement of
all pupils and all schools. A pupil ranking well above average may, in
fact, have less reason for self-satisfaction and complacency than a pupil
ranking below average, if the high-ranking pupil had educational advantages the other lacked.

There is merit in both these critisms, perhaps more in the second than
in the first, but it would be dangerous to accept them completely. No

pupil, no teacher, no schoolboard, no community should be continuously satisfied with their educational achievements, and few are. Information provided by standardized tests of achievement helps them focus their dissatisfactions more purposefully and take remedial action more constructively.

The second criticism is sometimes used in general terms as a rationalization for below average performance. It contains enough truth to be a persuasive argument for unsound interpretations of test results and for inaction when action is needed. On the basis of intelligence tests and other measures, we know it is unreasonable to expect the same achievement of all pupils and all schools. Unfortunately, the usual effort to obtain a standard of reasonable expectancy of achievement from intelligence test scores is based, I think, on some misconceptions about intelligence, achievement, and the educational process.

The important point to remember is that most pupils and many schools could achieve considerably more than they have achieved. Further, it is probably true that the pupils and schools which are below average in achievement have both the greatest need and the greatest opportunity to improve.

Understanding the causes of inferior achievement is an important prelude to effective remedial action. No child's potential and no school's potential for educational achievement is unlimited. But this should never be used as an excuse for inaction.

If standardized tests are valuable tools, why do many schools lag in using them effectively? Lack of full awareness of the potential value of test information and lack of training in how to use that information may be partly responsible. But there are also three common misconceptions about educational testing which may account for much of the skepticism about the value of tests and the reluctance to use them more extensively.

IMPORTANCE OF TANGIBLE OUTCOMES

The first of these misconceptions is the belief that the most important outcomes of education are too subtle, too complex, too subjective to be measured effectively. Elementary school teachers are less guilty on this score than some college professors who take off on flights of fancy when discussing intangible but supposedly essential outcomes of education.

Teachers of young children know that the development of skills in the tool subjects and the establishment of solid foundations for understanding and interest in the major fields of human knowledge are concrete, specific, important objectives. But some of them may feel that tests, especially objective standardized tests, fail "to get at" the real essentials of achievement in these skill and foundation subjects. This mystical devotion to a hidden reality of achievement which is more essential than overt ability to perform has never satisfied the research worker. He wants to know the nature of this hidden reality and what evidence there is that it is important.

DANGER OF OVEREMPHASIS ON ADJUSTMENT

The second misconception about educational testing arises from over-concern with the child's immediate happiness and self-satisfaction. Extreme supporters of this view often regard testing as an unfriendly, threatening, anxiety-generating process. They would shield the child from its stress and possible pain. I demur, and call as the first witness the physician.

Most of us learn to adjust to the physician's prescriptions, whether they are bad-tasting medicines, disinfectants that sting, shots that hurt, or even surgery. There is some emotional stress and discomfort, but the end result is usually increased health. To do what must be done a doctor needs courage, but this implies no lack of sympathy. What it does imply is farsighted concern for the ultimate welfare of the patient.

I have been appalled by the lack of this far-sighted attitude among some advocates of child-centered education. They talk as if the teacher's primary responsibility were to guard the child's ego against any bruises whatsoever. Let him achieve as much as he can without strain, they say, but be careful not to ask too much of him. Their excess of concern for protection of the child's present "security" may, however, encourage neglect of needed small readjustments until they accumulate into a crisis of major proportions.

Take the case of Sharon which illustrates a problem all too many schools and families have become unhappily acquainted with in recent years. Sharon was the third of four children in an upper middle-class family. Her early years at school were uneventful. Periodic descriptive reports indicated that she was adjusting well and making progress. If any standardized tests were given, the significance of the results was not reported to the parents.

Midway through the third grade, trouble developed. Sharon began to say she hated school and to seek escape by feigning illness. Investigation showed the basic problem was that Sharon couldn't read, at least not nearly as well as her classmates. They were beginning to refer to her as "dumb." The parents proposed that Sharon attend the reading clinic of a nearby university and perhaps get special individual instruction. The school staff counseled against such a step arguing that they could provide all the special help needed, now that the problem had been identified. Further, they said, much harm could be done if too much attention were paid to the problem. Better to treat it as casually and quietly as possible, they said.

Despite some misgivings, Sharon's parents agreed. For a while, things seemed to improve. Sharon was happier in school. She brought home reports of small triumphs, of special recognition and opportunities. The school reports, still couched in general, unthreatening phrases, indicated generally satisfactory progress. Then, near the end of Sharon's eighth grade year, trouble developed again. Her teacher recommended that she repeat the grade because of her serious reading disability. The special attention she had received had apparently taught her to learn by listening, but she had not learned effective self-direction in reading.

After some plain-speaking conferences between teacher and parents, Sharon did not fail. She did go to summer reading camps. She went on to high school and took five years to finish college instead of four.

If the school had had a systematic program of standardized testing and had reported the results regularly, Sharon's reading disability would probably have been identified before it was translated into an emotional and social problem. And once the difficulty was identified, if the school had been more concerned with Sharon's future welfare than her current happiness, the problem might well have been corrected before it affected her subsequent schooling. In education, as in medicine and justice, an excess of present sympathy can postpone or even defeat the procedures necessary for an individual's future welfare.

LIMITED VALUE OF PURELY LOCAL OBJECTIVES

. The third misconception about standardized educational achievement tests results in their avoidance or de-emphasis on the ground that this teacher's objectives or that school's objectives are uniquely different from those for which the standardized test was presumably built.

We all recognize that it is desirable for both teachers and schools to have freedom to experiment with new materials and methods and that it is unwise for them to be bound tightly to a rigidly prescribed curriculum. It is good that they can capitalize on their own unique talents and opportunities. But it is also necessary that they recognize their responsibilities to develop the same basic skills and fundamental understandings which other teachers and other schools are seeking to develop.

What constitutes a good elementary education today in Bangor, Maine, is not radically different from what constitutes a good elementary education in Los Angeles, California. Even if the ideal elementary education in one locality should differ from the ideal in another, it would be unwise to build an educational program around only the local needs. For it is certainly true that many of those educated in one place will spend most of their lives in some other.

One of the essential values of a well constructed standardized test is its reflection of expert consensus on nationwide objectives of achievement. Instead of asking how well the standardized test fits local objectives, the test selector should ask with how much competence the test constructors can speak concerning the common objectives of all schools. A teacher should not ask a standardized test to provide evidence on how well she has taught all the things she has tried to teach, but only on the things that all teachers ought to have taught! For those achievements which are truly and rightly unique to a particular school or teacher, locally constructed tests are the best answer.

WILL THE TEST MAKERS DICTATE CURRICULUM?

Many of those who mistrust the nationally developed standardized tests of achievement frequently express fear that the test makers will dictate the curriculum. There is some basis for this belief, but it should not be a source of anxiety. If the standardized test is taken seriously, it will certainly exert some influence on teaching. But if the test is constructed by competent experts, that influence should be more beneficial than harmful.

The content and emphasis of textbooks, courses of study, teaching methods, and tests of achievement should all be sanctioned by the same kind of authority—a consensus of expert judgments. If the test makers try, as many of them do, to catch and reflect in their tests a consensus of the judgment of curriculum specialists, it seems unreasonable to charge them with attempting to dictate curriculum developments. If standardized tests of achievements are supplemented by locally constructed tests, there is slight danger that the use of standardized tests will result in undesirable uniformity in curricula.

EXPERT TEST CONSTRUCTION

A well constructed standardized achievement test provides an independent, broadly based definition of *desirable goals* of achievement in *all* schools. This is one of its primary values. Two others are related to it. The first is expert, painstaking test construction. The second is independent, broadly based norms of achievement.

Those who prepare standardized tests, in consultation with subject-matter experts, usually are skilled in writing items. In addition, they pretest the items to identify those which are too difficult or too easy or which fail to discriminate clearly between high and low achievers. Careful attention is also given to the balance of the test among content areas and item types.

The result of the expertness and care applied to the construction of a standard test of educational achievement is usually a technically better test than a local teacher or group would be likely to create. The task it presents are those the pupils should be able to handle. The scores it yields discriminate reliably different levels of achievement. It is usually convenient to administer and score and is efficient and economical in its yield of useful information.

The provision of national, regional, or statewide norms for score interpretation is a third valuable contribution of the standardized achievement test. To secure accurate norms for clearly defined and widely appropriate reference groups is not a simple matter. It is even more difficult to present these norms so that they will be easy to use and to interpret properly.

These norms enable the user of a standardized test to obtain an external, broadly based standard for judging the achievements of pupils. Norms are not universal standards. Nor are they self-interpreting. An oversimplified approach to test norms can rob them of much of their potential usefulness. After the comparison of local achievements with external norms has been made and difference noted, one must still ask, "Is this good or bad?" and "Why do we seem to do so well, or poorly?" and "Under the circumstances, what should we do about the situation?" Standardized tests and their norms will not provide any automatic answers, but they can provide the basis for wise planning and for more reasonable decisions.

Schools exist to educate pupils, but it is the exceptional classroom teacher or school adminstrator who can report very precisely how much learning the pupils have acquired. Enrollment, attendance, and per pupil cost can be specified accurately and in detail, but the acquisition of skills, knowledge, and attitudes is not readily stated in statistical terms. Educational achievement is not easy to measure, and existing tests leave much to be desired. But relatively few schools and teachers are obtaining and using even a small fraction of the information on educational achievement that existing tests could provide. I am persuaded that competent teachers and school systems can improve their effectiveness rapidly by making good use of existing standardized systematic and skillful use of standardized tests should move any school toward higher levels of achievement.

A special and rather recent form of proficiency testing is that of readiness testing. Here the purpose is to ascertain how well an individual will profit from some subsequent course of training. Most such tests are used in educational settings and concern themselves, in particular, with programs in reading or mathematics. Their earliest use is typically with the entrance of the pupil into first grade. But there is no reason why this confinement to school settings need hold. All experiments in laboratory settings, whether with children or non-human subjects which concern themselves with internal mediating responses or learning sets, are dealing with readiness.

In the following selection by Jensen, the discussion centers around the two theoretical approaches to readiness: the earlier hypothesis of growth readiness which places little or no emphasis upon environmental inputs and the more recent notion of the cumulative learning model of mental development. Dr. Jensen is Professor of Educational Psychology and Research Psychologist at the Institute of Human Learning at the University of California at Berkeley. This "occasional paper" was published by the National Laboratory on Early Childhood Education in Urbana, Illinois, and was supported in part by a contract with the U.S. Office of Education and a grant from the Office of Economic Opportunity.

Dr. Jensen leaped into high public view with his long (invited) review of experimental results concerning genetically determined differences between black and white intelligence, especially as related to current educational programs for disadvantaged children. Any student interested in aptitude measurement should be aware of this unusual article, much too long to reproduce (but see pp. 369–380 for his discussion of genetic aspects of race difference, particularly black versus white). The contents of this article were widely discussed in the public press as well as in professional circles with many persons labeling Dr. Jensen's point of view as "racist."

In what follows, which is an exposition of the meaning and value of readiness, Dr. Jensen is discussing a far less controversial subject.

UNDERSTANDING READINESS*

Arthur R. Jensen

Recent research papers in child development and educational psychology reflect a renewal of interest in readiness among educational re-

* This occasional paper was produced pursuant to a contract with the Office of Education, U.S. Department of Health, Education, and Welfare. Contractors undertaking such projects under Government sponsorship are encouraged to express freely their professional judgment in the conduct of the project. Points of view or opinions stated do not, therefore, necessarily represent official Office of Education position or policy. Supported in part by a contract with the U.S. Office of Education (Contract OEC-3-7-070706-3118) and a grant from the Office of Economic Opportunity (Grants CG 9174 and CG 9995).

searchers. There is a new awareness of the importance of the really old notion of readiness and of the need to reexamine the diverse phenomena associated with this concept in light of recent theory and research in child development, individual differences, and the psychology of learning and instruction. The fact that empirical researchers in psychology and education are again seriously approaching the problems of readiness, now with more sophisticated theories and research methodologies than were available in the former heyday of the concept, is an important trend in the right direction.

A generation ago, readiness in a biological-maturational sense was of greater interest to educational psychologists and was regarded more seriously than it has been in the past decade, which has been dominated largely by conceptions derived from theoretical positions of extreme environmentalism and behavioristic learning theory. In its most extreme form, this view holds that the degree of readiness for learning at any given age is merely the product of the amount and nature of the learner's previous experience. Readiness is viewed as the amount of previous learning that can transfer to new learning.

There can be no doubt about the *fact* of readiness; that is, the common observation that certain kinds of learning take place much more readily at one age than at another. No one disputes this. Disagreements arise only when we try to *explain* readiness. The theoretical explanation of readiness is important, of course, because much of what we do about readiness in educational practice will depend upon our conception of its nature.

THE NATURE OF READINESS

For the sake of conceptual clarity, one can state two distinct theories of readiness. One theory can be called the *growth readiness* view of mental development. It is associated with such eminent psychologists as G. Stanley Hall and Arnold Gesell, and it holds that certain organized patterns of growth of neural structures must occur before certain experiential factors can effectively contribute to development. The rate of intellectual development is seen as due primarily to internal physiological mechanisms and their orderly, sequential growth, rather than to inputs from the environment.

The contrasting viewpoint emphasizes learning as the major causal factor in development. The simplest, most extreme statement of this position is simply that humans, like all mammals, possess the neural structures for the formation of associations between the sensory inputs from receptors and the output mechanism of the effectors. This is, in short, the capacity for acquiring stimulus-response connections or habits. The sets of habits which we identify as intelligent behavior are seen as being built up through the acquisition of habits and chains of habits which interact to produce complex behavior. Thus mental development is viewed as the learning of an ordered set of capabilities in some hierarchical or progressive fashion, making for increasing skills in stimulus differentiation, recall of previously learned responses, and generalization and transfer of learning. In recent years, this viewpoint has been most notably developed by Gagné (1965, 1968), who refers to it as the *cumulative learning* model of mental development.

Probably everyone who has attended to the relevant evidence in this field would agree that *both* the *growth readiness* and the *cumulative learning* theories are necessary for comprehending all the facts of the matter. These two aspects are not at all mutually exclusive but work hand in hand to produce the phenomenon we observe as cognitive development. There is little doubt that the physical maturation of the brain, particularly the cerebral cortex, underlies the development of particular cognitive abilities. The developmental sequence of these abilities or, more exactly, of the readiness to acquire them through interaction with the environment, is especially evident between birth and seven or eight years of age. In fact, we know that not all of the brain's potential neural connections are physiologically functionable until at least seven or eight years of age in the vast majority of children.

The orderly sequence of maturation of neural structures is such that the capability for certain kinds of learning and performance falls along an age scale. Standard intelligence tests, such as the Stanford-Binet, yield scores in terms of mental age and attempt to index the child's level of mental maturity. These standard indices, especially in childhood, unquestionably measure a composite of factors associated with both neurophysiological maturation and cumulative learning; there are more specialized tests which clearly measure more of one of these factors than of the others. Acquiring the names of objects—learning common nouns, for example—is highly dependent upon experience once the child begins to talk; the child's vocabulary of common nouns at a given age may thus be conceived of as cumulative learning. The ability to copy geometric forms of increasing complexity, however, seems to depend more upon maturational than upon experiential factors. For example, many children who can easily copy a circle or a square cannot copy a diamond, but the reverse is not true. There is a sequence or hierarchy in the emergence of some abilities. The average five-year-old can easily copy a square. But he must be six before he can easily copy a square containing a single diagonal, and he must be seven before he can copy a diamond. Intensive training in the specific act of copying a diamond is surprisingly difficult and generally ineffective in the average five-year-old. At seven, no training is necessary.

Everyone will agree, too, that these sequential stages of capability are not abrupt steps but that these are transitional stages from one to another. Some transitions are relatively rapid, so that in the preschool years an age difference of just a few months can make for quite striking differences in the child's learning capability for certain tasks.

LEVELS OF COMPLEXITY

In learning, as in perception, often the whole equals more than the sum of the parts. It is in the child's progressing ability to *integrate* the component subskills that the phenomenon called readiness is most apparent. Prior acquisition of the subskills is usually necessary but often not sufficient for learning a particular skill requiring the integration of the subskills. It is the integrative process, the development of a higher-order "master plan," that depends most upon the maturation of brain structures. The physical and mental *subskills* for drawing a diamond are clearly possessed by the five-year-old child. The abstract concept of a diamond, however, is still beyond him, and he therefore cannot integrate his subskills into the total performance of copying the figure of a diamond. He lacks the necessary program, the master plan, so to speak. If anyone doubts this, let him first try to teach a typical five-year-old to copy a diamond, and then to teach a seven-year-old. It is a highly instructive experience to the teacher and provides a most tangible demonstration of the meaning of readiness.

A task with more clearly defined subskills lends itself even more readily to a demonstration of the interactive effects of mental maturation and cumulative learning. Learning to play chess is a good example. I was able to observe the simultaneous roles of maturation and cumulative learning quite clearly while trying to teach my daughter to play chess when she was five years of age. At the time, I was especially interested in Gagné's formulation of cumulative learning in terms of learning hierarchies—the idea that each new step in learning is dependent upon the prior acquisition of certain subskills, and that learning takes place most efficiently when we insure that all relevant subskills have been mastered prior to the next-to-be-learned skill in the learning hierarchy. The notion of a hierarchy of skills seems clearly applicable to the teaching and learning of chess, and I proceeded carefully to teach my five-year-old daughter the game of chess with this hierarchical model in mind.

First, I had her learn to group the chess pieces into their two main categories, white and black. At five this was so easy for her that it hardly needed to be taught, as shown by the fact that she would spontaneously sort out the shuffled pieces in terms of their color when putting them away in the two compartments of the chess set's wooden storage box. If she had been only four years old, it might have been necessary to spend some time teaching her to categorize the items on the basis of color, but by five she had already acquired some concept of classes of objects that look alike in terms of some attribute—in this case, color. The next step was to learn the names of the six chess pieces, an example of paired-associates learning. Mastery of this was attained within a few trials and was accomplished with evident pleasure at having learned something new.

The next day's lesson consisted of learning the proper placement of the pieces on the chess board. This was learned, also with evident pleasure, in one brief session, but there was a slight retention loss before the next day, and further practice in placing the pieces was needed to bring this performance up to mastery. Then, one by one, the rules for moving each of the pieces were learned—another instance of paired-associate learning, but this time requiring practice with each piece in a number of different positions so that the general principle of each piece's movement could be acquired. This aspect of the learning also progressed quickly and easily. It seemed like fun to my daughter, and she appeared "motivated" and eager to learn more in the next lesson. Her learning had proceeded so smoothly and easily up to this point that I almost became convinced that if each step in the learning of the subskills of chess were carried to mastery and if interest and motivation persisted, each subsequent step would prove as easy as the preceding one. This was conspicuously not the case.

After the subskills of chess had been learned and the object of the game was explained and demonstrated repeatedly, we tried to play the game of chess, using all that had been learned up to that point. But a game did not emerge; good moves were reinforced by praise, illegal moves were prohibited and had to be taken back, poor moves resulted in the loss of a piece, and half the time bad moves were not made to result in a loss, in order to avoid too much discouragement. Further coaching resulted in no discernible improvement, there was no coordination or plan in the movement of pieces such that an actual chess game would result, and learning seemed to come to a standstill. Moreover, at this stage interest and motivation took such a slump that even some of the earlier acquired, simple component skills deteriorated. Further lessons led to boredom, inattentiveness, restlessness, and finally complete rejection of the whole enterprise. To continue would have required extreme coercion on my part, so we quit the lessons completely. A few weeks later we tried checkers, which she learned easily. It was sufficiently less complex than chess, and she had no trouble playing a reasonably good game. Learning and improvement in performance in checkers was a smooth, continuous process, and at no point did my daughter show signs of "turning off." Checkers became her favorite game for a time, and she often coaxed me and others to play with her.

What was the difference between chess and checkers? I doubt that I was a better teacher of checkers than of chess; I doubt that my daughter was more motivated to learn checkers than chess or that checkers was in some way more "relevant" to her than chess. I believe it was a difference in the complexity of checkers and chess and of the level of complexity that my child at age five could cognitively integrate into the total act of playing a game of checkers or chess.

A most instructive part of this experience to me was the rapidity of motivational slump and psychological "turn-off" when instruction persisted beyond the level of readiness. The same phenomenon must occur in the learning of school subjects as well as in the present chess example. I doubt also that what I observed could be explained entirely in terms of my having used inappropriate teaching methods at the final stage of the chess instruction.

Exactly one year later, when my daughter turned six, I again got out the chess set. By this time she had lost most of her negative reaction to it, and we ran through the component skills again; relearning was rapid. The only source of difficulty was some negative transfer from checkers; she now had to learn that chess pieces do not take other pieces by jumping over them but, rather, by displacing them on the same square. I believe she would have relearned faster had she never practiced checkers. But it was a trivial difficulty. What was interesting was that this time, though my instructional technique was no different from that used before, there was no hitch in the learning, and a smooth, easy transition was made from the learning of the subskills to learning to integrate them into playing a real game of chess. Simultaneously, there was a growing interest and motivation, and my daughter's skill in the game itself showed continuous improvement with practice. For many weeks thereafter, the first thing I heard from my daughter every night when I arrived home from the office was, "Daddy, let's play chess!"

This is a clear example of learning readiness in both of its aspects—the need to have already acquired the component subskills underlying the next level in the learning hierarchy and the need to have reached the level of cognitive development necessary for the integration of the subskills into a functional whole. Learning is a normal biological function. Children do not have to be cajoled, persuaded, coerced, manipulated, or tricked into learning. Given the opportunity and the appropriate conditions, including readiness, children simply learn. The most effective reinforcement for learning or the behaviors that promote learning (such as attention, effort, persistence, and self-direction) is the child's own perception of his increasing mastery of the skill he is trying to acquire. When this perception is lacking, learning bogs down, and external reinforcements or rewards are usually inadequate to maintain cognitive learning. The child's *efforts* are rewarded, but not the cognitive processes that lead to further mastery; and the end result is frustration and turning off in the particular learning situation. This reaction can become an attitude that generalizes to many similar learning situations; for example, school learning in general.

An important aspect of readiness is the child's ability to perceive discrepancies and approximations in his own behavior in relation to a good model or plan. It is becoming increasingly clear from the research on cognitive development that the child's capacity for plans increases with age and is underpinned by genetically coded neurophysiological developments. Any complex integrative activity—playing chess, reading with comprehension, doing arithmetic thought-problems—depends upon the development of these plans or cognitive structures. The child adapts his behavior to the model or plan and the self-perception of successive approximations provides the reinforcement (reward) that shapes behavior in the desired direction. This is the essence of cognitive learning. Although several years ago I believed that the child's learning of language was the chief instrument of his cognitive learning abilities and that these abilities were almost entirely dependent upon his use of language and his acquisition of habits of verbal mediation, my reading of more recent research in this field inclines me to reject this view. The evidence leads me to closer agreement with the position expressed by Sheldon White that ". . . the gathering evidence seems more and more to suggest that the child's progressive sophistication in language between five and seven is not the cause, but is rather the correlate of, his progressive sophistication in learning" (White, 1968, p. 3).

THE RELATIVITY OF READINESS

The age for readiness for some particular learning is rarely confined to a single point on a developmental scale for any given child. Readiness cannot be determined independently of the method of instruction. A child can evince readiness for learning to read, for example, at age three by one method of instruction and not until age six by another method. The materials and methods that will work at three will work at six, but the reverse may not be true. For example, most three-year-olds would not learn to read in the typical first grade classroom nor with the size of type typically used to print first grade primers, nor by a phonic method. Individual instruction, using very large, poster-sized type, and a "look-say" method will permit many three-year-olds to learn to read, although such reading at three is probably a quite different process psychologically than reading at six. In other words, what appears superficially as the same behavior may be acquired by different means and involve different psychological procsses at different developmental stages. The often superficial nature of the resemblance of the two behaviors can be observed in the extent and nature of the transfer of learning. The three-year-old who learns to read "leg," for example, will be at a loss when the new word "peg" is presented, and it will take as long to learn "peg" as it would to learn "can." For the six-year-old, reading need not be so much a form of audio-visual paired-associate rote learning as it is a form of problem-solving using phonetic mediators. Therefore there will be a high degree of transfer from "leg" to "peg".

Little is known about the extent to which the readiness factor can be minimized in learning by manipulating instructional techniques. Experiments on such tasks as copying a series of geometric figures of increasing complexity suggest that, at least in this realm, performance is far more dependent upon maturational factors than upon any variations that different instructional techniques can produce. Differences in instructional techniques in most forms of school learning may well be of maximum importance at the threshold of readiness, although beyond this threshold a variety of techniques may be relatively indistinguishable in their effectiveness.

IGNORING READINESS

What happens when we ignore the readiness of children who are of approximately the same chronological age but different readiness levels and attempt to teach all the children the same thing in the same way? Obviously we will observe marked individual differences in the speed and thoroughness with which the children learn, and we may be inclined to increase our efforts and persistence in teaching the slower learners in order to help them catch up to the others, or at least to try to achieve the same degree of mastery of the subject as attained by the faster children, even if it takes somewhat longer.

Aside from the accentuation of individual differences in the classroom, are there likely to be other effects of ignoring readiness with possibly greater psychological consequences than those of merely making more visible individual differences in scholastic performance? We do not have any firmly established answers to this question. However, recent animal research on readiness factors in learning and some of my own observations of certain classes in which many children appear not to be learning much of anything at all, despite heroic efforts of the teachers, lead me to hypothesize that ignoring readiness can have adverse psychological effects beyond merely not learning what is being taught at the time it is being taught.

These adverse effects seem to take two main forms: (*a*) The child may learn the subject matter or skill by means of the cognitive structures he already possesses; but because these structures are less optimal than more advanced structures in the sequence of cognitive development, the learning is much less efficient and results in the acquisition of knowledge and skills with lesser capability of transfer to later learning. The increasing breadth of transfer of learning is a chief characteristic of the sequence of cognitive development. (*b*) The second adverse effect of ignoring readiness by persisting in instruction beyond the child's present capability is to cause the phenomenon referred to earlier in the chess example as "turning off." This amounts to an increasing inhibition of the very behaviors that promote learning, and I believe it can become so extreme that it may eventually prevent the child from learning even those things for which he is *not* lacking in readiness.

"Learning to learn," or what psychologists call the acquisition of learning sets, is of greater educational importance, and requires more complex cognitive structures, than the learning of any specific associations or facts. All animals are capable of forming new associations between stimuli and responses, but only higher mammals are capable of learning set acquisition to any appreciable degree, and this capability is not easily demonstrated below the level of primates. Much research on learning sets has been conducted with monkeys and apes. This research clearly shows that learning to learn, more than any specific learning, is dependent upon maturational factors. Since a high degree of control can be maintained over the experiences of monkeys in the laboratory, it is possible to assess the relative importance of maturational and experiential variables for different kinds of learning and to study the consequences of forcing certain types of learning before the maturational factors are optimal for that particular learning.

Research on primates leaves no doubt that learning ability increases with age up to adulthood and that the asymptote of capability for various types of learning comes at later and later ages as the complexity of the learning task increases. The five-day-old monkey, for example, forms conditioned reflexes as rapidly as the adult monkey. The speed of learning object-discriminations, on the other hand, does not reach its maximum until about 150 days of age. When monkeys are given a *succession* of object discrimination problems, each involving different visual discriminations, the monkeys' learning speed gradually increases from one problem to the next. The first problems may require 100 to 200 trials to learn a single discrimination; but after the animal has learned to learn by being given a sequence of many different object discrimination problems, these discriminations may be learned in only one or two trials. In other words, the animal is said to have acquired a learning set for object discriminations and in this type of learning is capable of close to 100 percent efficiency; that is, learning in the fewest possible trials.

It is known that the speed with which learning sets are acquired depends upon the monkey's age; that is to say, its maturational readiness for learning set formation or interproblem learning. Young monkeys (60 to 90 days old) show much less readiness for learning set formation than older monkeys (150 to 300 days old), as reflected in the great differences in learning rates. The most interesting finding, however, is that the monkeys trained at the earlier, preoptimal age for learning set formation apparently do *not* eventually catch up with the older monkeys, even when they finally reach the same age as that at which the older monkeys were trained with much greater ease. In other words, the early training not only was less efficient, but it resulted in these young monkeys' attaining an asymptote at a lower level of proficiency than that attained by older monkeys with much less training. The too early training resulted in a low ceiling for the subsequent development of this particular ability (Harbow, 1959).

The shift in cognitive style in the second year of life in the rhesus monkey, described by Harlow, seems to have its counterpart in the human child between about five and seven years of age—the age at which children universally begin their formal schooling. Sheldon H. White (1965) has adduced a diversity of data in support of his hypothesis that adult mental organization is hierarchical, consisting of two main "layers": an associative layer laid down early in development and following conventional associative principles and a cognitive layer laid down in later childhood. The formation of the cognitive layer is most marked between the ages of five and seven. Between these ages children show a transition from a type of performance in learning situations characteristic of lower animals in similar situations to a type of performance characteristic of adult humans. Thus, it is during this period of most rapid qualitative changes in cognitive processes that consideration of readiness factors of the maturational type is of most importance. The period is better thought of as extending from age five to ages eight or nine, to include more or less the full range of individual differences in making this cognitive transition. Tests such as the Stanford-Binet, the Piagetian developmental tests, and the types of tests and indices described by Ilg and Ames (1964) are the best means now available for assessing readiness for cognitive learning in this age range.

As I mentioned before, the second major type of difficulty that can result when readiness is ignored is what I previously called "turning off"; that is to say, the extinction or inhibition of those forms of behavior which are essential aspects of learning—attention, self-directed effort, rehearsal, and active involvement. Signs of discouragement, waning interest, boredom, and the like are merely surface indicators of the inhibition of learning.

The psychological mechanism by which turning off comes about is well known in laboratory research on learning and was first described in detail by Pavlov under the names "experimental extinction" and "conditioned inhibition." It is a reasonable hypothesis that these processes operate in school when certain analogous conditions prevail in the learning situation. The essential condition is responding without reinforcement or with very inconsistent reinforcement. In animal learning, reinforcement or reward must be external; it is dispensed by the experimenter, usually as bits of food, to strengthen the responses defined as correct by the experimenter. Withholding reinforcement results in decrement or extinction of the response in question, and the stimuli that are present while this extinction process is underway become conditioned inhibitors; that is, the mere presence of these stimuli can come to inhibit the class of responses with which they were associated during extinction.

In humans, reinforcement can be external or internal, so to speak. External reinforcement in the pupil-teacher relationship generally involves both approval and praise by the teacher and "informative feedback" from the teacher as to the correctness or incorrectness of the child's responses. But more important in human cognitive learning is internal reinforcement resulting from the learner's self-perception of his own behavior and its approximation to self-perceived goals. Behavior is sustained and shaped by reinforcement or feedback. If there are no internalized standards or structures as a basis for feedback concerning the approximation of one's performance to the standard, then reinforcement must be external. A simple, clear-cut example is the comparison of a beginning student on the violin and a professional musician. The former must have a teacher to provide immediate feedback on the correctness or incorrectness of performance; the standard is in the teacher's head, so to speak, and not the pupil's. When the professional practices a new piece, on the other hand, his activities are reinforced by his successive approximations to his own internalized standards, which have been acquired through years of musical training, and the subtleties of which can only be referred to as musical talent.

Human cognitive learning (as contrasted with rote learning and motor learning) depends in large part on such internalized regulation of the learning process. The source of self-informative feedback is highly dependent on readiness, the capacity for plans or models to which the child's performance can achieve successive approximations. There is a difference in readiness, for example, between the child who reads by naming symbols (words) he has rote-learned and the child who perceives reading as making an effort to extract meaning from the printed words. Much of the activity of the latter child is self-instructional. Children who do not engage in self-instructional activity do not make normal progress in school. Forced practice in the absence of internal reinforcements, I suggest, can lead to extinction of the behavior being practiced.

Readiness in the cognitive sphere is largely the ability to conceptualize the learning task, to grasp the aim of one's efforts long before achieving mastery of the task. The relative ineffectiveness of shaping one's behavior to external requirements as compared with internal requirements is perhaps seen most dramatically in the child's efforts to copy geometric figures of varying difficulty. Unless the child can internalize a conceptual representation of the figure, he cannot copy it, even though the model is directly before him. Partly for this reason, as well as for its correlations with school readiness, the Ilg and Ames figure copying test is probably one of the most convincing and valuable measures of cognitive development in the preschool years and throughout the primary grades (Ilg and Ames, 1964).

CONCLUSION

Many school learning problems could be circumvented if more attention were paid to readiness in the primary grades, when children's learning is most easily turned off through extinction due to inadequate readiness. The risks of delaying instruction too long seem much less than the possible disadvantages of forcing instruction on a child who is still far from his optimal readiness for the subject of instruction.

We need much more experimentation on readiness; that is, trying the same instructional procedures over a much wider age range than is ever the case in traditional schools. It may well be that some sizeable proportion of children in our schools will, for example, be better readers at age twelve if they began reading instruction at age eight than if they began at age six, and this may apply to the learning of most scholastic skills. The high rate of reading failures and other deficiencies in basic scholastic skills found among high school graduates in groups called disadvantaged can hardly be explained in terms of deficiencies in basic learning abilities. It would seem necessary to invoke turn-off mechanisms at some early stage of their schooling to account for some of their marked educational deficiencies. Experimental programs of primary education that pay special attention to readiness factors in learning and actually *delay* formal instruction (meanwhile inculcating prerequisite experiential factors) until readiness is clearly in evidence are needed to test this hypothesis for its practical effectiveness in improving the ultimate educational achievements especially of children called disadvantaged. It is among this group that turning off in school is most evident.

I suggest that more of the factors which cause turning off are found within the school than outside the school and that among the prime causal factors is an inadequate recognition of the importance of readiness, both in terms of cognitive maturation and cumulative learning. Compared with the potential benefits of such experiments as suggested here in terms of the readiness concept, the risks seem almost trivial. It appears that considerably more bold and daring educational innovations are called for if we are to improve the outcomes of schooling for the majority of children called disadvantaged. The present large-scale programs of compensatory education, which so far have failed to yield appreciable scholastic gains among the disadvantaged, are psychologically and educationally probably still much too conservative. A variety of much more radical educational experiments, with the outcomes properly assessed, would seem to be indicated. At least a few such experiments should give extreme emphasis to readiness factors and to the avoidance of turn-off in school learning.

$$\triangledown \ \triangledown \ \triangledown$$

AN application for a position or an admissions blank for college entrance is not often thought of as a test, but by local research efforts such biographical inventories can take on many of the qualities of a validated measuring instrument. This is not surprising, since many such inventories contain items similar to personality measurements; in addition, they frequently ask for evidence of past achievements and interests. By doing an item analysis of all responses, by studying the extent to which these responses differentiate between a "success" and a "failure" group, by checking these data with a cross-validation group, one can then come up with a very good measuring instrument which has all the advantages of a standardized achievement test.

The earliest successful application of this technique was by the life insurance companies, who developed a weighted scoring system for certain items on a personal history blank which they found differentiated between their successful and unsuccessful salesmen. The Phoenix Mutual Life Insurance Company analyzed data for 500 men in the years 1919–21. It found that a mere 12 items differentiated the two groups, and the fantastic result was a reduction in their training failure rate from 90 to 30 percent (Russell & Cope, 1925). Goldsmith (1922) completed a similar research study for the Guardian Life Insurance Company, which after the establishment of a critical score eliminated 54 percent of the subsequent failures and retained 84 percent of the subsequent successes. The Aptitude Index, available only to members of the Life Insurance Agency Management Association, was first made available in 1938 and has undergone extensive cross-validation since then. It is basically a questionnaire about personal history data and also asks for self-ratings to which are applied weighted scores.

The technique has also been adapted, in a wide variety of settings, to concurrent validity situations. Kirchner and Dunnett (1957) used it to spot female office workers with long versus short-term employment records; Lindemann et al. (1959) studied hospital clinical records and discovered five demographic variables which predicted long versus short stay in a neuropsychiatric hospital; Ehrle (1964) was able to quantify biographical data to predict vocational rehabilitation success; McGrath (1960), in an interesting study to identify unprofitable groups of customers (whose cars were later repossessed), found that a weighted application blank would discriminate between good and poor credit risks. Anastasi and her co-workers at Fordham University (1960) were able to develop a valid scoring key with a simple, factual biographical inventory that would predict college success. Criterion correlations as high as .548 were obtained in cross-validation study. To illustrate such a concurrent validity study, the following report from Standard Oil Company of Indiana, dealing with a high ability group of subjects, is presented. Here the research competence and creativity, checked against three types of criteria, were assessed by means of personal history items. The report, slightly abbreviated from the original in the *Journal of Applied Psy-*

chology, 1961, was a cooperative research effort on the part of Smith, Albright, and Glennon from the Employment Relations Research Office of Standard Oil, and Owens from the Department of Psychology, Purdue University. Of these four, Dr. Owens has moved and is now Director of the Psychometric Laboratory at the University of Georgia's Institute for Behavioral Research.

THE PREDICTION OF RESEARCH COMPETENCE CREATIVITY FROM PERSONAL HISTORY

Wallace J. Smith, Lewis E. Albright,
J. R. Glennon, and William A. Owens

Traditionally, two different research designs have been employed by investigators in their use of biographical data. These are directly analogous to the present employee and follow-up methods of test validation. Exemplifying the latter are "weighted application blank" studies. In this approach, the pool of items for validation consists of those that appear on the employer's application form, filled out at the time of hiring by the criterion groups. Typically, the criterion used is job tenure, so that items are retained which discriminate the long and short tenure individuals. A validity coefficient based on the composite of surviving items would be a *predictive* validity estimate. The nature of the items retained, using this design, is almost always strictly demographic (age, marital status, number of dependents, etc.).

In the other design, which we will term the "personal history" approach, an instrument covering various background topics is administered to presently employed individuals who have been segregated into criterion groups. In contrast to the weighted application blank design, a diversity of criterion measures has been used; validity coefficients in these studies are *concurrent* validity estimates. Whereas, the weighted application blank is generally limited to factual items, the personal history questionnaire can include additionally items covering preferences, attitudes, and interpretation of experience.

The present study involves the attempt to validate an extensive personal history form with petroleum research scientists, using three different criteria of success in research work.

METHOD

Subjects

The *S*s for this study were volunteer male employees at the Standard Oil Company's largest research laboratory. All of them were college graduates, the majority possessing advanced degrees. The most common areas of educational specialization were chemistry and chemical engineering with a few individuals having degrees in other technical areas such as mathematics, physics, etc. The length of service of the group ranged from less than 1 year to over 20 years, the heaviest single concentration (30%) occurring in the one- to five-year interval. Seventy-six percent were less than 40 years of age. The number of Ss varied from 331 to 198 because of missing predictor or criterion data.

Predictor

The personal history questionnaire used was tailor-made for this study and consisted of 484 multiple-choice items. The items were assembled from various sources. The content of the questionnaire included home and family background, various aspects of present and previous jobs, athletic interests, school and college activities, etc.

Criteria

The criterion which was used initially in the study was a rating of the researchers on overall job performance made by their supervisors. These ratings are made periodically for administrative purposes; they were not collected specifically for this investigation. The rating scheme used is a seven-step forced-distribution system, such that ratings of 1 and 7 represent the high and low ends of the distribution, respectively. The percentages of Ss at each point on the distribution are as follows: 1, 10 percent; 2, 15 percent; 3, 15 percent; 4, 20 percent; 5, 15 percent; 6, 15 percent; 7, 10 percent. For purposes of item analysis, the 20 percent with ratings of 4 were eliminated, leaving the high and low 40 percent as criterion groups. Some evidence for the reliability of this criterion is the fact that any man's rating is the product of the judgment of several different supervisors. Also, it is reported that relatively little shift in rating occurs from year to year for most people.

Some time after the project was underway, it became possible to collect ratings regarding the creativity of the Ss. The rating instrument used was the Check-List Rating Scale for Creativity: Form C-1, as developed by Taylor (1958). This is a Thurstone-type scale of 24 descriptive items. The rater checks only those items that apply to or describe the ratee. The statements range in favorableness from "He shows signs of being one of the most creative men in this work that I have known" to "He never has an idea of his own to suggest." The reliability of the scale is suggested by Taylor's correlations, which averaged .83, between the creativity checklist ratings and descriptive ratings of the same individuals made 4 to 5 months later on "originality." The form was scored by computing the algebraic sum of the scale values. On this basis, individuals with checklist scores of -160 to -10 made up the low criterion group and those whose scores ranged from $+50$ to $+180$, the high group.

The third criterion consisted of the number of patent disclosures filed by each man during the five-year period 1954 to 1958 inclusive. (A patent disclosure is a document written by the technical man describing an idea which he regards as patentable. Before credit is received for the disclosure, it must be screened by an in-company patent advisory committee; after further processing it may eventually become a formal patent application.) This five-year span was chosen after an examination of the distribution of disclosures showed that this period of time included sufficient data to be reasonably reliable. Only those Ss were included in this part of the study who had been employed prior to 1954. Those who had no patent disclosures during the period were classified as low criterion individuals, those having eight or more as the high criterion group.

Procedure

Because of the length of the personal history questionnaire, the items were grouped into five "units" of approximately equal length. The units were given to the volunteer participants at the rate of about one per week. *S*s were allowed to complete the units during spare moments at their work places or to take them home if they wished. One unit was to be completed and returned before the next was given. Due to the voluntary nature of the project, normal turnover, travel schedules, etc. some attrition in numbers of *S* took place during the study.

For the item analysis, all criterion groups were subdivided randomly into validation and cross-validation samples. *N*s ranged from, 25 to 68, but were approximately equal for high and low samples for a given criterion and content unit. Using a program developed for the IBM 705, the significance of the difference in response percentages of the high and low criterion groups was computed for every response, validation and cross-validation samples separately. A scoring key was developed for each criterion from those items which discriminated in both the validation and cross-validation samples at or beyond the .10 level, making a compound probability requirement of .05 or less. The keyed items were given weights of $+1$ or -1 in accordance with the direction of discrimination.

RESULTS

Representativeness of Subjects

The fact that the *S*s were volunteers raised a question as to their representativeness of the entire professional staff in the laboratory. A check of representativeness was made by testing the distribution of obtained overall performance ratings against that expected under the forced-distribution system. This was done for all five questionnaire units. None of the five values of X^2 was significant at the .05 level, indicating that the sample was not disproportionately weighted with *S*s from one another rating category. This test was also made for the 100 randomly selected *S*s in the scoring sample, with nonsignificant results.

TABLE 21

INTERCORRELATIONS OF CRITERIA

	2	3
1. Overall performance rating	.534 ($N = 362$)	.187 ($N = 285$)
2. Creativity rating		.200 ($N = 251$)
3. Patent disclosures		

Intercorrelations of Criteria

Table 21 presents the intercorrelations of the three criteria. These values are based on the total numbers of Ss for whom the criterion data were available, regardless of whether they filled out the personal history questionnaire. As might be expected, the two sets of ratings correlate more highly with each other than either does with the patent disclosure criterion. However, all three of the coefficients shown are significant at the .01 level.

Validity and Reliability of Scoring Keys

The concurrent validity of the 37-item overall performance key was .613. Correspondingly, for the creativity and patent disclosure criteria the validities are .521 and .517, respectively, both based on 22 items. All of these coefficients far exceed the value required for significance at the .01 level.

The number of items indicated for each key may be somewhat misleading because the same item may discriminate on more than one criterion (although the same response is not necessarily scored each time). In fact, three items are included in all three keys. A total of 59 different items are scored.

An estimate of the reliability of some of these scored items was obtained when 25 researchers consented to retake two of the personal history units about 2 months after their original responses had been submitted. These two units contained 29 of the 59 discriminating items. The correlation of the 29-item scores obtained on the two administrations was .683. This value is similar in magnitude to those reported by other investigators with very large numbers of Ss.

DISCUSSION

The relatively high validities of the three scoring keys demonstrate the utility which the personal history technique can have with highly skilled individuals. As is often noted, aptitude and other types of tests which work well at lower ability levels may fail to discriminate in groups of this kind. Also, it would be difficult to find another instrument which would yield a better "rate of return" in predictive effectiveness per unit of testing time. For example, most applicants can easily complete the 59 keyed items in 30 minutes.

The only other studies in this general area of which the writers are aware are those by Mandell (1950), Stein (unpublished), and Taylor (1961). Mandell, using a 37-item inventory, was unable to discriminate chemists rated high and low on job performance by their superiors and colleagues. Taylor found that 20 out of 47 personal history items were significantly related to either or both of two criteria for 94 electronics engineers and scientists. The criteria were ratings of productivity and creativity. However, when he extended the scoring keys to a group of physicists, only chance relationships were obtained. Stein reports a number of biographical variables which differentiate significantly between his groups of "more" and "less" creative industrial research chemists. There were 23 individuals in each group, the groups being determined by rankings and ratings from superiors, colleagues, and subordinates. No cross-validation data are reported.

Although some of our "personal history" items are similar in nature to those found in tests of personality, interests, and values, it is felt that they engender less hostility on the part of the applicant and are less subject to faking than is characteristic of many such tests. For one thing, they are presented in context with other items which do require responses of a strictly factual nature. Also, the applicant may do himself as much harm as good by trying to appear the "Organization Man," due to the empirical weighting procedure used.

A review of the discriminating items suggests that a "self-confidence" factor may be what these items assess. This interpretation is reinforced by the frequency with which the high criterion groups say that they (a) have more readily taken advantage of opportunities presented them, (b) consider their achievements thus far to be greater than those of others with the same education, (c) work more quickly than others, and (d) prefer to have many things "on the fire" simultaneously. Also the high groups tend to have more education than their colleagues, have obtained it on scholarships or fellowships, have worked as teachers or instructors, have published at least one technical paper and devote much time to reading—suggesting the presence additionally of an "academic orientation" factor.

SUMMARY

A personal history questionnaire was administered to a group of petroleum research scientists employed in a research laboratory of the Standard Oil Company. The questionnaire items were analyzed and cross-validated against three criteria of research effectiveness: ratings of overall performance, ratings specifically on creativity (both made by supervisors of the researchers), and objective records of the number of patent disclosures produced by each man during a five-year period.

Three keys, totaling 59 items, were applied to a scoring sample of 100 randomly selected Ss. The concurrent validity estimates resulting were .613, .521, and .517 for overall performance ratings, creativity ratings, and patent disclosures, respectively. These results were interpreted as indicative of the value of the personal history technique with a highly select group.

A cautionary note should perhaps be appended to this presentation. Once the application blank items or the personal history data information has been studied, and scoring weights applied, it is unwise to allow such data to become old without reevaluation. Werni-mont (1962), for example, found that the validity of a weighted appli-cation blank for female clerical workers declined for the period 1954–59. His recheck showed that only three items retained predictive validity over this time span. It would thus be wise to review, every three to five years, the scoring weights assigned to biographical items.

$$\triangledown \ \triangledown \ \triangledown$$

A recent paper by Holtzman, which follows, is notable for the empha-sis given to criterion-referenced testing—especially in the area of achievement testing in schools—in contrast to norm-based testing techniques. Here is involved much "hardware" which has yet to be mass-produced. One should also note that such testing programs move away from the typical 50 percent item difficulty level which is customary with the more usual norm-based testing. The programs Holtzman describes here require extensive data banks and with the concomitant problem of preserving confidentiality which certain of these programs have handled in ingenious ways even to the deposi-tion of original identification numbers in a foreign country.

Dr. Holtzman is Professor of Psychology and Dean of the School of Education at the University of Texas; he is also Research Advisor to the Hogg Foundation for Mental Health also located at the University of Texas. The paper was his Presidential Address for Division 5 (Evaluation and Measurement) of the American Psychological Associ-ation at the Miami Beach meetings, September 1970, and which was later published in the June 1971 issue of the *American Psychologist.*

THE CHANGING WORLD OF MENTAL MEASUREMENT AND ITS SOCIAL SIGNIFICANCE

Wayne H. Holtzman

One of the great success stories of modern psychology is the development of objective tests for measuring human abilities that are of importance to society. During the past half century, the standardized mental test with nationally based norms has proven to be a highly effective instru-ment for selection and classification of men in the armed forces; for evaluation of educational progress within our school systems; for selec-tive admission of college students; for selection of employees within government, business, and industry; and for clinical assessment of individuals in need of psychological services. It is estimated that within American schools alone, over 250 million standardized tests of ability are administered each year (Brim *et al.,* 1969). It is a rare individual indeed, especially among children and young adults, who has not been evaluated by a standardized mental test, a test that has played a significant role in determining his place in society.

From World War I until the late 1950s, the testing movement enjoyed a degree of public acceptance it is unlikely to see again. Judging each person on the basis of his measured performance rather than on his family background, social status, or political connections has been a powerful agent of social change. Assuming unbiased, reliable measurement, what could be more just within the American concept of an egalitarian society than recognizing merit by objective tests of ability? Even today, college entrance examinations have made it possible for able but financially poor students to obtain scholarships in the best private colleges.

CRITICISMS OF TESTING

By the late 1950s, it became generally apparent that the large-scale normative use of objective tests for rewarding selected individuals among many in competition has serious social consequences of debatable value. The testing movement has always had its critics, but they failed to gain a foothold until the impact of adverse decisions based on tests had been felt by millions of individuals. In the post-Sputnik period, a growing number of critics have claimed that mental tests are unfair to the bright but unorthodox person, to the culturally disadvantaged, and to the naïve individual who lacks experience in taking standardized tests.

The growing controversies surrounding mental tests have become especially acute within educational institutions. It is generally recognized that the educated person enjoys the riches of society as well as enhanced self-esteem and personal development, while the person who prematurely drops out of school is cast into an inferior role. It is not surprising that the angry cries of black students are directed at normative tests that deprive them of entrance to the better colleges, jobs, and social positions.

A major dilemma arises in attempting to meet these criticisms. The traditional academic curricula of our schools and colleges are becoming increasingly dependent on verbal communication, verbal memory, and the same kind of abstract reasoning as measured by scholastic aptitude tests. Therefore, sufficiently high correlations arise between standardized multiple-choice aptitude tests and course examinations to justify the use of tests for prediction of academic achievement and selective admissions. The rapid growth of higher education and the greatly increased number of students per course have forced more and more instructors to employ multiple-choice objective examinations for grading students. As a result, the relevance of scholastic aptitude tests for prediction of academic grades has increased, rather than decreased, in recent years. The compelling economics of mass education and objective normative testing are exceedingly difficult to resist in a rapidly expanding system of higher education. Tests that are designed for normative use, whether for college admissions or course examinations, discriminate against those who are culturally different from the majority.

Such incidental discrimination might be more justifiable if there were a close correspondence between success in school and subsequent occupational success. But for a number of reasons, the correlation between grades and later success is too low to argue generally that measured performance in the traditional academic curriculum is that critical. The issue is made more complex by the fact that entry to many occupations is denied an individual who fails to complete the prescribed academic program, regardless of the program's relevance. The growing meritocracy built around traditional curricula that are uniformly prescribed, normative tests that are competitively graded, and restrictive credentials for job entry may be efficient means of building a technological society, but it does so by exacting a heavy toll on those members of society who fail to conform to the majority. The more tightly the meritocracy is drawn, the more self-fulfilling the prophecies.

EDUCATIONAL REFORM AND THE NEW TECHNOLOGIES

A way out of this dilemma may be closer at hand than many realize. The number of pressures within American society and new developments in measurement and instruction are moving in the same general direction. Led by students, spokesmen for minority rights, and concerned academicians, the general public is becoming increasingly aware of serious inequities within our educational system. As higher education becomes more essential to vocational advancement and personal fulfillment, the fruits of education cannot be denied to anyone who is motivated and capable of profiting from it.

The growing attacks on normative testing for college admission and course grading are having an impact as more and more individuals call for less emphasis on scholastic aptitude measures and more on other abilities and new forms of instruction. The kinds and variety of curricula recognized as appropriate for various forms of education are increasing markedly. Courses aimed at social problems and individual self-development are eroding the traditional, discipline-oriented curricula in many colleges. This new thrust may involve individual competencies in such things as social leadership, self-awareness, regard for human rights and social responsibilities, or other aspects of behavior that typically have not been important in traditional academic pursuits. As the curriculum moves through reform, there will be opportunities for new kinds of measurement as well.

Emphasis is being given in many circles to the idea of individualized instruction in which the learner moves at his own pace and at a time and place that is appropriate for him as an individual. The units of instruction emphasize self-paced learning with regular social reinforcement to maintain a high degree of motivation and relevance, coupled with the concept of continuous progress from one unit to the next. These "microcurriculum units" or modules have fairly well-defined behavioral objectives or performance criteria by which mastery can be recognized. The curriculum itself is viewed in a more global manner as consisting of strings of modules arranged according to an explicit hierarchy of values that are in harmony with the future goals of individual development. In many fields of learning, these specific modules involve training objectives where criterion testing for standardized mastery is employed rather than normative testing for measuring individual differences. Much of what goes on in education is susceptible to treatment in this form. The broader educational objectives differ considerably from one individual to the next in order to maximize potentiality for individual development.

A major force for social change in educational reform is the emergence of new educational technology and related techniques of measurement. Keeping track of a person moving at his own pace in a continuous progress environment, where the particular branching of the curriculum is tailor-made for the student's own learning aptitudes and level, requires a computer to manage the curriculum and assist with the instruction. In a traditional setting, the instructor keeps a record of how well each student does on each achievement test for the course, while the periodically collected scores from standardized normative tests are stored centrally. When instruction is individualized, testing must be done more frequently and at different times for each student. In many cases, performance testing and instruction are so closely interwoven that they appear as one integrated learning activity. Except for periodic testing at a later date to determine how much a person has retained, even the conceptual nature of measurement shifts from a normative basis, where each person is compared with a general population, to a criterion-referenced basis, where the only decision made is whether or not the student has achieved the desired objective for a specific instructional module. Not only are more short tests given, but many more have to be constructed, again requiring a computer for generating tests from item pools as well as scoring and storing them for each student.

Several large-scale programs of individualized instruction are sufficiently advanced to demonstrate the feasibility and power of this approach to educational reform. Now in its fourth year of operation under the leadership of John Flanagan, and jointly developed by the American Institutes for Research and Westinghouse Learning Corporation, Project PLAN consists of over 1,000 modules divided across nine operating grades and four subject-matter areas (Dunn, 1969). Each teaching unit is coded as to reading difficulty, required teacher supervision, media richness, required social involvement, and a number of other characteristics. A profile is prepared for each student containing measures of abilities, interests, aspirations, and background data for use by the computer in matching the curriculum to the student. The combination of normative measurement on nationally standardized tests for initial guidance and placement of the student and criterion-referenced tests for assessing progress in mastering the curriculum modules is especially noteworthy. Experience to date with over 10,000 students indicates that most individuals like the new freedom provided by PLAN, and that learning proceeds at a faster pace.

A still more detailed form of individualized instruction can be found in the program of individually prescribed instruction developed by Glaser and associates at the University of Pittsburgh's Learning Research and Development Center (Cooley & Glaser, 1969). A specific lesson plan is prescribed individually for each child every day, depending on his performance and desires of the previous day. Thousands of curriculum modules are stored and retrieved manually by clerks at the end of each day until the experimental system can be perfected and stored electronically in computers. Interwoven with each module is a criterion-referenced achievement test that provides a basis for decision making in selecting the next module.

A recent study by Ferguson (1969) serves to illustrate computer-assisted branched testing with elementary arithmetic materials in the Pittsburgh individually prescribed instruction program. A model was developed and tested in which items are selected on the basis of previous responses and are thus tailored to the competencies of the student. A learning hierarchy of prerequisite relationships among 18 objectives in addition and subtraction was formulated on the basis of previous studies. Two major sequences emerged as dominant in the hierarchy, one involving only addition skills and the other exclusively concerned with subtraction. A third sequence integrated both addition and subtraction. Initially, an examinee was presented with a randomly generated item for the specific objective being tested. The computer scored his response as correct or incorrect and generated another item. The process continued until a sufficient number of items had been answered for the computer to make a decision regarding the individual's proficiency on the objective. The decision model involved assigning a priori probability values to the two types of error constituting incorrect decisions and applying Wald's sequential probability ratio test to terminate the testing on the objective in question. Selection of the next objective to be tested depended on the examinee's proficiency on the first objective as well as the proposed learning hierarchy. When given to 75 students in grades 1–6 at the Oakleaf Elementary School, Pittsburgh, Pennsylvania, the sequential branched testing method proved to be three times as efficient as a fixed-length conventional test, requiring, on the average, only 52 items instead of 150.

A sequential branched testing procedure proves far superior to conventional testing when one has a computer for generating and scoring items, a suitable communication terminal for interaction of computer and examinee, and a good basis for arranging the skills to be tested in a learning hierarchy. The procedure is ideally suited to criterion-referenced testing but is of questionable value where normative testing is employed. As Lord (1970) has demonstrated, little is to be gained by the use of tailored testing with conventional items for normative measurement except in the case of best and worst students.

Integrating the elements of programmed learning and sequential branched testing into a single curriculum requires a computer for electronic storage and retrieval of the material to be learned, the test items for measuring mastery, and the instructional branching strategy for both the curriculum and the tests. Suitable multimedia teaching terminals with visual display devices, light pens, audio units, and typewriters under either student or computer control, depending on the nature of the curriculum and purpose of the student, must be provided in large numbers at reasonable cost before computer-assisted instruction, testing, and guidance can become operational. Several major companies are now designing hardware configurations that will soon have the required functional capabilities for fully implementing computer-assisted instruction. It is now fairly certain that the cost of such a system can be sharply reduced by mass production to the point where it is economically feasible to think of large-scale implementation (Alper & Bitzer, 1970). Psychological laboratories for computer-assisted instruction at Stanford University, the University of Texas, the University of Illinois, Florida State University, System Development Corporation, the Mitre Corporation, and a dozen other universities and research institutes have already demonstrated the feasibility of this new technology as well as its dramatic impact on individual learning in many areas.

Such new technologies as Project PLAN, individually prescribed instruction, and computer-assisted instruction are highly promising in their eventual impact on educational practices and the concomitant measurement of standardized mastery using criterion-referenced tests instead of normative testing for competitive selection. Successful prototypes have been developed, but these represent only a small beginning compared to what must be done in the way of research and development before individualized instruction in the true sense of the term can be properly implemented on a large scale.

NATIONAL ASSESSMENT OF EDUCATIONAL CHANGE

Still another important departure from standardized normative measurement of individual differences in mental abilities grows out of the increased concern for developing a national system of social indicators, measures that reflect the quality of life, the rate of educational progress, and the value of human resources for the nation as a whole as well as for different regional, ethnic, and socioeconomic groups. A recent report of the Behavioral and Social Sciences Survey Committee (1969) has recommended the establishment of a system of social indicators by the federal government that would lead to an annual social report for measuring changes in many aspects of society. A step in this direction has already been taken by the National Assessment of Educational Progress, a project of the Education Commission of the States (Womer, 1970).

Under the leadership of Ralph Tyler and support from the Carnegie Corporation, the Exploratory Committee on Assessing the Progress of Education began in 1964 to collect information about the knowledge and skills held by 9-, 13-, and 17-year-olds and of young adults in 10 subject areas taught in schools. After five years of planning and public debate as to the merits of the project, National Assessment launched its first annual survey for all four age levels in three subject areas—citizenship, science, and writing. The national sample contained a total of approximately 100,000 persons carefully chosen on a stratified random basis involving 52 sampling units from each of four geographic regions.

The first step in preparing materials for National Assessment was to determine a list of educational objectives for each subject. Using these objectives as guides, various measurement research organizations took responsibility for preparing exercises designed to assess what young people actually know. A variety of approaches —questionnaires, interviews, observations, and performance tasks—were employed in addition to traditional multiple-choice and short answer questions similar to those used in standardized mental tests.

Five important distinctions can be made between the National Assessment exercises and multiple-choice items employed in normative tests. First, the assessment exercises are designed to discover what defined segments of the nation's population can do or what they know, rather than to distribute people normatively according to measured individual differences. For example, what percentage of the 9-year-olds in the country know that most plants get most of their water directly from the soil? Or know how to report a fire? Or report that they had ever taken part in some organized civic project to help other people? Does this percentage shift significantly across different segments of the population or over time?

Second, while items in a test are summed to give a score for each individual, exercises in National Assessment are each analyzed in their own right by pooling data across individuals. For this reason, it is particularly important that the exercises be meaningful to specialist and layman alike, that they be directly related to the stated objectives, and that they have high content validity. Extensive review sessions involving a variety of judges were held for every exercise retained for National Assessment.

Third, the exercises are designed for a broad range of difficulty in order to report to the American public examples of knowledges, skills, and understandings that are common to almost all American youth of a given age, examples that are common to a typical or average American youth, and examples that are common to only the most knowledgeable youth. Ideally, one third of the exercises should be passed by most of the population, one third by about half, and one third by only a small percentage. By contrast, item difficulty level in the typical normative test is likely to hover near the 50 percent level or to be evenly distributed throughout the range.

Fourth, all exercises, except those in reading, are presented aurally as well as visually, so that no one is severely penalized in responding, say, to citizenship or science questions.

And fifth, the exercises are assembled in heterogeneous packages with different sets of exercises given to different individuals on a sampling basis. A package for 17-year-olds last year, for example, contained seven multiple-choice science exercises, three free response citizenship exercises, and one essay exercise for writing. Exercises are packaged in any convenient fashion that adds up to no more than 50 minutes of assessment time for each person. Items in a normative test, on the other hand, are assembled in relatively homogeneous scales so that they can be added together to give a reliable score.

Unlike most measurement applications in psychology and education, in National Assessment a person is never asked to record his name. Responses are clustered and analyzed by sex, age, race, region, community, and family characteristics in order to obtain censuslike information about the educational progress of various segments of the population. Repeated applications in the years ahead will provide a wealth of data dealing with change over time—data that should be useful in national planning, particularly when examined together with other social indicators.

Individuals and schools approached by National Assessment were given the option of declining to participate in order to respect their rights to privacy. Exceedingly few refused to participate under these permissive conditions, testifying to the wisdom of this policy. My own experience in soliciting the cooperation of 13,000 high school students in a probability statewide sample (Moore & Holtzman, 1965) and in asking for the continued participation of 420 families in a longitudinal study of personality development (Holtzman et al., 1968) has been similarly favorable. Unbiased samples can be obtained in most measurement studies without coercion of even a mild sort. National Assessment provides an exemplary model of how one should proceed in order to protect the privacy of individual participants and their freedom to decline.

Preserving the confidentiality of data is a related problem that continues to worry many thoughtful individuals. As we move into large-scale programs with extensive, centralized data banks stored in computers, the possibility of harm to an individual cannot yet be completely eliminated. The files that may do greatest damage to the individual are those that are kept secret from him but not from those who can take action affecting him. While much of the national concern expressed in recent congressional hearings deals with personal information that psychologists are unlikely to find interesting, specific attention has been directed at potential abuses of individual privacy involving psychological test data, biographical information, and social attitudinal data typically employed in psychological research. The proper balance between protecting the individual against the misuse of information about himself and collating data to help solve major social, economic, and educational problems has not yet been achieved. On the other hand, continuation of the present highly decentralized systems will not cure present abuses of individual privacy, although it will prevent the integration of information required for future social development. Properly developed centralized data banks can eventually assure greater protection for the individual while also providing essential information for basic research as well as future national planning.

One interesting solution to the problem of protecting the confidentiality of data from individual respondents is the Link system that has been devised for the national study of college student characteristics by the American Council on Education's Cooperation Institutional Research Program (Astin & Boruch, 1970). Measurement data and biographical information on several hundred thousand college freshmen are collected each year as part of an ongoing educational data bank. Initially, a more or less traditional system was instituted. Two physically separate tape files were created, one containing the student's answers to research questions together with an arbitrary identification number, and a second containing only the student's name and address and the same arbitrary number. The first tape with the research data file was openly accessible for analysis. The second tape with the name and address file was locked in a vault and used only to print labels for follow-up mailings. The original questionnaires and punched cards were then destroyed.

Good as it may seem, this system still did not offer complete protection against government subpoena or unauthorized disclosure by staff members with access to both files. A third file, the Link file, was created which contained two sets of numbers—the original arbitrary identification numbers from the research data file, and a completely new set of random numbers which were substituted for the original identification numbers in the second file. The final step in establishing the new system was to deposit the new Link file at a computer facility in a foreign country with a firm agreement that the foreign facility would never release it to anyone, including the American Council on Education. Follow-up mailing tapes now have to be prepared by the foreign facility. There is no way that anyone can identify individual responses in the research file.

Such elaborate steps to guarantee the complete confidentiality of personal information in research files may seem far too expensive. Why go to this extreme when the chances are exceedingly remote that any harm could be done to an individual by using a more traditional system? The reason for foolproof data files is that the public demands it. However unlikely, there does exist the possibility of court subpoena or improper invasion of privacy when the data files and decoding files are under the control of the same organization.

RECOGNITION OF SOCIAL, CULTURAL, AND LINGUISTIC VARIABILITY

One of the most important changes of the past decade in the field of mental measurement as well as in society as a whole is the greatly increased respect for social, cultural, and linguistic variability among different kinds of people. Until recently, the "American way of life" was defined almost entirely by middle-class values of white, English-speaking people of largely western-European origin. In general, school curricula, symbols of social status and privilege, occupations, the more highly valued life styles, and to some extent even suggested definitions of intelligence, all conformed to the dominant values of which most Americans were proud. The forgotten minorities were expected to adjust to these values if they were to enjoy the fruits of the nation. As recently as 10 years ago, school principals in the Southwest often pointed proudly to the fact that the speaking of Spanish by Mexican-American children was prohibited on their school grounds, English being the only permissible language in which to receive an education.

The emergence of black culture, the Chicano movement, and the stirring of the American Indian as well as other forgotten groups in the wake of desegregation and civil rights legislation have forced white America to reexamine its soul. The result in the field of mental measurement has been a recognition and acceptance of cultural variability, a search for new kinds of cognitive, perceptual, and affective measures by which to gauge mental development, and a renewed determination to contribute significantly to the task of overcoming educational and intellectual deprivation.

A generation ago, the typical study involving mental measurement and social variability consisted of giving tests, standardized largely on middle-class whites, to people of other ethnic, linguistic, and socioeconomic backgrounds. Countless individual and group differences were observed and classified in a descriptive manner. Today, more attention is given to devising procedures for measurement and evaluation which are indigenous to the culture under study. Illustrative of this new approach is the work of Freeberg (1970) who developed a test battery specifically tailored in content, format, and administration to disadvantaged adolescents drawn largely from the black and Puerto Rican ghettos of New York. The extensive six-year longitudinal study of 2,000 Headstart children undertaken last year by the Educational Testing Service also contains a large variety of new measures that are specifically designed for culturally disadvantaged children (Anderson, 1969). The problem with most such tailored procedures is that they may be just as ill-suited for use with other markedly different individuals as are tests standardized on middle-class whites when employed for assessing educationally disadvantaged children.

The most difficult methodological problems arise in cross-cultural research where two or more distinctly different cultures are compared systematically. The translation, calibration, and administration of psychological measures across cultures require close and continual collaboration of specialists from each culture who have learned to trust each other fully. In a similar manner, measurement across subcultures within a given nation requires the full participation of representatives from each subculture, a condition that is met by all too few investigators thus far. In spite of such problems, studies dealing systematically with cultural, social, and linguistic variability are growing rapidly in number while also increasing greatly in the power of their research designs. Is it too much to hope that by the end of the coming decade the lingering ethnocentrism of the testing movement will disappear?

In the short span of this article, it has been possible to highlight only selected topics within the broad field of mental measurement. It should be obvious to even the casual observer of trends in the field that other areas also deserve attention. It is worth noting that every one of the new advances reviewed is heavily dependent on the modern electronic computer for its implementation. Fundamental to the changing world of mental measurement is the rapid growth in power, versatility, and accessibility of high-speed computers. Large-scale testing; new educational technology such as individually prescribed instruction, sequential branched testing within the curriculum, Project PLAN, and computer-assisted instruction; national assessment of educational change and the development of a system of social indicators; new techniques for preserving the confidentiality of personal data; and even new programs for assessing the mental development of culturally different people—all require a computer for implementation.

In focusing primarily on the social implications of new advances, it is easy to overlook the numerous theoretical and methodological contributions to the field of measurement and evaluation that have been made in the past few years. New techniques of scaling, test theory, factor analysis, and multivariate experimental designs are being produced and extended in a lively manner. The immediate social significance of these developments may not be readily apparent because of their indirect, long-range nature as basic research contributions. And yet, without the continued, vigorous support of such theoretical and methodological advances, the truly great potentiality of the changing world of measurement would fail to materialize. Each of the promising new developments surveyed above is heavily dependent on the solution of difficult basic research problems before it can be fully realized to the benefit of society. There is every reason to be optimistic about the next 10 years in the field of mental measurement, given the recognized social significance of new developments and the rapid rate at which basic work is advancing.

PART TEN

Automation, Computers, and Multivariate Techniques

COMPUTERS more and more take over complex functions formerly managed by individuals. Large colleges and universities now are involved with extensive testing in over- and underachieving students—achievement, that is, measured by grade point average and whether it is significantly above or below the earlier predicted grade point average—computerized ways may now be found to provide feedback to individual students. With large college enrollments, extensive normative studies can be completed; multiple regression analyses come later. The counseling staff or faculty advisers formerly summarized entrance test data to students; now this task has been computerized. The following report is from Pennsylvania State University, where profile data plus predicted grade point average, expressed in terms of probability, is succinctly presented to the individual student. The study originally appeared in *Educational and Psychological Measurement* for 1958. All three authors were at that time associated with Pennsylvania State University. Dr. Zeigler is currently Professor of Psychology at the University of Illinois, Dr. Bernreuter is in private practice, and Dr. Ford is Professor of Psychology and Dean of the College of Human Development at Pennsylvania State University.

A NEW PROFILE FOR INTERPRETING ACADEMIC ABILITIES

Martin L. Ziegler, Robert G. Bernreuter,
and Donald H. Ford

A method of profiling and lucidly reporting a student's academic abilities was delivered at the Pennsylvania State University in early 1956 to meet the needs of a new comprehensive freshman counseling program introduced at that time. One of the shortcomings of the previous counseling program was the difficulty in communicating to students, parents, and faculty the student's relative class standing and his predicted achievement levels. Under the old system, the student's test results and predicted averages were reported on IBM cards. The predicted averages, however, could be reported on those cards only through a range of twelve intervals of one fourth of a grade point each, and there was no way to indicate the standard error of prediction. Under these conditions, the misconception often arose among the interviewees that the student could achieve neither better nor worse than the range predicted on the card. The new method attempted to ensure correct interpretation of the test results.

The new method also attempted to take into account the uncertainty of many entering freshmen concerning which curriculum they should pursue. To provide for this, multiple regression equations were formulated for two major curriculum groups—a "science" group (curriculums requiring mathematics beyond college trigonometry) and a "nonscience" group (curriculums not requiring advanced mathematics). Depending upon the student's expressed interest in regard to these areas, his test scores were compared with those of other entering freshmen in that area and predictions were made of his probable academic attainment. In cases in which the student was more certain of his goals and evinced an interest in one of the specific colleges within the University, the counselor similarly had available to him the information necessary for comparison of his scores with those of other students showing an interest in that college and for prediction of his probable achievement within that college. An extensive manual was prepared for the counselor which contained—for all tests and subtests—the percentile ranks, means, standard deviations, sten scores (half standard deviation units from the mean), and beta weights multiplied by the test scores. These various measures were computed separately for each of the nine colleges. Accordingly, the counselor could plot on the profile the student's test scores as related to any specific college and portray for him how his performance compared with that of other freshman entering that college. In addition, beta weights could be located and summed so that the student could be shown what his probability of success was within the particular college.

THE PROFILE

Figure 12 shows the complete profile developed for the counselor's use in the interview. For purposes of illustrating the way in which it appears in actual use, a fictious case was set up on IBM and is printed on the profile. At the top of the profile appear the student's name, his student number, his high school rank reported in quintiles, the year in which the test was administered, sex, and the semester in which the student is enrolled.

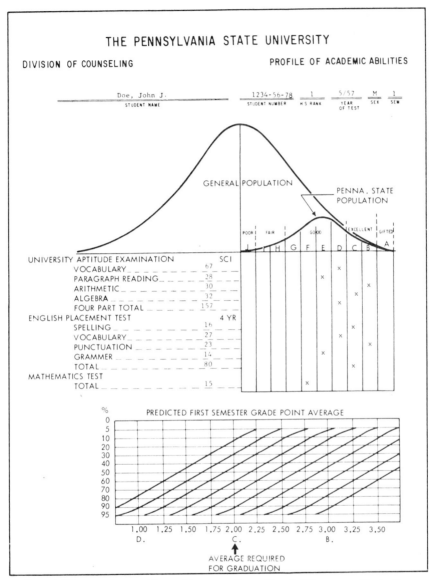

FIG. 12. The complete profile used in counseling with a fictitious case illustration.

The method for reporting test scores consists of using two curves: the smaller curve shows the distribution of academic ability scores of Pennsylvania State University students; the larger, distribution of scores that would be earned on the same test by persons in general. This technique communicates to the student how his overall and specific scores compare with other Penn State freshman students, and how thay compare with the general population. Since the prospective freshman is almost always superior to the average member of the general population, this method can be reassuring for students and parents; especially is this true in the case of a student who scores in the fair or poor range of Penn State students. The profile does show, however, that such a student must expect to meet relatively keen competition and would have to work diligently to earn satisfactory grades.

The "SCI" appearing on the line of the profile opposite "University Aptitude Examination" means that the performance of the student is being compared with that of other students planning to enter one of the "science" curriculums; an "N SCI"would indicate comparison with students entering a "nonscience" curriculum. The raw test scores beside each subtest on the profile make it possible for the counselor, by referring to the manual, to locate sten scores and make predictions of the student's achievement within any college.

The second graph on the profile is an abac showing the predicted grade point averages. On the abscissa are intervals of grade point averages from 1.00 (equal to a "D") through 3.50 (equal to a "B+"). A 4.00 (or "A") does not appear on the graph since it cannot be predicted, because of regression, that any one will have a fifty-fifty chance of earning that average. On the ordinate are percentage values from zero to 100. The ogives plotted on the graph show the standard error of the predicted grade point average for the middle 90 percent of the predictive range. The standard error has been presented in this way since extreme scores—the upper and lower five percent—tended to fluctuate widely and not in relationship to achieved grades.

Predicted averages were derived through multiple regression equations utilizing high school average and scores on the University aptitude examination. The abac was then constructed by plotting predicted averages against achieved first semester averages. This procedure was carried out on two separate groups; results obtained for both groups were very similar and both corresponded to the standard error of the coefficient of multiple correlation.

In order to determine the appropriate ogive for a particular student the multiple prediction was machine computed and the letter "X" printed on the slanted line within the appropriate predicted grade point average interval. In all cases the "X" appears at the 50 percent level since the student has a fifty-fifty chance of exceeding or falling below that point.

An illustration will demonstrate how the abac is used. It can be seen from Figure 12 that an "X" identifies the ogive to be read for the particular student. The "X," in this illustration, is placed between the grade point average values 2.25 to 2.50 and, as always, at the 50 percent level. Thus it can be determined and explained to the student that 50 percent of the students whose predicted grade point average falls between 2.25 and 2.50 may be expected to earn grade point averages which fall within or *above* that cell, and 50 percent may be expected to earn grade point averages which fall within or *below* that cell.

Similarly, any other probability may be determined and explained to the student. For example, by reading the same ogive at its top extreme it is seen that only five percent of students with a predicted grade point average between 2.25 and 2.50 may be expected to exceed a grade point average of 3.25, and that 95 percent will probably fall below that level. Or, it may be explained by referring to the required Penn State graduation average of 2.00 and reading upward to the same ogive and then across, that about 75 percent of the students who scored in the interval of 2.25 to 2.50 may be expected to attain or exceed the graduation requirement.

The profile has been favorably received by students, counselors, and adminstration during its year of use. For all, it has appeared to provide a ready interpretation of test scores and an understanding of potentiality for achievement.

SUMMARY

A new method of illustrating and communicating test results by means of a profile has been reported. By this method it is possible to show a student how his academic abilities compare with those of his classmates, and how they compare with people in general. His relative abilities within two broad curriculum groups—a "science" and a "nonscience" group—or within specific colleges of the University are also readily communicated to him. A more effective means of reporting predicted grade point averages has also been presented.

The multiple regression technique here is clearly an advance. Still more sophisticated techniques are now coming to the fore, particularly multivariate procedures. The older ways of presenting a series of profiles to the student—say, one profile obtained from an aptitude test battery, such as the DAT, and then a second profile obtained from the Strong Vocational Interest Blank, and then perhaps a third profile obtained from, say, the Allport-Vernon-Lindzey Study of Values—only compound the statistical errors inherent in all these measurements, and they cause considerable confusion to the individual. As a recent paper by Sprinthall (1967) states, univariate or bivariate procedures for analysis of data are insufficient when it comes to dealing with complex issues. Discriminant function analysis, or multivariate procedures, where one simultaneously handles many variables, is the answer now proposed. Project TALENT is an excellent example of extensive use of such procedures (see pp. 319–333 of this book). Thus, when one wants to compare an individual's set of scores to the scores of people in a wide variety of groups—for example, the Strong Vocational Interest Inventory or the Pennsylvania State University method using various curricula—discriminant analysis is the appropriate technique. The result points up the similarities of the individual's scores to the group he most resembles. Aside from Project TALENT, the Harvard Studies in Career Development (see Sprinthall for a brief summary of these studies) have also made wide use of such analyses.

COMPUTERS can be made to do far more than mere clerical reporting or summarizing. Not only are regular class achievement tests now scored by machines; in addition, computers can now be programmed to do all the work in both reporting and evaluating guidance programs. Extensive test data—aptitude and achievement data of all sorts—pile up and are summarized on the cumulative record. Computers can be programmed to handle all this mass of data with great speed and efficiency.

In the past, many professional people expressed alarm at so much automation. At the Educational Testing Service's Invitational Conference on Testing, Traxler (1953) expressed concern over the presumed takeover of test scoring machines for psychological and educational testing, and the subsequent production of "the multiple-choice mind." Traxler was talking about what might now be labeled the Model-T version of scoring machines. Regardless, he is probably correct when he remarks that he believes many teachers have accepted objective measurement, "perhaps with quiet resignation," and are not at all comfortable with the thought that despite the skill and resourcefulness and imagination and stimulation they bring to their work, in the end the achievements of their students (and indirectly their own success) is to be evaluated by how well their students respond to a single type of test item.

Now with testing programs proliferating at a rapid rate, more extensive use of computer-based systems can now be made. But all too often the key people see such programs as simple automation of clerical tasks (such as reporting of scores). When at the Center for Research in Careers at Harvard University, Professor Cooley (now Co-Director of the Learning Research and Developmental Center at the University of Pittsburgh) prepared the following paper dealing with a computer measurement system in which one could ask questions that would assist guidance people in interpreting the data at hand. Briefly, he proposed that we shift from the system of merely recording sets of numbers on student records to a procedure of "flashing red lights," which then indicate when a student seems to be in some special difficulty. Statistically, this means multivariate analysis. The paper is also of interest because if deals with the serious business of career decision and vocational choice. It is also one of the many reports emanating from Project TALENT.

The 1962 Fall issue of the *Harvard Educational Review* was entirely concerned with a critical and scholarly examination of guidance when the focus was on the search for theoretical models and substantiating evidence. This series of papers was later expanded (one of the additions was this paper by Cooley) into a special monograph edited by Mosher, Carle, and Kehas (1965). Dr. Cooley's original article appeared in the *Harvard Educational Review*, Fall, 1964.

A COMPUTER MEASUREMENT SYSTEM
FOR GUIDANCE

William W. Cooley

For some time psychologists have been convincing guidance workers that one test score alone is not sufficient evidence to conclude much of anything about a student. Their recommendation was to consider several test scores as a profile of the student. This resulted in the familiar "parallel stalks" model, each stalk standing for a test, with a line passing from stalk to stalk representing a particular student's score combination. Although this gives the impression that all the test score information available on a student is being considered simultaneously, anyone who has worked with this approach knows that it is only a slight graphical improvement over this same set of scores recorded in a cumulative record. *What has been needed is a summary of this test score evidence with respect to particular questions, questions with educational and career relevance for each student.*

I certainly do not visualize a system where the student's test scores are the input and prescribed curriculum and career are the output. Rather, the input consists of test scores, grades, biographical (including family) information, *and* the student's school and career plans. Output from the system would include, for example, certain information regarding students who appear to have high risk plans. The actual form of this computer output could include explanatory paragraphs, if that seemed desirable. The task of the guidance program then, given this information about their plans, and about themselves in relation to those plans.

One key component of the output would be the probable success and satisfaction associated with a particular student plan. Most students seem quite willing and able to make plans and to discuss their plans in terms of probabilities. Interviews with the 700 boys of the *Scientific Careers Study,* a five-year study of career development, consistently found them talking in terms of their chances of doing this or that (Cooley, 1963). "Although I would rather be a doctor, I think I have a better chance of getting into a dental school." "With my grades, what are my chances of making it as a physicist?" "Do boys like me tend to go into law?" The students seemed to be continually searching for the type of data which a computer-measurement system could provide them.

Perhaps a specific example would help to clarify the points being made here. A case was drawn form the *Scientific Careers Study,* and it illustrates a frequent guidance problem. Selection of the case was quite simple. A brief inspection of computer output quickly identified several students with the characteristics needed. The files of that five-year study contained folders on each of the 700 boys, and each folder contained about 100 scale scores, 4 questionnaires and 2 interviews. Only with the aid of the computer can students with particular combinations of characteristics be identified quickly and easily from a file of data this extensive.

The Case of Robert S.

Bob S. was first contacted in the 8th grade. Our file contains his achievement data prior to 8th grade, as well as the data which were collected from grades 8 to 12 as part of the study.

Bob lives with his natural mother and stepfather. He has two younger brothers and no sisters. His father is a typewriter repairmen and his mother does not work.

Ability and achievement information available on Bob when he was in 8th grade gave every indication that he had the potential for further schooling beyond 12th grade. A multivariate statistical summary of his ability and achievement profile indicated that about 83 percent of the boys with his particular combination of scores do enter some type of college.

Interest and temperament data available indicate that Bob "looks" very much like other boys who have entered careers in some field of science and technology. Of the boys with his pattern of interest, 73 percent enter some science-technical field. About one half of the boys who responded to the Temperament Survey as he did were pursuing careers in science-technology.

A summary of socioeconomic data showed that 87 percent of the boys with Bob's family background do not go to college. These data include such variables as parents' education, father's occupational level, and the parents' expectations with respect to further schooling for the boy.

Notice that the numbers reported above tell something about Bob with respect to such questions as whether he is likely to go to college and/or become an engineer. Those percentages can be thought of as the probabilities associated with a particular type of prediction based upon a certain set of data. The data upon which these predictions are based were available when Bob was in 8th grade. Previously used techniques tend to report test results in terms like, "Bob did better on the mathematics test than did 50 percent of his classmates," or perhaps simply, "Bob received a score of 500 on the SCRAP mathematics test." It is difficult to decide what to think about such test scores. They are static. No implications are discernible.

Bob's career plans when first contacted in eigth grade were to enter the Coast Guard. He had an uncle and a cousin in the Coast Guard and felt "they had a good life." Otherwise, he might become an airline pilot. At grade 9, he was still talking about the Coast Guard but was also considering becoming a mechanic or engineer. He thought it might be a good idea to be a mechanic in the service because it is "more organized and less chances of business collapsing." In 10th grade he talked about "becoming a mechanical engineer because he liked to work on cars." This goal continued through 11th grade, but when he was last contacted in grade 12 he was planning to enter the service after high school graduation and become an airplane mechanic.

The point of this particular case is to illustrate a high risk in the sense that if Bob developed realistic college goals later during high school (as he did during grades 10 and 11), he would discover that his eighth and ninth grade behavior (e.g. course selection) was not consistent with those goals.

PROGRAMMED EXPERIENCES

By a systematic examination of several different types of data, a variety of potential problem cases can be uncovered today among a very large group of students. A computer measurement system could allow the early identification of potential problems, soon enough to do something about it. The problem then is what to do once a trouble spot has been observed. The recommendation here is to develop a system of *programmed experiences*.

In Bob's case, for example, general mechanical-technical orientation was quite clear. What was not clear was the level at which he might operate. A sequence of experiences could be designed to show the broad range of jobs open to boys like Bob, including the training required. For common problems, such as this one, films could be an excellent method. Included in these experiences would be some indication of the types of financial aid available to boys like Bob, so that college is not unrealistically discounted too early for financial reasons.

Included in his program of experiences would be a talk with a counselor. In fact, this might be the first experience in the sequence, to make sure that the established measurement computer system did not miss something important, and to examine the prescribed sequence to see if it made sense. It is beyond the scope of this paper to consider other facets of the counseling interview. The plea here is that we do not rely so exclusively on such talks for either diagnosis or "treatment."

The concept of programming experiences perhaps needs further clarification, especially its difference from programmed instruction. Programmed instruction appears to be a very useful technique for teaching students many routine skills, such as arithmetic. Although some workers have attempted to adapt this stimulus-response technique to guidance, it might be more useful to adopt the concept of program, but broaden the units to be programmed. Instead of the sequences of separate one sentence stimuli needed to take a student through the intricacies of arithmetic, programmed experiences would lead him through the types of experiences needed in order to develop a realistic concept of what a mechanical engineer does, what training he needs to have, what special abilities he has, the current and projected employment situation, etc. Such experiences might include work experience, meeting role models, visiting plants and laboratories, etc. Computer measurement techniques are now developed to the point where they can be used to help the guidance programmer decide which students seem to need what types of experiences.

Additional Applications

At this point, it might be useful to survey other types of problems which a computer measurement system could easily uncover.

The college placement function is a big consumer of counselor time. College finding services, for example, have demonstrated that much of this problem can be automated. Also, the computer measurement system could identify trouble spots which, if acted upon immediately, the counselor could easily help remedy. If not identified early, the problem could grow until the student's situation required extensive remedial action.

One case occasionally observed is the student who is planning to apply to only two colleges and the chances of his being accepted at either one is something like one chance in one thousand. It would not be difficult to develop experiences which could point out to the student the desirability of *also* applying to a college for which he has a much higher probability of being admitted. Counselors are already using a type of intuitive estimate of such probabilities, so they should welcome assistance in this area.

The case just mentioned illustrates the problem of "over-aspiring," whereas Bob's problem, cited earlier, was a type of "under-aspiring." Both are frequent problems in educational and vocational planning, and if identified early, they might be remedied with suitable student experiences. The student may decide not to change his plans, but at least he will know he is pursuing a high risk path. He may even decide to do something about some of the predictors (e.g., grades), thus changing his probability in that way. The main thing is that he have a rational basis for whatever plan he develops. As Kogan and Wallach (1964) have recently shown, the amount of risk a person is willing to take is a function of his personality, and this aspect could also be built into the computer measurement system.

Another area in which an active computer measurement system could accomplish much is in the analysis of student achievement. It is now possible for schools to develop a type of dynamic norm, which would make it possible to detect, for example, a student whose achievement growth curve has suddenly slacked off. If this is done on a continuous basis, problems can be anticipated before they became serious, such as leading to another dropout. The need for dynamic norms is considered in the next section.

A computer measurement system could perform other very important diagnostic functions. Testing programs of the past have tended to assess "how much" the student knows, instead of asking what missing skills or concepts are interfering with his school progress. Perhaps a few weeks' review of fractions would help fill a gap which is currently giving some students trouble in shop work, for example.

THE NEED FOR DYNAMIC NORMS

Although there have been several factors which have limited the effective use of measurement in guidance, the problem of obtaining sufficient normative data has been one of the more serious problems. For one thing, norms have been allowed to get out of date. Funds are only now becoming available in the amounts needed to provide their continued updating. Another problem is that norms have been insufficiently developed, limiting the questions which can be asked. Norms are needed which are based upon multiple observations of the same students over time, and these need to be developed on a continuous basis. Also, counselors have not had the information needed for understanding the validity of test scores or the predictive implications of particular test score combinations.

Project TALENT (Flanagan *et al.*, 1962 and 1964) has shown that it is now possible to develop truly representative norms. These norms are also dynamic in the sense that they are based upon follow-up data which make it possible to ask questions about the subsequent educational or vocational implications of current behavioral and environmental observations, including the current plans of the student.

At regular intervals (say every three years), a five percent sample of schools could be selected for participation in a national "norming" study. The students would take a battery of tests which broadly sampled student behavior and determined their plans.

Periodic follow-up studies could then determine the pattern of events which followed the testing. The first follow-up might be conducted five years later, when most of the original group will have graduated from high school. This is more or less the current plan of Project TALENT, and so the feasibility of such an operation is now being demonstrated.

The computer measurement system being proposed here is completely dependent upon obtaining such adequate normative data. The *Scientific Careers Study* (Cooley, 1963) has shown the potential utility and validity of the probability predictions for individual students based upon multivariate information, but only the *techniques* used there have generalizability. The actual prediction equations from that study are appropriate for a very restricted population (boys of above average ability in Eastern Massachusetts). Undertakings such as Project TALENT can now provide the type of normative data which has been lacking.

This proposed, periodic, mass testing program may sound expensive.

It certainly is when viewed in terms of amount of money which has previously been spent on establishing norms and other validating information for tests. Yet it would cost only about $500,000 annually,* which is about what it would cost to add only 50 more counselors to the entire United States, a number which would not even make a dent in the current student-counselor ratio. If we really want to learn more about students from the millions of dollars annually spent on school testing programs, if we want to provide the type of information which students seem to want and need, then such undertakings seem necessary and feasible.

The skeptic may also claim that, although computers and multivariate methods are available today, they are out of the financial reach of most school systems. There are ways to solve this financial problem, however. Through establishment of regional data processing centers such as the New England Education Data Systems (NEEDS) project, a center computer facility is able to service many school systems, including the analysis of test scores for guidance purposes. In a few years each school could be directly connected to a central computer by a remote typewriter-type terminal which would enable school personnel to ask questions of their school data stored at the central computer center.

THEORETICAL BASIS

The discussion thus far has been more or less exclusively about rather vague operations. By now the reader is probably concerned about the theoretical basis for this type of wild talk. Actually there are several bases, depending upon the area of application for the computer measurement system. Perhaps it would be useful to examine the view of man which is behind the recommendations for applications in the area of student educational and vocational planning.

The basic proposition is that different plans are appropriate for different people. This proposition required a taxonomy for plans and people, and a method for dealing with relationships between types of plans and kinds of people.

Factor theory provides a more operational basis for talking about people differences and their relationship to plans. In the factorial conceptualization of human behavior, personality has its locus in an m-dimensional space. An individual's personality is his unique location in this space, the location determined by the total pattern of the m behavioral measures which are available for that individual. In this context, personality encompasses all behavior, including intellectual functioning. People who have similar patterns of scores will occupy similar regions of this m-dimensional space. That is, people who behave similarly have similar personalities. Career planning and decision making

---

* Estimate based on approximate Project TALENT budget.

is one aspect of behavior. People with similar personalities *tend* to make similar type of career decisions. Once the regions of the personality space occupied by people who have made particular types of career decisions are defined, the probability that another person will made a certain decision can be estimated.

Before this theoretical position can be further developed, it is necessary to explain that the test space concept and the probability classification procedures which are the analytical techniques employed in the factor approach advocated here.

Say, for example, the task is to distinguish future scientists from nonscientists, Figure 13 represents a one-dimensional test space. An individual's location along axis X depends upon his score on test X. The height of the curve for the scientist group at some point, for example at x_1, is the frequency with which scientists receive that particular score on X. Knowing only the test score, you would predict that the person was a nonscientist if the score was low, and a scientist if the score was high. Knowing the heights of the two curves at score x_1, it is possible to compute the proportion of people receiving that score who are scientists, and the proportion who are nonscientists. With new test scores, from a person for whom the scientist-nonscientist designation is unknown, the proportions became probabilities of group membership for that person.

For example, if one third of the people having a score of x_1 are nonscientists, and two thirds are scientists, then the probability that a person with score x_1 is a scientist is .67 and .33 is the probability of nonscientist. This assumes that the two categories exhaust the possibilities for the population under consideration. If the areas under the two curves are equal, this also assumes that the two groups exist in equal numbers within that population. These two conditions (that there are only two categories of people in the mixed population and that they are of equal frequency), are peculiar to this example and are not limitations of the technique.

Of course, a single test score yields inadequate information, so a method is needed for handling more than one test score. Consider the next most simple case, that of two tests. This results in a two-dimensional space similar to Figure 14. In this space, each individual can be represented as a point with a unique location depending upon his combination of scores on X_1 and X_2. This time questions can be asked

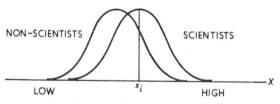

NON-SCIENTISTS   SCIENTISTS

LOW x_i HIGH

FIG. 13. A one-dimensional test space.

about people receiving a *particular combination* of test scores: what proportion are scientists, and what proportion are nonscientists. These proportions are computed from the relative densities of "scientist points" and "nonscientist points" for a given score combination.

The importance of score combinations can be seen in this example. A score of x_1 on test X_1 could have different implications depending upon the score X_2. High scores on X_2 with x_1 on X_1 indicate the student is more like a nonscientist. Low scores on X_2 with a score of x_1 on X_1 indicate greater similarity to the scientist group. If a score on X_2 is viewed alone, nothing can be concluded about the student's resemblance to these two groups. Multivariate procedures make use of this combinational aspect of scores.

Consider another example. If a decision between two alternatives has been made by individuals located in the behavioral space, such as A college preparatory curriculum in high school, and B, noncollege preparatory, the behavioral space will contain regions in which many individuals chose A over B, other regions in which B was preferred to A. There may be at least some A choosers in all regions of the personality space, but the A density varies from region to region. Comparison of the density of A choosers to B choosers at a particular point in the space determines the probability that choice A will be made by persons at or near that point. This scheme of analysis is generalizable to decision making situations involving more than two alternatives and/or two variables. Each new variable adds a new axis to the system. The bivariate normal distributions for three groups on tests X_1 and X_2 are outlined in Figure 15. Once the means and dispersions of these three groups have been estimated, the probability that individual i is a member of group A, B, or C can also be estimated. The computations become rather extensive as the number of variables increases, but this is where the computer comes in.

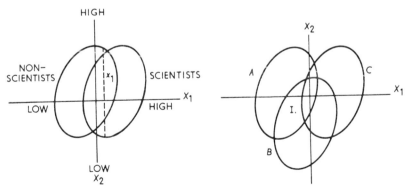

FIG. 14. A two-dimensional test space.
FIG. 15. Three group dispersions in a two-dimensional space.

Mathematically the analytic task is handled by employing the algebra of matrices and vectors. A vector is a row or column of numbers. In a column vector of scores, each number represents a test score for someone. A row vector, if it contains m-scores, locates an individual in an m-dimensional space. If there are N such vectors, representing N people sampled from a population, the region of the test space occupied by that population can be estimated from the sample by assuming that the distribution of points in the population is multivariate normal. The center of the swarm of points is represented by the vector of sample means (called the centroid), and the dispersion of the points about the centroid is described by the variance-covarience matrix. This is the essence of multivariate analysis.

It is certainly not necessary for counselors to become familiar with the details of this type of multivariate analysis. The nature of these techniques was hinted at here for purposes of illustrating the type of thinking and analysis behind the computer output that would monitor student plans. To actually see how such techniques are applied in analysis of data, the reader might consult Cooley and Lohnes (1962) for computational details and Cooley (1963) for career research applications.

SUMMARY

As recently as 1960, participants at a conference on measurement and research (Traxler, 1961) have pleaded that counselors and teachers be taught how to interpret test scores in relation to all other data available on the same student. Although this is a noble goal, it is unrealistic. Even if they had the follow-up data which would make predictive interpretations possible, people are just not able to process that much information reliably.

It is possible to achieve this goal of sounder interpretation by use of the computer, methods of multivariate analysis, and results of continuous, normative, longitudinal studies. I do not mean to imply that such a system is ready to be installed tomorrow in any school that wants a computer measurement system. The point is that, for the first time, the parts are all clearly discernible and feasible.

This paper and these arguments seem necessary because of the emphasis today on the counseling process. There seem to be too few people in guidance today who are concerned with the role of measurement in guidance and the ways in which new techniques might assist counselors in the task of helping our millions of students through school and into careers. The hope is that this type of article might stimulate renewed action along these lines.

HELM (1967) has proposed, in a similar vein, what he terms a "black box model" where computer programs are written to simulate the counseling process. He begins with the development of a special computer language to produce written evaluations of psychometric test data obtained from an extensive battery of ability and interest and personality measures. Working with clinical psychologists who were engaged in interpreting this complex battery, and with all test scores converted to a standard range of zero to 9, Helm developed a list of rules to be fed into the computer. For example, if a score in the range of 6 to 9 on a measure of social responsibility is obtained plus a score between 5 to 7 on a scale measuring interest in supervisory tasks, then the following sentence would be produced: he appears to be willing to assume supervisory responsibilities. One application of this scheme involved a complex set of some 100 specifications or rules for the computer for a profile based on 70 test scores. The psychologist himself composes a paragraph of test interpretation and this is then compared with that produced by the computer. In some instances, the computer output is such as to simulate the psychologist's own performance in the clinical situation very well (for two examples, see Helm, 1967, pp. 50–51). Other applications of this type of work involve the performance of a counselor interacting with a ninth grade student in a guidance situation (Coulson and Cogswell, 1965) and a program which conducts a psychotherapy session at the console of a computer (Weizenbaum, 1966).

Mention has already been made of Project TALENT, probably the most ambitious longitudinal survey of aptitudes and abilities and plans that has ever been attempted. No volume on psychological testing would be complete without at least a summary presentation of this research under the general direction of John C. Flanagan. The project began auspiciously in 1957, when plans were made for two days of testing in a representative sample of approximately 1,000 high schools in the United States. Testing was commenced in 1960, when over 2,000 test and questionnaire items were administered to 400,000 grade 9 and grade 12 students. Long range plans call for follow-ups 1, 5, 10, and 20 years after the expected date of the students' high school graduations. Because of the enormous size of this project, all data are handled by computers. The theoretical orientation of the research is that of classical trait and factor theory: certain traits are measured, the high school students are then followed up, and relationships are sought between the traits exhibited by these students in school and their subsequent vocational behavior. This criterion behavior includes their career plans and decisions, the degree of their job satisfaction and their job sucess. The study is another example of multivariate analysis, making possible consideration of patterns that occur in the data rather than analysis of only one trait at a time.

The following report concerns the sampling problems involved and the final test battery that was selected. It has been taken from the initial announcement about Project TALENT (Flanagan et al., 1962).

Dr. Flanagan, well known former Director of the Army Air Force Aviation Psychology Research program, is now the Director of Project TALENT, whose headquarters are in Palo Alto, California.

PROJECT TALENT SAMPLE

John C. Flanagan

We decided that a sample involving five percent of the high school enrollment, or between 400,000 and 500,000 students, would be large enough to provide a sturdy base for our contemplated research structure. Such a sample had the dimensions to satisfy many research needs of the present and future. For one thing, we knew that we would be studying many different groupings and subgroupings of individuals and schools. To do this adequately, the initial size of the sample had to be large enough so that it could be divided, subdivided, then divided again and still yield substantial information. Later, as follow-up studies progressed, the original facts collected would be broken down for students who did and did not go to college; for those who did and did not finish college; for students who trained for many different professions and occupations; for those who succeeded and those who failed in their chosen field; for those who achieved high standing and renown—and, at the other end of the scale, for those who ran into trouble with society.

But there is still another reason the sample needed to be so large. We knew that a good percentage of this number would go into clerical jobs, sales work, mechanics; a smaller percentage would become lawyers, doctors, nurses, and teachers. But few indeed would become nuclear physicists, research chemists, or theoretical mathematicians. Yet, we would want to trace the factors in the career development of these future high level specialists. Out of a half million students, probably no more than 2,000 would become Ph.D.s; of these there might be 100 mathematicians and 200 physicists. A large sample would be necessary if we were to draw these future specialists into our study.

Another question that had to be settled was whether to choose the sample on the basis of school systems, separate schools, or individual students. In many of the studies to be carried out with Project TALENT data, the schools would be the focus of concern. Student achievement and future success would be studied in relation to large and small schools, public and private schools, conventional and experimental curricula, and so on. For this reason—as well as for the sake of administrative efficiency—we established the school as the sampling unit.

How many schools would we need in order to draw a sample consisting of five percent of high school students? Five percent of the schools? Theoretically, yes—and, as it turned out, we did give the tests in approximately one out of every twenty schools. But it wasn't as simple as that.

The sizes of public high schools differ radically—from less than a hundred students to more than 5,000. The small high schools dotting the rural countryside are far more numerous than very large city high schools. To emphasize the contrast, the total enrollment of several dozen rural schools may fall far below the enrollment of one city school. To select one out of every 20 schools in the country without consideration of size differences would have resulted in so few large public high schools— and so very many small schools— that our later research on the effects of school size would have been inconclusive. The solution was to invite one out of every 20 medium-sized public high schools to particpate in the study; one out of every 13 very large schools; and one out of 50 small schools. We invited one out of 20 private and parochial schools, regardless of size, to participate in Project TALENT.

To adjust for these variations, our statistical procedures called for "weighting" the schools in the analysis of the data obtained from them. Only by applying appropriate weights to the data can results be obtained which permit sound inferences about the total population of high schools or high school students.

The decisions made so far controlled the dimensions of the sample to be selected, but they did not control exactly which schools were to be included.

From various sources, primarily the U.S. Office of Education, we had obtained the names and addresses of all high schools in the United States—some 26,000 schools—along with their enrollment figures. It was from these official sources that we had to select approximately one out of every 20 schools. But which ones? We were face to face with the sampling problem.

In order to avoid biases, it is necessary to select the sample in a random manner. A characteristic of a simple random sample is that every member of an entire group has an equal chance of being in the sample. The laws of chance operate in such a way that a random sample will tend to be representative in all resects of the group as a whole.

Random sampling can be improved by a procedure known as stratified random sampling. This consists in dividing the entire group into smaller groups, according to one or more characteristics, and then using a strictly random selection method within each classification. To classify, or "stratify," the total group according to certain characteristics before drawing the random sample makes it more representative in certain respects and less representative in none. In view of this admirable feature, stratified random sampling was the method used in selecting schools to participate in Project TALENT.

There is a limit, of course, to the number of characteristics that can be singled out for such special handling, even in a survey as comprehensive as Project TALENT. We wanted to select only the most important characteristics and through stratifying, take out insurance, so to speak, that the sample would be truly representative in regard to these characteristics.

The first important characteristic to be singled out was an obvious one involving the type of school—public, parochial, or private. In our groupings we included all Roman Catholic high schools in the parochial classification. Other church-affliated schools were put in the private school group.

We also wanted to be certain that we would have proper geographical representation. There is a big difference in schools because of differences in the economy of the region and the nature of the population. There are also differences in schools because the various state departments of education set different requirements for curricula, teacher certification, and graduation. Still another significant factor is whether the school is in a very large city or a relatively small community. For these reasons, we first grouped schools into broad geographical areas and then subgrouped them by states, our basic geographic units. These were New York, Chicago, Los Angeles, Philadelphia, and Detroit. Such treatment assured us of having proper large city representation.

We next took steps to insure that the sample would reflect the differences in school size. Size is certainly one of the most important variables among schools. For one thing, a small school cannot offer as varied a curriculum as a large school except at greater cost per pupil. We therefore divided the public high schools into the following four groups according to grade 12 enrollment: (a) those with less than 25 seniors; (b) those with 25–99 seniors; (c) those with 100–399 seniors; (d) those with 400 or more seniors. One reason for this particular division was to set up two groups that would, and two that would not, meet the minimum size standards for schools recommended by educational authorities.

Another characteristic singled out for special attention among public high schools was the student-holding power of the schools. In some schools many students drop out before graduation; in others nearly all stay to graduate. Since we assume that there are major differences between schools with high and low holding power, we wanted to be sure we had proper representation of each type. This stratification was made by computing a retention ratio for each school. The ratio was the number of students who graduated in 1958 to the number of students in the 10th grade in 1959. This information provided a separation of schools into categories on the basis of whether (at one end of the scale) nearly all students graduate, or whether (at the other extreme) very few students graduate.

The machine that did the actual selection work (IBM-650) was given considerable human prompting on how to make a random choice from each category. For instance, the machine was instructed to take into account the different sampling ratios that had been set up for schools of different sizes. Instead of picking one in 20 as for medium-sized schools, the machine was programmed to pick out one out of 13 very large schools and one out of 50 very small schools.

Parochial and private schools were stratified (separately) into the 56 geographical units, but there were too few of these nonpublic schools to make it desirable to stratify them on school size and holding power, too.

The ninth grader was, of course, and important individual in our study. But America's public secondary school organization sometimes places the ninth grader in a four-year public high school and sometimes in a three-year junior high school. Not all graduates of a particular junior high school go to a particular senior high school, and not all tenth graders in a senior high school come from the same junior high school. This gave rise to complications in obtaining a representative sample of ninth graders. However, a solution to the problem was found. Where junior high schools or groups of junior high schools were clearly and unambiguously associated with a senior high school that had been selected, the ninth graders in those junior high schools were put in the sample. In communities where the situation was not so clear cut, the coordinators helped in deciding what junior high schools would include the maximum number of ninth grade students who would go to the selected high school and the minimum number who would go to any other senior high school. A small supplementary sampling of the remaining junior high schools, together with a procedure for adjusting school weights, provided the means for mathematically correcting any minor inaccuracies that might have resulted from the approximation procedure described above for selecting the junior high schools.

One important phase of Project TALENT was to collect information on an entire age group, the 15-year-olds. This meant that the data had to be obtained not only for the 15-year-olds in high schools, but also for 15-year-olds still in grade 8 or below, already in college, or not in school at all. We decided that the non-high-school 15-year-olds to be included in the study were to be residents of areas served by one tenth of the public senior high schools selected in the sample. The schools selected in the sampling phase were divided into ten subsamples which would be as close to equivalent in terms of the stratification variables as could reasonably be achieved. One of these ten subsamples (designated "Subsample 0") was then selected to include the non-high school 15-year-olds for study. These non-high school 15-year-olds are not intended to be considered part of the regular sample, which consists entirely of high school students. However, they will supplement the 15-year-olds in the regular sample to provide a picture of the entire age group—the total group of 15-year-old Americans.

Two other special groups require mention at this point. The first consisted of two small groups of schools trying experimental courses in mathematics. The two experimental programs were developed by Dr. Max Beberman of the University of Illinois and Dr. E. G. Begle, formerly of Yale University. The performance of students in this new type of program will be compared with that of matched groups of students who take conventional mathematics courses.

Another special group are the schools in Knoxville, Tennessee, and in the surrounding county, Knox County. Two schools were drawn as part of the regular sample in this area, but as a result of the special interest of the school authorities there it was possible to arrange to test every student in every school—public, parochial, and private—in the entire Knoxville and Knox County area, not only in grades 9 through 12, but also in grade 8. This very comprehensive testing in a concentrated area, over a five-grade range, will make possible many special studies that could not otherwise be carried out.

A total of 23 tests, 3 inventories, 2 themes (5 minutes apiece for students to write on 2 topics—the meaning of high school and my view of an ideal occupation). The composition of the final battery is shown in Table 22.

The first one-year follow-up has been published (Flanagan & Cooley, 1966) and certain implications for high school guidance programs are already very apparent. What follows is a summary of some of these findings, for both boys and girls, with data concerning the stability of their career plans. These data have been abstracted from Bulletin No. 5 (July, 1966), from the Project TALENT offices.

TABLE 22

COMPOSITION OF THE FINAL PROJECT TALENT BATTERY

Aptitude and Achievement Tests

1. Information Test	12. Creativity
2. Memory for Sentences	13. Mechanical Reasoning
3. Memory for Words	14. Visualization in Two Dimensions
4. Disguised Words	15. Visualization in Three Dimensions
5. English: Spelling	16. Abstract Reasoning
6. Capitalization	17. Mathematics: Arithmetic Reasoning
7. Punctuation	18. Introductory
8. English Usage	19. Advanced
9. Effective Expression	20. Arithmetic Computation
10. Word Functions in Sentences	21. Table Reading
11. Reading Comprehension	22. Clerical Checking

23. Object Inspection

Miscellaneous	*Inventories*
Preference Test	Student Activities Inventory
Themes	Interest Inventory
	Student Information Blank

AFTER HIGH SCHOOL

During the four-year period of Project TALENT's one-year follow-up studies, the percentage of young people reporting further education after high school increased from 57 to 68 percent. The first section of this bulletin concerns the relationships between data collected from these young people when they were in high school and their educational experiences after high school.

Comparisons of Students Attending Various Schools

The percentile scores on selected Project TALENT variables for various post high school educational groups are shown in Figures 16 and 17.

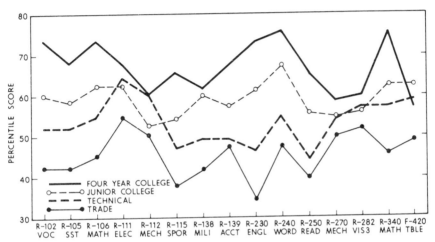

FIG. 16. Post-high school educational groups (males).

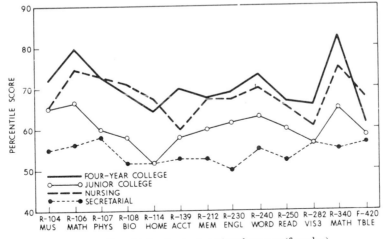

FIG. 17. Post-high school educational groups (females).

Figure 16 presents the percentile scores of young men tested in 1960 as eleventh graders who later entered four-year colleges, technical schools, or trade schools. As indicated in Figure 16, the four-year college group scored highest on 13 of the 15 tests. Their score on Mechanical Information was equaled by the technical institute group, while their Table Reading score was below that obtained by the junior college and technical institute groups. The young men attending trade school scored lowest on each of the tests.

Figure 17 presents the percentile scores of the young woman from the same grade who entered four-year colleges, junior colleges, nursing, or secretarial schools. On eight of the 13 tests, the four-year college group had the highest percentile scores. The nursing school students scored highest on Biological Science Information, Home Economics Information, and Table Reading. Their scores on Physical Science Information and Memory for Words were the same as those obtained by the young women attending a four-year college. The percentile scores of the junior college students were either the same as or lower than those of the nursing students. Below the junior college group on most variables were the secretarial school students.

Probability of Entering a Four-Year College

Using general academic ability and socioeconomic level as predictor variables, Table 23 presents the probabilities that a grade 11 male will later enter a four-year college. These probabilities range from .06 for low socioeconomic and low ability scores to .87 for high socioeconomic and ability scores. Table 24 presents the probabilities of a grade 11 female

TABLE 23

PROBABILITY OF A MALE ENTERING A FOUR-YEAR COLLEGE

Ability Quarter	Socioeconomic Quarter			
	Low 1	2	3	High 4
Low 1	.06	.12	.13	.26
2	.13	.15	.29	.36
3	.25	.34	.45	.65
High 4	.48	.70	.73	.87

TABLE 24

PROBABILITY OF A FEMALE ENTERING A FOUR-YEAR COLLEGE

Ability Quarter	Socioeconomic Quarter			
	Low 1	2	3	High 4
Low 1	.07	.07	.05	.20
2	.08	.09	.20	.33
3	.18	.23	.36	.55
High 4	.34	.67	.67	.82

attending college. As expected, these probabilities are generally lower than those for males. They range from .07 for low scores on both variables to .82 for high socioeconomic and ability scores.

As can be seen, a high socioeconomic score only partially compensates for a low ability score in predicting which students enter college. In other words, the ability score facilitates college entrance to a considerably greater degree than does socioeconomic level. For example, the probability of a young man with a high ability score and a low socioeconomic score entering college is .48. The college attendance probability of a young man with a high ability score and a low socioeconomic score entering college is .48. The college attendance probability of a young man with a low ability score and a high socioeconomic score is only .26.

JOBS AFTER HIGH SCHOOL

Young people who went directly to work after high school have also been a concern of Project TALENT. Of the noncollege high school graduates, approximately two thirds held full-time jobs one year after graduation. The greatest percentages of young men were employed as skilled or unskilled workers, while smaller percentages held jobs in clerical or sales occupations. Approximately 70 percent of the females were clerical or sales workers; 15 percent were employed as service workers.

Comparisons of Jobs Held by High School Graduates and Dropouts

Comparisons of the work experiences of high school graduates and dropouts have shown that the difference between the two groups is not in the percentages employed, but in the kinds of jobs held. For example, from both the ninth and tenth grade classes of 1960, the percentage of male dropouts with full-time jobs was the same as the percentage of employed male graduates not attending college.

However, of the young men from the class tested in tenth grade, more dropouts than graduates were protective, skilled, service, and unskilled workers; fewer dropouts than graduates held jobs in clerical or sales work.

Of the young men from the ninth grade class, the dropouts were more likely than the noncollege high school graduates to hold unskilled, outdoor, and protective jobs. However, fewer male dropouts than graduates were employed in skilled and clerical or sales work.

Of the young women from both classes, greater percentages of dropouts than graduates had skilled, service, and unskilled jobs. In contrast, female dropouts were less likely than the young women who completed high school to be clerical or sales workers. In fact, only 34 percent of the female dropouts from grade 10 held clerical or sales jobs compared to 72 percent of the graduates. From the class tested in ninth grade, 21 percent of the young women who dropped out of high school were clerical or sales workers, while 68 percent of the female graduates held similar jobs.

Holding Power of Jobs Varies

A study of 35 jobs held by young men, both graduates and dropouts from high school, has shown that occupations have different degrees of holding power. In other words, workers in some occupations are much more likely than those in other occupations to make careers of their present jobs.

For example, 63 to 88 percent of the barbers (percentages varied from class to class), 58 to 74 percent of the farmers and ranchers, 48 to 58 percent of the printers, and 39 to 59 percent of the photographers planned to remain in their present fields. These four groups had the highest stability of the 35 occupations studied.

Those employed in the crafts had slightly lower stability percentages— approximately 30 to 45 percent of the plumbers, carpenters, electricians, electronic technicians, machinists, and mechanics planned similar careers. Of those in business at the managerial level, 36 to 45 percent indicated they would remain in their present jobs. And 29 to 38 percent of the salesmen planned to continue careers in sales.

Among those with the lowest stability percentages were factory and assembly line workers (5 to 9%), general clerical workers (4 to 5%), farm or ranch laborers (1 to 4%) and waiters or busboys (0 to 2%).

CAREER PLANS

Stablility of Career Plans

One of the original goals of Project TALENT was to achieve a better understanding of the career plans made by young people. Through the 1960 testing and the four one-year follow-up studies, much progress has already been made toward this goal. One aspect of career plans—their stability from high school to one year after high school— will be discussed in this section of the bulletin using comparisons of the plans indicated by 15-, 16-, 17-, and 18-year-old high school students and the plans indicated by these same young people on the one-year follow-up questionnaires. At the time of the follow-up studies, these young people were about 19 years of age.

The overall stability of career plans made in grades 9, 10, 11, and 12 is shown in Table 25.

Some plans were more stable than others. For the boys, for example, careers as clergymen and physicians showed a high degree of stability. Of those twelfth grade boys planning careers in those fields, over 50 percent had the same plans after high school. The twelfth grade boys expecting to be teachers, writers, and farmers also showed better than

TABLE 25

PERCENTAGES OF YOUNG PEOPLE HAVING CAREER PLANS ONE YEAR AFTER HIGH
SCHOOL SIMILAR TO PLANS MADE IN GRADES 9, 10, 11, 12

	Males	Females
Grade 9	16.8	26.1
Grade 10	18.9	28.7
Grade 11	25.0	36.4
Grade 12	31.4	41.2

average stability in their plans. Forty-four to 49 percent of these young men reported the same plans one year later. Career plans in engineering, dentistry, pharmacy, law, art or entertainment, and skilled occupations were between 30 and 40 percent stable from grade 12 to one year after high school.

As Table 25 has indicated, the overall stability of plans made by young men decreased from 31 (grade 12) to 17 percent (grade 9). For ninth grade boys, only one career, businessman, was still planned by more than 30 percent of the boys who chose it in high school. Only 18 percent of the very large number of boys in the ninth grade planning careers as engineers still intended to work in this field four years later.

For the girls, teacher and housewife were the only career plans showing more than 50 percent stability from any grade level to one year after high school. Careers with more than 40 percent stability included office worker, nurse, beautician, and artist or entertainer.

This high degree of instability of the plans of boys and girls in 9th, 10th, 11th, and 12th grade raises the question as to whether the new career plans were closely related or generally unrelated to the initial careers goals. Inspection of some of the plans of individuals initially in large groups such as those intending to be engineers has indicated quite clearly that there was no pattern to the new plans which could be predicted from the initial plans with better than chance success. This emphasizes the necessity of turning to more stable characteristics of the individual, such as those measured by the 1960 battery of tests, to predict his ultimate career plans rather than depending upon his initial selection to provide important clues. The following section of this bulletin will illustrate how 1960 data can aid in these predictions.

Predicting Career Plan Changes

Using an individual's stated plans, his scores on the 1960 TALENT tests, and the techniques of multiple discriminant analysis and probability classification, Project TALENT has attempted to predict changes in career group membership. These changes come about when an individual perceives a discrepancy between what he thinks of himself and what he thinks of his plans for an occupation.

The most difficult aspect of this research has been determining the criterion to be predicted, since there is a seemingly infinite number of ways to classify career plans. Project TALENT's schemes for classifying plans have been developed by considering: (a) the test profile similarity of more specific career groups (i.e., boys planning either physics or chemistry were grouped into Physical Science because their 1960 TALENT profiles were similar), (b) the types of educational decisions students have to make as they move toward these various careers (there is no point in making finer distinctions in career planning earlier than required by the educational system), and (c) the types of back-and-forth changes which tend to be made in career planning.

One classification scheme used in our recent follow-up report makes two basic distinctions: (a) whether the career is science-technology or people oriented, and (b) whether or not a college education is necessary. The science-technology oriented careers requiring a college education ared divided into Physical Science (mathematician, physical scientist, engineer, scientific aide) and Medicine-Biology (biological scientist, nurse, physician, pharmacist, dentist, medical technician). The people oriented careers which require college training include two groups— Humanities (social scientist, social worker, clergyman, teacher) and Business College (accountant, lawyer, businessman, government, salesman). The careers for which a college education is not necessary are divided into technical (aviation, engineering aide, medical technician, skilled worker, structural worker) and Business Noncollege (government, salesman, accountant, service worker, businessman, office worker).

One study conducted using this six group criterion determined that the TALENT ability measures were more highly related to follow-up plans than to plans in grade 9. That is, the later plans tended to be more consistent with ability profiles than were the earlier grade 9 plans.

Measures of vocational interest, on the other hand, tended to be more highly related to grade 9 plans than to follow-up plans. This is explained by the theory that both interest responses and stated plans are a function of the student's current self-concept and his current sterotypes of work and workers. As these change during high school, so will both stated plans and inventoried interests. We are currently exploring this question in greater detail using data available for a subsample of grade 9 students who were retested with the TALENT battery in grade 12.

These and other findings have demonstrated that the TALENT tests are relevant to the process of career development. It is also becoming quite clear that procedures based upon these results and the results of subsequent Project TALENT follow-up studies can aid in the development of a much improved system of school guidance.

IMPLICATIONS FOR GUIDANCE

The great number of career plan changes that take place during and immediately following high school suggest that plans formed in high school are unrealistic for one reason or another. This is an unfortunate phenomenon since educational decisions made during and immediately following high school are based upon these unrealistic (or at least unstable) plans.

There is really no concern if a boy changes his career goal from physics to mathematics between grade 10 and grade 12 because the high school preparation of future physicists and future mathematicians is similar. On the other hand, if a tenth grade boy planning to go into business later decides in twelfth grade to become an astronautical engineer, he will be rather set back if he has not taken the necessary mathematics options during high school.

These practical guidance considerations are based on the following principles: (a) there is no single high school curriculum appropriate for all students, (b) the appropriateness of a curriculum depends in part upon career plans of the student, (c) different career plans are appropriate for different students, and (d) the appropriateness of a career plan depends upon the abilities and motives of the student and the projected supply and demand characteristices of the job market.

Because of the number of students to be served and the volume of information to be processed, at least partial automation of school guidance services is necessary if these principles are to be followed. One computer measurement system of guidance has already been proposed by Cooley (see pp. 310–318). A major function of this system would be to give each student a good projection of his possible vocational future. Project TALENT would be useful in the development of such a system. First of all, the results of the follow-up studies described earlier have provided evidence of the predictive validity of the TALENT variables for membership in various post high school occupational, educational, and career plan groups. A measurement system using these data could, for example, take a boy's test scores and return to him the probability of future membership in each of the six occupational categories discussed earlier. These probabilities would sum to one. A particular boy might get this set of probabilities:

1. Physical Science—.70
2. Medicine–Biology—.03
3. Humanities—.02
4. Business College—.04
5. Technical—.20
6. Business Noncollege—.01

This information does not tell the boy that he must become a physical scientist. It informs him that in a group of boys who share his measured characteristics, one year out of high school, most plan to be physical scientists, some intend to be technicians, and very few plan careers in the other four areas. He is not forced to react in any particular way, but he may choose to incorporate the information into his planning for his future.

Project TALENT can also aid in the development of a computerized system of guidance by providing a model for future career follow-ups. These follow-ups could be carried out by local school districts or by a central agency established by the Office of Education. Information obtained through these studies could then be systematically given to all local guidance programs.

Other TALENT contributions to a computer measurement system will include:

(1) the phrasing of a comprehensive, coherent trait-and-factory theory of adolescent personality
(2) the delineation of a measurement system related to that theory
(3) the packaging of computer programs for the data processing and analytical operations of a school measurement system
(4) an effort through content analysis of school courses, achievement tests, and vocational positions to synthesize the common element of curriculum and guidance sciences.

The Project TALENT Data Bank is now only one of such data banks available for researchers to mine. The feature that distinguishes it (Schoenfeldt, 1970) from others is that new subjects are not being added; instead, additional data are continually being collected on the 400,000 original participants. A research person wanting to study some long-range process, such as career development, can avoid the long wait between collection of data and the later behavior he hopes to study. Astin and Myint (1971) are a very recent example of this in their study of some 5,400 women during the five-year period after high school. This sample consisted of females in the TALENT Data Bank who had been tested in 1960 at which time they were seniors in high school; they had been followed up in the fall of 1961 (one year after high school) and again in 1966 (about 5 years after high school). With respect to patterns of stability and change in career plans over time, brighter women either maintained or raised their vocational aspirations whereas the less academically capable women planned on less demanding careers.'

What is termed the "follow-back technique" has become an increasingly popular application of the TALENT data. This procedure capitalizes on the premise that approximately five percent of those born between 1942 and 1946 participated in the 1960 testing. As an illustration of this, a university could retrieve the TALENT participants who registered at their institution and then combine college performance measures with TALENT scores.

Readers might also be interested in a rather unusual use of TALENT data which also employed this "follow-back" method (Lipe, 1970). A large commercial airline supplied the names of some 4,800 current and recently terminated stewardesses to the American Institute for Research in Palo Alto. From such a large list of airline stewardesses, names of those enrolled in high school in 1960 might be compared with all Project TALENT subjects. Project TALENT tested a five percent stratified random sample of USA high school students; thus about five percent of the airline stewardesses who attended high school in 1960 might be located. And this was the case. A total of 27 performance ratings were supplied for these girls, typically ratings by the initial employment interviewer, instructor evaluations during training (for example, svelteness), actual job performance data, termination data where available. From the point of view of measurement, the principal conclusion of the study was that trait validity obtained in this manner was very low. Terminators, incidentally, for reasons other than marriage, tended to be young women who reported more "scholastic type" activities in high school.

Schoenfeldt also has remarked that an objection frequently heard against this data bank concept is that one seldom finds data in existing archives that are exactly what the investigator would have collected himself. Thus one would tend to study questions for which data are already in the bank rather than to seek data for the important questions of concern to the individual researcher. At times this might well be the case; Schoenfeldt feels this is an inadequate reason to abandon the data bank concept. He reports that experience at TALENT suggests more often than not that the available data are appropriate for investigating hypotheses posed by outside persons with many and varied interests. At TALENT, for example, over 80 research projects were completed in the first four years of the data bank. "More often than not, the research process is one of successive approximations. For this reason, the qualified conclusions resulting from studies that require some compromises can be of substantial value" (p. 614).

Currently (January, 1975), the most recent of Project TALENT publications is the *Career Data Book* (Flanagan *et al.,* 1973) which reports a five year follow-up of approximately 100,000 students in 1960 by means of a mailed questionnaire. About one third of this group completed and returned the requested information. (A representative sample of nonrespondents was also selected and tracked down to ascertain how nonrespondents differed from respondents.) These students, responding to the questionnaire five years after completing high school, thus provided results to indicate only career preparation and entry and not ultimate success. Profiles are presented for each of 138 occupations organized into 12 career groups. A revision of this *Career Data Book* is planned for sometime in 1976 which will then report results for an 11-year follow-up.

▽ ▽ ▽

PERHAPS even more remarkable is the imminence of computer grading of essay type examinations. A preliminary report of this development was presented at the 1966 Invitational Conference on Testing Problems, sponsored by the Educational Testing Service. (And possibly even more ingenious was Stone's paper, presented at this same conference, in which he showed a computer playing the role of a psychotherapist). Because these yearly conferences offer interesting discussions, often of new techniques in only preliminary stages and not yet ready for final journal publication, listeners are provided with advance information concerning new testing developments and strategies. The conference proceedings are always published later in monograph form.

The following is an abbreviated version of a progress report by Dr. Ellis Page, presented by the author as "a description, clouded though it may be, of the view from where we stand." It is taken from the published conference proceedings (Page, 1966). Dr. Page is Professor of Educational Psychology and Director of the Bureau of Educational Research at the University of Connecticut. During 1966–67 he was on part-time leave as Visiting Scientist to the Massachusetts Institute of Technology Computation Center.

GRADING ESSAYS BY COMPUTER*

Ellis B. Page

It was a meeting at Harvard in late 1964† that started me tossing and turning and losing sleep about the whole field of essay grading by computer. *Why not?* I kept wondering, and little by little the necessary research design began to emerge. Once you ask the question *Why not?* and begin investigating this field, you might be astonished at how rich the background material is—and how much of it is virtually unknown to psychologists. You find yourself at a disciplinary interface, involving not only psychometrics and statistics, but also linguistics, English composition, computer science, educational psychology, natural language analysis, curriculum, and more. This interdisciplinary aspect sometimes makes communication more complicated, since what will seem elementary to one segment of an audience will seem impossibly recondite to another.

The reactions to our effort have been fantastic. Our work has attracted a certain amount of attention in national news media, ranging from the favorable to the outraged. On one hand, there is the inevitable

* This work has been supported by the U.S. Office of Education (Research Branch), the College Entrance Examination Board, the National Science Foundation (through the Computing Center), the University of Connecticut, and the Massachusetts Institute of Technology.

† See Stone *et al.*, *The General Inquirer* (1966).

disbelief and dread of occupational replacement, and, perhaps, something still deeper. My own favorite press reaction (possibly because I am a former English teacher) is one in a recent issue of a teachers' journal, which carried a drawing of this monster, an essay grading machine. The machine was depicted at work with flailing arms (apparently losing some papers), glaring eyes, and thick sensual lips. The author of the accompanying article (Roby, 1966) wrote of a "cynical dehumanizing which, fully achieved, would reduce language to the terrifying 'duckspeak' of Orwell's nightmare world." He claimed that *human* essay grading is good *because* it is subjective—that is, because one teacher will not agree with another!

On the other hand, there have been many reactions to our work which were embarrassingly favorable, with such a wistful optimism about what we could do to help that some instructors at the University of Connecticut have called our bureau about grading their midterm exams!

The reality of our study, of course, lies somewhere between the impossible and the operational. We are not grading routine exams and will not be next year either. There are some good, hard problems on the way to this goal, but we feel the future is bright. Let us see whether, after having been brought up to date, you will share this optimism.

We may conceive our general problem as resembling Figure 18. As the column heads indicate, we are interested in *content* (what is said) and in *style* (the way it is said). Obviously, these columns are not mutually exclusive, but the simplification may be useful.

Similarly, the rows are not mutually exclusive either. But their general meaning must be mastered to understand what is being attempted. The first row refers to the simulation of the human product, without any great concern about the way this product was produced. It refers to actuarial optimization, a pragmatic approach to the simulation of the behavior of qualified judges. The bottom row, on the other hand, refers to the master analysis of the essay, to the sort of knowledgeable and detailed description of the essay, and of its various parts, which might emerge when competent judges apply advanced analytic skills.

We have coined two terms to describe this difference. Since the top row is concerned with ap*prox*imation, we speak of the computer varia-

	I Content	II Style
A. Rating Simulation	I (A)	II (A)
B. Master Analysis	I (B)	II (B)

FIG. 18. Possible dimensions of essay grading.

bles employed as *proxes*. Since the bottom row is concerned with the true in*trin*sic variables of interest, we speak of such variables as *trins*.

A trin, then, is a variable of intrinsic interest to the human judge, for example, "aptness of word choice." Usually a trin is not directly measurable by present computer strategies. And a prox is any variable measured by the computer, as an approximation (or correlate) of some trin such as the proportion of uncommon words used by a student (where common words are discovered by a list look-up procedure in computer memory).

So far in our investigations, we have concentrated on the top row of Figure 18 looking for actuarial strategies, seeking out those proxes which would be of most immediate use in the simulation of the final human product. This does not mean that we have no interest in the trins. But many people have a misguided view of simulation. They imagine that a more microscopic strategy really does things in some "human" way. This is usually an illusion. The principal difference between strategies is often just in the size of bite, in the temporal scope of behavior chosen to be the target. For example, suppose we tried to imitate judges at a number of points along the behavioral continuum, picking up the essay, for example, then reading the title, and so on until we reach the eventual decision concerning overall grade. Suppose we imitated 10 such different choice points en route to this grade. That would perhaps seem a more accurate simulation of the process. Within each of these 10 behavioral blocks, however, we would still be using algorithms which had little to do with the "real" human procedures. In other words, *all* computer simulation of human behavior appears to be product simulation rather than process simulation. And the two fields of psychological simulation, on the one hand, and artificial intelligence, on the other, are not necessarily so very far apart as some would claim.

In adopting the overall, terminal strategy described here, we have not abandoned a goal of more refined analysis, nor of simulation closer to the human process itself. Indeed, we are pushing in much more deeply, as my later comments will suggest. But for the first attempts, we evolved a general research design, which we have more or less followed to date:

1. Samples of essays were judged by a number of independent experts. For our first trial, there were 276 essays written by students in grades 8 to 12 at the University of Wisconsin High School, and judged by at least four independent persons. These judgments of overall quality formed the trins.

2. Hypotheses were generated about the variables which might be associated with these judgments. If these variables were measurable by a computer, and feasible to program within the logistics of the study, they became the proxes of the study.

3. Computer routines were written to measure these proxes in the essays. These were written in FORTRAN IV, for the IBM 7040 computer, and are highly

modular and mnemonic programs, fairly well documented.

4. Essays were prepared for computer input. In the present stage of data processing, this means that they were typed by clerical workers on an ordinary key punch. They were punched into cards which served as input for the next stage.

5. The essays were passed through the computer under the control of the program which collected data about the proxes. Various counts (see Table 26) were made for the whole essay and were transcribed into scores, which then constituted the input for the final analysis.

TABLE 26

VARIABLES USED IN PROJECT ESSAY
GRADE 1-A FOR A CRITERION OF
OVERALL QUALITY

A. Proxes	B. Corr. with Criterion	C. Beta wts.	D. Test-Ret. Rel. (Two essays)
Title present	.04	.09	.05
Av. sentence length	.04	−.13	.63
Number of paragraphs	.06	−.11	.42
Subject-verb openings	−.16	−.01	.20
Length of essay in words	.32	.32	.55
Number of parentheses	.04	−.01	.21
Number of apostrophes	−.23	−.06	.42
Number of commas	.34	.09	.61
Number of periods	−.05	−.05	.57
Number of underlined words	.01	.00	.22
Number of dashes	.22	.10	.44
No. colons	.02	−.03	.29
No. semicolons	.08	.06	.32
No. quotation marks	.11	.04	.27
No. exclamation marks	−.05	.09	.20
No. question marks	−.14	.01	.29
No. prepositions	.25	.10	.27
No. connective words	.18	−.02	.24
No. spelling errors	−.21	−.13	.23
No. relative pronouns	.11	.11	.17
No. subordinating conjs.	−.12	.06	.18
No. common words on Dale	−.48	−.07	.65
No. sents. end punc. pres.	−.01	−.08	.14
No. decl. sents. type A	.12	.14	.34
No. decl. sents. type B	.02	.02	.09
No. hyphens	.18	.07	.20
No. slashes	−.07	−.02	−.02
Aver. word length in ltrs.	.51	.12	.62
Stan. dev. of word length	.53	.30	.61
Stan. dev. of sent. length	−.07	.03	.48

6. These scores were then analyzed for their multivariate relationship to the human ratings, were weighted appropriately, and were used to maximize the prediction of the expert human ratings. This was all done by use of a standard multiple regression package.

The resulting data, summarized briefly in Table 26 for 272 students, suggest the nature and performance of some of the early proxes. Column A gives the names of the proxes employed. Some were based upon careful analysis and hypothesis. Others (such as the less common punctuation marks) were recorded only because they were naturally produced by the computer programs. Column B shows their correlation with the criterion, the overall human judgment. Column C shows the beta weights for predicting the criterion, when all 30 proxes were employed. And Column D shows what could be called the "test-retest" reliability of the proxes. These coefficients in Column D are based on two different essays on different topics written about a month apart by the same high school students.

The overall accuracy of this beginning strategy was startling. The proxes achieved a multiple correlation coefficient of .71 for the first set of essays analyzed and, by chance, achieved the identical coefficient for the second set. Furthermore, and this is, of course, important, the beta weightings from one set of essays did a good job of predicting the human judgments for the second set of essays written by the same youngsters. All in all, the computer did a respectable "human-expert" job in grading essays, as is visible in Table 27.

Here we see the results of a cross-validation. These are correlations between judgments of 138 essays done by five "judges," four of them human and one of them the computer. The computer judgments were the grades given by the regression weightings based on 138 *other* essays by *other* students. This cross-validation, then, is very conservative. Yet, from a practical point of view, the five judges are indistinguishable from one another. In eventual future trials, we expect the computer will correlate *better* with the human judges than will the other humans.

However useful such an overall rating might be, we of course still wish greater *detail* in our analysis. We have therefore broadened the

TABLE 27

WHICH ONE IS THE COMPUTER?

Intercorrelation Matrix Generated by the Cross-Validation of the Computer Program

	Judges				
	A	B	C	D	E
A		51	51	44	57
B	51		53	56	61
C	51	53		48	49
D	44	56	48		59
E	57	61	49	59	

TABLE 28*

COMPUTER SIMULATION OF HUMAN JUDGMENTS
FOR FIVE ESSAY TRAITS
(30 PREDICTORS, 256 CASES)

A. Essay Traits	B. Hum.-Gp. Reliab.	C. Mult. R	D. Corr. (Atten.)	E. Shrunk. Multi. R
Ideas or Content	.75	.72	.78	.68
Organization	.75	.62	.64	.55
Style	.79	.73	.77	.69
Mechanics	.85	.69	.69	.64
Creativity	.72	.71	.78	.66

* Col. B represents the reliability of the human judgments of each trait, based upon the sum of eight independent ratings, August 1966. Col. C represents the multiple regression coefficients found in predicting the pooled human ratings with 30 independent proxes found in the essays by the computer program of PEG-IA. Col. D presents these same coefficients, corrected for the unreliability of the human groups. (Cf. Mc-Nemar, 1962, p 153.) Col. E presents these coefficients, both corrected for the unreliability and shrunken to eliminate capitalization on chance from the number of predictor variables. (Cf. McNemar, 1962, p. 184.) Note: Cols. C, D, and E differ from the original text. Dr. Page reported a data-processing error to the editor and kindly supplied revised data. The conclusions of the article are not altered from the original.

analysis to five principal traits commonly believed important in essays. For our purpose they may be summarized as: *ideas, organization, style, mechanics,* and *creativity.* We had a particular interest in *creativity,* since some have from the beginning imagined that our study would founder on this kind of measure. "You might grade mechanics all right," someone will say, "but what about originality? What about the fellow who is really different? The machine can't handle him!"

Therefore, this summer we called together a group of 32 highly qualified English teachers from the schools of Connecticut to see how *they* would handle *creativity* and these other traits. Most had their master's degrees and extensive experience in teaching high school English, and all had the recommendation of their department chairmen. Each of 256 essays was rated on a five-point scale on each of these five important traits, by eight such expert judges, each acting independently of the other.‡ To investigate each of these five ratings, then, the same 30 proxes were again employed, with the results shown in Table 28.

In our rapidly growing knowledge, Table 28 may have the most to say to us about the computer analysis of important essay traits. Column A, of course, gives the titles of the five traits. Column B shows the rather low reliability of the group of eight human judges, computed by analysis of variance. This is the *practical* reliability of these pooled judgments.

‡ For a study of this size, the random assignment of essays to judges, to periods, and to sessions turned out to be a formidable task, and once again the computer was called in. This was our first experience of using the computer to *design* a study as well as to analyze one. We discovered some interesting things in the process and recommend this idea to the consideration of others.

We get higher reliabilities when we subtract from the error term the variances attributable to period, session, and judge; but it would be misleading to do so in this present comparison, since these adjustments were not made preparatory to the machine grading regression analysis. Here in Column B it seems that *creativity* is less reliably judged by these human experts than are the other traits, even when eight judgments are pooled. And *mechanics* may be the most reliably graded of these five traits. Surely, then, *humans* seem to have a harder time with *creativity* than with *mechanics*.

Now what of the computer? Column C shows the raw multiple correlations of the proxes with these rather unreliable group judgments. These were the coefficients produced by the standard regression program. If a really fair comparison is to be made among the traits, however, the criterion's unreliability should be taken into account. And this results in the corrected multiple coefficients appearing in Column D. Here such difficult variables as *creativity* and *organization* no longer seem to suffer; the computer's difficulty is apparently in the criterion itself, and is therefore attributable to human limitations rather than to those of the machine or program. Column E simply shows the same coefficients after the necessary shrinking to avoid the capitalization on chance which is inherent with multiple predictors. Column E, then, exhibits what we might expect on cross-validation of a similar set of essays, if we were predicting a perfectly reliable set of human judgments.

Now there are standard beginning questions which people almost inevitably ask at this point if our subject is new to them: What about the input problem? What about subject-matter grading? What about the student who tries to con the machine? What about detailed feedback to the student? And so on. These are all valid questions, and we have written our answers in the January issue of *Phi Delta Kappan* (Page, 1966). For most people these answers appear to be satisfactory.

But we are not presenting the results here as a terminal achievement against which to measure this sort of work. On the contrary, this is a temporary reading taken in the middle of the research stream. In the meantime, we go on with other strategies. Don Marcotte, for example, has recently developed an interesting phrase analyzer and has discovered that clichés, as usually listed, are pretty irrelevant in such essay grading. We have this summer studied some problems of style, parallelism, and certain semantic questions. We are exploring various dictionary and parsing options which lie before us. Recently we located what may be the most promising parsing program and used it to run certain essays. There are some fascinating studies done by people in artificial intelligence and information retrieval, which may have something different to offer in the near future. And we are interested in improving our statistical strategies as well. We are looking at the proxes themselves through factor analysis and stepwise regression. And then there is the question of extending the strategy to the humanities. One of the questions raised by scholars is whether it will handle various authors. A cartoon reflecting this question was printed in the *Phi Delta Kappan* and picked up by the *New York Times*. It is shown in Figure 19.

The machine is anthropomorphic and it seems embarrassed about "flunking Hemingway." Well, we are key punching some passages from Hemingway and other standard authors to find out how the program handles them! In any case these present results are, as I pointed out above, the merest way station, but they may indicate to most of you, as they do to us, that workers in this field will not be wasting their time.

There are many tantalizing problems in such research. One of the greatest is the effort toward psychologically deepening the work and making it more humanoid in process. Of considerable relevant interest to us, and to workers in related fields, is the possible verbal education of a computer. The solution will probably lie *not* in trying to *program* all the linguistic responses to be made by the computer. Rather, the solution may consist in programming only a certain set of quasi-psychological procedures, designed to enable the computer to learn on its own (i.e.— to gain literary *experience*) by reading in and correctly processing a great amount of appropriate text, making use of automated dictionaries and other aids while doing so. We dream of producing, in other words, the well-read computer. Part of our success to date has occurred through

Great Scot! It's just flunked Hemingway.

FIG. 19.

Cartoon by Margaret McGarr reproduced by permission of *Phi Delta Kappan*.

allowing the computer itself, in the multiple regression program, to determine which analytic weightings are valuable. What we hope is that somehow an expansion of this strategy of computer education can be undertaken. This is a very hard problem but a fascinating one and a number of people, in one field and another, are very interested in it.

And finally, a statement of present methodological bias: We believe that the work should not surrender to the purist on the one hand, who might claim that permanent improvement can be made only by a thorough mastery of theoretical concepts. Nor to the complete empiricist on the other, who may conceive that trial and error activities, with a poorly understood response surface, can lead to useful mastery of the underlying psychometric realities. No, a compromise would be more faithful to the professional history of my readers. Indeed, such a compromise between practical educational utility, on the one hand, and intriguing psychological and statistical depth, on the other, may be the very foundation on which our profession of measurement has flourished. In this new venture of grading essays by computer, competent measurement people, especially those with a love of language, should play an important role.

▽ ▽ ▽

PART ELEVEN

Testing of the Disadvantaged: Bias, Discrimination, and Differential Validities

A group of black Federal employees filed suit in Washington, D.C., charging that the principal test (the Federal Service Entrance Examination) that qualifies college graduates for employment and promotion was culturally and racially discriminatory. The plaintiffs said that in 1969 about half of the 100,000 individuals who were administered this examination made scores above 70 and with a disproportionally low percentage of blacks and other minority individuals "passing." Somewhat ironically it should be noted that the testing procedure had been already under attack by the Federal Government itself: the Equal Employment Opportunity Commission had suggested to numerous private employers that they overhaul, and in many cases get rid of, tests that in effect exclude minorities.*

Four New York City high schools with a national reputation for academic excellence also became embroiled in a controversy over traditional entrance tests. The charge was, again, that the admissions tests were "elitist" in nature and discriminated against racial minorities. Enrollment at these four special schools was, on the average, 25 percent nonwhite as compared with 51 percent nonwhite for all other New York City high schools. The issue went to the legislature in Albany where the Assembly, by a vote of 107 to 35, passed a bill which would, in effect, prevent the New York City Board of Education from making any significant change in the admissions procedures for these four schools. †

---

* *New York Times*, February 5, 1971.

† A quota of 14 percent of minority group students was retained for the "Discovery" program whereby gifted and highly motivated disadvantaged students not doing well on standardized tests are admitted.

Again in New York and this time the Board of Examiners of the New York City school system—the local licensing agency for some 55,000 teachers and 4,000 supervisors—was told by the U.S. District Court that the examinations used violated the equal protection clause of the 14th Amendment. The Court ruled that the tests discriminated against blacks and Puerto Ricans and also stated, perhaps equally importantly, that the tests were not truly job-related. Judge Mansfield wrote that "the existence of such de facto racial discrimination is further confirmed by the fact that only 1.4 percent of the principals and 7.2 percent of the assistant principals in New York City schools are black or Puerto Rican." The suit was brought by the N.A.A.C.P. Legal Defense and Educational Fund on behalf of two acting principals, one black and the other Puerto Rican.§

Even the United States Supreme Court has become involved. On March 8, 1971, Chief Justice Burger said that the required employment of high school graduates and the use of a general intelligence test by the Duke Power Company's Dan River Station in North Carolina effectively prevented blacks from job placement or advancement and that these requirements were, again, not job-related. The 13 black employees, who brought the suit, did say, however, that they would not object to tests which measured the ability of workers to perform on the job.

The American Psychological Association considered the issue so important that it set up a Task Force on Employment Testing of Minority Groups with Dr..Brent Baxter as Chairman together with a distinguished group of industrial and measurement consultants. The report of this task force should be carefully read by all who become involved with job testing of the disadvantaged (A.P.A., 1969).

Manpower development programs learned early that disadvantaged persons performed poorly on employment tests and so were frequently not admitted to various training programs. Labor Department experimental and demonstration (E & D) manpower projects studied this problem and came up with a variety of practical procedures. Mr. Joseph Seiler, Chief of the Division of Experimental Operative Research, Office of Research and Development, Manpower Administration, U.S. Department of Labor, describes some of these projects. What follows is a condensation of his article from the March, 1971, issue of the *Vocational Guidance Quarterly*.

PREPARING THE DISADVANTAGED FOR TESTS

Joseph Seiler

A number of E&D projects have been designed to explore the possibility of developing methods for assessing the job potentials of the disadvan-

---

§ *New York Times,* July 18, 1971.

taged. Most projects, however, have recognized the substantial cost and time required to develop new assessment approaches, the slender chances of convincing employers and guidance personnel to drop or change their vocational appraisal instruments, and the great immediate need to enhance test-taking skills of the poor.

As a result, experimental work has been concentrated on finding ways to prepare hard-to-employ individuals for taking employment and related aptitude and intelligence tests. "Pretesting orientation" activities have identified difficulties encountered by the disadvantaged in taking tests and potential approaches for overcoming them.

Disadvantaged persons usually come to employers and employment agencies to get a job, not to be tested, counseled, or trained. The relatively high dropout rate during the first two weeks of manpower programs reflects their rejection of a variety of services which they do not feel help them get a job.

Many People Fear Tests

Their resistance to taking tests is seen in the high number who do not appear for scheduled tests. In one survey to find out why, some applicants said they thought that "taking a test" was like a medical exam which required undressing. One applicant, when told he would take a "test battery," associated it with having to know about electricity. In addition to such misunderstandings, applicants expressed their fear of failing the tests.

Fear of tests is not limited to any particular socioeconomic class, but is particularly severe among the disadvantaged. Not only do they lack experience with tests, their few past tries at testing have produced low scores which often have been used to deny them jobs or training opportunities. And too often their limited education makes it difficult for them to understand test content.

To overcome these disabilities, pretesting orientation for the disadvantaged should: (a) help them understand the need for testing and give them confidence in taking tests, (b) teach test-taking mechanics and procedures, and (c) improve language skills and other abilities that will help overcome culture and education bias in tests.

The third objective is clearly the most difficult to achieve and has been given the least attention. It does not lend itself to the fairly quick and easy solutions developed to achieve the other two. More importantly, it points to the paradox of building a person's attitude, confidence, and procedural know-how so he can take tests which themselves are not valid in measuring true abilities for members of all ethnic groups. This paradox remaining, testing difficulties of the disadvantaged have been eased through a variety of E&D experiences with pretesting orientation.

The disadvantaged person must be prepared for formal tests by experiences which will motivate him to report and take them with minimum fear and suspicion about what they will reveal and how they will be used. To develop positive attitudes and confidence, E&D projects have found the following of value:

Fully explain why the tests are given and how they can help. For example, when being considered for a training program, the applicant should be shown how test results help determine the assignments which can best use his valuable time.

Applicant and counselor should decide jointly on the use of testing for specific reasons—say for placement in the proper remedial education class. In addition, the counselor should assure the applicant that test scores will be kept confidential and that overall findings will be interpreted to him.

Letting the applicant have a look at sample tests is useful in showing him how specific tests have relevance to jobs. Later the significance of tests can be better perceived by the applicant when he learns, through visits to companies and discussions with employer representatives, about the specific jobs and employers which require the tests.

Expose applicants to nonthreatening test settings. To bolster applicants' confidence, counselors should, in small group sessions, give practice test-taking without time limits, answer questions in a reassuring and approving manner, and explain errors. Also helpful is role playing, whereby applicants test each other to become familiar with tests and to understand better why they are required.

A project in California reported that informal exposure to tests combined with building confidence by constantly stressing the great success by past trainees has helped establish a "self-fulfilling prophecy." In two and one-half years, only one trainee failed to pass the written and performance tests required to earn the Class I license for professional truck drivers.

If most applicants are from a particular ethnic group, it is desirable that persons explaining tests be members of the same group. This enhances rapport with the applicants and reduces their test anxiety and resistance.

After these preparations, applicants are ready to learn to improve their knowledge of test mechanics and procedures (assuming their basic literacy skills are at least fifth grade level). This has been accomplished by E&D projects in the following ways:

Further practice in test-taking—Disadvantaged applicants should be given intensive drill. These practice tests should use items and instruction similar to those the applicants will face in formal testing. They should concentrate on instruction in marking answers on separate answer sheets, comprehension of various oral and written directions, and development of speed in working against time. The practice should be conducted in a nonthreatening atmosphere (as in the earlier sessions) and under standard testing conditions. If possible, these sessions should take place in the same room where formal testing usually occurs.

Sufficient drill should be conducted to permit complete familiarization with practice items. Ample time is needed for applicants to ask questions and receive full explanations and to allow immediate checking and correction of practice answers. Use of various published materials on how to take tests and of discontinued test forms also may be helpful.

State employment service offices have found it helpful to give disadvantaged applicants one and one-half hours of test-taking practice before giving them the General Aptitude Test Battery (GATB). Individuals vary in their degree of familiarity with GATB test content and in their ability to understand test-taking directions; exercises are designed to minimize the impact of these differences on test scores.

Brief Tutoring Helpful

Sample test exercises closely resemble their GATB counterparts for measuring numerical and verbal aptitude, spatial relations, clerical and form perception, and other aptitudes. The actual computerized GATB answer sheet is used in recording answers.

The test practice is supervised by an examiner but his presentation of pretesting orientation materials and instructions is purposely informal to aid in gaining good rapport. Also, the examiner gives the group, at the appropriate time, correct answers to all the questions. Applicants are allowed to check their own answer sheets and hold group discussions on any aspect of the test.

Tutoring. A number of E&D projects have found it useful to tutor disadvantaged applicants briefly in various subjects (not to be confused with remedial education which will be discussed later). These short sessions enable applicants to brush up on academic and other abilities they have not used for some time. Tutoring usually involves practice exercises in arithmetic, spelling, grammar, and reading. Some tutoring centers around the logic, concepts, and principles underlying tests of verbal analogies, spatial relations, and abstract reasoning.

‖ For special use with disadvantaged groups, a nonreading edition of the GATB is now available (Droege *et al.*, 1970). Specially devised tests were developed as substitutes for certain GATB tests (example: Matrices for the GATB General Learning Ability measure, Picture-Word Matching for the GATB Verbal Aptitude). Other original GATB tests, already mostly nonverbal, such as Place-Turn and Assembly-Disassemble were retained in the new edition.

The Psychological Corporation has also developed The Fundamental Achievement Series (Bennett & Doppelt, 1969) for the disadvantaged. A verbal and numerical test with items based on everyday experiences that simulate real life situations is presented (example: can the worker tell how much his lunch will cost?). The FAS tests are administered via tape recordings to eliminate examiner bias. Many easy questions were deliberately included to minimize feelings of frustration on the part of the examinee. Two forms of the test are available. See also the Psychological Corporation's Test Service Bulletin 57 by these same authors.

An E&D project in Washington, D.C. tutored trainees in spatial relations. It was found that their three-dimensional conceptualization of two-dimensional picture diagrams could be improved through the use of special paper and sheet metal objects which could be twisted and shaped to match the two-dimensional diagrams. Also, by using foldable transparencies with an overhead projector, trainees learned to perceive the relationship between sides and angles in three-dimensional space.

Giving applicants "test-taking hints" also is a popular form of tutoring. An E&D project in Tennessee found it useful to give instructions on how to choose answers and when to guess on true-false, multiple-choice, and matching answer type tests. Examinees had not previously been aware of differing test scoring rules and formulas, the advisability of answering the easier questions first, and finding correct answers by the process of elimination.

Service Rejects Aided

State employment service offices give applicants the brochure, "Doing Your Best on Aptitude Tests." It illustrates some rules for taking aptitude tests and contains sample items found on such tests. Also, it presents test-taking hints in a concise, colorful, handy form.

Special Curriculum. Some E&D projects have found useful a commercially marketed practice test package consisting of a sound tape used with a test workbook during a 30-minute teaching session. The tape recording presents test instructions and practice questions and, after applicants take the tests, reviews the answers. Also, there is a booklet of practice tests which trainees can take and score at home after completing the programmed portion of the course. The tape and booklets cover five kinds of objective tests. The tests are designed for practice and familiarization only; no provision is made for interpreting scores.

One E&D project in North Carolina analyzed the questions and underlying principles of the Bennett Mechanical Comprehension Test and the Wonderlic Personnel Test, two very different instruments. For each test, a separate pretesting course was developed with special learning units given approximately five hours a week for five weeks.

The special course increased scores on the Bennett from an average of 18 before orientation to 55 afterwards, on the Wonderlic from 11 to 30. At initial testing only 2 of 26 trainees were able to score at the level required by employers, while all but 2 trainees made the grade after the pretesting orientation. The size of these gains may be suspect because the samples were small and the men had taken the same tests at the outset, but they point to the potential value of special instruction developed around specific types of knowledge required by particular tests.

Extensive Remedial Education. This is essential for people with below fifth grade literacy levels if they are to take traditional highly verbal, timed paper-and-pencil tests. Comprehension of such tests usually requires at least sixth grade reading abilities. In addition, without such ability it is highly doubtful that examinees can develop adequate motivation and confidence, or can be instructed effectively in the mechanics of test-taking.

Several E&D projects have served young men 17 to 22 years of age, all of whom were Armed Forces volunteers rejected as unqualified for military service because of academic deficiencies. The projects clearly demonstrated that through brief classroom training these youth could be upgraded to meet Armed Forces entrance requirements. Coach class training provided youth with special curricula similar to the types of subject content in the Armed Forces Enlistment Screening Test and Armed Forces Qualifications Test.

An E&D project in San Francisco showed that a comprehensive one-year program could prepare highly disadvantaged jobseekers to pass the Civil Service examination for postal clerks and carriers. The program combined pretesting orientation with temporary employment, job-related remedial education, and human relations training for job supervisors. Of the 513 who entered the program, 416 took the exam within a year after entrance and 263 passed; the average program cost per success was $235.

The 513 temporary employees were hired without being tested and without reference to educational qualifications. Their special status expired after one year, by which time they had to pass the regular Civil Service examination to remain employed. They attended class (without pay) two hours a day, five days a week. Average literacy level for the group at hire was less than sixth grade. Pretest orientation sessions used several published tests on how to pass the Postal Clerk Carrier exam, as well as intensive practice in following test instructions, using answer sheets, and learning to work under time pressure.

Extended Effort Required

The San Francisco project demonstrated the value of temporary employment as a motivator for the disadvantaged to improve their academic and test-taking skills. This effort is no longer E&D but is now a regular activity of the manpower program in San Francisco.

E&D experiences across the country support the conclusion that pretesting orientation can enhance the ability of the disadvantaged in test taking. However, the appropriate methods for, and scope of, such activity will vary depending on the character of the vocational test to be taken and the education and testing experience of the job applicant.

E&D work does not support the common notion that pretesting orientation is a one-shot hour long activity focused on general test-taking considerations. Rather, it should be an extended experience in which the applicant must develop trust in those who are giving the test, skills in the specific types of test directions, questions, and content he will ultimately face in formal testing.

All this concern with the disadvantaged is rather new. Campbell (1971) sees this "discovery" of minority and disadvantaged groups as "another fad." He remarks that before 1968, there was almost no mention of such group training problems. A case in point, he says, is the *Training and Development Journal,* the principal journal for practitioners: in 1967, there was one article dealing with minority group training; in 1968, there were two; and in 1969, there were 15. "As a fad, Blacks had caught on. If the fad runs its typical course, there will be a flood of descriptive articles, with a few small-scale empirical investigations mixed in, and the whole business will soon be replaced by some other hot topic. However, in this particular case the consequences are tragic. The problem will not go away" (Campbell, 1971, p. 566).

Studies of blacks in New York City and Detroit confirm the conventional wisdom that if a training program does not lead directly to jobs, morale suffers and attitudes toward such training programs become much more negative. A typical by-product here (as in Detroit where a literacy training program was organized) was the extreme lack of confidence generated by the feeling of being hopelessly undereducated.

Campbell feels the best and most informative research is that reported by Hodgson and Brenner (1958). Two studies for Lockheed Aircraft are summarized, one in California and the other in Georgia. The bulk of the training at both plants was job-related but with some remedial training in reading and shop mathematics. The Georgia program ran for 12 weeks and included 72 hours of psychodrama and role playing; it was oriented to fairly high level training in sheet metal. The California program was only four weeks long, was geared toward specific training for specific jobs, and participants were paid a full wage for that job. There was also considerable individual counseling but no role playing nor psychodrama. Three quarters of the Georgia sample were black and two thirds were 21 years or younger; all were male. The California sample was older and evenly divided among blacks, Mexican-Americans, and whites; both males and females were included. The unique thing about both samples was that the applicants had to meet four of the following five criteria: (a) school dropout, (b) unemployed head of the household, (c) income less than $3000 during the last 12 months, (d) poor work history, (e) no primary work skills. At the California site, 70 percent of the applicants were turned down because they were not "hard core" enough or because their arrest records were overwhelmingly severe. None of these trainees could meet traditional company hiring standards. Dropout rates for the training period were, surprisingly, very low. After four months on the job, the turnover was only about 10 percent in both samples, which was significantly below the normal level. A study of the California group showed no difference in quantity or quality of work between trainees and regular employees. The authors attribute the success of the training to appropriate instructional methods, frequent recognition and reinforcement, training content that was directly linked to a specific job, and jobs that were not "dead end" (Campbell, 1971, pp. 586–587).

These Hodgson and Brenner reports, it should be noted, did not make use of psychological tests. The inclusion of aptitude or ability measures then will involve something more than unfair discrimination because differences in test validity intrude. Thus a measure might be significantly valid in each of two ethnic groups, but the degree of validity might differ markedly. Kirkpatrick *et al.* (1968) in a series of studies on fairness and validity of personnel tests for different ethnic groups, a study sponsored by the Ford Foundation, point to these differential validity data but also stress that mean job criterion performance must also be considered. These authors remark that, for example, a test might be quite valid for both whites and blacks, and blacks obtain lower mean test scores, the test would not then be unfairly discriminatory if blacks also earned proportionately lower criterion scores. Should this same test not be valid for either group, but blacks obtain lower test scores and proportionately lower criterion scores, the test would again not be unfairly discriminatory. "Thus, regardless of the validity of a test, unfair discrimination will occur only if the predicted criterion scores of one ethnic group are lower than their actual criterion scores" (Kirkpatrick *et al.*, 1968, p. 7). These authors, all members of the Department of Psychology at New York University at the time of the two-year study, after a survey of the relevant industrial testing literature, were finally able to locate only five situations that were even minimally suitable for such comparisons and where the necessary cooperation could be obtained. These five studies are also of interest because of the employment of a moderator variable of cultural status. This was a measure derived from a factor analysis of various personal background data (parental education, educational and occupational history of the individual and such) on employees resulting in a score for each individual, which served as an index of cultural status. In the end, however, this index turned out to be too simplistic because the real psychological dynamics of cultural status were not tapped.

Kirkpatrick *et al.* (1968) report five studies, mostly involving small samples of whites and blacks. In three of the four studies, relatively few instances (about 24%¶) of unfairness could be detected. The largest study, involving performance of white and black students on the National League of Nursing's admissions test (a college aptitude and achievement battery required for entrance into most Schools of Nursing) clearly discriminated against blacks. But here, however, the measure of cultural deprivation was probably inadequate because the index, when used as a moderator variable, did not improve

¶ Editor's calculation from data in Kirkaptick *et al.* Summary Table (1968, p. 27). In study 5, unfairness could not be tested.

prediction. The authors concluded that a general statement on fairness or unfairness could not be made. Fairness must be checked for each situation, each job performance criterion, each ethnic group, and each test employed. It would also be a wise precaution to utilize separate prediction equations for each ethnic group. The authors conclude that an objective and valid selection measure, properly used by a conscientious personnel manager, is an effective safeguard against unfair discrimination. Badly needed here are better measures of "cultural disadvantage," which means going beyond simple biographical information.

Testing in all of these five studies was minimal and long-term effects, such as upgrading on the job, were not studied. One additional report which did deal with job upgrading was done for the Bell Telephone Company (Grant & Bray, 1970), where an extensive test battery was employed and where a geographically spread sample of workers was utilized and also—an unusual feature in such research—where the training given would also include material normally taught later in the employee's career. The program is therefore a program for the screening of candidates for upgrading. The results show aptitude measures in a "happier" vein. The program consisted of seven levels, each succeeding level being more complex than the preceding one. Each subject was tested preceding each level on the content of that level. If he passed this pretest, he then went directly to the pretest for the next level. If he fails to pass this pretest, he then goes through the training for that level and, when ready, takes a posttest. All of the training was programmed. The candidate is given the needed materials and then proceeds through the sequence at his own pace. Telephone companies in Detroit, Philadelphia, Washington, Chicago, and San Francisco were involved, each of whom agreed in advance to employ 100 men of which half would be blacks. The test battery was extensive: The ETS School and College Ability Test (Level 2), Bennett Mechanical Comprehension (Form BB), Bell System Qualification Test III (a task similar to locating a trouble spot in an electrical circuit), DAT Abstract Reasoning, the Crawford Small Parts Dexterity Test. The statistical treatment was complex: multiple correlation coefficients and expectancy tables were computed for all test variables against the highest level of training passed for each company sample, for the combined company samples, and for minority and nonminority samples separately and combined. Attention here will only be given to the minority versus nonminority findings. (The original report should be consulted for other interesting results: for example, two of the aptitude measures—SCAT and AR—predicted just about as well as did the entire test battery.) Scores of nonminority and minority subjects on the five aptitude tests showed no differences that were significant and, likewise, the correlation coefficients between the aptitude measures and highest level of training passed were not statistically different (.05 level). The slopes of the regression lines for minority versus nonminority groups were practically identical, the latter being lower but parallel to the former. The authors concluded, however, that for employment purposes the effects were not of sufficient magnitude to warrant the use of different regression lines.

Mention was previously made of the CCNY College Discovery Program, 80 percent of these students coming from minority groups. Recently a predictive study of college performance of these Discovery students, where they were compared with regular matriculants, has appeared (Dispenzieri et al., 1971). The Discovery sample was composed of 492 students who had entered the CCNY program in 1966. The second group consisted of 257 regular matriculants randomly selected from the fall 1966 entering class. A wide variety of predictor variables was utilized: three measures of achievement motivation, the Brown-Holtzman Study Habits Inventory, two general ability tests (the WAIS and the Otis Group Intelligence Scale) plus other more specific ability measures (the DAT Space Relations Test and the Preliminary Scholastic Aptitude Test). Attitudes were sampled via an Intellectual-Pragmatism scale and the reality of the student's aspiration level was measured. The Watson-Glaser Critical Thinking Appraisal was given as well as other indices of cognitive style (a social desirability scale, the Christie Machiavellianism Scale (duplicity, distrust in people, etc.)). Criteria employed were grade point averages at the end of both the first and second semesters, total credits earned, and (for the Discovery students) graduation from college.

In a word, a wealth of data was gathered and with very disappointing results. Multiple-regression analyses for the Discovery group for the three criterion variables (GPA, credits earned, graduation) showed that the predictors could account for only between 17 and 22 percent of the variance in any criterion. The authors confess that, other than personal histories, it is difficult to think of other predictors that might pay off. The unrealistic overaspirations of many of the Discovery students was noted as well as the low esteem in which they held their instructors and college requirements. There would appear to be considerable frustration here, what with their need to prove their academic worth, their fear of failure, and their need to reduce anxiety about their abilities. The authors suggest these students may attempt to reduce their anxiety in a self-defeating manner. The simple measure used here of the discrepancy between expected college average and high school average proved to be an adequate index of unrealistic aspiration.

The study ends on the note, long ago emphasized by Guthrie's learning theory, that the best predictor appears to be past performance: you do what you did the last time. In fact, high school average yielded a higher correlation with the criteria for Discovery students than for regular matriculants (example: first year GPA—.38 and .16 respectively.**

** An allied problem to testing with disadvantaged or minority groups is that of testing in developing nations. Testing procedures that work well in Western cultures often fail elsewhere. Ortar (1963) has shown that test items that work well in USA may even work very ineffectively in Europe. Schwarz (see pp. 26–34) has discussed this

To end on a cautionary note and with some pessimism despite the highly favorable results regarding blacks from the Grant and Bray (1970) study previously summarized are results from the following studies. Everybody is now much aware of the need for training and employment of the hard core unemployed. Rosen and Turner (1971) remark that many companies have rushed into such programs literally on a trial-and-error basis.

A recent report, with rather depressing results, is that of Friedlander and Greenberg (1971) working in Cleveland, Ohio with a federally funded Concentrated Employment Program there known as AIM-JOBS. The group studied there was largely male, black, of relatively low educational level, and obviously unemployed (for an average of 15 weeks) prior to the program. The group went through a two-week orientation program before job placement where attitudes toward work were studied, a variety of biographical/demographical variables were collected, and the job climate was assessed. Of the 428 men who completed the orientation program, a mere 147 (31%) were working in business organizations six months later. A control group, matched for age, education, area of residence, and work history was used for comparison purposes. One of the most surprising results here was the high negative relationship ($r = -.60$) between the supervisor's evaluation of the reliability of the hard core unemployed individual and the number of weeks he continued on the job: those who stayed on the job tended to be rated as less reliable ("does not show up every day," "does not show up on time") by their supervisor. The authors conclude that the work effectiveness and behavior of these hard cores depends primarily on the social climate in which they are placed and work (how they are treated, how much support they receive both from peers and their supervisor). Increasing the supportiveness of this climate seems to be the major avenue for increasing the performance and the retention of these workers. Most hard core programs focus instead on trying to get these individuals to adapt to the predominantly white middle-class culture. The underlying assumption here (often unstated) is that the hard core unemployed culture is defective and accordingly deviant. Wellman (1968, and cited by Friedlander & Greenberg) describes a program similar to AIM-JOBS as follows:

> The desire for work was not the problem. The real problem was what the program demanded of the young men. It asked that they change their manner of speech and dress, that they ignore their lack of skills and society's lack of jobs, and that they act as if their arrest records were of no consequence in obtaining a job. It asked, most importantly, that they pretend *they*, and not society, bore the responsibility for their being unemployed. TIDE (the program) didn't demand much of the men: only that they become white (p. 13).

It is within such hard core programs that such cross-cultural issues get acted out both by the dominant culture and the disadvantaged

---

problem regarding Africa. The reader is referred to this and other papers in the earlier section on "Test Administration Problems."

minority. Friedlander and Greenberg confess to "some pessimism" about other programs where the intention is to change the attitudes and values of the hard core group to fit our own social structure. "Indeed, the social structure as it is represented by the climate in most organizations may be more a cause than a cure for the hard-core unemployed's inappropriate work behavior" (p. 295).

▽ ▽ ▽

MOST testing with disadvantaged groups interprets the typical results in terms of cultural deficits. Looking at such groups and taking measurements of their performance, the researcher then typically makes certain inferences about underlying competencies and capacities. Critics of this strategy have pointed out that this involves an attitude of ethnocentrism—as when we make distinctions between "standard" and "substandard" English. Recent research, especially with communication systems, has strongly challenged this "deficit" hypothesis and stressed, instead, a "difference" hypothesis. The great bulk of research about language differences has involved blacks but this may well also be the case with the Appalachian child or the American Indian or, for that matter, the white child residing in the inner city. As various language specialists are now insisting, we need massive research concerning the different varieties of nonstandard English. The "deficit" hypothesis is thus seen to be the result of an ethnocentric bias; instead, and especially in our schools, it should be recognized that cultural distinctions really do exist among people and that to be different is not necessarily to be disfavored.

The following article by Cole and Bruner, which appeared in the 1971 issue of the *American Psychologist*, deals directly with this "difference" issue. The material was originally prepared for the 1972 *National Society for the Study of Education Yearbook on Early Childhood Education*. Dr. Cole is Professor of Psychology at the Rockefeller University; Dr. Bruner is Professor of Psychology and Director of the Center for Cognitive Studies at Harvard University.

CULTURAL DIFFERENCES AND INFERENCES ABOUT PSYCHOLOGICAL PROCESSES

Michael Cole and Jerome S. Bruner

DEFICIT INTERPRETATION

Perhaps the most prevalent view of the source of ethnic and social class differences in intellectual performance is what might be summed up under the label "the deficit hypothesis." It can be stated briefly, without risk of gross exaggeration. It rests on the assumption that a community under conditions of poverty (for it is the poor who are the focus of attention, and a disproportionate number of the poor are members of minority ethnic groups) is a disorganized community, and this disorganization expresses itself in various forms of deficit. One widely agreed upon source of deficit is mothering; the child of poverty is assumed to lack adequate parental attention. Given the illegitimacy rate in the urban ghetto, the most conspicuous "deficit" is a missing father and, consequently, a missing father model. The mother is away at work or, in any case, less involved with raising her children than she should be by white middle-class standards. There is said to be less regularity, less mutuality in interaction with her. There are said to be specialized deficits in interaction as well—less guidance in goal seeking from the parents, less emphasis upon means and ends in maternal instruction, or less positive and more negative reinforcement.

More particularly, the deficit hypothesis has been applied to the symbolic and linguistic environment of the growing child. His linguistic community as portrayed in the early work of Basil Bernstein (1961), for example, is characterized by a restricted code, dealing more in the stereotype of interaction than in language that explains and elaborates upon social and material events. The games that are played by poor children and to which they are exposed are less strategy bound than those of more advantaged children (Eifermann, 1968); their homes are said to have a more confused noise background, permitting less opportunity for figure-ground formation (Klaus & Gray, 1968); and the certainty of the environment is sufficiently reduced so that children have difficulty in delaying reinforcement (Mischel, 1966) or in accepting verbal reinforcement instead of the real article (Zigler & Butterfield, 1968).

The theory of intervention that grew from this view was the idea of "early stimulation," modeled on a conception of supplying nutriment for those with a protein deficiency or avitaminosis. The nature of the needed early stimulation was never explained systematically, save in rare cases (Smilansky, 1968), but it variously took the form of practice in using abstractions (Blank & Solomon, 1969), in having dialogue where the referent objects were not present, as through the use of telephones (Deutsch, 1967), or in providing secure mothering by substitution (Caldwell *et al.*, 1970).

A primary result of these various deficits was belived to express itself in the lowered test scores and academic performance among children from poverty backgrounds. The issue was most often left moot as to whether or not this lowered test performance was easily reversible, but the standard reference was to a monograph by Bloom (1964) indicating that cognitive performance on a battery of tests, given to poor and middle-class children, yielded the result that nearly 80 percent of the variance in intellectual performance was accounted for by age 3.

DIFFERENCE INTERPRETATION

Such data seem to compel the conclusion that as a consequence of various factors arising from minority group status (factors affecting motivation, linguistic ability, goal orientation, hereditary proclivities to learn in certain ways—the particular mix of factors depends on the writer—minority group children suffer intellectual deficits when compared with their "more advantaged" peers.

There is a body of data and theory that controverts this contention, casts doubt on the conclusion that a deficit exists in minority group children, and even raises doubts as to whether any nonsuperficial *differences* exist among different cultural groups.

There are two long standing precedents for the view that different groups (defined in terms of cultural, linguistic, and ethnic criteria) do not differ intellectually from each other in any important way. First, there is the anthropological "doctrine of psychic unity" (Kroeber, 1948) which, on the basis of the "run of total experience," is said to warrant the assumption of intellectual equality as a sufficient approximation to the truth. This view is compatible with current linguistic anthropological theorizing, which concentrates on describing the way in which different cultural/linguistic groups categorize familiar areas of experience. By this view, different conclusions about the world are the result of arbitrary and different, but equally logical, ways of cutting up the world of experience. From this perspective, descriptions of the "disorganization" of minorities would be highly suspect, this suspicion arising in connection with questions like, Disorganized from whose point of view?

Anthropological critiques of psychological experimentation have never carried much weight with psychologists, nor have anthropologists been very impressed with conclusions from psychological tests. We have hypothesized elsewhere (Cole *et al.*, 1971) that their mutual indifference stems in part from a difference in opinion about the inferences that are warranted from testing and experimentation, and in part because the anthropologist relies mainly on data that the psychologist completely fails to consider: the mundane social life of the people he studies. As we shall see, these issues carry over into our criticism of the "deficit" theory of cultural deprivation.

A second tradition that calls into question culturally determined group difference in intelligence is the linguist's assertion that languages do not differ in their degree of development (Greenberg, 1963), buttressed by the transformationalist's caution that one cannot attribute to people a cognitive capacity that is less than is required to produce the complex rule-governed activity called language (Chomsky, 1966).

Although Chomskian linguistics has had a profound effect on psychological theories of language and cognitive development in recent years, psychological views of language still are considered hopelessly inadequate by working linguists. This criticism applies not only to psycholinguistic theory but to the actual description of linguistic performance on which theory is based. Needless to say, the accusation of misunderstanding at the descriptive level leads to accusations of absurdity at the theoretical level.

A third tradition that leads to rejection of the deficit theory has many sources in recent social sciences. This view holds that even when attempts have been made to provide reasonable anthropological and linguistic foundations, the conclusions about cognitive capacity from psychological experiments are unfounded because the performance produced represents a complex interaction of the formal characteristics of the experiment and the social/environmental context that determines the subject's interpretation of the situation in which it occurs. The need for "situation-bound" interpretations of experiments is emphasized in such diverse sources as sociology (Goffman, 1964), psychology (Brunswick, 1958), and psycholinguistics (Cazden, 1970). This is an important issue, which we will return to once illustrations of the "antideficit" view have been explored.

Perhaps the most coherent denial of the deficit position, coupled with compelling illustrations of the resourcefulness of the supposedly deprived and incompetent person, is contained in Labov's attack on the concept of "linguistic deprivation" and its accompanying assumption of cognitive incapacity (Labov, 1970).

It is not possible here to review all of Labov's evidence. Rather, we have abstracted what we take to be the major points in his attack.

1. *An assertion of the functional equality of all languages.* This assertion is applied specifically to his analysis of nonstandard Negro English, which has been the object of his study for several years. Labov provided a series of examples where young blacks who would be assessed as linguistically retarded and academically hopeless by standard test procedures enter conversations in a way that leaves little doubt that they can speak perfectly adequately and produce very clever arguments in the process.

2. *An assertion of the psychologist's ignorance of language in general and nonstandard dialects in particular.* Labov's particular target is Carl Bereiter (Bereiter & Englemann, 1966) whose remedial teaching technique is partly rationalized in terms of the *inability* of young black children to use language either as an effective tool of communication or thinking. Part of Labov's attack is aimed at misinterpretations of such phrases as *"They mine,"* which Labov analyzed in terms of rules of contraction, but which Bereiter made the mistake of referring to as a "series of badly connected words" (Labov, 1970, p. 171). This "psychologist's deficit" has a clear remedy. It is roughly equivalent to the anthropological caveat that the psychologist has to know more about the people he studies.

3. *The inadequacy of present experimentation.* More serious criticism of the psychologist's interpretaton of "language deprivation" and, by extension, his whole concept of "cultural deprivation" is contained in the following, rather extensive quote:

this and the preceding section are designed to convince the reader that the controlled experiments that have been offered in evidence (of Negro lack of competence) are misleading. The only thing that is controlled is the superficial form of the stimulus. All children are asked, "What do you think of capital punishment?" or "Tell me everything you can about this." But the speaker's interpretation of these requests, and the action he believes is appropriate in response is completely uncontrolled. One can view these test stimuli as requests for information, commands for action, or meaningless sequences of words. . . . With human subjects it is absurd to believe that identical stimuli are obtained by asking everyone the same question. Since the crucial intervening variables of interpretation and motivation are uncontrolled, most of the literature on verbal deprivation tells us nothing of the capacities of children (Labov, 1970, p. 171).

Here Labov is attacking the experimental method as usually applied to the problem of subcultural differences in cognitive capacity. We can abstract several assertions from this key passage: (*a*) Formal experimental equivalence of operations does not insure de facto equivalence of experimental treatments; (*b*) different subcultural groups are predisposed to interpret the experimental stimuli (situations) differently; (*c*) different subcultural groups are motivated by different concerns relevant to the experimental task; (*d*) in view of the inadequacies of experimentation, inferences about lack of competence among black children are unwarranted.

These criticisms, when combined with linguistic misinterpretation, constitute Labov's attack on the deficit theory of cultural deprivation and represent the rationale underlying his demonstrations of competence where its lack had previously been inferred.

One example of Labov's approach is to conduct a rather standard interview of the type often used for assessment of language competence. The situation is designed to be minimally threatening; the interviewer is a neighborhood figure and black. Yet, the black 8-year-old interviewee's behavior is monosyllabic. He is a candidate for the diagnosis of linguistically and culturally deprived.

But this diagnosis is very much situation dependent. For at a later time, this same interviewer goes to the boy's apartment, brings one of the boy's friends with him, lies down on the floor, and produces some potato chips. He then begins talking about clearly taboo subjects in dialect. Under these circumstances, the mute interviewee becomes an excited participant in the general conversation.

In similar examples, Labov demonstrated powerful reasoning and debating skills in a school dropout and nonlogical verbosity in an acceptable, "normal" black who has mastered the forms of standard English. Labov's conclusion is that the usual assessment situations, including IQ and reading tests, elicit deliberate, defensive behavior on the part of the child who has realistic expectations that to talk openly is to expose oneself to insult and harm. As a consequence, such situations *cannot* measure the child's competence. Labov went even further to assert that far from being verbally deprived, the typical ghetto child is

bathed in verbal stimulation from morning to night. We see many speech events which depend upon the competitive exhibition of verbal skills—sounding, sing-ing, toasts, rifting, louding—a whole range of activities in which the individ-ual gains status through the use of language. . . . We see no connection be-tween the verbal skill in the speech events characteristic of the street culture and success in the school room (Labov, 1970, p. 163).

Labov is not the only linguist to offer such a critique of current theories of cultural deprivation (see, e.g., Stewart, 1970). However, Labov's criticism raises larger issues concerning the logic of compara-tive research designs of which the work in cultural/linguistic deprivation is only a part. It is to this general question that we now turn.

COMPETENCE AND PERFOMANCE IN PSYCHOLOGICAL RESEARCH

The major thrusts of Labov's argument, that situational factors are important components of psychological experiments and that it is diffi-cult if not impossible to infer competence directly from performance, are not new ideas to psychologists. Indeed, a concern with the relation between *psychological process* on the one hand and *situational factors* on the other has long been a kind of shadow issue in psychology, surfacing most often in the context of comparative research.

It is this question that underlies the often berated question, What do IQ tests measure? and has been prominent in attacks on Jensen's (1969) argument that group differences in IQ test performance are reflective of innate differences in capacity.

Kagan (1969), for example, pointed to the work of Palmer, who regularly delays testing until the child is relaxed and has established rapport with the tester. Jensen (1969, p. 100) himself reported that significant differences in test performance can be caused by differential adaptation to the test situation.

Hertzig *et al.* (1968) made a direct study of social class/ethnic differ-ences in response to the test situation and demonstrated stable differ-ences in situational responses that were correlated with test perform-ance and were present even when measured IQ was equivalent for subgroups chosen from the major comparison groups.

Concern with the particular *content* of tests and experiments as they relate to inferences about cognitive capacity occurs within the same context. The search for a "culture-free" IQ test has emphasized the use of universally familiar material and various investigators have found that significant differences in performance can be related to the content of the experimental materials. Price-Williams (1961), for example, demonstrated earlier acquisition of conservation concepts in Nigerian children using traditional instead of imported stimulus materials and Gay and Cole (1967) made a similar point with respect to Liberian classification behavior and learning.

Contemporary psychology's awareness of the task and situation-specific determinants of performance is reflected in a recent article by Kagan and Kogan (1970). In a section of their paper titled "The Significance of Public Performance," they are concerned with the fact that "differences in quality of style of public performance, although striking, may be misleading indices of competence" [p. 1322].

Although such misgivings abound, they have not yet crystallized into a coherent program of research and theory nor have the implications of accepting the need to incorporate an analysis of situations in addition to traditional experimantal manipulations been fully appreciated.

EXTENDED IDEA OF COMPETENCE

Labov and others have argued forcefully that we cannot distinguish on the basis of traditional experimental approaches between the underlying competence of those who have had a poor opportunity to participate in a particular culture and those who have had a good oportunity and between those who have not had their share of wealth and respect and those who have. The crux of the argument, when applied to the problem of "cultural deprivation," is that those groups ordinarily diagnosed as culturally deprived have the same underlying competence as those in the mainstream of the dominant culture, *the differences in performance being accounted for by the situations and contexts in which the competence is expressed.* To put the matter most rigorously, one can find a corresponding situation in which the member of the "out culture," the victim of poverty, can perform on the basis of a given competence in a fashion equal to or superior to the standard achieved by a member of the dominant culture.

A prosaic example taken from the work of Gay and Cole (1967) concerns the ability to make estimates of volume. The case in question is to estimate the number of cups of rice in each of several bowls. Comparisons of "rice estimation accuracy" were made among several groups of subjects, including nonliterate Kpelle rice farmers from North Central Liberia and Yale sophomores. The rice farmers manifested significantly greater accuracy than the Yale students, the difference increasing with the amount of rice presented for estimation. In many other situations, measurement skills are found to be superior among educated subjects in the Gay and Cole study. Just as Kpelle superiority at making rice estimates is clearly not a universal manifestation of their superior underlying competence, the superiority of Yale students in, for example, distance judgments is no basis for inferring that their competence is superior.

We think the existence of demonstrations such as those presented by Labov has been salutary in forcing closer examination of testing situations used for comparing the children of poverty with their more advantaged peers. And, as the illustration from Gay and Cole suggests, the argument may have quite general implications. Obviously, it is not sufficient to use a simple equivalence-of-test procedure to make inferences about the competence of the two groups being compared. In fact, a "two-groups" design is almost useless for making any important inferences in cross-cultural research. From a logical view, however, the conclusion of equal cognitive competence in those who are not members of the prestige culture and those who are its beneficiaries is often equally unwarranted. While it is very proper to criticize the logic of assuming that poor performance implies lack of competence, the contention that poor performance is of *no* relevance to a theory of cognitive development and to a theory of cultural differences in cognitive development also seems an oversimplification.

Assuming that we can find test situations in which comparably good performance can be elicited from the groups being contrasted, there is plainly an issue having to do with the range and nature of the situations in which performance for any two groups can be found to be equal.

We have noted Labov's conclusion that the usual assessment of linguistic competence in the black child elicits deliberate defensive behavior and that he can respond effectively in familiar nonthreatening surroundings. It may be, however (this possibility is discussed in Bruner, 1970), that he is unable to utilize language of a decentered type, taken out of the context of social interaction, used in an abstract way to deal with hypothetical possibilities and to spell out hypothetical plans (see also Gladwin, 1970). If such were the case, we could not dismiss the question of different kinds of language usage by saying simply that decontextualized talk is not part of the natural milieu of the black child in the urban ghetto. If it should turn out to be the case that mastery of the culture depends on one's capacity to perform well on the basis of competence one has stored up, and to perform well in particular settings and in particular ways, when plainly the question of differences in the way language enters the problem solving process cannot be dismissed. It has been argued, for example, by Bernstein (1970) that it is in the nature of the very social life of the urban ghetto that there develops a kind of particularism in which communication usually takes place only along concrete personal lines. The ghetto child, who by training is likely to use an idiosyncratic mode of communication, may become locked into the life of his own cultural group, and his migration into other groups consequently becomes the more difficult. Bernstein made clear in his most recent work that this is not a question of capacity but, rather, a matter of what he calls "orientation." Nevertheless, it may very wll be that a ghetto dweller's language training makes him unfit for taking jobs in the power and prestige-endowing pursuits of middleclass culture. If such is the case, then the issue of representativeness of the situations to which he can apply his competence becomes something more than a matter of test procedure.

A major difficulty with this line of speculation is that at present we have almost no knowledge of the day-to-day representativeness of different situations and the behaviors that are seen as appropriate to them by different cultural groups. For example, the idea that language use must be considered outside of social interactions in order to qualify as abstract, as involving "cognition," is almost certainly a psychologist's fiction. Until we have better knowledge of the cognitive components that are part of social interactions (the same applies to many spheres of activity), speculations about the role of language in cognition will have to remain speculations.

In fact, it is extraordinarily difficult to know, except in a most superficial way on the basis of our present knowledge of society, what is the nature of situations that permit control and utilization of the resources of a culture by one of its members and what the cognitive skills are that are demanded of one who would use these resources. It may very well be that the very definition of a subculture could be put into the spirit of Lévi-Strauss' (1963) definition of a culture:

What is called a subculture is a fragment of a culture which from the point of view of the research at hand presents significant discontinuities in relation to the rest of that culture with respect to access to its major amplifying tools.

By an amplifying tool is meant a technological feature, be it soft or hard, that permits control by the individual of resources, prestige, and defence within the culture. An example of a middle class cultural amplifier that operates to increase the thought processes of those who employ it is the discipline loosely referred to as "mathematics." To employ mathematical techniques requires the cultivation of certain skills of reasoning, even certain styles of deploying one's thought processes. If one were able to cultivate the strategies and styles relevant to the employment of mathematics, then that range of technology is open to one's use. If one does not cultivate mathematical skills, the result is "functional incompetence," an inability to use this kind of technology. Whether or not compensatory techniques can then correct "functional incompetence" is an important, but unexplored, question.

Any particular aspect of the technology requires certain skills for its successful use. These skills, as we have already noted, must also be deployable in the range of situations where they are useful. Even if a child could carry out the planning necessary for the most technically demanding kind of activity, he must not do so if he has been trained with the expectancy that the exercise of such a skill will be punished or will, in any event, lead to some unforeseen difficulty. Consequently, the chances that the individual will work up his capacities for performance in the given domain are diminished. As a result, although the individual can be shown to have competence in some sphere involving the utilization of the skill, he will not be able to express that competence in the relevant kind of context. In an absolute sense, he is any man's equal, but in everyday encounters, he is not up to the task.

The principle cuts both ways with respect to cultural differences. Verbal skills are important cultural "amplifiers" among Labov's subjects; as many middle class school administrators have discovered, the ghetto resident skilled in verbal exchanges is a more than formidable opponent in the battle for control of school curriculum and resources. In like manner, the Harlem youth on the street who cannot cope with the verbal battles described by Labov is failing to express competence in a context relevant to the ghetto.

These considerations impress us with the need to clarify our notion of what the competencies are that underlie effective performance. There has been an implicit, but very general, tendency in psychology to speak as if the organism is an information-processing machine with a fixed set of routines. The number and organization of these routines might differ as a function of age, genetic makeup, or environmental factors, but for any given machine, the input to the machine is processed uniformly by the routines (structures, skills) of the organism.

Quite recently, psychologists have started to face up to the difficulties of assuming "all things are equal" for different groups of people (concern has focused on difference in age, but the same logic applies to any group comparisons). The study of situational effects on performance has forced a reevaluation of traditional theoretical inferences about competence. This new concern with the interpretation of psychological experiments is quite apparent in recent attempts to cope with data inconsistent with Piaget's theory of cognitive development. For example, Flavell and Wohlwill (1969) sought to distinguish between two kinds of competence: First, there are "the rules, structures, or 'mental operations' embodied in the task and . . . (second, there are) the actual mechanisms required for processing the input and output" (p. 98). The second factor is assumed to be task specific and is the presumed explanation for such facts as the "horizontal decalages" in which the same principle appears for different materials at different ages. The *performance* progression through various stages is presumably a reflection of increases in both kinds of competence, since both are assumed to increase with age.

The same general concern is voiced by Mehler and Bever (1968). They ask,

How can we decide if a developmental change or behavioral difference among adults is really due to a difference in a structural rule, to a difference in the form of the expressive processes or a difference in their quantitative capacity (p. 278)?

Their own work traces the expression of particular rules in behavior and the way the effect of knowing a rule ("having a competence") interacts with dependence on different aspects of the input to produce "nonlinear trends" in the development of conservation-like performance.

Broadening psychological theory to include rules for applying cognitive skills, as well as statements about the skills themselves, seems absolutely necessary.

However, the extensions contemplated may well not be sufficient to meet all of Labov's objections to inferences about "linguistic deprivation." In both the position expressed by Flavell and Wohlwill and by Mehler and Bever, "competence" is seen as dependent on situational factors and seems to be a slowly changing process that might well be governed by the same factors that lead to increases in the power of the structural rules or competence, in the older sense of the word. Yet in Labov's example, the problem is considerably more ephemeral; Labov gives the impression that the subjects were engaged in rational problem solving and that they had complete control over their behavior. He is claiming, in effect, that they are successfully coping with *their* problem; it simply is not the problem the experimenter had in mind, so the experimenter claims lack of competence as a result of his own ignorance.

Acceptance of Labov's criticisms, and we think they should be accepted, requires not only a broadening of our idea of competence, but a vast enrichment of our approach to experimentation.

NECESSITY OF A COMPARATIVE PSYCHOLOGY OF COGNITION

If we accept the idea that situational factors are often important determinants of psychological performance, and if we also accept the idea that different cultural groups are likely to respond differently to any given situation, there seems to be no reasonable alternative to psychological experimentation that bases its inferences on data from comparisons of both experimental and situational variations.

In short, we are contending that Brunswik's (1958) call for "representative design" and an analysis of the "ecological significance" of stimulation is a prerequisite to research on ethnic and social class differences in particular and to any research where the groups to be compared are thought to differ with respect to the process under investigation prior to application of the experimental treatments.

Exhortations to the effect that college sophomores with nonsense syllables and white rats in boxes are not sufficient objects for the development of a general psychological theory have produced, thus far, only minor changes in the behavior of psychologists. The present situations seem to *require* a change.

An illustration from some recent cross-cultural research serves as an illustration of one approach that goes beyond the usual two-group design to explore the situational nature of psychological performance.

Cole *et al.* (1971, p. 4) used the free-recall technique to study cultural differences in memory. The initial studies presented subjects with a list of 20 words divided into four familiar, easily distinguishable categories. Subjects were read the list of words and asked to recall them. The procedure was repeated five times for each subject. A wide variety of subject populations was studied in this way; Liberian rice farmers and school children were the focus of concern, but comparison with groups in the United States was also made.

Three factors of the Kpelle rice farmers' performance were remarkable in these first studies: (*a*) The number recalled was relatively small (9–11 items per list); (*b*) there was no evidence of semantic or other organization of the material; (*c*) there was little or no increase in the number recalled with successive trials.

Better recall, great improvement with trials, and significant organization are all characteristic of performance of the American groups above the fifth grade.

A series of standard experimental manipulations (offering incentives, using lists based on functional rather than semantic classes, showing the objects to be remembered, extending the number of trials) all failed to make much difference in Kpelle performance.

However, when these same to-be-recalled items were incorporated into folk stories, when explicit grouping procedures were introduced or when seemingly bizarre cuing procedures were used, Kpelle performance manifested organization, showed vast improvements in terms of amount recalled, and gave a very different picture of underlying capacity. Cole *et al.* (1971) concluded that a set of rather specific skills associated with remembering disconnected material out of context underlies the differences observed in the standard versions of the free-recall experiment with which they began. Moreover, they were able to begin the job of pinpointing these skills, their relevance to traditional activities, and the teaching techniques that could be expected to bring existing memory skills to bear in the "alien" tasks of the school.

CONCLUSION

The arguments set forth in this study can now be brought together and generalized in terms of their bearing on psychological research that is "comparative" in nature—comparing ages, cultures, subcultures, species, or even groups receiving different experimental treatments.

The central thesis derives from a reexamination of the distinction between competence and performance. As a rule, one looks for performance at its best and infers the degree of underlying competence from the observed performance. With respect to linguistic competence, for example, a single given instance of a particular grammatical form could suffice for inferring that the speaker had the competence to generate such instances as needed. By the use of such a methodology, Labov demonstrated that culturally deprived black children, *tested appropriately* for optimum performance, have the same grammatical competence as middle class whites, although it may be expressed in different settings. Note that negative evidence is mute with respect to the status of underlying capacity—it may require a different situation for its manifestation.

The psychological status of the concept of competence (or capacity) is brought deeply into question when one examines conclusions based on standard experiments. Competence so defined is both situation blind and culture blind. If performance is treated (as it often is by linguists) only as a shallow expression of deeper competence, then one inevitably loses sight of the ecological problem of performance. For one of the most important things about any "underlying competence" is the nature of the situations in which it expresses itself. Herein lies the crux of the problem. One must inquire, first, whether a competence is expressed in a particular situation and second, what the significance of that situation is for the person's ability to cope with life in his own milieu. As we have had occasion to comment elsewhere, when we systematically study the situational determinants of performance, we are led to conclude that cultural differences reside more in differences in the situations to which different cultural groups apply their skills than to differences in the skills possessed by the groups in question (Cole *et al.*, 1971, Ch.7).

The problem is to identify the range of capacities readily manifested in different groups and then to inquire whether the range is adequate to the individual's needs in various cultural settings. From this point of view, cultural *deprivation* represents a special case of cultural difference that arises when an individual is faced with demands to perform in a manner inconsistent with his past (cultural) experience. In the present social context of the United States, the great power of the middle class has rendered differences into deficits because middle class behavior is the yardstick of success.

Our analysis holds at least two clear implications of relevance to the classroom teacher charged with the task of educating children from "disadvantaged" subcultural groups.

First, recognition of the educational difficulties in terms of a *difference* rather than a special kind of intellectual disease should change the students' status in the eyes of the teacher. If Pygmalion really can work in the classroom (Rosenthal & Jacobson, 1968), the effect of this change in attitude may of itself produce changes in performance. Such difference in teacher attitude seems to be one prime candidate for an explanation of the fine performance obtained by Kohl (1967) and others with usually recalcitrant students.

Second, the teacher should stop laboring under the impression that he must create new intellectual structures and start concentrating on how to get the child to *transfer* skills he already possesses to the task at hand. It is in this context that "relevant" study materials become important, although "relevant" should mean something more than a way to motivate students. Rather, relevant materials are those to which the child already applies skills the teacher seeks to have applied to his own content. It requires more than a casual acquaintance with one's students to know what those materials are.

Psychologists concerned with comparative research, and comparisons of social and ethnic group differences in particular, must take seriously the study of the way different groups organize the relation between their hands and minds; without assuming the superiority of one system over another, they must take seriously the dictum that man is a cultural animal. When cultures are in competition for resources, as they are today, the psychologist's task is to analyze the source of cultural difference so that those of the minority, the less powerful group, may quickly acquire the intellectual instruments necessary for success of the dominant culture, should they so choose.

PERHAPS the most famous and controversial statement is that of Jensen (1969) which stresses a "difference" hypothesis on the genetic basis. Jensen's data and discussion are far too extensive to present here, except for a short section specifically devoted to race differences. In brief, Jensen feels that a unidimensional concept of intelligence is no longer adequate and that the size of score differences between lower- and middle-class children is not always a function of the test's "cultural loading." Some of the *least* culturally loaded tests show big differences between lower- and middle-class children. Jensen reports at least two dimensions must be postulated to understand socioeconomic class differences: one of these axes represents the degree of cultural loading of the text; the other axis, conceptualized as orthogonal to the culture-loading axis, represents a continuum ranging from "simple" associative learning to complex conceptual learning. Level I (associative ability) is tapped mostly by tests such as digit span, serial rote learning, paired associate learning; Level II (conceptual ability) involves a real transformation of the stimulus input before an overt response can be made (concept learning and problem solving would be good examples here). Lower-class children, whether white, black, or Mexican-American, perform Level I tasks as well or better than middle-class children within the same IQ range. Level II abilities show increasing socioeconomic class differences with groups of increasing age and are thus less often encountered in the disadvantaged.

Jensen stated flatly that compensatory education had failed. His main point, as Tyler (1972) has pointed out, was sometimes lost in the "acrimonious" exchanges: that the pattern of mental abilities may differ in different races and the blacks and other lower-class persons appear to be equal to whites on the kind of associative memory measured by digit span tests. Jensen felt that this kind of ability to memorize could be seen as an educational asset but his critics saw this as relegating blacks to a sort of second-class ability status. A strong statement by the Society for the Psychological Study of Social Issues repudiated the Jensen position and the major part of the next two issues of the *Harvard Educational Review* was devoted to discussions by psychologists and educators who disagreed with Jensen's conclusions.

What follows is the brief section from the very long Jensen article that touches off all the controversy: the section devoted directly to the topic of race differences. This specific section has now been greatly expanded into a 400-page volume published by Methuen in London and, simultaneously, by Harper & Row in New York with the title *Educability and Group Differences* (1973). Dr. Jensen is Professor of Educational Psychology at the University of California at Berkeley.

RACE DIFFERENCES

Arthur R. Jensen

The important distinction between the *individual* and the *population* must always be kept clearly in mind in any discussion of racial differences in mental abilities or any other behavioral characteristics. Whenever we select a person for some special educational purpose, whether for special instruction in a grade school class for children with learning problems, or for a "gifted" class with an advanced curriculum, or for college attendance, or for admission to graduate training or a professional school, we are selecting an *individual,* and we are selecting him and dealing with him as an individual for reasons of his individuality. Similarly, when we employ someone, or promote someone in his occupation, or give some special award or honor to someone for his accomplishments, we are doing this to an individual. The variables of social class, race, and national origin are correlated so imperfectly with any of the valid criteria on which the above decisions should depend, or, for that matter, with any behavioral characteristic, that these background factors are irrelevant as a basis for dealing with individuals—as students, as employees, as neighbors. Furthermore, since as far as we know, the full range of human talents is represented in all the major races of man and in all socioeconomic levels, it is unjust to allow the mere fact of an individual's racial or social background to affect the treatment accorded to him. All persons rightfully must be regarded on the basis of their individual qualities and merits, and all social, educational, and economic institutions must have built into them the mechanisms for insuring and maximizing the treatment of persons according to their individual behavior.

If a society completely believed and practiced the ideal of treating every person as an individual, it would be hard to see why there should be any problems about "race" per se. There might still be problems concerning poverty, unemployment, crime, and other social ills, and, given the will, they could be tackled just as any other problems that require rational methods for solution. But if this philosophy prevailed in practice, there would not need to be a "race problem."

The question of *race* differences in intelligence comes up not when we deal with individuals as individuals, but when certain identifiable *groups* or subcultures within the society are brought into comparison with one another *as groups or populations*. It is only when the groups are disproportionately represented in what are commonly perceived as the most desirable and the least desirable social and occupational roles in a society that the question arises concerning average differences among groups. Since much of the current thinking behind civil rights, fair employment, and equality of educational opportunity appeals to the fact that there is a disproportionate representation of different racial groups in the various levels of the educational, occupational, and socioeconomic hierarchy, we are forced to examine all the possible reasons for this inequality among racial groups in the attainments and rewards generally valued by all groups within our society. To what extent can such inequalities be attributed to unfairness in society's multiple selection purpose? ("Unfair" meaning that selection is influenced by intrinsically irrelevant criteria such as skin color, racial or national origin, etc.) And to what extent are these inequalities attributable to really relevant selection criteria which apply equally to all individuals but at the same time select disproportionately between some racial groups because there exist, in fact, real average differences among the groups—differences in the population distributions of those characteristics which are indisputably relevant to educational and occupational performance? This is certainly one of the most important questions confronting our nation today. The answer, which can be found only through unfettered research, has enormous consequences for the welfare of all, particularly of minorities whose plight is now in the foreground of public attention. A preordained, doctrinaire stance with regard to this issue hinders the achievement of a scientific understanding of the problem. To rule out of court, so to speak, any reasonable hypotheses on purely ideological grounds is to argue that static ignorance is preferable to increasing our knowledge of reality. I strongly disagree with those who believe in searching for the truth by scientific means only under certain circumstances and eschew this course in favor of ignorance under other circumstances, or who believe that the results of inquiry on some subjects cannot be entrusted to the public but should be kept the guarded possession of a scientific elite. Such attitudes, in my opinion, represent a danger to free inquiry and, consequently, in the long run, work to the disadvantage of society's general welfare. "No holds barred" is the best formula for scientific inquiry. One does not decree beforehand which phenomena cannot be studied or which questions cannot be answered.

GENETIC ASPECTS OF RACIAL DIFFERENCES

No one, to my knowledge, questions the role of environmental factors, including influences from past history, in determining at least some of the variance between racial groups in standard measures of intelligence, school performance, and occupational status. The current literature on the culturally disadvantaged abounds with discussion—some of it factual, some of it fanciful—of how a host of environmental factors depresses cognitive development and performance. I recently co-edited a book which is largely concerned with the environmental aspects of disadvantaged minorities (Deutsch, Katz & Jensen, 1968). But the possible importance of genetic factors in racial behavior differences has been greatly ignored, almost to the point of being a tabooed subject, just as were the topics of venereal disease and birth control a generation or so ago.

My discussion with a number of geneticists concerning the question of a genetic basis of differences among races in mental abilities have revealed to me a number of rather consistently agreed upon points which can be summarized in general terms as follows: Any groups which have been geographically or socially isolated from one another for many generations are practically certain to differ in their gene pools, and consequently are likely to show differences in any phenotypic characteristics having high heritability. This is practically axiomatic, according to the geneticists with whom I have spoken. Races are said to be "breeding populations," which is to say that matings within the group have a much higher probability than matings outside the group. Races are more technically viewed by geneticists as populations having different distributions of gene frequencies. These genetic differences are manifested in virtually every anatomical, physiological, and biochemical comparison one can make between representative samples of identifiable racial groups (Kuttner, 1967). There is no reason to suppose that the brain should be exempt from this generalization. (Racial differences in the relative frequencies of various blood constituents have probably been the most thoroughly studied so far.)

But what about behavior? If it can be measured and shown to have a genetic component, it would be regarded, from a genetic standpoint, as no different from other human characteristics. There seems to be little question that racial differences in genetically conditioned behavioral characteristics, such as mental abilities, should exist, just as physical differences. The real questions, geneticists tell me, are not whether there are or are not genetic racial differences that affect behavior, because there undoubtedly are. The proper questions to ask, from a scientific standpoint, are: What is the direction of the difference? What is the magnitude of the difference? And what is the significance of the difference—medically, socially, educationally, or from whatever standpoint that may be relevant to the characteristic in question? A difference is important only within a specific context. For example, one's blood type in the ABO system is unimportant until one needs a transfusion. And some genetic differences are apparently of no importance with respect to any context as far as anyone has been able to discover—for example, differences in the size and shape of ear lobes. The idea that all genetic differences have arisen or persisted only as a result of natural selection, by conferring some survival or adaptive benefit on their possessors, is no longer generally held. There appear to be many genetic differences, or polymorphisms, which confer no discernible advantages to survival.*

---

* The most comprehensive and sophisticated discussion of the genic-behavior analysis of race differences that I have found is by Spuhler and Lindzey (1967).

NEGRO INTELLIGENCE AND SCHOLASTIC PERFORMANCE

Negroes in the United States are disproportionately represented among groups identified as culturally or educationally disadvantaged. This, plus the fact that Negroes constitute by far the largest racial minority in the United States, has for many years focused attention on Negro intelligence. It is a subject with a now vast literature which has been quite recently reviewed by Dreger and Miller (1960, 1968) and by Shuey (1966), whose 578 page review is the most comprehensive, covering 382 studies. The basic data are well known: on the average, Negroes test about 1 standard deviation (15 IQ points) below the average of the white population in IQ, and this finding is fairly uniform across the 81 different tests of intellectual ability used in the studies reviewed by Shuey. This magnitude of difference gives a median overlap of 15 percent, meaning that 15 percent of the Negro population exceeds the white average. In terms of proportions of variance, if the numbers of Negroes and whites were equal, the differences *between* racial groups would account for 23 percent of the total variance, but—an important point—the differences *within* groups would account for 77 percent of the total variance. When gross socioeconomic level is controlled, the average difference reduces to about 11 IQ points (Shuey, 1966, p. 519), which, it should be recalled, is about the same spread as the average difference between siblings in the same family. So-called "culture-free" or "culture-fair" tests tend to give Negroes slightly lower scores, on the average, than more conventional IQ tests such as the Stanford-Binet and Wechsler scales. Also, as a group, Negroes perform somewhat more poorly on those subtests which tap abstract abilities. The majority of studies show that Negroes perform relatively better on verbal than on nonverbal intelligence tests.

In tests of scholastic achievement, also, judging from the massive data of the Coleman study (Coleman *et al.*, 1966), Negroes score about 1 standard deviation (SD) below the average for whites and Orientals and considerably less than 1 SD below other disadvantaged minorities tested in the Coleman study—Peurto Rican, Mexican-American, and American Indian. The 1 SD decrement in Negro performance is fairly constant throughout the period from grades 1 through 12.

Another aspect of the distribution of IQs in the Negro population is their lesser variance in comparison to the white distribution. This shows up in most of the studies reviewed by Shuey. The best single estimate is probably the estimate based on a large normative study of Stanford-Binet IQs of Negro school children in five Southeastern states, by Kennedy, Van De Riet, and White (1963). They found the SD of Negro children's IQs to be 12.5, as compared with 16.4 in the white normative sample. The Negro distribution thus has only about 60 percent as much variance (i.e., SD^2) as the white distribution.

There is an increasing realization among students of the psychology of the disadvantaged that the discrepancy in their average performance cannot be completely or directly attributed to discrimination or inequalities in education. It seems not unreasonable, in view of the fact that intelligence variation has a large genetic component, to hypothesize that genetic factors may play a part in this picture. But such an hypothesis is anathema to many social scientists. The idea that the lower average intelligence and scholastic performance of Negroes could involve, not only environmental, but also genetic, factors has indeed been strongly denounced (e.g., Pettigrew, 1964). But it has been neither contradicted nor discredited by evidence.

The fact that a reasonable hypothesis has not been rigorously proved does not mean that it should be summarily dismissed. It only means that we need more appropriate research for putting it to the test. I believe such definitive research is entirely possible but has not yet been done. So all we are left with are various lines of evidence, no one of which is definitive alone, but which, viewed all together, make it a not unreasonable hypothesis that genetic factors are strongly implicated in the average Negro-white intelligence difference. The preponderance of the evidence is, in my opinion, less consistent with a strictly environmental hypothesis than with a genetic hypothesis, which, of course, does not exclude the influence of environment or its interaction with genetic factors.

We can be accused of superficiality in our thinking about this issue, I believe, if we simply dismiss a genetic hypothesis without having seriously thought about the relevance of typical findings such as the following:

FAILURE TO EQUATE NEGROES AND WHITES IN IQ AND SCHOLASTIC ABILITY

No one has yet produced any evidence based on a properly controlled study to show that representative samples of Negro and white children can be equalized in intellectual ability through statistical control of environment and education.

SOCIOECONOMIC LEVEL AND INCIDENCE OF MENTAL RETARDATION

Since in no category of socioeconomic status (SES) are a majority of children found to be retarded in the technical sense of having an IQ below 75, it would be hard to claim that the degree of environmental deprivation typically associated with lower-class status could be responsible for this degree of mental retardation. An IQ less than 75 reflects more than a lack of cultural amenities. Heber (1968) has estimated on the basis of existing evidence that IQs below 75 have a much higher incidence among Negro than among white children at every level of socioeconomic status, as shown in Table 29. In the two highest SES categories the estimated proportions of Negro and white children with

TABLE 29

<small>Estimated Prevalence of Children with IQs Below 75 by Socioeconomic Status (SES) and Race Given as Percentages (Heber, 1968)</small>

SES	White	Negro
High 1	0.5	3.1
2	0.8	14.5
3	2.1	22.8
4	3.1	37.8
Low 5	7.8	42.9

IQs below 75, are in the ratio of 13.6 to 1. If environmental factors were mainly responsible for producing such differences, one should expect a lesser Negro-white discrepancy at the upper SES levels. Other lines of evidence also show this not to be the case. A genetic hypothesis, on the other hand, would predict this effect, since the higher SES Negro offspring would be regressing to a lower population mean than their white counterparts in SES, and consequently a larger proportion of the lower tail of the distribution of genotypes for Negroes would fall below the value that generally results in phenotypic IQs below 75.

A finding reported by Wilson (1967) is also in line with this prediction. He obtained the mean IQs of a large representative sample of Negro and white children in a California school district and compared the two groups within each of four social class categories: (a) professional and managerial, (b) white collar, (c) skilled and semiskilled manual, and (d) lower class (unskilled, unemployed, or welfare recipients). The mean IQ of Negro children in the first category was 15.5 points below that of the corresponding white children in SES category 1. But the Negro mean for SES 1 was also 3.9 points below the mean of white children in SES category 4. (The IQs of white children in SES 4 presumably have "regressed" upward toward the mean of the white population.)

Wilson's data are not atypical, for they agree with Shuey's (1966, p. 520) summarization of the total literature up to 1965 on this point. She reports that in all the studies which grouped subjects by SES, upper-status Negro children average 2.6 IQ points *below* the low-status whites. Shuey comments: "It seems improbable that upper and middle-class colored children would have no more culture opportunities provided them than white children of the lower and lowest class."

Duncan (1968, p. 69) also has presented striking evidence for a much greater "regression-to-the-mean" (from parents to their children) for high status occupations in the case of Negroes than in the case of whites. None of these findings is at all surprising from the standpoint of a genetic hypothesis, of which an intrinsic feature is Galton's "law of filial regression." While the data are not necessarily inconsistent with a possible environmental interpretation, they do seem more puzzling in terms of strictly environmental causation. Such explanations often seem intemperately strained.

INADEQUACIES OF PURELY ENVIRONMENTAL EXPLANATIONS

Strictly environmental explanations of group differences tend to have an ad hoc quality. They are usually plausible for the situation they are devised to explain, but often they have little generality across situations, and new ad hoc hypotheses have to be continually devised. Pointing to environmental differences between groups is never sufficient in itself to infer a causal relationship to group differences in intelligence. To take just one example of this tendency of social scientists to attribute lower intelligence and scholastic ability to almost any environmental difference that seems handy, we can look at the evidence regarding the effects of "father absence." Since the father is absent in a significantly larger proportion of Negro than of white families, the factor of "father absence" has been frequently pointed to in the literature on the disadvantaged as one of the causes of Negroes' lower performance on IQ tests and in scholastic achievement. Yet the two largest studies directed at obtaining evidence on this very point—the only studies I have seen that are methodologically adequate—both conclude that the factor of "father absence" versus "father presence" makes no independent contribution to variance in intelligence or scholastic achievement. The sample sizes were so large in both of these studies that even a very slight degree of correlation between father absence and the measures of cognitive performance would have shown up as statistically significant. Coleman (1966, p. 506) concluded: "Absence of a father in the home did not have the anticipated effect on ability scores. Overall, pupils without fathers performed at approximately the same level as those with fathers— although there was some variation between groups" (groups referring to geographical regions of the U.S.). And Wilson (1957, p. 177) concluded from his survey of a California school district: "Neither our own data nor the preponderance of evidence from other research studies indicate that father presence or absence, *per se*, is related to school achievement. While broken homes reflect the existence of social and personal problems, and have some consequence for the development of personality, broken homes do not have any systematic effect on the overall level of school success."

The nationwide Coleman study (1966) included assessments of a dozen environmental variables and socioeconomic indices which are generally thought to be major sources of environmental influence in determining individual and group differences in scholastic performance—such factors as: reading material in the home, cultural amenities in the home, structural integrity of the home, foreign language in the home, preschool attendance, parents' education, parents' educational desires for child, parents' interest in child's school work, time spent on homework, child's self-concept (self-esteem), and so on. These factors are all correlated—in the expected direction—with scholastic performance within each of the racial or ethnic groups studied by Coleman. Yet, interestingly enough, they are not systematically correlated with differences *between* groups. For example, by far the most environmentally disadvantaged groups in the Coleman study are the American Indians. On every environmental index they average *lower* than the Negro samples, and overall their environmental rating is about as far below the Negro average as the Negro rating is below the white average. (As pointed out by Kuttner [1968, p. 707], American Indians are much more disadvantaged than Negroes, or any other minority groups in the United States, on a host of other factors not assessed by Coleman, such as income, unemployment, standards of health care, life expectancy, and infant mortality.) Yet the American Indian ability and achievement test scores average about half a standard deviation higher than the scores of Negroes. The differences were in favor of the Indian children on each of the four tests used by Coleman: nonverbal intelligence, verbal intelligence, reading comprehension, and math achievement. If the environmental factors assessed by Coleman are the major determinants of Negro-white differences that many social scientists have claimed they are, it is hard to see why such factors should act in reverse fashion in determining differences between Negroes and Indians, especially in view of the fact that *within* each group the factors are significantly correlated in the expected direction with achievement.

EARLY DEVELOPMENTAL DIFFERENCES

A number of students of child development have noted the developmental precocity of Negro infants, particularly in motoric behavior. Geber (1958) and Geber and Dean (1957) have reported this precocity also in African infants. It hardly appears to be environmental, since it is evident in nine-hour-old infants. Cravioto (1966, p. 78) has noted that the Gesell tests of infant behavioral development, which are usually considered suitable only for children over four weeks of age, "can be used with younger African, Mexican, and Guatemalan infants, since their development at two or three weeks is similar to that of Western European infants two or three times as old." Bayley's (1965a) study of a representative sample of 600 American Negro infants up to 15 months of age, using the Bayley Infant Scales of Mental and Motor Development, also found Negro infants to have significantly higher scores than white infants in their first year. The difference is largely attributable to the motor items in the Bayley test. For example, about 30 percent of white infants as compared with about 60 percent of Negro infants between 9 and 12 months were able to "pass" such tests as "pat-a-cake" muscular coordination, and ability to walk with help, to stand alone, and to walk alone. The highest scores for any group on the Bayley scales that I have found in my search of the literature were obtained by Negro infants in the poorest sections of Durham, North Carolina. The older siblings of these infants have an average IQ of about 80. The infants up to 6 months of age, however, have a Developmental Motor Quotient (DMQ) nearly one standard deviation above white norms and a Developmental IQ (i.e., the non-motor items of the Bayley scale) of about half a standard deviation above white norms (Durham Education Improvement Program, 1966–67, a, b).

The DMQ, as pointed out previously, correlates negatively in the white population with socioeconomic status and with later IQ. Since lower SES Negro and white school children are more alike in IQ than are upper SES children of the two groups (Wilson, 1967), one might expect greater DMQ differences in favor of Negro infants in high socioeconomic Negro and white samples than in low socioeconomic samples. This is just what Walters (1967) found. High SES Negro infants significantly exceeded whites in total score on the Gesell developmental schedules at 12 weeks of age, while low SES Negro and white infants did not differ significantly overall. (The only difference, on a single subscale, favored the white infants.)

It should also be noted that developmental quotients are usually depressed by adverse prenatal, perinatal, and postnatal complications such as lack of oxygen, prematurity, and nutritional deficiency.

Another relationship of interest is the finding that the negative correlation between DMQ and later IQ is higher in boys than in girls (Bayley, 1966, p. 127). Bronfenbrenner (1967, p. 912) cites evidence which shows that Negro boys perform relatively less well in school than Negro girls; the sex difference is much greater than is found in the white population. Brenfenbrenner (1967, p. 913) says, "It is noteworthy that these sex differences in achievement are observed among Southern as well as Northern Negroes, are present at every socioeconomic level, and tend to increase with age."

PHYSIOLOGICAL INDICES

The behavioral precocity of Negro infants is also paralleled by certain physiological indices of development. For example, x-rays show that bone development, as indicated by the rate of ossification of cartilage, is more advanced in Negro as compared with white babies of about the same socioeconomic background, and Negro babies mature at a lower birth weight than white babies (Naylor & Myrianthopoulos, 1967, p. 81).

It has also been noted that brain wave patterns in African newborn infants show greater maturity than is usually found in the European newborn child (Nilson & Dean, 1959). This finding especially merits further study, because there is evidence that brain waves have some relationship to IQ (Medical World News, 1968), and because at least one aspect of brain waves—the visually evoked potential—has a very significant genetic component, showing a heritability of about .80 (uncorrected for attenuation) (Dustman & Beck, 1965).

MAGNITUDE OF ADULT NEGRO-WHITE DIFFERENCES

The largest sampling of Negro and white intelligence test scores resulted from the administration of the Armed Forces Qualification Test (AFQT) to a national sample of over 10 million men between the ages of 18 and 26. As of 1966, the overall failure rate for Negroes was 68 percent as compared with 19 percent for whites (*U.S. News and World Report*, 1966). (The failure cut-off score that yields these percentages is roughly equivalent to a Stanford-Binet IQ of 86.) Moynihan (1965) has estimated that during the same period in which the AFQT was administered to these large representative samples of Negro and white male youths, approximately one-half of Negro families could be considered as middle class or above by the usual socioeconomic criteria. So even if we assumed that all of the lower 50 percent of Negroes on the SES scale failed the AFQT, it would still mean that at least 36 percent of the middle SES Negroes failed the test, a failure rate almost twice as high as that of the white population for all levels of SES.

Do such findings raise any question as to the plausibility of theories that postulate exclusively environmental factors as sufficient causes for the observed differences?

This nature-nurture issue in regard to intelligence is very much alive and will remain so. Hebb suggested in a letter to the *American Psychologist* that many of Jensen's detractors were dogmatic, emotional, and illogical but that Jensen himself had employed a "misleading" concept of heritability. The nub of Hebb's argument was that if 100 boys were reared in barrels and fed through the bunghole until, say, age 12 (as Mark Twain once proposed), their IQ variance would be essentially zero because of the homogeneity of the reading conditions and thus making it seem that heredity is all. But this statistic would overlook the fact that all the boys would probably show low IQs as a result of the environmental restriction. Jensen, in reply, stated that it is Hebb's notion of hereditability that was "confused"—in fact, was "nonsense." Hereditability proportions always refer, he wrote, to specific populations; Hebb has left consideration of the boys in the barrel the moment he begins to compare them with other boys (reared under home conditions and predicted to have a mean IQ of 100). Another determination of heritability is required for the analysis Hebb wants: an analysis of twin-pairs reared in barrels in comparison with twin-pairs reared at home and with twin-pairs reared under disparate conditions. As Jensen phrases it, in a population with such heterogeneous environments, consisting of homes and barrels, we should expect the value of h_2 (heritability) to be comparatively small, reflecting the greater variance as a result of the extreme environmental variation.

Furthermore, as Tyler remarked in her 1972 *Annual Review* article, the finding—contrary to what most people assume as true—that blacks are less handicapped on verbal than on performance tests was corroborated in a study by Caldwell and Smith (1968) involving 420 black children in the south. Verbal IQ was significantly higher than performance IQ. Wysocki and Wysocki (1969) obtained the same sort of result when testing black and white veterans, the racial differences turning out to be greater on performance than on verbal tests. And, in support of the Jensen theory, blacks scored significantly higher than whites on the digit span test. Yet Baughman and Dahlstrom (1968), in an intensive study of black and white children in a rural southern setting and utilizing the Primary Mental Abilities tests, found black children scored a little higher on the culture-fair test than on an individual test of intelligence that was more verbal in content. It is clear, writes Tyler, that the final word on pattern differences between blacks and whites has not yet been said.

Bodmer and Cavalli-Sforza, two geneticists writing in the *Scientific American* (1970) shortly after the Jensen article had appeared, do not exclude the possibility of a genetic component in the mean difference in IQ between American whites and blacks. But they state that the only way to provide strong support for this view would be a comparison of large samples of black and white children brought up in identical environments. In view of the fact of the prevalence of racial prejudice in American society, such a comparison is not currently possible.

Cronbach, in an important and recent article (1975) prepared originally for the American Academy of Arts and Sciences, has summarized the past five decades of public controversy over mental testing. He goes back to the period of World War I when, in the spring of 1917, Lewis Terman went to Washington with materials designed for a group test of intelligence which his student, Arthur Otis, had constructed. (This later became the famous Army Alpha Examination.) Today, Cronbach points out, the critics of such testing are vociferous and the Jensen controversy is perhaps the noisiest. Jensen's long article for the *Harvard Educational Review* (1969)—some 50,000 words—was put together at the request of the editors in two months. Cronbach traces the lengthy controversy that resulted and his article is well worth perusal. One of his summary paragraphs is worth quoting in full: "Since Eden, there have been uncertainties about whether knowledge is good. In the scientific ethic, and even more in the vision of social science held by the Progressives, knowledge is created to be made available. But there is a higher knowledge that records the effects of knowledge, and there is a social science still to be built that will clarify when and how knowledge is likely to be used to exploit or corrupt or dehumanize" (1975, p. 13).

▽ ▽ ▽

PART TWELVE

Measurement and
Policy Issues

ANOTHER one of the *Briefs* delivered to the CEEB's Commission on Tests was the following paper by Thresher. It addresses itself largely to the topic of admissions testing and is a plea for the abandonment of the usual psychometric orientation and, in its place, to install a student-centered testing philosophy. The core proposal here is to institute a wide range of self-administered and self-scored achievement tests and to make these available to students in large numbers. This would lead to the eventual disappearance of the Board's Scholastic Aptitude Test (SAT) and other similar college admission tests. As a starter, however, these self-scored tests would be employed as a supplement to the present College Board program. The article, and this entire point of view, is one of a growing number of protests against normative testing for purposes of college admission and grading.

Dr. Thresher, the proponent of these rather radical proposals, is Director of Admissions Emeritus at Massachusetts Institute of Technology; he also served as Vice Chairman to the CEEB's Commission on Tests.

A PROPOSAL FOR SELF-SCORED, SELF-ADMINISTERED TESTS

B. Alden Thresher

The principle of symmetry that forms the central theme of the Commission's recommendations can be implemented in a number of ways, all calculated to increase the student's knowledge and understanding of himself, the educational opportunities open to him, and the world around him. The present brief suggests a single mode that seems promising. It is not proposed that this replace all other kinds of testing, but rather that it be initiated and experimented with seriously with the idea that it might come to form an important part of the Board's armamentarium of tests. In this mode psychometry would be less central to the operation than it now is. The psychologist and statistician would remain important auxiliaries, but the teacher would be the central and determining influence to a much greater extent than at present.

Every teacher knows that the best time to get an idea across is right after students have taken a test on the subject and are keyed up, alert, and questioning. A discussion at this juncture can be unusually fruitful because it falls on prepared ground. It is unsound not to utilize this important principle. I think it is possible to go further and say it is demeaning, unethical, and educationally unsound to subject a student to a test without discussing it with him, or if this is not feasible, at least providing him with a reasoned analysis of it as soon as possible afterwards. If no discussion takes place, the student reads the signal; they are more interested in judging me that in educating me. This lack of education follow-through constitutes one of the major drawbacks of the present mode of testing. Present tests not only miss entirely the opportunity to extend and deepen understanding of the particular subject being tested. They have the more serious defect of failing to reinforce in the student the habit of questioning, discussing, developing ramifications of thought, comparing frames of reference, and viewing in more than one perspective. In general there is a complete failure to open out the subject by any play of the intellect. The habit of dropping all further concern with a topic once the "right" answer is found is damaging to the life of the mind. The student never comes within sight of the idea that no subject is ever permanently closed off from discussion, no conclusion forever final and irreversible. It is this antiintellectual effect of the prevailing test mode that constitutes the most serious defect in a system that otherwise has much to commend it. Measurement is not without its uses, but has come to crowd out other and more subtle but more important objectives.

Proposals to meet this situation have included branching tests and tests that seek to determine the student's reasons for having chosen certain answers to a previous test. These have some merit, but neither meets the central problem because no reasoned analysis ensues. The central proposal here, therefore, is that self-administered and self-scored tests be instituted and made available to students in great profusion.

The testimony heard by the Commission from teachers on test committees was most illuminating. They were doing a skilled job constructing items with real teaching merit. The more they followed their teaching impulse, the more frustrated they became, because there was no opportunity for the student to benefit from this devoted effort. Only a tiny residue of "measurement" came out of the whole process. There is a kind of tragic irony in thus setting good teachers to do a job that throws away most of their talent and skill. One could tell from their remarks that they sensed it.

Under the present proposal, every time a test committee generates a test item, they would produce an accompanying reasoned discussion about the choice of an answer. This would go beyond the simple justification for the "right" answer as now given for the illustrative questions in the explanatory booklets prepared for the tests. Possible reasons for choosing alternative answers would be discussed, taking account of how a student with a different frame of reference might approach the question. Some item analysis and pretesting statistics might be included. In other words what is now compulsively and secretively covered up would be thrown open and the student invited to participate in the exercise of reason. Both test and statistics would be put in a public domain.

Depending on the use and purpose of the test, the student's access to the reasoned explanation could be deferred by varying degrees. Two principal cases suggest themselves: (a) For truly self-administered and self-scored tests, the discussion could be put at the back of the test booklet, either with a seal or with uncut pages. The student, if he really wishes a self-appraisal, could be told to read this material, preferably as soon as possible after finishing the test. (b) For truly "adversary" testing in the present mode, with measurement the prime purpose, the discussion could be distributed to testees at the end of the test, or even sent to them later.

ADVANTAGES OF THE STUDENT-CENTERED APPROACH

1. The problem of speededness vanishes in a self-scored test except as retained at the student's option. It could and should be moderated in any tests that continue to be conducted in the completely adversary mode with the student as defendant.

2. In a self-scored test the security problem vanishes. If the student wishes to cheat, he cheats only himself and would probably also cheat at solitaire.

3. The student would no longer feel threatened or manipulated, or be a defendant in a process carried on not necessarily for his benefit. Even in the adversary version, he would not be flying completely blind.

4. The test committees could at last feel that they are functioning as teachers. Especially impressive was the testimony heard of the Commission from the history and physics people, who seemed to me to be suffering from frustration as good teachers not allowed to teach. A score is, after all, a minimum information device, and critics are undoubtedly right in objecting that this is not an adequate summary of any student, even within the limited area that the test purports to measure.

5. Self-tests and quizzes have an immense psychological appeal as is apparent from the number constantly appearing in the popular press

both in serious and frivolous contexts. To test oneself answers a deep human need. It helps the individual answer the, to him, all important question: "How am I doing?"

6. Face validity or curricular validity would be restored as a major criterion for test items, and a corresponding reduction could occur in the kind of statistical pretesting and time analysis now carried on. Along with this would go a reduction in the emphasis on precise measurement, or rather the pretense of it. Granted that evaluation has its place, it cannot be, as applied to the individual and his prospects, more than a very rough guide. Marianne Moore has put it in a nutshell: "Why dissect destiny with instruments more highly specialized than components of destiny itself?" Pyschometrics has gained an importance that should go rather to the processes of teaching and learning, not simply to their results.

7. Finally, the proposal for self-scored tests recognizes the basic principle that the best way to encourage the student to become a responsible person intellectually is to treat him as if he were one, not to fence him with safeguards that imply that he is expected to try to beat the game.

It will be objected that the proposal to accompany tests with a (printed) discussion of the question falls far short of the ideal give and take of oral face-to-face discussion. This is a valid objection, yet the proposal at least represents a vast improvement over the present system in which the student drops his answers into the void and they are never heard from again—a situation nicely calculated to stifle intellectual curiosity. It would be well worth while to experiment on a small scale with groups meeting for oral discussion within a day or two after a test. Face-to-face discussion would give an opportunity to gauge the true psychological and intellectual atmosphere in which the tests are enveloped, and would, I think, introduce a wholesome nonpsychometric element. The student, instead of being an "it," to whom an instrument is "administered" could be looked over by an experienced teacher alert to the psychodynamics of the group, and the student (probably to his amazement) could respond, react, answer back, and have his views taken seriously.

OBSTACLES AND PROBLEMS

1. By far the biggest obstacles to this proposal would be a complete reversal in the viewpoint and habits of thought characteristic of all testing organizations. These, in their whole origin and purpose are psychometrically oriented, instead of being primarily oriented to the teaching and intellectual values in tests. I would hope that the Commission on Tests might, with the co-operation of Educational Testing Service (ETS), set in motion a searching study of this problem to see how far it might be made practicable to carry out changes of the kind suggested. It will inevitably require a fresh initiative in a direction quite different

from the present. Most important of all, it will bring into consideration a range of intellectual values that by their very nature cannot be made to stand or fall by the conventional "validity study" techniques. They will have to be appraised, in the end, by a global judgment in which teachers and students participate.

2. It would be necessary to increase the output of test items enormously. I recall being shown some years ago a file at ETS containing something of the order of 100,000 reserve items for the Scholastic Aptitude Test (SAT). These presumably have not in most cases been pretested or subjected to item analysis or even to committee consideration. The policy has been to keep under lock and key a limited bank of test items carefully screened and pretested and to economize by reusing them at subsequent test administrations. This miserly and secretive policy treats knowledge as if it were a closed and secret matter, hidden from the public eye in the custody of a hieratic group. Nothing could be further from the spirit of free inquiry and universal publication.

I propose doing just the opposite. The object would be to flood the market with more test items than either student or coaching schools could possibly deal with individually, so that it would be less trouble to study the subject than to coach or memorize individual items. These would be in the public domain, protected by their great numbers. This ought to go far to put the coaching schools out of business.

To produce test items on the scale I am contemplating would require the services of a much larger number of experienced teachers and a complete restructuring of the present group of small committees, who by their own testimony to the Commission are hard put to produce even the items now needed for various dates and adminstrations. I would see this as a unique and priceless opportunity to involve actively many more teachers in the testing process, which should be the natural complement to teaching. The College Board has been plagued for years with the recurring criticism that active teachers do not feel they have any genuine part in the testing operation. The Board with all its works remains to almost all secondary school teachers a remote, inapproachable power whose actions are past understanding and are usually arbitrary and unreasonable. One can picture a new situation in which teachers in general are invitee to contribute items, subject to screening by an expanded committee. A history teacher could say to a class: "Here are some questions I have proposed to the College Board Committee. Do you want to discuss them? Perhaps one will turn up on the test." The proposal would bring Educational *Testing* Service a step nearer to becoming *Educational* Testing Service.

Pretesting and statistical item analysis would presumably still be needed, but on a reduced scale especially for the fully self-administered and self-scored tests. Greater participation by teachers would go along with greater emphasis on face validity, and a reduction of the homogenizing tendency of statistical item analysis. Measurement might be crude, but with discussion and reasoned analysis playing a part, educational ends would be better served. Even "adversary" testing might well be affected by this trend. It might well be possible to drop from Board test scores the third digit, which has always misled the public by a spurious pretense at precision.

3. Introducing self-scored tests would, I think, lead to an eventual phasing out of the College Board SAT, as contrary in principle to the teaching objective. A test that one cannot study for is an affront to the student in appearing to brand him with an evaluation that no effort of his can hope to change. The eventual phasing out of the SAT would leave a body of tests along the lines of the College Board's Achievement Tests now in use, perhaps with added subjects, perhaps with smaller and more numerous modules, and with considerable choice open to the candidate. These would continue to serve such member colleges as wished to make use of them. It is essential that no Board member college feel that anything is being forced on it unwillingly, and the SAT would presumably continue for some time, unless a general strike against it by minority group students should put it out of business.

The ETS view is that Achievement Tests have, over the years, come to be more and more like aptitude tests because there are more items on the methodology of each subject and fewer factual items. This tendency exists, yet to draw this conclusion from it puts the cart before the horse. There will be increasing need in the future for people competent in data management and in the art of learning how to learn, people who retain plasticity and mental flexibility. These qualities, methodological though they may be, will increasing constitute the subject matter of education. Aptitude tests should be reduced to achievement tests in the sense of reporting mastery of profitable knowledge and skills. For example, the Achievement Test in English Composition and the verbal sections of the SAT report simply a mastery of standard English and have a high intercorrelation.

The basic objective should be to get the student's intellect working and to make it second nature to him to use his intellect. To get a precise measurement is by comparison of secondary importance. A rough quantitative appraisal may actually be better because it is not yet known what qualities might be usefully quantified, or how much of the apparent precision in test scores is, as has been frequently alleged, spurious or premature.

4. Any proposal to phase out the SAT, the mainstay of the Board's income, must raise serious financial questions. Under the general approach proposed above, there would seem to be three mitigating factors: (a) Phasing out would be gradual, on the assumption that some member colleges would want to continue the SAT, for a time at least. (b) Then, if the SAT were eventually dropped, member colleges who might wish to

continue "adversary" testing (and this number would probably be large for some time) could make a greater use of the new Achievement Test. This use would go far to replace SAT revenues lost. (c) A more difficult problem would be maintaining a flow of the self-scored and self-administered tests to students and of financing them. The most obvious device would be to make the purchase of one or more of these prerequisite to taking an Achievement Test of the adversary type.

It would be premature to go into detail on these proposals at this stage. I believe that it is desirable, however, for the College Board to take a careful look at the broad principle involved: an increase in emphasis on the educational and intellectual aspects of testing, partly to supplement, partly to replace the exclusively measurement emphasis. Even if there should seem to be a good case for continuing tests as adverse procedures, the educational aspect could still be concurrently developed. Enlightened admissions policies in the colleges will be a prime requisite, and the Board can take the lead in encouraging them.

Self-scored and self-administered tests would ease the over-emphasis on test *scores* as an aid to guidance. Although guidance will, for a long time, require the dubious strategems of college choicemanship, it can be given also a needed impulse in the truly educational dimension. The student can begin to see that the important thing is not where he goes to college, but what he does when he gets there. He can begin to develop some critical sense about his own efforts. He can test himself or, if he wishes to retain this option, have himself tested in a manner that engages, respects and develops his growing intellectual powers. This is an introduction to the life of reason, as opposed to an attitude of "find out what they want and give it to them." I hope very much that it may be possible to work out some device that will bring some of this spirit into the Board's operations and even into testing at large. I offer the above as a first, groping effort in this direction.

RECOMMENDATIONS

It is recommended that the College Entrance Examination Board:

1. Supplement its present programs with self-administered and self-scored tests, made available to students in great profusion, and accompanied, under various degrees of delayed availability, by reasoned discussions about the choice of an answer for each item.

2. Draw teachers, particularly those in secondary schools, into large scale participation in the production both of these tests and of tests in the conventional "adversary" mode.

3. Stress face or curricular validity in the selection of test items, stress items of teaching merit.

4. Invite, experimentally at least, groups of students who have taken a test soon thereafter to participate in an oral discussion of the test under the Board's auspices.

To end on a general policy theme, we are reproducing here in its entirety a position statement of the American Psychological Assoication which clearly applies to issues such as the invasion of privacy, bias in the assessment of disadvantaged or minority groups, and other public or civil rights issues. The basic, fundamental issue running through all these issues is that of relevance. This position statement was adopted by the APA Board of Directors in January 1970, the initial draft of which was written by Dr. Leona Tyler of the University of Oregon. The statement appeared in the March 1970 issue of the *American Psychologist*. The editor of this book feels this is a fitting note upon which to conclude this volume.

PSYCHOLOGICAL ASSESSMENT AND PUBLIC POLICY

American Psychological Association

The nature of man and of society makes it necessary that we attempt to assess psychological characteristics. Individual human beings differ from one another in a variety of ways; society requires a variety of diverse contributions from its members. The more accurately we can judge each person's suitability for potential roles consistent with his interests, the more successfully a society will function. Accurate assessment brings benefits to the individual as well by enabling him to locate the particular kinds of situations in which he can function most effectively as he seeks education, employment, medical and psychological services, and fuller personal development.

In attempting to understand others and to predict how they will function under various circumstances, all of us utilize a great variety of assessment methods—observations, careful or casual, interviews, formal or informal, and comments and recommendations based on varying degrees of acquaintance with the person being judged. Specialized psychological assessment techniques have been developed as refinements on these general methods or as supplements to them. What such specialized techniques add is some indication of the validity and usefulness of the information. They also provide some degree of *standardization of conditions* under which observations are made or samples of behavior obtained and, where possible, some *quantification* of the findings. This makes possible systematic comparisons of the individual's characteristics with those of reference or norm groups. But the psychological procedures are similar in many ways to the more informal appraisals of people that constantly go on.

SPECIAL FEATURES OF PSYCHOLOGICAL ASSESSMENT

Because techniques of psychological assessment are *instruments* designed and built for specific tasks, they require specialized knowledge if they are to be used correctly. One cannot choose the most appropriate instrument for a particular purpose or make valid interpretations of the scores or protocols that respondents produce unless he possesses such knowledge. It is much more than a matter of proper administration and scoring procedures. Indeed, for conventional objective tests, little more is needed than adherence to the instructions for administering and scoring. It is the body of research information associated with an instrument that furnishes the basis for decisions about what it does and does not measure or reveal, how accurate or reliable it is under various circumstances, and what special cautions must be observed in its use.

The accumulation of this essential information requires the cooperation of large numbers of persons, persons who are not themselves being assessed for any particular purpose. Millions of men, women, and children, for example, have taken intelligence and achievement tests as participants in research projects designed to establish test validity and to develop norms. Persons in all walks of life have filled out interest inventories, attitude scales, and personality questionnaires in order to furnish the data psychologists needed to develop scoring systems and scaling procedures. A test or other standardized assessment instrument represents this total effort, not simply the intentions of its author. It cannot lead to sound inferences about an individual's characteristics unless this research has been done and the person interpreting the test is familiar with it.

Often a test is used solely as a predictor of probably successful performance, as in selecting candidates for job or school. In this case the score is treated as if it provides no information on the person's chazracteristics other than likelihood of success. No interpretations of test performance or inferences about personal characteristics are required for this kind of use. Although a practitioner employing a test for such purposes need not be familiar with the supporting research, the person responsible for prescribing its use should be.

Information derived from instruments used in psychological assessment as well as the instruments themselves become *dated*, and their significance may change markedly over time. A person's score or protocol indicates only his present status, and while it may constitute a basis for predicting future status, such predictions have not turned out to be very accurate except over short periods of time. Although dated or obsolete information should not be used for decision-making purposes, it may be valuable for research and should be retained using adequate coding procedures to protect the identity of the individual. The instruments themselves also require frequent updating to replace obsolete items and stimuli and to insure that norms are representative of the appropriate segments of the population.

A special difficulty in psychological assessment, particularly when used in employment or placement rather than treatment situations, is the problem of faking and response sets. It has been obvious from the beginning to anyone who examines a typical personality inventory or questionnaire that it is quite possible for respondents to falsify their answers. In circumstances where one wishes to make a good impression, the *social desirability* response set may have a considerable effect on the scores from which inferences are to be made. This and other effects of various response sets have been exhaustively studied, and ways of at least partially controlling them have been developed. The appropriate use of techniques for psychological assessment requires a thorough familiarity with this body of research knowledge.

Several policy implications follow from these essential features of psychological assessment. First, the individual assessed should be protected against unwarranted *inferences* by persons not equipped with the requisite background of knowledge. It cannot be expected that psychiatrists, classroom teachers, personnel managers, or heads of government agencies will have this kind of expertise, although some of them may possess it. Normally, therefore, arrangements will need to be worked out for collaboration with psychologists who have specialized in the kinds of assessments being conducted.

Second, the individual assessed should be protected against unfavorable evaluation based on obsolete information. This is a problem not peculiar to psychological assessment methods. An old letter of recommendation may be fully as damaging as a low IQ recorded on one's record, although the quantitative appearance of the latter makes it less apparent, perhaps, that it is no longer relevant. All proposals for data banks and permanent record systems must grapple with this problem and provide appropriate safeguards for verifying the accuracy of the records and for discarding periodically the obsolete information.

Third, the individual must be protected against unnecessary intrusions into his privacy. The assessment procedures used should be intelligently selected for particular purposes. Unnecessary tests should not be administered, and unnecessary questions should not be asked.

Fourth, whatever policies are set up to insure these kinds of protection should be of such a nature as to maintain conditions that will facilitate the research on which new and improved assessment procedures can be based. Flat prohibitions of certain kinds of tests or questions would retard research on the ways in which such tests and questions might be validly used. To require the destruction of all records of test scores and protocols along with the interpretations derived from them would make impossible some very significant kinds of longitudinal research on personality. The objective of whatever policies are adopted should be to protect the right of each individual to be soundly evaluated, realizing that to do this requires a constant effort to improve the techniques by means of which evaluations are made. The proper control is to vest responsibility in the person carrying out the assessment rather than to place arbitrary restrictions on the methods he is permitted to use.

ADDITIONAL PROBLEMS IN PERSONALITY ASSESSMENT

While not differing in principle from the assessment of abilities, the assessment of personality (sometimes called noncognitive) characteristics involves extra complications related to policy issues. In instruments for personality assessment, the relationship of the respondent's test behavior to his behavior in life situations is more indirect that it is in the typical ability testing situation, where the items to which he is responding are often samples of the problems he must solve in the world outside the testing room. Whether the instrument for assessing personality requires the individual to answer questions about his attitudes, symptoms, and feelings, or whether it asks him to read meaning into inkblots or tell stories about ambiguous pictures, the psychologist's task of *validating* the instrument is a complex and difficult one. The fact that there is as yet no general agreement about what the most important personality traits are adds to the difficulty.

A special problem that may arise in personality assessment is that some of the item content is drawn from areas of human experience most likely to be regarded as private, so that such assessment techniques are especially likely to raise questions about whether a respondent's right to privacy has been infringed. For a variety of reasons it has seemed necessary or important to include some inquiry into the individual's sexual and religious ideas in instruments designed for personality assessment. Interpretations of these measures are dependent on the context in which they were standardized. If there is too much deviation from the standardized contexts by eliminating items, some distortion might be introduced into interpretations.

In formulating policies to deal with these problems, the basic requirement is the one emphasized in the previous section—that decisions about what assessment procedures are to be used and how they are to be handled should be based on recommendations form persons competent to make them—ordinarily a psychologist with specialized training in assessment. It is the responsibility of organizations and agencies in which assessment is carried on to place such persons in charge of the operations. It is the responsibility of universities and colleges to educate them in such a way that they can carry out this complex task. It is the responsibility of professional societies, such as the American Psychological Association, to formulate standards and ethical codes controlling their activity. Many states have statutory procedures for qualifying psychologists who meet legally established standards of competence and ethical conduct controlling their activity. Legal proscriptions of certain kinds of tests, items, or procedures can only handicap them in their efforts to make sound, relevant judgments about individuals.

The central concept governing what information is to be obtained from a person whose characteristics are to be assessed for a particular purpose is *relevance*. In employment situations, for example, inquiry about family, sexual, or religious matters should be carried on only if its relevance to the employee's fitness for the position in question has been established; in such instances its use may be justifiable. Always, however, relevance must be weighed and justified in terms of socially accepted values and principles.

The right of an individual to decline to be assessed or to refuse to answer questions he considers improper or impertinent has never been and should not be questioned. This right should be pointed out to the examinee in the context of information about the confidentiality of the results. Whenever possible, he should be told who will have access to the information and for what purposes. The burden of proof that assessment techniques are relevant to the situation falls on the professional person responsible for the undertaking. His competence is the foundation on which the whole structure must rest.

BIBLIOGRAPHY

ALBEE, G. W. The short, unhappy life of clinical psychology. *Psychol. Today,* 1970, 4 (4), 42–43, 74–75.

ALPERT. D., & BITZER, D. L. Advances in computer-based education. *Science,* 1970, **167,** 1582–90.

AMERICAN PSYCHOLOGICAL ASSOCIATION. Job testing and the disadvantaged. *Amer. Psychologist,* 1969, **24,** 637–50.

AMERICAN PSYCHOLOGICAL ASSOCIATION: Psychological Assessment and public policy. *Amer. Psychologist,* 1970, **25,** 264–66.

AMERICAN PSYCHOLOGICAL ASSOCIATION. *Technical Recommendations for Psychological and Diagnostic Techniques.* Washington, D.C.: American Psychological Association, 1954.

AMERICAN PSYCHOLOGICAL ASSOCIATION. *Standards for Educational and Psychological Tests and Measurements.* Washington, D.C.: American Psychological Association, 1974.

ANASTASI, A. (Ed.). *Testing Problems in Perspective.* Washington, D.C.: American Council on Education, 1966.

ANASTASI, A., MEADE, M. J., & SCHNEIDERS, A. A. *The Validation of a Biographical Inventory as a Predictor of College Success.* Princeton, N.J.: Educational Testing Service, 1960.

ANDERSON, S. B. The ETS-OEO longitudinal study of disadvantaged children. In *Untangling the Tangled Web of Education.* Princeton, N.J.: Educational Testing Service, 1969.

APPEL, V., & FEINBERG, M. R. Recruiting door-to-door salesmen by mail. *J. Appl. Psychol.,* 1969, **33,** 362–66.

ASTIN, A. W. *Who Goes Where to College?* Chicago: Science Research Associates, 1965.

ASTIN, A. W., & BORUCH, R. E. A "Link" system for assuring confidentiality of research data in longitudinal studies. *ACE Research Reports,* 1969, 5 (3).

ASTIN, H. S., & MYINT, T. Career development of young women during the post-high school years. *J. Counsel. Psychol.,* 1971, **18,** 369–93.

BARNES, E. H. The relationship of biased test responses to psychopathology. *J. Abnorm. Soc. Psychol.,* 1955, **51,** 286–90.

BARNES, E. H. Response bias and the MMPI. *J. Consult. Psychol.,* 1956, **20,** 371–74.

BAUGHMAN, E. E., & DAHLSTROM, W. G. *Negro and White Children.* New York: Academic Press, 1968.

BAYLEY, N. Comparisons of mental and motor test scores for ages 1–15 months by sex, birth order, race, geographical location and education of parents. *Child Dev.,* 1965, **36,** 379–411.

BAYLEY, N. Learning in adulthood: the role of intelligence. In H. J. Klausmeier, & C. W. Harris (Eds.), *Analyses of Concept Learning.* New York: Academic Press, 1966, pp. 117–38.

BECHTOLDT, H. P. Construct validity: a critique. *Amer. Psychologist,* 1959, **14,** 619–29.

BECKER, S., LERNER, M., & CARROLL, J. Conformity as a function of birth order, payoff, and type of group pressure. *J. Abnorm. Soc. Psychol.,* 1964, **69,** 318–23.

BEHAVIORAL AND SOCIAL SCIENCES SURVEY

COMMITTEE. *The Behavioral and Social Sciences: Outlook and Needs.* Washington, D.C.: National Academy of Sciences, 1969.

BENNETT, G. K., & DOPPELT, J. E. *The Fundamental Achievement Series.* New York: Psychological Corporation, 1969.

BERDIE, R. F. Validities of the Strong Vocational Interest Blank. In W. L. Layton (Ed.), *The Strong Vocational Interest Blank: Research and Uses.* Minneapolis: University of Minnesota Press, 1960, pp. 18–61.

BEREITER, C.; & ENGLEMANN, S. *Teaching Disadvantaged Children in the Preschool.* Englewood Cliffs, N.J.: Prentice-Hall, 1966.

BERKOWITZ, L. *Aggression, a Social Psychological Analysis.* New York: McGraw-Hill, 1962.

BERKOWITZ, L., & DANIELS, L. Responsibility and dependency. *J. Abnorm. Soc. Psychol.,* 1963, **66**, 429–36.

BERKOWITZ, L., KLANDERMAN, S., & HARRIS, R. Effects of experimenter awareness and sex of subject and experimenter on reactions to dependency relationships. *Sociometry,* 1967, **27**, 327–37.

BERNSTEIN, B. Social class and linguistic development: a theory of social learning. In A. H. Halsey, J. Floyd, & C. A. Anderson (Eds.), *Education, Economy and Society.* Glencoe, Ill.: Free Press, 1961.

BETTLEHEIM, B. H. A study in rehabilitation. *J. Abnorm. Soc. Psychol.,* 1949, **44**, 231–65.

BLANK, M., & SOLOMON, F. A tutorial language program to develop abstract thinking in socially disadvantaged preschool children. *Child Dev.,* 1969, **40**, 47–61.

BLOCK, J. *The Q-sort Method in Personality Assessment and Psychiatric Research.* Springfield, Ill.: Charles C Thomas, 1961.

BLOOM, B. S. *Stability and Change in Human Characteristics.* New York: Wiley, 1964.

BLUM, M. L., & APPEL, V. Consumer versus management reaction in new package development. *J. Appl. Psychol.,* 1961, **45**, 222–24.

BODMER, W., & CAVALLI-SFORZA, L. L. Intelligence and race. *Scientific Amer.,* 1970, **223**, 19–29.

BORING, E. G. *Sensation and Perception in the History of Experimental Psychology.* New York: Appleton-Century-Crofts, 1942.

BORING, E. G. The role of theory in experimental psychology. *Amer. J. Psychol.,* 1953, **69**, 169–84.

BRAYFIELD, A. H. Congress and social science. *Amer. Psychologist,* 1967, **22**, 877–1041.

BREUER, J., & FREUD, S. *Case Histories* (original publication 1895; English translation by J. Strachey.) In J. Strachey (Ed.), *The Standard Edition of the Complete Psychological Works of Sigmund Freud.* Vol. 2, London: Hogarth Press, 1955, pp. 19–181.

BRIDGMAN, P. W. *The Logic of Modern Physics.* New York: Macmillan, 1927.

BRIM, O. G., JR., GLASS, D. C., NEULINGER, J., FIRESTONE, I. J., & LERNER, S. C. *American Beliefs and Attitudes about Intelligence.* New York: Russell Sage Foundation, 1969.

BRONFENBRENNER, U. The psychological costs of quality and equality in education. *Child Dev.,* 1967, **38**, 909–25.

BRUNER, J. S. On perceptual readiness. *Psychol. Rev.,* 1957, **64**, 123–54.

BRUNER, J. S. *Poverty and Childhood.* Merrill-Palmer Institute Monographs, 1970.

BRUNER, J. S., & TAJFEL, H. Cognitive risk and environmental change. *J. Abnorm. Soc. Psychol.,* 1961, **62**, 230–41.

BRUNSWIK, E. *Representative Design in the Planning of Psychological Research.* Berkeley: University of California Press, 1958.

BRYAN, J. H., & TEST, M. A. Models and helping: naturalistic studies in aiding behavior. *J. Pers. Soc. Psychol.,* 1967, **16**, 400–407.

BRYAN, W. L., & HARTER, N. Studies on the telegraphic language: the acquisition of a hierarchy of habits. *Psychol. Rev.,* 1899, **6**, 345–75.

BRYDEN, M. P. A non-parametric method of item and test scaling. *Educ. Psychol. Measmt.,* 1960, **20**, 311–15.

BURTT, H. E. An experimental study of early childhood memory. *J. Genet. Psychol.,* 1932, **40**, 287–95.

BURTT, H. E. An experimental study of early childhood memory: final report. *J. Genet. Psychol.*, 1941, **58**, 435–39.

BYRD, R. E. *Alone*. New York: Putnam's, 1938.

CALDWELL, B. M., WRIGHT, C. M., HONIG, A. S., & TANNENBAUM, J. Infant day care and attachment. *Amer. J. Orthopsychiatry*, 1970, **40**, 397–412.

CALDWELL, M. B., & SMITH, T. A. Intellectual structure of southern Negro children. *Psychol. Rep.*, 1968, **23**, 63–71.

CAMPBELL, D. P. The 1966 revision of the Strong Vocational Interest Blank. *Personnel & Guidance J.*, 1966, **45**, 744–49.

CAMPBELL, D. P. Stability of interests within an occupation over thirty years. *J. Appl. Psychol.*, 1966, **50**, 51–56.

CAMPBELL, D. P. *Handbook for the Strong Vocational Interest Blank*. Stanford, Calif.: Stanford University Press, 1971.

CAMPBELL, D. P. *Manual for the Strong-Campbell Interest Inventory (T325 Merged Form)*. Stanford, Calif.: Stanford University Press, 1974.

CAMPBELL, D. T. Recommendations for APA test standards regarding construct, trait, or discriminant validity. *Amer. Psychologist*, 1960, **15**, 546–53.

CAMPBELL, D. T., KRUSKAL, W. H., & WALLACE, W. P. Seating aggregation as an index of attitude. *Sociometry*, 1966, **29**, 1–15.

CAMPBELL, J. P. Personnel training and development. In P. H. Mussen, & M. R. Rosenzweig (Eds.), *Annual Review of Psychology*. Vol. 22, Palo Alto: Annual Reviews Inc., 1971., pp. 565–602.

CANNON, W. B., & WASHBURN, A. L. An explanation of hunger. *Amer. J. Psychol.*, 1912, **29**, 441–54.

CAPLOW, T. *The Sociology of Work*. Minneapolis: University of Minnesota Press, 1954.

CARKHUFF, R. R., & BERENSON, B. G. *Beyond Counseling and Therapy*. New York: Holt, Rinehart and Winston, 1967.

CATTELL, R. B. *Personality and Motivation Structure and Measurement*. Yonkers-on-Hudson, N.Y.: World Book Company, 1957.

CATTELL, R. B. *The Scientific Analysis of Personality*. Baltimore, Md.: Penguin Books, 1965.

CATTELL, R. B., SAUNDERS, D. R., & STIC, G. *Handbook for the 16 PF Questionnaire*. Champaign, Ill.: Institute for Personality and Ability Testing, 1957.

CAZDEN, C. The neglected situation. In F. Williams (Ed.), *Language and Poverty*. Chicago: Markham Press, 1970.

CENTRA, J. A. The college environment revisited: current descriptions and a comparison of three methods of assessment. *College Entrance Examination Board Research and Development Reports, RDR-70-71, 1*. Princeton, N.J.: Educational Testing Service, August 1970.

CHASE, C. I., & LUDLOW, H. G. (Eds.) *Readings in Educational and Psychological Measurement*. New York: Houghton Mifflin, 1966.

CHOMSKY, N. *Cartesian Linguistics*. New York: Harper & Row, 1966.

CLARK, W. W., & TIEGS, E. W. *Technical Report on the California Achievement Tests, 1957 Edition*. Los Angeles: California Test Bureau, 1958.

COHEN, L. D., KIPNIS, D., KUNKLE, E. C., & KUBZANSKY, P. E. Observations of a person with congenital insensitivity to pain. *J. Abnorm. Soc. Psychol.*, 1955, **51**, 333–38.

COLE, M., GAY, J., GLICK, J., & SHARP, D. W. *The Cultural Context of Learning and Thinking*. New York: Basic Books, 1971.

COLLEGE ENTRANCE EXAMINATION BOARD. *Report of the Commission on Tests: I. Righting the Balance, II. Briefs*. Princeton, N.J.: 1970.

COLEMAN, J. S. et al. *Equality of Educational Opportunity*. Washington, D.C.: U.S. Department of Health, Education and Welfare, 1966.

COMREY, A. L. An operational approach to some problems in psychological measurement. *Psychol. Rev.*, 1950, **57**, 217–28.

COMREY, A. L. Mental testing and the logic of measurement. *Educ. Psychol. Measmt.*, 1951, **11**, 323–34.

COOKE, M. K., & KIESLER, D. J. Prediction of college students who later require personal counseling. *J. Counsel. Psychol.*, 1967, **14**, 346–49.

COOLEY, W. W. *Career Development of Sci-*

entists. Cambridge, Mass.: Harvard Graduate School of Education, 1963.

COOLEY, W. W. A computer-measurement system for guidance. *Harvard Educ. Rev.*, 1964, **34**, 559–72.

COOLEY, W. W., & GLASER, R. The computer and individualized instruction. *Science*, 1969, **166**, 574–82.

COOLEY, W. W., & LOHNES, P. R. *Multivariate Procedures for the Behavioral Sciences.* New York: Wiley, 1962.

COULSON, J. E., & COGSWELL, J. F. Effects of individualized instruction on testing. *J. Educ. Measmt.*, 1965, **1**, 59–64.

CRAVIOTO, J. Malnutrition and behavioral development in the preschool child. *Preschool Child Malnutrition,* National Health Science, Public, 1966, 1282.

CRONBACH, L. J. Response sets and test validity. *Educ. Psychol. Measmt.*, 1946, **6**, 475–94.

CRONBACH, L. J. Further evidence on response sets and test design. *Educ. Psychol. Measmt.*, 1950, **10**, 3–31.

CRONBACH, L. J. Assessment of individual differences. *Annu. Rev. Psychol.*, 1956, **7**, 173–96.

CRONBACH, L. J. *Essentials of Psychological Testing.* New York: Harpers, 1949.

CRONBACH, L. J. Five decades of public controversy over mental testing. *Amer. Psychologist.*, 1975, **30**, 1–14.

CRONBACH, L. J., & GLESER, G. C. *Psychological Tests and Personnel Decisions* (2nd ed.). Urbana: University of Illinois Press, 1965.

CULLER, E., & METTLER, F. A. Conditioned behavior in a decorticate dog. *J. Comp. Psychol.*, 1934, **18**, 291–303.

CURETON, E. E. Validity, reliability, and baloney. *Educ. Psychol. Measmt.*, 1950, **10**, 94–96.

DANET, B. N. Prediction of mental illness in college students on the basis of "nonpsychiatric" MMPI profiles. *J. Consult. Psychol.*, 1965, **29**, 577–80.

DARLEY, J., & LATANÉ, B. Bystander intervention in emergencies: diffusion of responsibility. *J. Pers. Soc. Psychol.*, 1967, **6**, 400–07.

DATEL, W. E. Socialization scale norms on military samples. *Military Med.*, 1962, **127**, 740–44.

DECHARMS, R., & MOELLER, G. Values ex-

pressed in American children's readers: 1800–1950. *J. Abnorm. Soc. Psychol.*, 1962, **64**, 136–42.

DEUTSCH, M. *The Disadvantaged Child.* New York: Basic Books, 1967.

DINGLE, H. Book review of *Measurement: Definitions and Theories,* edited by C. W. Churchman and P. Ratoosh. *Scientific Amer.*, 1960, **202**, 189–92.

DISPENZIERI, A., GINIGER, S., REICHMAN, W., & LEVY, M. College performance of disadvantaged students as a function of ability and personality. *J. Counsel. Psychol.* 1971, **18**, 298–305.

DOMINO, G. *Personality patterns and choice of medical speciality.* Unpublished Ph.D. dissertation, University of California, Berkeley, 1967.

DRAKE, L. E. Interpretation of MMPI profiles in counseling male clients. *J. Counsel. Psychol.*, 1956, **3**, 83–88.

DRAKE, L. E. MMPI patterns predictive of underachievement. *J. Counsel. Psychol.*, 1962, **9**, 164–67.

DRAKE, L. E., & OETTING, E. R. An MMPI pattern and a suppressor variable predictive of academic achievement. *J. Counsel. Psychol.*, 1957, **4**, 245–47.

DRASGOW, J., & BARNETTE, W. L., JR. F—K in a motivated group. *J. Consult. Psychol.*, 1957, **21**, 399–401.

DREGER, R. M., & MILLER, K. S. Comparative psychological studies of Negroes and whites in the United States. *Psychol. Bull.*, 1960, **57**, 361–402.

DROEGE, R. C., SHOWLER, W., BEMIS, S., & HAWK, J. Development of a nonreading edition of the General Aptitude Test Battery. *Measmt. Eval. Guidance,* 1970, **3**, 45–53.

DUBOIS, P. H. A test-dominated society: China, 115 B.C.–1905 A.D. *Proceedings of the 1964 Invitational Conference on Testing Problems.* Princeton, N.J.: Educational Testing Service, 1965, pp. 3–11.

DUKES, W. F. $N = 1$. *Psychol. Bull.*, 1965, **64**, 74–79.

DUNCAN, O. D., FEATHERMAN, D. L., & DUNCAN, B. *Socioeconomic background and educational achievement: extensions of a basic model.* Final Report, Project 5-0074, U.S. Department of Health, Education and Welfare, May 1968.

DUNN, J. A. The accomodation of individual differences in the development of personal programs of study. In J. C. Flanagan (Chairman), *Project PLAN: a computer-supported individualized education program.* Symposium presented at the meeting of the American Psychological Association, Washington, D.C., September 1969.

DURHAM EDUCATIONAL IMPROVEMENT PROGRAM, 1966–1967.(a)

DURHAM EDUCATIONAL IMPROVEMENT PROGRAM, RESEARCH, 1966–1967.(b)

DUSTMAN, R. E., & BECK, E. C. The visually evoked potential in twins. *Electroencephalogr. Clin. Neurophysiol.,* 1965, **19**, 570–75.

DVORAK, B. J. Differential occupational ability patterns. *Bull. Emplyt. Stabilization Res. Inst.,* 1953, **3**, (8). Minneapolis: University of Minnesota Press.

DVORAK, B. J. The general aptitude test battery. *Personnel & Guidance J.,* 1956, **35**, 145–52.

EBBINGHAUS, H. *Uber das Gedächtnis.* Leipzig: Duncker & Humblot, 1885. (*Memory: A Contribution to Experimental Psychology.* English translation by H. A. Ruger and C. E. Bussenius. New York: Teachers College, Columbia University, 1913.)

EBEL, R. L. Standardized achievement tests: uses and limitations. *National Elementary Principal,* 1961, **40**, 29–32.

EHRLE, R. A. Quantification of biographical data for predicting vocational rehabilitation success. *J. Appl. Psychol.,* 1964, **48**, 171–74.

EHRLICH, M. *The Selective Role of Aggression in Concept Formation.* Unpublished Ph.D. thesis, New York University, 1961.

EIFERMANN, R. *School Children's Games.* Washington, D.C.: Department of Health, Education and Welfare, 1968.

EISEN, N. H. Some effects of early sensory deprivation on later behavior: the quondam hard-of-hearing child. *J. Abnorm. Soc. Psychol.,* 1962, **65**, 338–42.

ENGLISH, H. B., & ENGLISH, A. *A Comprehensive Dictionary of Psychological and Psychoanalytical Terms.* New York: Longmans, Green, 1958.

ERIKSON, E. Identity and uprootedness in our time. In E. Erikson (Ed.), *Insight and Responsibility.* New York: Norton, 1964.

EVANS, J. Miller. *J. Abnorm. Soc. Psychol.,* 1950, **45**, 359–79.

FENZ, W. D., & EPSTEIN, S. Gradients of physiological arousal in parachutists as a function of approaching jump. *Psychosom. Med.,* 1967, **29**, 33–51.

FERGUSON, R. L. *Computer-assisted criterion-referenced testing.* Working Paper 49, Learning Research and Development Center, University of Pittsburgh, 1969.

FLANAGAN, J. C., & COOLEY, W. W. *Project TALENT One-Year Followup Studies.* University of Pittsburgh, School of Education, 1966.

FLANAGAN, J. C., DAILEY, J. T., SHAYCOFT, M. F., GORHAM, W. A., ORR, D. B., & GOLDBERG, I. *Design for a Study of American Youth.* Boston: Houghton Mifflin, 1962.

FLANAGAN, J. C., DAILEY, J. T., SHAYCOFT, M. F., GORHAM, W. A., ORR, D. B., GOLDBERG, I., & NEYMAN, C. A. *The American High-School Student.* Pittsburgh: Project TALENT Office, 1964.

FLANAGAN, J. C., TIEDEMAN, D. V., WILLIS, M. B., & McLAUGHLIN, D. H. *The Career Data Book.* Palo Alto, Calif.: American Institutes for Research, 1973.

FLAVELL, J. H., & WOHLWILL, J. F. Formal and functional aspects of cognitive development. In D. Elkind, & J. H. Favell (Eds.), *Studies in Cognitive Development.* New York: Oxford University Press, 1969.

FLYNN, J. T., & GARBER, H. (Eds.) *Assessing Behavior: Readings in Educational and Psychological Measurement.* Reading, Mass.: Addison-Wesley, 1967.

FRANK, J. D. Discussion of H. J. Eysenck, "The effects of psychotherapy." *Int. J. Psychiatry,* 1965, **1**, 288–90.

FRANK, J. D., GLIEDMAN, L. H., IMBER, S. D., STONE, A. R., & NASH, E. H. Patient's expectancies and relearning as factors determining improvement in psychotherapy. *Amer. J. Psychiatry,* 1958, **115**, 961–68.

FREEBERG, N. E. Assessment of disadvantaged adolescents: a different approach to research and evaluation measures. *J. Educ. Psychol.,* 1970, **61**, 229–40.

FRIEDLANDER, F., & GREENBERG, S. Effect of job attitudes, training, and organization climate on performance of the hardcore unemployed. *J. Appl. Psychol.*, 1971, 55, 287–95.

GAGNE, R. M. Contributions of learning to human development. *Psychol. Rev.*, 1968, 75, 177–91.

GALTON, F. *Hereditary Genius*. New York: Appleton, 1870.

GARFIELD, S. L., & AFFLECK, D. C. A study of individuals committed to a state home for the retarded who were later released as not mentally defective. *Amer. J. Ment. Defic.*, 1960, 64, 907–15.

GAY, J., & COLE, M. *The New Mathematics and an Old Culture*. New York: Holt, Rinehart and Winston, 1967.

GEBER, M. The psycho-motor development of African children in the first year, and the influence of maternal behavior. *J. Soc. Psychol.*, 1958, 47, 185–95.

GEBER, M., & DEAN, R. F. A. The state of development of newborn African children. *Lancet*, 1957, 1, 1216–19.

GEISSER, S. A note on McQuitty's index of concomitance. *Educ. Psychol. Measmt.*, 1958, 18, 125–28.

GHISELLI, E. E. *The Validity of Occupational Aptitude Tests*. New York: Wiley, 1966.

GOLD, R. Janitors versus tenants: a status-income dilemma. *Amer. J. Sociology*, 1952, 58, 486–93.

GLADWIN, T. *East is a Big Bird*. Cambridge: Belnap Press, 1970.

GOFFMAN, E. The neglected situation. In J. Gomperz, & D. Hymes (Eds.), The ethology of communication. *Amer. Anthrop.*, 1964, 66 (6, Part 2), 133–36.

GOLDBERG, L. R. Review of the California Psychological Inventory. In O. K. Buros, (Ed.), *Seventh Mental Measurements Yearbook*. Highland Park, N.J., Gryphon Press, 1972, p. 49.

GOLDMAN, M., HORWITZ, M., & LEE, F. L. Alternative classroom standards concerning management of hostility and effects on student learning. *ONR Technical Report*, Washington, D.C.: Office of Naval Research, 1954.

GOLDSCHMID, M. L. The prediction of college major in the sciences and the humanities by means of personality tests.

Unpublished Ph.D. dissertation, University of California, Berkeley, 1965.

GOLDSMITH, D. B. The use of personal history blanks as a salesmanship test. *J. Appl. Psychol.*, 1922, 6, 149–55.

GOODSTEIN, L. D. Save the baby ... and some of the bathwater. *Prof. Psychol.*, 1970, 1, 271–74.

GOODSTEIN, L. D. Review of Iscoe and Spielberger (Eds.), "Community Psychology: Perspectives in Training and Research." *Contemp. Psychol.*, 1971, 16, 503–05.

GOUGH, H. G. The F minus K dissimulation index for the Minnesota Multiphasic Personality Inventory. *J. Consult. Psychol.*, 1950, 14, 408–13.

GOUGH, H. G. *Manual for the California Psychological Inventory*. Palo Alto, Calif.: Consulting Psychologists Press, 1957.

GOUGH, H. G. Theory and measurement of socialization. *J. Consult. Psychol.*, 1960, 24, 23–30.

GOUGH, H. G. A cross-cultural analysis of the CPI femininity scale. *J. Consult. Psychol.*, 1966, 30, 136–41.

GOUGH, H. G. Appraisal of social maturity by means of the CPI. *J. Abnorm. Psychol.*, 1966, 71, 189–95.

GOUGH, H. G. Graduation from high school as predicted from the California Psychological Inventory. *Psychol. Schools*, 1966, 3, 208–16.

GOUGH, H. G., & SANDHU, H. S. Validation of the CPI socialization scale in India. *J. Abnorm. Soc. Psychol.*, 1964, 68, 544–47.

GOUGH, H. G., WENK, E. A., & ROZYNKO, V. A. Parole outcome as predicted from the CPI, the MMPI and a base expectancy index. *J. Abnorm. Psychol.*, 1965, 70, 432–41.

GRANT, D. L., & BRAY, D. W. Validation of employment tests for telephone company installation and repair occupations. *J. Appl. Psychol.*, 1970, 54, 7–14.

GREENBERG, J. *Universals of Language*. Cambridge: M. I. T. Press, 1963.

GRONLUND, N. E. *Readings in Measurement and Evaluation*. New York: Macmillan, 1968.

GUION, R. M. Personnel selection. *Annu. Rev. Psychol.*, 1967, 18, 191–216.

HAGGARD, E. A. Isolation and personality. In P. Worchel & D. Byrne (Eds.), *Personality Change*. New York: Wiley, 1964, pp. 433–69.

HARLOW, H. F. The development of learning in the rhesus monkey. *Amer. Scientist*, 1959, 47, 459–79.

HARRIS, F. R. National Social Science Foundation: proposed Congressional mandate for the social sciences. *Amer. Psychologist*, 1967, 22, 904–10.

HARTSHORN, H., & MAY, M. A. *Studies in Deceit*. New York: Macmillan, 1928.

HARTSHORN, H., & MAY, M. A. *Studies in Service and Self Control*. New York: Macmillan, 1929.

HARTSHORN, H., & MAY, M. A. *Studies in the Organization of Character*. New York: Macmillan, 1930.

HATHAWAY, S. R. A coding system for MMPI profiles. *J. Consult. Psychol.*, 1947, 11, 334–47.

HATHAWAY, S. R., & McKINLEY, J. C. *Manual for the Minnesota Multiphasic Personality Inventory*. New York: Psychological Corporation, 1943.

HATHAWAY, S. R. & MONACHESI, E. D. *Analyzing and Predicting Juvenile Delinquency with the MMPI*. Minneapolis: University of Minnesota Press, 1953.

HAYES, K. J., & HAYES, C. Imitation in a home-raised chimpanzee. *J. Comp. Physiol. Psychol.*, 1952, 45, 450–59.

HEBER, R. Research on education and habilitation of the mentally retarded. Peabody College, Nashville, Tenn., June 1968.

HEINEMANN, E. G. Photographic measurement of the retinal image. *Amer. J. Psychol.*, 1961, 74, 440–45.

HELLER, K., MYERS, R. A., & KLINE L. V. Interviewer behavior as a function of standardized client roles. *J. Consult. Psychol.*, 1963, 37, 117–22.

HELM, C. Computer simulation techniques for research on guidance problems. *Personnel & Guidance J.*, 1967, 46, 47–52.

HERTZIG, M. E., BIRCH, H. G., THOMAS, A., & MENDEZ, O. A. Class and ethnic differences in the responsiveness of preschool children to cognitive demands. *Monogr. Soc. Res. Child Dev.* 1968, 33 (1, Serial 117).

HOCH, E. L., ROSS, A. O., & WINDER, C. L. Conference on the psychological preparation of clinical psychologists: a summary. *Amer. Psychol.*, 1966, 21, 42–51.

HODGSON, J. D., & BRENNER, M. H. Successful experience: training hard core unemployed. *Harvard Bus. Rev.*, 1968, 46 (5), 148–56.

HOLLAND, J. L. Explorations of a theory of vocational choice and achievement: II. A four-year prediction study. *Psychol. Rep.*, 1963, 15, 547–94.

HOLLAND, J. L. *Making Vocational Choices*. Englewood Cliffs, N.J.: Prentice-Hall, 1973, 125–159.

HOLTZMAN, W. H., DIAZ-GUERRERO, R., SWARTZ, J. D., & LARA TAPIA, L. Cross-cultural longitudinal research on child development: studies of American and Mexican school children. In J. P. Hill (Ed.), *Minnesota Symposia on Child Psychology*. Vol. 2. University of Minnesota Press, 1969, 125–159.

HUNT, H. F. The effect of deliberate deception on the Minnesota Multiphasic Personality Inventory. *J. Consult. Psychol.*, 1948, 12, 396–402.

ILG, F. L., & AMES, L. B. *School Readiness*. New York: Harper & Row, 1964.

ISCOE, I., & SPIELBERGER, C. D. (Eds.), *Community Psychology: Perspectives in Training and Research*. New York: Appleton-Century-Crofts, 1970.

JACOBSON, E. Electrical measurements of neuromuscular states during mental activities: VI. A note on mental activities concerning an amputated limb. *Amer. J. Physiol.*, 1931, 96, 122–25.

JENSEN, A. R. How much can we boost IQ and scholastic achievement? *Harvard Educ. Rev.*, 1969, 39, 1–123.

JENSEN, A. R. *Educability and Group Differences*. New York: Harper & Row, 1973.

JENSEN, M. B. Mental deterioration following carbon monoxide poisoning. *J. Abnorm. Soc. Psychol.*, 1950, 45, 146–53.

JONES, M. C. A laboratory study of fear: the case of Peter. *J. Genet. Psychol.*, 1924, 31, 308–15.

KAGAN, J. Inadequate evidence and illogical conclusions. *Harvard Educ. Rev.*, 1969, 39, 274–77.

KAGAN, J., & KAGAN, N. Individuality

and cognitive performance. In P. Mussen (Ed.), *Manual of Child Psychology*. New York: Wiley, 1970.

KATZ, I., ROBERTS, O. S., & ROBINSON, J. M. Effects of difficulty, race of administrator, and instructions on Negro digit-symbol performance. *ONR Technical Report*, Washington, D.C.: Office of Naval Research, 1963.

KATZ, I., ROBINSON, J. M., EPPS, E. G., & WALY, P. The influence of race of the experimenter and instructions upon the expression of hostility by Negro boys. *J. Soc. Issues*, 1964, 20, 54–59.

KAY, B. R. The use of critical incidents in a forced-choice scale. *J. Appl. Psychol.*, 1959, 43, 269–70.

KELLOGG, W. N., & KELLOGG, L. *The Ape and the Child*. New York: McGraw-Hill, 1933.

KELLY, E. L. Review of the California Psychological Inventory. In O. K. Buros (Ed.), *Sixth Mental Measurements Yearbook*. Highland Park, N.J.: Gryphon Press, 1965, pp. 168–70.

KELLY, J. G. Review of Stern's "People in Context." *Contemp. Psychol.*, 1971, 16, 320–23.

KENNEDY, W. A., VAN, DE RIET, V., & WHITE, J. C., JR. A normative sample of intelligence and achievement of Negro elementary school children in the Southeastern United States. *Monogr. Soc. Res. Child Dev.*, 1963, 28, (6).

KIRCHNER, W. K., & DUNNETTE, M. D. Applying the weighted application blank technique to a variety of office jobs. *J. Appl. Psychol.*, 1957, 41, 206–208.

KIRK, B. Extra-measurement use of tests in counseling. *Personnel & Guidance J.*, 1961, 39, 658–61.

KIRKPATRICK, II., J., EWEN, R. B., BARRETT, R. S., & KATZELL, R. A. *Testing and Fair Employment*. New York: New York University Press, 1968.

KLAUS, R., & GRAY, S. The early training project for disadvantaged children: a report after five years. *Mongr. Soc. Res. Child Dev.*, 1968, 33, (4).

KLEIN, G. S., BARR, H. L., & WOLITSKY, D. L. Personality. *Annu. Rev. Psychol.*, 1967, 18, 467–560.

KLEINMUNTZ, B. MMPI decision rules for the identification of college maladjustment: a digital computer approach. *Psychol. Monogr.*, 1963, 77, (Whole No. 577).

KLUCKHOLM, F. R. Dominant and substitutive profiles of cultural orientations: their significance for the analysis of social stratification. *Soc. Forces*, 1950, 28, 376–93.

KOGAN, N., & WALLACH, M. A. *Risk-Taking: A Study in Cognition and Personality*. New York: Holt, Rinehart & Winston, 1964.

KOHL, H. *36 Children*. New York: New American Library, 1967.

KREBS, D. L. Altruism—an examination of the concept and a review of the literature. *Psychol. Bull.*, 1970, 73, 258–302.

KROEBER, A. L. *Anthropology*. New York: Harcourt, Brace, 1948.

KUTTNER, R. E. Biochemical anthropology. In R. E. Kuttner (Ed.), *Race and Modern Science*. New York: Social Science Press, 1967, pp. 197–222.

LABOV, W. The logical non-standard English. In F. Williams (Ed.), *Language and Poverty*. Chicago: Markham Press, 1970.

LAWLER, E. E., III, & HACKMAN, J. R. Impact of employee participation in the development of pay incentive plans: a field experiment. *J. Appl. Psychol.*, 1969, 53, 467–71.

LEFCOURT, H. M. Serendipitous validity study of Gough's Social Maturity Index. *J. Consult. Clin. Psychol.*, 1968, 32, 85–86.

LENNEBERG, E. H. Understanding language without ability to speak: a case report. *J. Abnorm. Soc. Psychol.*, 1962, 65, 419–25.

LESHNER, S. S. *Situational evaluation of sub-marginal claimants*. In "Documents of Interest to Vocational Consultants," Section VI, U.S. Department of Health, Education and Welfare, Social Security Administration, Bureau of Hearings and Appeals. Mimeographed, November 1965.

LÉVI-STRAUSS, C. *Structural Anthropology*. New York: Basic Books, 1963.

LINDEMANN, J. E., FAIRWEATHER, G. W., STONE, G. B., SMITH, R. S., & LONDON, I. T. The use of demographic characteristics in predicting length of neuropsychiatric hospital stay. *J. Consult. Psychol.*, 1959, **23**, 85–89.

LIPE, D. Trait validity of airline stewardess performance ratings. *J. Appl. Psychol.*, 1970, **54**, 347–52.

LORD, F. Some test theory for tailored testing. In W. H. Holtzman (Ed.), *Computer-assisted Instruction, Testing and Guidance.* New York: Harper & Row, 1970.

LORGE, I. Gen-like: halo or reality. *Psychol. Bull.*, 1937, **34**, 545–46.

MAAS, J. B. Patterned scales expectation interview: reliability studies on a new technique. *J. Appl. Psychol.*, 1965, **49**, 431–33.

MACKINNON, D. W. The personality correlates of creativity: a study of American architects. In G. E. Nelson (Ed.), *Proceedings of the XIV International Congress of Applied Psychology.* Copenhagen: 1961, Vol. 2, pp. 11–39.

MACMEEKAN, A. M. *The Intelligence of a Representative Group of Scottish Children.* London: University of London Press, 1940.

MANDELL, M. Selecting chemists for the federal government. *Personnel Psychol.*, 1957, **41**, 206–8.

MARTIN, W. A. P. Competitive examinations in China. *N. Amer. Rev.*, 1870, **111**, 62–77.

MASLING, J. The effects of warm and cold interaction on the interpretation of a projective protocol. *J. Proj. Tech.*, 1957, **31**, 377–83.

MASLING, J. The effects of warm and cold interaction on the administration and scoring of an intelligence test. *J. Consult. Psychol.*, 1959, **25**, 336–41.

MAYFIELD, E. C. The selection interview—a re-evaluation of published research. *Personnel Psychol.*, 1964, **17**, 239–60.

MCARTHUR, C. Long-term validity of the Strong Interest Test in two subcultures. *J. Appl. Psychol.*, 1954, **38**, 346–53.

MCCURDY, H. G. La belle dame sans merci. *Charact. & Pers.*, 1944, **13**, 166–77.

MCGRATH, J. J. Improving credit evaluation with a weighted application blank. *J. Appl. Psychol.*, 1960, **44**, 325–26.

MCNEMAR, Q. Sampling in psychological research. *Psychol. Bull.*, 1940, **37**, 331–65.

MCNEMAR, Q. *Psychological Statistics* (3rd ed.), New York: Wiley, 1962.

MCNEMAR, Q. Lost: our intelligence: Why? *Amer. Psychologist*, 1964, **19**, 871–82.

MCREYNOLDS, P. (Ed.) *Advances in Psychological Assessment.* Vol. 1, Palo Alto, Calif.: Science and Behavior Books, 1968.

MEEHL, P. E. *Clinical versus Statistical Prediction.* Minneapolis: University of Minnesota Press, 1954.

MEEHL, P. E. When shall we use our heads instead of the formula? *J. Consult. Psychol.*, 1957, **4**, 268–73.

MEEHL, P. E. The cognitive activity of the clinician. *Amer. Psychol.*, 1960, **15**, 19–27.

MEGARGEE, E. I. (Ed.). *Research in Clinical Assessment.* New York: Harper & Row, 1966.

MEGARGEE, E. I. *The California Psychological Inventory Handbook.* San Francisco: Jossey-Bass, 1972.

MEHLER, J., & BEVER, T. The study of competence in cognitive psychology. *Int. J. Psychol.*, 1968, **3**, 273–80.

MEHRENS, W. A., & EBEL, R. L. *Principles of Educational and Psychological Measurement.* Chicago: Rand McNally, 1967.

MERRIT, C. B., & FOWLER, R. G. The pecuniary honesty of the public at large. *J. Abnorm. Soc. Psychol.*, 1948, **43**, 90–93.

MILLS, R. B., MCDEVITT, R. J., & TONKIN, S. Situational tests in metropolitan police recruit selection. *J. Crim. Law, Criminology & Police Sci.*, 1966, **57**, 99–106.

MISCHEL, W. Theory and research on the antecedents of self-imposed delay of reward. In B. A. Maher (Ed.), *Progress in Experimental Personality Research.* Vol. 3, New York: Academic Press, 1966.

MIZUSHIMA, K., & DE VOS, G. An application of the California Psychological Inventory in a study of Japanese delinquency. *J. Soc. Psychol.*, 1967, **71**, 45–51.

MOORE, B. M., HOLTZMAN, W. H. *Tomorrow's Parents.* Austin: University of Texas Press, 1965.

MOSHER, R. I., CARLE, R. F., & KEHAS, C. D. *Guidance: An Examination.* New York: Harcourt Brace, 1965.

MOYNIHAN, D. P. *The Negro Family*. Washington, D.C.: Office of Policy Planning and Research, U.S. Department of Labor, 1965.

MURPHY, G. *Historical Introduction to Modern Psychology*. New York: Harcourt Brace, 1949.

NARROL, H. H., & LEVITT, E. E. Formal assessment procedures in police selection. *Psychol. Rep.*, 1963, 12, 691–94.

NAYLOR, A. E., & MYRIANTHOPOULOS, N. C. The relation of ethnic and selected socioeconomic factors to human birthweight. *Ann. Hum. Genet.*, 1967, 31, 71–83.

ORNE, M. T. On the social psychology of the psychological experiment: with particular reference to demand characteristics and their implications. *Amer. Psychologist*, 1962, 17, 776–83.

ORTAR, G. R. The transfer of psychological diagnostic measures from one culture to another. *Acta Psychol.*, 1963, 21, 218–30.

OSEAS, L. "Give the first natural answer." *J. Counsel. Psychol.*, 1966, 13, 454–58.

OSS ASSESSMENT STAFF. *Assessment of Men*. New York: Rinehart, 1948.

PACE, C. R. Methods of describing college cultures. *Teach. Coll. Rec.*, 1962, 63, 267–77.

PACE, C. R. *Preliminary Technical Manual for CUES: College & University Environment Scales*. Princeton, N.J.: Educational Testing Service, 1963.

PACE, C. R. Selective higher education for diverse students. In E. J. McGrath (Ed.), *Universal Higher Education*. New York: McGraw-Hill, 1966.

PACE, C. R. A program for providing information about colleges to applicants. In *Report of the Commission on Tests: II. Briefs*. New York: College Entrance Examination Board, 1970, pp. 87–97.

PAGE, E. B. The imminence of grading essays by computer. *Phi Delta Kappan*, 1966, 47, 238–43.

PAGE, E. B. Grading essays by computer: progress report. *Proceedings of the 1966 Invitational Conference on Testing Problems*. Princeton, N.J.: Educational Testing Service, 1967, pp. 87–100.

PAYNE, D. A., & McMORRIS, R. F. *Educational and Psychological Measurement: Contributions to Theory and Practice*. Waltham, Mass.: Blaisdell Publishing Company, 1967.

PERVIN, L. A. A twenty-college study of student and college interaction using the TAPE (transactional analysis of personality and environment): rationale, reliability and validity. *J. Educ. Psychol.*, 1967, 58, 290–302.

PETERSON, D. R., QUAY, H. C., & ANDERSON, A. C. Extending the construct validity of a socialization scale. *J. Consult. Psychol.*, 1959, 23, 182.

PIERCE, R. C. Note on testing conditions. *J. Consult. Psychol.*, 1963, 27, 536–37.

PILIAVIN, I. M., RODIN, J., & PILIAVAN, J. A. Good Samaritanism: an underground phenomenon? *J. Pers. Soc. Psychol.*, 1969, 13, 289–99.

PRICE-WILLIAMS, D. R. A. A study concerning concepts of conservation of quantities among primitive children, *Acta Psychol.*, 1961, 18, 297–305.

PRINCE, M. *The Dissociation of a Personality*. New York: Longmans, Green, 1905.

RAPAPORT, D. *Diagnostic Psychological Testing*. Chicago: Year Book Publishers, 1946.

RICHARDSON, M. W. The relation between the difficulty and the differential validity of a test. *Psychometrika*, 1936, 1, 33–49.

ROBY, K. E. A voice against computer correction of themes. *The Maine Teacher*, 1966, 27, 19–20.

ROHRER, J. H. *Human Adjustment to Antarctic Isolation*. Arlington, Va.: Armed Services Technical Information Agency Publication AD 246610, 1960.

ROSEN, E. George X: the self-analysis of an avowed fascist. *J. Abnorm. Soc. Psychol.*, 1949, 44, 528–40.

ROSEN, H., & TURNER, J. Effectiveness of two orientation approaches in hard-core unemployed turnover and absenteeism. *J. Appl. Psychol.*, 1971, 55, 296–301.

ROSENBAUM, M., & BLAKE, R. Volunteering as a function of field structure. *J. Abnorm. Soc. Psychol.*, 1955, 50, 193–96.

ROSENTHAL, R. Experimenter attributes as determinants of subjects' responses. *J. Proj. Tech.*, 1963, 27, 324–31.

ROSENTHAL, R. Experimenter outcome-orientation and the results of the psychological experiment. *Psychol. Bull.*, 1964, 61, 405–12.

ROSENTHAL, R. Covert communication in the psychological experiment. *Psychol. Bull.*, 1967, 67, 356–67.

ROSENTHAL, R., & JACOBSON, L. *Pygmalion in the Classroom.* New York: Holt, Rinehart and Winston, 1968.

ROSENWALD, G. C. The assessment of anxiety in psychological experiments. *J. Abnorm. Soc. Psychol.*, 1961, 63, 666–73.

ROTTER, J. B. *Clinical Psychology* (2nd ed.). Englewood Cliffs, N.J.: Prentice-Hall, 1971.

ROWE, P. M. Individual differences in selection decisions. *J. Appl. Psychol.*, 1963, 47, 304–307.

RUCH, F. L. A technique for detecting attempts to fake performance on the self-inventory type of personality test. In Q. McNemar & M. A. Merrill (Eds.), *Studies in Personality.* New York: McGraw-Hill, 1942, pp. 229–34.

RUCH, F. L., & RUCH, W. W. The *K* factor as a (validity) suppressor variable in predicting success in selling. *J. Appl. Psychol.*, 1967, 51, 201–204.

RUCH, G. M. Recent developments in statistical procedures. *Rev. Educ. Res.*, 1933, 3, 39–40.

RUSSELL, W., & COPE, G. V. Method of rating the history of achievements of applicants. *Publ. Personnel Stud.*, 1925, 3, 202–19.

SANDHU, H. S. An instrument for measuring delinquency potential: validation of socialization scale (or delinquency scale) in India. *J. Correct. Work*, 1960, 7, 92–101.

SARASON, S. B., DAVIDSON, K. S., LIGHTHALL, F. F., WAITE, R. R., & RUEBUSH, B. K. *Anxiety in Elementary School Children.* New York: Wiley, 1960.

SATTLER, J. M., & THEYE, F. Procedural, situational and interpersonal variables in individual intelligence testing. *Psychol. Bull.*, 1967, 68, 347–60.

SAWYER, J. Measurement and prediction, clinical and statistical. *Psychol. Bull.*, 1966, 66, 178–200.

SCHAFER, R. *The Clinical Application of Psychological Tests.* New York: International Universities Press, 1948.

SCHAIE, K. W. The effect of age on a scale of social responsibility. *J. Soc. Psychol.*, 1959, 50, 221–24.

SCHEFLEN, K. C., LAWLER, E. E., III, & HACKMAN, J. R. Long-term impact of employee participation in the development of pay incentive plans: a field experiment revisited. *J. Appl. Psychol.* 1971, 55, 182–86.

SCHOENFELDT, L. F. Data archives as resources for research, instruction and policy planning. *Amer. Psychologist*, 1970, 25, 609–16.

SCHOPLER, J., & BATESON, N. The power of dependence. *J. Pers. Soc. Psychol.*, 1965, 2, 247–54.

SCHWARZ, P. A. *Aptitude Tests for Use in the Developing Nations.* Pittsburgh: American Institute for Research, 1961.

SCHWARZ, P. A. Adapting tests to the cultural setting. *Educ. Psychol. Measmt.*, 1963, 23, 673–86.

SECHREST, L. Incremental validity: a recommendation. *Educ. Psychol. Measmt.*, 1963, 23, 153–58.

SEILER, J. Preparing the disadvantaged for tests. *Voc. Guidance Quart.* 1971, 19, 201–205.

SELLS, S. B. A model for the social system for the multiman extended duration space ship. *NASA Report No. NGR 44-009-008* (undated).

SHUEY, A. M. *The Testing of Negro Intelligence* (2nd ed.). New York: Social Science Press, 1966.

SIEGMAN, W. W. Personality variables associated with admitted criminal behavior. *J. Consult. Psychol.*, 1962, 26, 199.

SMILANSKY, S. The effect of certain learning conditions on the progress of disadvantaged children of kindergarten age. *J. Sch. Psychol.*, 1968, 4, 68–81.

SMITH, E. E. Obtaining subjects for research. *Amer. Psychologist*, 1962, 17, 577–78.

SMITH, P. C., & KENDALL, L. M. Retranslation of expectations: an approach to the construction of unambiguous anchors for rating scales. *J. Appl. Psychol.*, 1963, 47, 149–55.

SMITH, W. J., ALBRIGHT, L. W., GLENNON, J. R., & OWENS, W. A. The prediction of research competence and creativity from personal history. *J. Appl. Psychol.*,

1961, 45, 59–62.

SOCIETY FOR PSYCHOLOGICAL STUDY OF SOCIAL ISSUES. Guidelines for testing minority group children. *J. Social Issues*, 1964, 20,127–45.

SORENSON, W. W. Test of mechanical principles as a suppressor variable for the prediction of effectiveness on a mechanical repair job. *J. Appl. Psychol.*, 1966, 50, 348–53.

SPRINTHALL, N. A. Test interpretation: some problems and a proposal. *Voc. Guidance Quart.*, 1967, 15, 248–56.

SPUHLER, J. N., & LINDZEY, G. Racial differences in behavior. In J. Hirsch (Ed.), *Behavior-Genetic Analysis*. New York: McGraw-Hill, 1967, pp. 366–414.

STAFF, COUNSELING CENTER, UNIVERSITY OF MARYLAND. A check-list for recording test-taking behavior. *J. Counsel. Psychol.*, 1960, 7, 110–19.

STERN, G. G. *People in Context: Measuring Person-Environment Congruence in Education and Industry*. New York: Wiley, 1970.

STEWART, L. H. Social and emotional adjustment during adolescence as related to the development of psychosomatic illness in adulthood. *Genet. Psychol. Monogr.*, 1963, 65, 175–215.

STEWART, W. A. Toward a history of American Negro dialect. In F. Williams (Ed.), *Language and Poverty*. Chicago: Markham Press, 1970.

STONE, P. J. An interactive inquirer. *Proceedings of the 1965 Invitational Conference on Testing Problems*. Princeton, N.J.: Educational Testing Service, 1967, pp. 63–79.

STONE, P. J., DUNPHY, D. C., SMITH, M. S., & OGILVIE, D. M. *The General Inquirer: A Computer Approach to Content Analysis*. Cambridge, Mass.: M. I. T. Press, 1966.

STRATTON, G. M. Vision without inversion of the retinal image. *Psychol. Rev.*, 1897, 4, 341–60, 463–81.

STRONG, E. K., JR., *Vocational Interests of Men and Women*. Stanford, Calif.: Stanford University Press, 1943.

STRONG, E. K., JR. Twenty-year follow-up of medical interests. In L. L. Thurstone (Ed.), *Applications of Psychology*. New York: Harper & Brothers, 1952, pp. 111–30.

STRONG, E. K., JR. *Vocational Interests 18 Years after College*. Minneapolis: University of Minnesota Press, 1955.

STRONG, E. K., & TUCKER, A. C. Use of vocational interest scales in planning a medical career. *Psychol. Monogr.*, 1952, 66, (Whole No. 341).

SUPER, D. E. *Appraising Vocational Fitness*. New York: Harper, 1949.

SUPER, D. E. The use of multifactor test batteries in guidance. *Personnel & Guidance J.*, 1956, 25, 2–8.

SZASZ, T. S. *The Ethics of Psychoanalysis*. New York: Basic Books, 1965.

TANNER, J. M. *The Physique of the Olympic Athlete*. London: Allen & Unwin, 1964.

TAYLOR, D. W. Variables related to creativity and productivity among men in two research laboratories. In C. W. Taylor & F. Barron (Eds.), *Scientific Creativity*. New York: Wiley, 1963, pp. 228–50.

TERMAN, L. M. The intelligence quotients of Francis Galton in childhood. *Amer. J. Psychol.*, 1917, 28, 209–45.

TERMAN, L. M., & MERRILL, M. A. *Measuring Intelligence*. New York: Houghton, Mifflin, 1937.

TESKA, P. T. The mentality of hydrocephalics and a description of an interesting case. *J. Psychol.*, 1947, 23, 197–203.

THIGPEN, C. H., & CLECKLEY, H. A case of multiple personality. *J. Abnorm. Soc. Psychol.*, 1954, 49, 135–51.

THISTLETHWAITE, D. L. *Effects of College Upon Student Aspirations*. U.S. Office of Education, Cooperative Research Project No. 0-098. Nashville, Tenn.: Vanderbilt University, 1965.

THRESHER, B. A. A proposal for self-scored, self-administered tests. In *Report of the Commission on Tests. Vol. 2, Briefs*. Princeton, N.J.: College Entrance Examination Board, Box 592, 1970, pp. 146–54.

TRAXLER, A. E. Impact of machines and devices on developments in testing and related fields. *Proceedings of the 1953 Invitational Conference on Testing Problems*. Princeton, N.J.: Educational Testing Service, 1954, pp. 139–46.

TRAXLER, A. E. (Ed.). *Measurement and Research in Today's Schools*. Washington, D.C.: American Council on Education, 1961.

TYLER, L. E. Human Abilities. In P. H. Mussen & M. R. Rosenzweig (Eds.), *Annual Review of Psychology 1972*. Palo Alto, Calif.: Annual Reviews, Inc., pp. 177–206.

U.S. DEPARTMENT OF LABOR, BUREAU OF EMPLOYMENT SECURITY. *Guide to the Use of the General Aptitude Test Battery*. Washington, D.C.: Government Printing Office, 1958.

U.S. DEPARTMENT OF LABOR, BUREAU OF EMPLOYMENT SECURITY. *GATB Norms for Ninth and Tenth Grades*. Washington, D.C.: Government Printing Office, 1959.

VINCENT, C. *Unmarried Mothers*. New York: Free Press, 1961.

WALLACE, J. An abilities conception of personality: some implications for personality measurement. *Amer. Psychologist*, 1966, 21, 132–38.

WALTERS, C. E. Comparative development of Negro and white infants. *J. Genet. Psychol.*, 1967, 110, 243–51.

WATSON, J. B., & RAYNER, R. Conditioned emotional reactions. *J. Exp. Psychol.*, 1920, 3, 1–4.

WEBB, E. J. Unconventionality, triangulation and inference. *Proceedings of the 1966 Invitational Conference on Testing Problems*. Princeton, N.J.: Educational Testing Service, 1967, pp. 34–43.

WEBSTER, E. C. *Decision Making in the Employment Interview*. Montreal: Industrial Relations Centre, McGill University, 1964.

WEIZENBAUM, J. ELIZA—a computer program for the study of natural language communication between man and machine. *Communications of the ACM* (Association for Computing Machinery), 1966, 1, 36–45.

WELLMAN, D. The wrong way to find jobs for Negroes. *Trans-action*, 1968, 5, 9–18.

WELSH, G. S. *Preliminary Manual for the Welsh Figure Preference Test*. Palo Alto, Calif.: Consulting Psychologists Press, 1959.

WERNIMONT, P. F. Re-evaluation of a weighted application blank for office personnel. *J. Appl. Psychol.*, 1962, 46, 417–19.

WHITE, S. H. Evidence for a hierarchical arrangement of learning processes. In L. R. Lipsitt, & C. C. Siker (Eds.) *Advances in Child Development and Behavior*. Vol. 2, New York: Academic Press, 1965, pp. 187–200.

WICKERT, F. R. An adventure in psychological testing abroad. *Amer. Psychologist*, 1957, 5, 86–88.

WILSON, A. B. Educational consequences of segregation in a California community. In *Racial Isolation in the Public Schools*, Volume 2 of a report by the U.S. Commission on Civil Rights. Washington, D.C.: U.S. Government Printing Office, 1967.

WOMER, F. G. *What is National Assessment?* Denver, Colo.: Education Commission of the States, 1970.

WYSOCKI, B. A., & WYSOCKI, A. C. Cultural differences as reflected in Wechsler-Bellevue Intelligence (WBII). *Psychol. Rep.*, 1969, 25, 95–101.

YATES, A. J. The application of learning theory to the treatment of tics. *J. Abnorm. Soc. Psychol.*, 1958, 56, 175–82.

YERKES, R. M. The mind of a gorilla. *Genet. Psychol. Monogr.*, 1927, 2, 1–193.

ZEIGLER, M. L., BERNREUTER, R. G., & FORD, D. H. A new profile for interpreting academic abilities. *Educ. Psychol. Measmt.*, 1958, 18, 583–88.

ZIGLER, E., & BUTTERFIELD, E. Motivational aspects of changes in IQ test performance of culturally deprived nursery school children. *Child Dev.*, 1968, 39, 1–14.

ZUBIN, J. Clinical versus actuarial prediction: a pseudo-problem. In A. Anastasi (Ed.), *Testing Problems in Perspective*. Washington, D.C.: American Council of Education, 1966, pp. 625–37.

Author Index

Subject Index